Visual Basic™ 4.0 Internet Programming

Carl Franklin

WILEY COMPUTER PUBLISHING

John Wiley & Sons, Inc.

New York • Chichester • Brisbane • Toronto • Singapore

For my daughter, Emmeline, and my wife, Gretchen, who have both been patiently putting up with me working so hard. I love you very much, Gretchen. Emmy, please don't blurp on Daddy's book!

Publisher: Katherine Schowalter
Editor: Philip Sutherland
Managing Editor: Angela Murphy
Text Design & Composition: Benchmark Productions, Inc.

Designations used by companies to distinguish their products are often claimed as trademarks. In all instances where John Wiley & Sons, Inc. is aware of a claim, the product names appear in initial capital or all capital letters. Readers, however, should contact the appropriate companies for more complete information regarding trademarks and registration.

This text is printed on acid-free paper.

This publication is designed to provide accurate and authoritative information in regard to the subject matter covered. It is sold with the understanding that the publisher is not engaged in rendering legal, accounting, or other professional service. If legal advice or other expert assistance is required, the services of a competent professional person should be sought.

Library of Congress Cataloging-in-Publication Data:
Franklin, Carl.
    Visual Basic Internet programming / by Carl Franklin.
      p. cm.
    Includes index.
    ISBN 0–471–13420–1 (pbk : alk. paper)
    1. Microsoft Visual BASIC. 2. Internet (Computer network)
  I. Title.
    QA76.73.B3F72 1996
    005.7'1262--dc20   96–14111

Printed in the United States of America

10 9 8 7 6 5 4 3 2 1

CONTENTS

■■■■ FOREWORD

I've heard some people say that an expert is not someone who knows everything, but someone who knows how to find information when it is needed. They are wrong. Perhaps this was true once, but today it's not hard to find information, especially with high-speed, full-text searches of online databases or CD-ROMs. And it's really not that hard to filter out the key information that you are looking for after performing such a search.

But understanding what you've found—ah!—that can be a problem. You see, I believe that a true expert is not someone who knows a great deal, or someone who knows how to find information. True experts are persons who understand the fundamentals of their field very, very well. So well that for them, it is simple.

I've found that when tackling a new subject, especially a complex subject, the real problem is building that core understanding—the conceptual framework in which you can fit the knowledge that you acquire. I still remember the day, many years ago, when I first understood the concept of a "Class." It was a Freshman Computer Science language class and I had spent weeks struggling with the concept. My homework assignments were travesties of software design, were buggy, and were leading me rapidly towards a low grade in the class. Then one day, I got it. It clicked. I suddenly understood classes—why they existed and the tradeoffs involved in using them. It was more than just understanding the syntax for using them in a particular language or for particular projects—I really, really understood classes. When Visual Basic 4.0 showed up with support for classes (of a sort), it took very little effort to take full advantage of them. I already understood the underlying concepts; it was just a matter of fitting the VB4 specific knowledge into the conceptual framework that I had built so long ago.

If you were to choose a random software designer from a crowd and ask how he or she feels about the current state of technological change in our industry, you might hear "exciting," "interesting," or similar glowing terms. Give the same programmer a shot of truth serum and you might hear the terms "intimidating," "overwhelming," and even "terrifying." I was at a conference recently where Jon Roskill, a manager at Microsoft, brought up the term "technological downpour." Boy, did that hit home! Things are changing so quickly that you need to work as hard as you can just to keep up—like the Red Queen in "Through the Looking Glass," you have to run as fast as you can just to stay in place. If you want to get ahead you must run even faster. The results: stress, burnout, and the constant fear that you're falling farther and farther behind.

I'd been feeling that way about the Internet. It seemed that the entire universe had gone insane with Internet hype, and that everyone out there knew more about it than I did. And that I had only limited time available to understand it, or I would be left hopelessly behind.

So there I was. I felt the need to learn about the Internet—not just to learn about it, but to become an "expert." Not an expert in the sense of knowing everything about the Internet, but in the sense of having the conceptual framework on which I could build. Finding information was not a problem; there are probably no more than several hundred books in print about the Internet. I needed to gain that core knowledge that would allow me to really understand all of the information that I would soon be exploring.

So when Carl Franklin asked me to write the foreword for this book, it came at a perfect time. I had bits and pieces of knowledge—many Internet related terms were vaguely familiar to me, but I didn't really understand them. I've known Carl for several years and knew about his long-standing interest in communication of all forms, so I had hopes that his book might help me to build further on my understanding of the fundamentals.

I read the manuscript over the course of just a few days and discovered something. I said earlier: An expert understands the fundamentals of a subject so well that it seems simple. Well, a great teacher also has the ability to convey a subject so that it becomes simple to the student. In other words, a great teacher has the ability to help a student to build a conceptual framework for themselves. In effect, the student becomes an expert as well. You've probably read books and met teachers who managed to make their subjects seem incredibly complex and intimidating. This might make them seem smarter or more capable, but it does little for the student. I'm glad to report that Carl is not one of these but is, in fact, one of the great ones.

Having read this manuscript, I can't say that I could write a VB web client or server off the top of my head, or that I could Internet mail enable an application with no effort. But I'll say this: I now have absolute confidence in my ability to learn to do all of these things quickly and to read and understand the myriad of references and specifications that are available. I may not know the specifics of how to perform a particular task on the Internet, but I understand clearly now, for the first time, how those tasks are accomplished. In fact, for many tasks this book will serve as the starting point, since it is full of easily understood, practical applications of Internet programming. This book tied together the fragmentary knowledge that I had already picked up and wrapped it together into a clear and consistent framework—the conceptual framework that is a key towards making further progress. In other words, as intimidating as the Internet seemed just a few days ago, today I realize that it's all really quite simple.

I may not be an Internet programming expert today, but you can bet that I'll be one very, very soon. Thanks, Carl.

DANIEL APPLEMAN

■■■ PREFACE

Communications Programming

I have always wanted to write a book about communications programming that did not have 19 chapters full of hardcore technical mumbo-jumbo and only one or two chapters of practical application of that knowledge. Instead, this book covers the technical details of internet programming in full in one or two chapters, and the rest of it deals with the practical application of that technology in Programmer-Technospeak, which is enough like English to understand and yet able to convey precise technical ideas.

I find it ridiculous that the technical information that comes with most high-tech equipment (be it electronic music products (the worst!), clock radios, or software components), is often the least helpful. Why is that? Why is it that I shell out good money for a parallel/serial port board, and its documentation consists of a four-inch sheet of paper written in some foreign language with a diagram that looks like it was scribbled by a nine-year old?

There has always been somewhat of a lack of VB programmers who are hip in communications, and I submit that there are two reasons, the second being an outcome of the first. The first reason is because the documentation made available to them on the subject has always been sorely lacking. I remember before I got serious as a programmer looking through the BASIC keyword index that came with my friend's Tandy laptop, seeing statements like "COM(x) ON" and then on the next page "ON COM(x)" and thinking to myself, *this is crazy*! How can a programmer be expected to figure this out? The second reason for the apparent dearth of VB comm programmers is that there is so much technology beyond the programmer's control that must be supported that they usually end up jumping off a tall building into a vat of mayonnaise before ever really having the chance to become an expert.

Traditionally, serial port programming has been a nightmare. The real nightmare exists at the hardware level. There are so many things that get in the way of the programmer implementing good clean communications because a lot of the hardware details (forgive me for getting too technical), like parity, stop bits, flow control, and so on, are left up to the programmer, as if the programmer really knows what the heck to do with these settings. Therefore, the programmer does what everyone else does: *Let the user decide!* There's a lame idea if I ever heard one. Does your father-in-law who just got his modem and wants to get online know what flow control is? Should he even *have* to? It would be nice if the answer were *no*, but that is usually not the case. Once an option (like flow control) is given to the user, then every system has to have the same option in order to be flexible. It's only because different machines use different serial port settings that the options have to be there in the first place; the natural extension of serial port technology dictates that in order to be omniflexible, one has to present the user with every possible option.

Fortunately, the low-level details of modems and the world that they inhabit are being absorbed by today's new high-tech operating systems like Windows 95, Windows NT, and OS/2 Warp, so that the modem becomes not just a means for you to connect to an online service, but a tool that the entire operating system can leverage as just another transport mechanism for getting data from point A to point B.

Today you can install Windows 95, let the operating system detect your modem, and it is automatically configured for you. Within five or ten minutes you are surfing the net! Remote Access (RAS) lets you use a modem to make a network connection. Where there was one Zmodem there is now FileCopy.

Client/Server and Peer-to-Peer Networking

If you were at all paying attention in the late 1980s to early 1990s, you have probably heard the term *client/server*. Client/server is a name for the idea that the systems of the future should share the processing between a client and a server. This movement grew as the microcomputer became more powerful. The corporate client/server relational database system has been the primary recipient of this label. The client application provides all of the application-specific processing (like the presentation of data, reports, and so on) while the server's sole task is to interpret queries and return requested data to the client in a raw format. This is the prime example of balancing the processing load between the client and the server machines.

Up until the client/server model hit the scene, the existing model was the timesharing system. These systems placed all of the processing on a mainframe or minicomputer. The terminals that connected to the brain were considered *dumb*, or having no processing task except to communicate with the server. The server shares time with each terminal in a loop, checking each logged-in terminal for tasks that need to be attended to one by one.

The term client/server is really a buzzword to describe systems in which there are clearly defined client machines and server machines. Applying this model to something like the World Wide Web is not entirely appropriate. At any one time you are hitting a Web server with a Web client application, but then you can quickly jump from server to server, which is more like the behavior of a peer-to-peer system.

As the Internet grows and our ideas of computing evolve, you will see the term *client/server* phased out and replaced by the term *distributed computing* or *peer-to-peer*, meaning that there can be many servers or combinations of both client and server. In any event, these are just words. They are not rules. You do not need to design a system that fits the previous definition of what a system should be. That type of attitude stagnates progress, and does not encourage creative problem solving.

Why Use Visual Basic?

I am often asked why anyone would want to use Visual Basic code with a simple WinSock control to access the Internet instead of just buying a good set of Internet tools. It's a good question, and you may think that I am just trying to get you to buy this book by saying "use Visual Basic," but this isn't true. The Internet is always changing. The protocols that you use to access it are subject to revision. There's no time to wait for a tool vendor to play catchup. You need control. With the WinSock tools and Visual Basic code in this book you will be able to keep up with the current technology and always be ready to make modifications if need be. You'll be able to create new protocols and new applications that use the same Internet techniques that the big web browsers do, and more.

There seems to be a big myth that writing for the Internet is difficult. This is so much baloney it's not even funny. One big reason for this concept is that there is so much money to be made in the market, the Internet tools people want you to think you can't handle writing it yourself. The truth is that you will have one hundred times more trouble writing a simple serial port script than you will writing a complete Usenet newsreader. With the code included in this book, all you have to do is pop it in. You also have the added benefit of the source code, which you can modify and upgrade if need be.

Who Should Read This Book

If you are an intermediate-level Visual Basic programmer who is thirsty for Internet knowledge and how to apply it to your Visual Basic applications, then this book is for you. This book assumes that you have an intermediate knowledge of Visual Basic 4.0 and have written at least one medium-sized application with it. You do not need any prior knowledge of communications or communications programming.

Requirements

In order to use the software for the Internet, you must be running Windows 3.11 with a TCP/IP and WinSock driver (included on the CD-ROM), Windows 95, or Windows NT. The software in this book was developed with Visual Basic 4.0 32-bit, although the source code works with both VB 32 and 16 bit.

The Internet Is Hot—Go Get 'Em!

There's no doubt about it—the Internet is a hot topic these days. I don't think this is a fad that will go away any time soon. The public's reaction has been too strong for it to just go away. The face of the Internet will be constantly changing, and that's good for you as a developer, but the underlying network is here to stay.

Now is the time to take advantage of the tools and knowledge that are available so you can be prepared to ride the wave of Internet development that is upon us. In this book, I have given you the knowledge. You now have the power to marry Visual Basic and the Internet, so go write some code.

Acknowledgments

Many people have helped me in my never-ending quest for knowledge. In particular, many people helped me put this book together, and I wish to thank them wholeheartedly here and now.

Gary Wisniewski

Steve Cramp

Trent Henson

Jonathan Woods

Scott Granados

1

THE INTERNET

Attack of the Buzzwords!

"**H**ey, can you show me how to surf the net?"

"Sure, let's check out the web! We can download some MPEGs!"

"Wow, I feel like a warrior of cyberspace! We're zooming down the Information Superhighway, just like those AT&T commercials!"

The Internet will go down in history as the big public discovery of the 1990s, even though it's been around for years. From the late 1970s, when the Internet was started, until the early 1990s, the Internet had been primarily the domain of UNIX users, mostly at universities and research facilities around the world. Only recently has the Internet been made available to a wide array of Windows users, who've been flooding it with traffic. Once it became widely available to Windows users in early 1993, the Internet began to see a steady increase in use that would result in numbers so mind-blowing that the Internet may have run out of assignable addresses by the time you read this book!

The Internet is vast. There are tens of thousands of computers connected by it all over the world. I say connected *by* it and not *to* it because the Internet is not a computer, it's a network. It is not the computers but the *medium* by which computers communicate with each other.

There are lots of ways to access data on the Internet. The most popular way is via the World Wide Web ("the web"). The World Wide Web is a collection of published pages that have links to each other within them. For example, there might be a page all about gardening, with pictures of flowers and trees. At the bottom of the page, there could be a list of related pages all over the world that show up as hypertext (underlined and colored) links. One click on a link, and you're instantly connected to another computer, which could be anywhere on the Internet all over the world. That page may have links to a few other pages, and you can keep going and going until you just can't take it anymore! This activity is called *surfing the net* and is the primary cause of computer widowdom all over America, besides cola-breath of course.

The biggest problem that users of the Internet face, and which has generated the most complaints, is that people can't find what they are looking for with any degree of ease. Sometimes, specific information cannot be found at all. The reason is the incredible diversity of user interface on Internet host computers.

As an example of this, the Library of Congress catalog is accessed by Telnet, a text-based terminal in which the user interface is custom to the program, much like a DOS program. Many universities publish papers on Gopher servers, a hierarchy of menus and documents, the design of which varies from host to host. At each potential source of information there is a learning curve, and therein lies the problem. The World Wide Web is nice because everything is graphical and mostly easy to understand, but it suffers from the same problem. There are no rules to how you present information. The WWW user interface takes less time to learn than Telnet or Gopher, but the problem still exists.

From what I have gathered, many programmers are at first slightly afraid of the Internet. You may have had some experience or heard horror stories about implementing serial communications either under DOS or Windows. I can tell you from experience it is not an easy task. The coding part is pretty much straight ahead, but there are so many low-level issues that have to be addressed with modems that it can get pretty hairy to support a serial-enabled application.

I have gotten calls from fellow programmers who are knee-deep in supporting Windows serial port applications (such as bulletin board systems, terminal programs, or custom applications that communicate through the serial port) complaining that their software doesn't work with a particular modem, or that a particular modem doesn't hang up when you try to disconnect, or whatever. The developer ends up being a liaison between the customer and the modem company, which is always a pleasant situation to be in. Kind of like a whipping boy for both parties.

The fact is that application software developers should not have to support hardware. The reason for this big mess with modems and software is because the serial port driver talks directly to the hardware, and there are no layers between them to do any kind of robust error handling. Today, most modems have error handling built right in, but some don't! What happens when a modem with error handling connects to one without it? No error handling! The result: Software developers have to do extra error handling in their app to support modems that don't handle errors during the transmission of data. It shouldn't have to be that way, and fortunately it isn't.

I am here to tell you that you can now write communications software the way you have always wanted to. That is, with the knowledge that when you receive data there is no line noise in it, and it is exactly what was sent to you. If you want to send a file, just send the data. It's easier than writing to a file. Using the tools in this book, you can write an application that can communicate with another application anywhere in the world using a modem, a network connection, wireless, or what have you. You don't even need to use the Internet to benefit from this technology. Your application is separated from the physical layer and will work on any machine that uses the TCP/IP protocol. As my friend Al would say, this is all good news.

I foresee a few existing communications technologies falling by the wayside:

1. Direct serial port access
2. DDE (Dynamic Data Exchange)
3. NetDDE (Network DDE)
4. Mailslots

Without getting too much ahead of myself, the method by which you as a Visual Basic programmer will access the Internet is Windows Sockets (or WinSock). The tools included with this book make this extremely easy. The good news is that WinSock isn't just for the Internet. You can just as easily communicate with another application on the same machine, as you can with an app on your LAN, or within your domain, or anywhere in the world. A domain is simply a larger group of smaller groups of computers. You can develop both the client and the server applications on your desktop. When you move them to separate locations the only thing that changes is the Socket, or the address of the applications. Add to that a robust network architecture that does error checking for you so you can concentrate on writing software. Sounds nice, huh?

It is easy to see why WinSock will replace direct serial port access: reliability and abstraction. By using WinSock you can support a wider market than can those who use only modems to communicate. Not only that, but you remove yourself from the hardware. There are at least two layers between your application and the hardware, and sometimes three, as you will read shortly. The new generation of operating systems utilizes the modem directly. If your customer has trouble with the modem, they contact the modem manufacturer, or if there is a problem with the network software, they contact Microsoft (or the network software manufacturer). You like this idea, I'm sure.

DDE programming is always frustrating. The reason for this is applications that expose functionality via DDE do not follow any kind of standards. The implementation presents a learning curve for each application that uses it. For example, manipulating data in an Excel spreadsheet is very different from sending a fax with WinFax Pro. Also, there isn't any liaison between your application and a DDE server application. This lends itself to errors beyond the scope of most VB programmers. DDE was actually a steppingstone to OLE (Object Linking and Embedding),

Microsoft's interapplication communication system. I actually foresee OLE (Object Linking and Embedding) as being a direct replacement for DDE, but WinSock can be used in the absence of OLE.

You may not have heard of Mailslots. Mailslots is a network API for interapplication communications on a basic send-and-receive level. There has been at least one shareware VBX for Mailslots, but that's all I've ever seen. You don't hear much about it. I have tried using it and it didn't live up to my expectations. Presumably for the same reason DDE doesn't always work, there isn't any abstraction between your app and another app, and there is no reliability intelligence built into Mailslots.

Let me expound on the possibilities in software for the next ten or so years. Because the PC is the most widely used personal computer in the world, and seeing that the PC's major operating systems now have built-in support for the Internet (Windows 95, OS/2 Warp, and Windows NT), there is no reason not to take advantage of the connectivity that automatically exists among all PCs running these operating systems.

Picture this: You wake up in the morning, pour some coffee, rub the fruitcake out of your eyes, and sit down at the PC equipped with Windows 95 and a modem. There is a little icon on your desktop that looks like a newspaper. You click it, and you are reading a summary of the daily news. You sip your coffee. You observe the wallpaper bitmap on the Windows desktop, a satellite weather photo taken just 15 minutes ago. You look at it, noticing a storm approaching from the East. You open the shade and see it's snowing like crazy (for those of you not familiar with snow, it's what happens when rain freezes). Realizing that the roads are closed, you resign yourself to a little chat with your electronic pen-pal in Barbados. You double-click an icon that says "SuperChat" on the desktop. You pick your friend's name from a list and within a few seconds you see your friend's greeting at the top of the window, "Hello there, what's up?" You type, "Not much, what are you doing?" Your friend replies, "Sitting on my porch looking at the ocean and soaking up the Sun, how about you?" You type, "Sitting in my office watching the snow fall and feeling the heat from the furnace on my feet."

Well, dream no more. After reading this book, you will be writing applications just like these, and even cooler ones.

Protocols and Data

Upon looking in *Webster's Dictionary* for the word *protocol*, I found a slew of different meanings ranging from "first sheet of a papyrus roll bearing data of manufacture" to "glue" to "record or minute" to "code." In the context of computers and networking, a protocol is a set of codes or rules; a method by which data is moved between devices.

The simplest example of a real-world protocol that I can think of is calling information for somebody's phone number. It starts with you dialing 411. The operator then answers and says "what city please?" You reply with the name of a city. The operator then says, "yes?" prompting you to say the name of the party whose number you are looking for. The operator looks up the number and gives it to you.

There is a set of rules that must be followed for a communication to be effective. If you did not know the rules, you might get the wrong number, or it just might take more time for you to get the right number. Can you imagine what would happen if you were following one set of rules, and the operator was following another? Actually, this premise has been used as the basis of many famous comedy routines:

OPERATOR:	"What city please?"
ME:	"Yes, I'll have a Jumbo with extra cheese, small fries, and a medium Coke."
OPERATOR:	"Excuse me?"
ME:	"Oh, I'm sorry, make that a large fry."
OPERATOR:	"What city?!"
ME:	"Oh, I see . . . make it a number 1 meal!"
OPERATOR:	"*What city*?!"
ME:	"What?"
OPERATOR:	"What city does the party live in?"
ME:	"The party's at my house in Mystic."

OPERATOR:	"And the name in Mystic?"
ME:	"Franklin, Carl Franklin. . . . Why do you want my. . ."
OPERATOR:	"The number is 555-5742."
ME:	"You mean, I have to take a *number*!? How long is the wait?"

Have you ever tried to upload a file to someone manually with a terminal program, and the other person has no idea what they're doing? You say to them, "Use the Zmodem protocol," and they pick Ymodem by accident. You both start the transfers and nothing happens. Why? Because one of you is waiting for the city name, and the other is ordering a Jumbo with extra cheese. The protocols don't match.

Using a protocol in networking isn't any different than using a protocol to transfer a file with a modem. The only difference is that network protocols are used to move all forms of data, not just files, between machines on the network, in real time.

Which brings me to the data itself. Different protocols have different names for "chunks" of data: messages, packets, streams, datagrams. These are all names for the same thing—a definable chunk of data that is passed through and processed by the network and its protocols.

You can write your own protocol if you wish. A protocol does not have to have incredibly complex algorithms. It can be as simple as one machine sending another machine a one-byte command, and the other machine sending back n bytes of data based on the command it received. In this book, we will be implementing popular protocols used on the Internet as Visual Basic code, which you can reuse in your own applications. These protocols are documented at the Internet Network Information Center (Inter NIC) in documents called RFC documents.

RFC stands for Request For Comments, a collection of public documents which act both as an open forum for new ideas pertaining to the Internet, and as a source of documentation of existing protocols. RFCs are numbered. The CD-ROM that comes with this book contains all of the RFCs in their current form as of the first quarter of 1996.

Protocol Stacks
and the OSI Model

If you are not familiar with what a protocol stack is, and are merely interested in how to write applications in Visual Basic that access the Internet, I am here to tell you that you can skip over this section with a clear conscience. Understanding the protocol stack is not crucial for successful Internet VB programming. However, knowledge of these concepts can help you understand where your Visual Basic application fits in the big picture.

The term *stack* comes from the conception of the OSI (Open Systems Interconnection) Reference Model, a conceptual framework for the design and implementation of computer networks developed in the early 1980s by the ISO (International Standards Organization). Although the Internet doesn't adhere exactly to the OSI Reference Model, the model is a useful way to understand how all networks operate.

The essence of the OSI model is a layer-cake metaphor, in which there are seven discrete layers. At each layer a function is performed by any number of protocols when data is transmitted between applications on a network. At the top is your application, at the bottom is the hardware, and everything in between supports the top and bottom layers. Think of data originating in the source application, moving down the stack to the hardware and up the stack at the destination application. Figure 1.1 shows the seven layers. From bottom to top they are: Physical, Data Link, Network, Transport, Session, Presentation, and Application. Each layer has its own responsibilities. You would not expect code at the Application layer to manipulate hardware directly. That is a no-no for proper network operation. These responsibilities will become clear shortly, unless of course you are reading in the dark.

At the Physical layer, there are cables, wires, and other electronic gadgets through which data travels. The responsibility at the Physical layer is for the circuits to be designed and implemented correctly. Data should move free of interference and noise, and the signal should be as strong as possible. You get the idea.

The Data Link layer defines the format of transmitted data relative to the Physical layer, including the logistics of how data is moved around. How are

Application Layer
Applications that use the network

Presentation Layer
Standardizes data presentation
to the applications

Session Layer
Manages sessions between
applications

Transport Layer
Provides end-to-end error
detection and correction

Network Layer
Manages connections across the
network for the upper layers

Data Link Layer
Provides reliable data delivery
across the physical link

Physical Layer
Defines the physical characteristics
of the network media (hardware)

▰▰▰▰ **Figure 1.1** OSI model.

machines identified? How do you package data so that it is recognizable by other machines? The answers to these questions are different depending on the Physical layer (LAN, T1 line, modem, etc.). The DataLink layer doesn't do the actual sending and receiving of data, it is just concerned with how data is packaged and interpreted from the Physical layer. You may be familiar with the word *packet*. A packet is a unit of data that is defined by the DataLink layer. It is also what you do to a suitcase.

The Network layer is responsible for moving packets of data from point A to point B. For the Internet, this is handled by routing packets through the path of least resistance, so to speak, so that they get to their final destination in the most efficient manner. The IP (Internet Protocol) handles this problem on the Internet.

The Transport layer is concerned with managing the transmission of data from point A to point B. This is where the actual delivery of data takes place. In the case of the Internet, this is accomplished by TCP (Transmission Control Protocol) or UDP (User Datagram Protocol), which we will talk about shortly.

The Physical, Data Link, Network, and Transport layers of the OSI Reference Model make up what are called the lower layers of the stack. The top three layers from bottom to top are the Session layer, the Presentation layer, and the Application layer.

The Session layer is utilized in a local area network and is responsible for things such as managing when the network is accessed so that no two users attempt to access it at the exact same time, and basically providing an applications-oriented data stream to the session user.

The Presentation layer determines the format of data transmitted by applications. For example, ASCII is the most common format of transmitted data. Any data encryption such as PGP (Pretty Good Privacy) is done at the Presentation layer. Data compression and expansion is also handled at this layer.

The Application layer is where your Visual Basic application resides. Programs such as terminals, electronic mail readers, Web browsers, and so forth all transmit and receive data on top of the Presentation layer of the OSI Reference Model.

TCP/IP

TCP/IP is a collection (or suite) of protocols whose name stands for two of its primary protocols, TCP (Transmission Control Protocol) and IP (Internet Protocol).

Just to help avoid unnecessary embarrassment, the proper pronunciation is to spell out the letters: T-C-P-I-P, and not to say "Tick-pip" or some such nonsense. TCP resides at the Transport layer, and IP at the Network layer. What we call TCP/IP is not limited to these two protocols, but instead describes the entire suite of protocols used with the Internet.

Both Windows 95 and Windows NT ship with Microsoft's 32-bit TCP/IP drivers, which are very nice. Several third-party companies offer similar drivers at a price, and I am not saying anything negative about those companies, but it seems to me that the days of charging an arm and a leg for Windows TCP/IP drivers are numbered, seeing that Microsoft ships a complete stack with the operating system. You can call it unfair if you like, but I'm not complaining that Microsoft is saving me money.

Names and Addresses

IP uses a special addressing scheme to identify a connection. I use the word *connection* because although we identify computers by IP address, the address actually defines the connection between the computer and the network. Don't let it throw you, though. For all intents and purposes we can identify each computer on the network by its IP address.

An IP address is made up of four 8-bit numbers (from 0 to 255) separated by periods. For example, the IP address of the machine running Carl & Gary's Visual Basic Home Page is 199.204.192.200.

Because it is more difficult to remember numbers than it is to remember names, every IP address can have a name. The name of Carl & Gary's server is www.apexsc.com. The rightmost word in the name is called the *top-level domain*. Inside the United States, the top-level domain defines the type of organization. For example, gov = government, com = commercial organization, edu = educational institution, net = network, org = noncategorized organization, and so on. Outside the United States, though, the top-level domain usually identifies the country or continent. For example, jp = Japan, uk = United Kingdom, and so forth.

IP addresses and names of domains are issued by the Internet Network Information Center (InterNIC). For a nominal fee you can apply to register a domain name, which can then have several machines, the exact number of which is defined by the class of domain you register. Without spending too much time on this, different classes of IP addresses exist for accommodating a small or large group of computers in a given domain. For more information you can connect to the NIC's web site at www.internic.net.

Ports

An IP address identifies a host machine (or gateway) on the Internet. An IP port identifies an application running on an Internet host machine. Unlike serial communications, where you may have four ports, there is no functional limit to the number of IP ports you can have. This is because a port is just a number. If you were to count the number of applications running on your machine right now (or whenever you are at your machine), and assign each application a number, you have grasped the concept of an IP port. It simply identifies an application.

There are some applications that will always have the same port number, and you will see why in a minute. In order to access an application on an Internet host machine you need to know the machine name (or IP address), and you need to know the port number. If you have those two pieces of information, you can communicate with that host application.

For example, all World Wide Web servers communicate on port 80. This makes it easy for clients like Netscape and MS Internet Explorer to jump from web server to web server in an instant. The port is a given—80. The only piece of information needed to connect to a web server is the machine name or IP address. Once connected you can use the Hypertext Transfer Protocol (HTTP) to communicate with the web server, retrieving documents, graphics, music, video, or whatever is available.

There are quite a few reserved ports when using TCP/IP. Here is a list of some of the more popular Internet applications and the ports they use:

1. HTTP (WWW)   80
2. FTP   20 and 21
3. Gopher   70
4. SMTP (email)   25

5. POP3 (email)   110
6. Telnet   23
7. Whois   43
8. Finger   79

Name Resolution

As previously stated, any connection that has an IP address can also have a name. Names are not required but they do make it easier for people to access machines on the network. The network doesn't understand names, though. It understands IP addresses.

There are two methods for resolving names into addresses. The old method, still in use, is to store all names and addresses in a text file called HOSTS. In UNIX, this table is accessible in a shared directory. In Windows this file exists in the \WINDOWS directory of each machine on the network. It is up to the user (usually) to edit this file if need be.

The file format is incredibly simple. On each line, specify an IP address followed by at least one space, and then one or more names separated by at least one space. For example, you might have an entry for Carl & Gary's VB Home Page:

```
199.204.192.200    www.apexsc.com
```

The disadvantage of this system is pretty obvious. Name resolution is a global issue; it is not local to your machine. If everyone in the world used a HOSTS file for name resolution, you'd have to give everybody your IP address and machine name, and they would have to make an entry before they even connected to you. If your IP address changes, everyone's HOSTS file needs to be updated. The advantage of using the HOSTS file system is primarily for systems that do not use the Internet, but use TCP/IP on a local network. It serves as a quick solution to name resolution when there is no other option.

The currently used method for resolving names is using a system called the Domain Name System (DNS). DNS is a distributed database that contains IP addresses for all registered Internet hosts.

Sockets

A socket is simply the combination of an IP address and port. It can be said, therefore, that a socket identifies an application running anywhere on the Internet. This idea originates from the Berkeley Software Distribution system, created at the University of California at Berkeley. In this system, there lives an API (Application Programming Interface) called Berkeley Sockets, which is widely used in the world of UNIX programming for Internet communications.

When you hear the word *socket*, it may mean several things. First and foremost, it refers to the combination of an IP address and port, as in the above definition. However, it can also refer to Berkeley Sockets, a set of functions for UNIX programmers that provides Internet access. There is one other definition of sockets, though, and that is Windows Sockets, a similar set of functions for Windows programmers that provides Internet access. The Windows Sockets 1.1 API (or WinSock) is consistent with release 4.3 of the Berkeley Software Distribution, and also provides Windows-specific routines to aid in the process of writing Windows applications that communicate via the Internet. When I refer to a socket, I mean a WinSock socket connection, existing of an IP address and a port.

The reason WinSock is so cool is because of its high-level accessibility. There are only 44 functions in WinSock 1.1, the current version at the time of this writing, so implementation is fairly straight ahead in a C/C++ environment.

But what about Visual Basic? As you would expect, there are a few people (including Microsoft) trying to make WinSock programming even easier by creating DLLs, VBXs, and OCXs that simplify access to the API. As of this writing I have not seen any high-level WinSock DLLs, but I have seen two or three shareware VBXs, and a few shareware OCXs. I am also aware of several larger add-on vendors creating WinSock OCXs. I can tell you from experience that the best one I've seen so far is a shareware VBX and OCX called DSSOCK, from Dolphin Systems in Toronto, Canada. The OCX works exactly the same as the VBX, so you can write an application for both 16-bit (VB3) and 32-bit (VB4) platforms. The latest versions of DSSOCK.VBX and .OCX are included with this book, and all of the sample code uses them. DSSOCK has about 22 custom properties and 7 custom events, so as you can imagine the implementation is fairly simple and straight ahead.

The TCP/IP Model

Although TCP/IP's implementation closely resembles the OSI Reference Model, the most widely accepted description of the TCP/IP model (although there are many) has four layers: Application, Host to Host, Internet, and Network Access (see Figure 1.2). At each layer, a special header is tacked onto each packet as it passes down the stack. When data comes up the stack at the receiving application, the header information is stripped off at each layer. This process is called *encapsulation*.

At the lowest level in the TCP/IP model is the Network Access layer. It provides the functionality of the Physical, Data Link, and Network layers of the OSI model. Its functions include mapping IP addresses to physical network addresses, and encapsulating IP datagrams (packets) into data that the local network understands. Because TCP/IP works with many different types of networks, the Physical layer of

Application Layer
Applications and processes that use the network

Host To Host Transport Layer
Provides end-to-end data delivery services

Internet Layer
Defines the datagram and handles the routing of data

Network Access Layer
Consists of routines for accessing physical networks

▮▮▮▮ **Figure 1.2** TCP model.

the Internet is not handled by TCP/IP. In the case of Windows, TCP/IP's Network Access layer is in the form of a network driver.

The Internet layer sits right above the Network Access layer, and is really the heart of TCP/IP. The Internet Protocol, or IP, does most of the work at this layer. IP provides the framework for the delivery of data from point A to point B. IP is a connectionless protocol, meaning that it does not have to have an acknowledgment of connection (or handshake) from the other side to begin sending data. IP instead relies upon other protocols (namely TCP) to handle this important function. IP also does not do any error handling. Again, this task is left to other protocols.

Let's say you have a Visual Basic command called TCP_Print that sends a string of data to the host you are currently connected to via TCP/IP. Let's say we call this command with a 1024-byte string. The task is to send 1024 bytes from your application to your host application, which for the sake of argument, let's say, is a simple data terminal running on a Windows NT machine in the back office of a brewery in Munich (hey, this is my fantasy). IP breaks the data into several datagrams, each with a header containing, among other things, the IP address and port of the terminal application in Germany. The IP sends each datagram to a gateway that is connected to both the local network and an Internet Access Provider's network. The term *gateway* can mean any machine that passes on received datagrams, but in this case I am talking specifically about an IP router, which is an intelligent device whose sole purpose is to move datagrams to and from other connections. IP looks at the destination address and decides where to send the datagram so that it will arrive at its destination the fastest. This ability to determine the path of least resistance is what makes IP and the Internet extremely efficient and reliable. If a router goes down, IP just finds a new route. This characteristic was extremely important to the designers of TCP/IP. The network must be able to adapt to the prospect of numerous gateways being shut down (or blown up) in the event of nuclear war. As you can see, they did it right.

I know, I know, this book is about Visual Basic. You don't really need to know how TCP/IP works to write applications that use it, but bear with me. When you understand how rich this protocol is, it may change the way you approach writing VB applications, as you will see shortly.

The layer of the TCP/IP model directly above the Network layer is called the Host-to-Host Transport layer. The two most important protocols used here are TCP (Transmission Control Protocol) and UDP (User Datagram Protocol). TCP provides reliable data transmission and error correction for moving data from source to destination. UDP is a connectionless datagram delivery protocol that does not perform reliability checking or error correction, it simply moves data blindly from point A to point B.

You might be wondering "what good is UDP if it's not reliable?" Plenty, actually: Since UDP does not do any special handling of data, it is faster than TCP. Also, UDP is useful for sending small blurbs of the same piece of data over and over again, like the timeserver protocol on port 37. When you connect to a timeserver on port 37 you receive a string containing the time of day (GMT) over and over again. It does not matter if one of those time packets did not make it to your application; you'll get the next one.

TCP, on the other hand, is a connection-based error-handling protocol, and is widely used throughout the Internet for moving data around. TCP verifies that data was sent across the network and that it is received in the proper sequence. When datagrams are sent across the network, they may arrive at the destination in random order. If there are five datagrams in a transmission, the destination may receive number three first, then number four and five, followed by two and then one. This is not uncommon because, if you remember, IP routes datagrams according to the path of least resistance at the time of transmission. This is the really amazing part of TCP/IP. Fifty percent of your datagrams may have arrived by way of New Zealand, 25 percent by way of the United Kingdom, and 25 percent by way of Australia. To me, that's just incredible.

The Application layer of the TCP/IP model is the same as in the OSI model, except that it performs all functions above the OSI model Transport layer, which include the Presentation layer (how data is formatted and recognized) and the Session layer (synchronizing access to the network, etc.). Among the most widely known application protocols at this layer are HTTP (Hypertext Transport Protocol), which is the language of the World Wide Web; FTP (File Transfer Protocol), the most common way of accessing files through the Internet; SMTP (Simple Mail Transfer Protocol), which deals with moving email messages around; and NNTP (Network News Transfer Protocol), which is used by Usenet News clients and servers.

For more information on the inner-workings of TCP/IP, I suggest the following book: *TCP/IP Network Administration*, by Craig Hunt (O'Reilly & Associates, ISBN: 0-937175-82-X).

Hey, wake up! Class dismissed.

CHAPTER

2

WINSOCK

PROGRAMMING

Introduction

In this chapter, you will learn about DSSOCK, the shareware VBX and OCX included with this book. You will learn how to create both client and server applications quickly and easily.

DSSOCK was first released as a shareware VBX. The implementation is the best I've ever seen, but you should be aware that unregistered copies exhibit a quite annoying splash screen when loaded into memory. It will cost you a fee for the registered version, which does not have a splash screen. In my opinion, it is well worth it considering that some commercial vendors of TCP/IP and/or WinSock controls charge runtime royalties on top of your standard commercial product price. If you are just going to mess around with WinSock and the Internet, you may be willing to live with the splash screen, but it is not wise to ship a commercial application that displays someone else's logo when it starts up. If you wish to purchase a registered copy of DSSOCK, you can call, write, or email Dolphin Systems at:

Dolphin Systems
13584 Kennedy Road North
Inglewood, Ontario
CANADA LON 1KO

Phone:	905-838-2896
Fax:	905-838-0649
CompuServe:	70471,137
Email:	stephenc@idirect.com

I should point out that as I write this book there is no such thing as an absolutely free fully functional Windows Sockets custom control. By the time this book hits the stores Microsoft may have created a WinSock VBX and OCX, but this is just speculation on my part and is in no way founded on fact. One nice thing about this control is that the OCX version is exactly the same as the VBX version, except that it's an OLE control. For this reason, the code in this book is written using the current state of the art (Visual Basic 4.0). Each sample program has a 32-bit and a 16-bit version.

Why Not Use the WinSock API?

This is a good question. Ambitious programmers may want to use the WinSock API directly from Visual Basic, but I advise against this approach because it requires polling for received data in Visual Basic, which is much slower than using a custom control. Also, it is much easier to use a custom control than to have to deal with the details of WinSock in VB. You don't gain *any* technical advantage by using the WinSock API in VB, and you certainly don't gain speed. All you gain is an increase in your learning curve as well as in your development time.

Registering DSSOCK32.OCX on Your System

From Visual Basic 4.0 (32-bit), create a new project by selecting New Project from the File menu. Since this is the first time you are using DSSOCK, it is not yet a registered OLE control on your system. Before you can load the control into 32-bit VB, you must register it. This is done from Visual Basic's Custom Controls Dialog Box (see Figure 2.1). Pop up the box by either pressing Ctrl-T or selecting Custom Controls from the Tools menu.

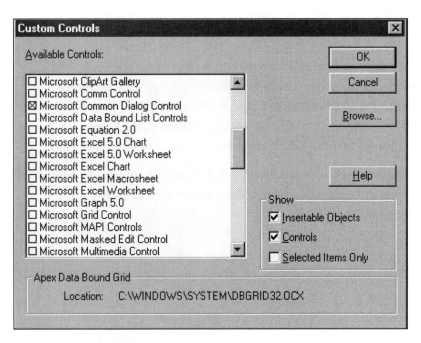

■■■■■■■ **Figure 2.1** Custom Controls.

The Custom Controls dialog box pops up and displays a list of all registered OLE controls. To add DSSOCK to the list, click the Browse button. Navigate to your \WINDOWS\SYSTEM directory and select DSSOCK32.OCX by either double-clicking on it, or single-clicking on it and then clicking the OPEN button (see Figure 2.2). Make sure that the entry "dsSocket TCP/IP control" is checked off in the list, and click the OK button. DSSOCK is now registered on your machine as an OLE server. If you have not installed the CD-ROM software, do so before attempting to register DSSOCK.

DSSOCK.BAS

DSSOCK.BAS is a module containing global constants, types, variables, arrays, and a few simple utility functions that are always coming in handy.

SocketConnect

The SocketConnect function is a nice wrapper for everything that needs to happen when you connect to a host machine. Here is the syntax:

```
Dim nErrCode As Integer
nErrCode = SocketConnect(dsSocket, lPort, szHostAddress, nTimeout)
```

Where dsSocket is the socket control, lPort is the port number of the host application, szHostAddress is a string containing either a host name such as www.apexsc.com or a DOT address such as 199.204.199.200, and nTimeout is the number of seconds you want it to wait for a connection before it gives up. If no nTimeout value is specified, it will wait forever and your program will be hooped (that's Latin for really messed up).

The only requirement of SocketConnect is that you must set gnConnected to True in the DSSOCK control's Connect event procedure, and set gnSendReady to True in the SendReady event:

```
Private Sub DSSocket1_Connect ()
    gnConnected = True
End Sub


Private Sub DSSocket1_SendReady ()
    gnSendReady = True
End Sub
```

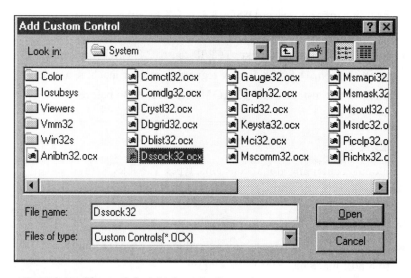

■■■■■■■■ **Figure 2.2** Add Custom Controls.

IsDotAddress

IsDotAddress is another useful function in DSSOCK.BAS. You pass it a string and it tells you whether or not it's a valid IP address. A valid IP address must have four numbers ranging from 0 to 255 separated by periods. The following strings will cause IsDotAddress to return false:

Invalid IP address	Reason:
this.is.not.legal	characters are not allowed
100.2A.11.33	contains the letter A
100.14.7	only three numbers specified
199.22..3	missing the third number
80.-2.40.8	contains a negative number
256.120.20.13	contains a number greater than 255

Getting Started with DSSOCK

Place a DSSOCK control on Form1. You can do this by selecting Form1, and then double-clicking the DSSOCK Toolbox icon, or single-clicking the DSSOCK Toolbox icon and dragging the control on Form1. If the Toolbox is not visible (on the left-hand side of the screen), you can make it visible by selecting Toolbox from the View menu.

Let's start out by looking at two properties: LocalDotAddr and LocalName. LocalDotAddr contains the IP address (sometimes called the Dot Address) of the local machine, and LocalName contains the machine name. As a first exercise, add the following code to Form1's Form_Load event to display the IP address and machine name:

```
Private Sub Form_Load

    Caption = DSSocket1.LocalDotAddr & " - " & DSSocket1.LocalName

End Sub
```

Run the application by either pressing F5, clicking the Run button, or selecting Start from the Run menu. This program simply displays the local IP address and machine name in the caption. The LocalDotAddr and LocalName properties are both string properties (see Figure 2.3).

■■■■■■■■■■ **Figure 2.3** Local IP address.

Making a Sockets Connection

This book comes with a starter project called WINSOCK.VPP, which contains a form with a DSSocket control on it and DSSOCK.BAS. Load the WINSOCK project now, and save it as a new project.

Place a second DSSOCK control on Form1. Next, add a new form to the project (Form2) and place a DSSOCK control on it. Add a command button to both Form1 (name = btnEnd, caption = "End") and Form2 (name = btnAction, caption = "Connect"). Size the forms so they appear as they do in Figure 2.4. If you have not already done so, set the startup form to Form1. The task here is for Form1 to open up a server socket on an arbitrary port and have a client socket connect to it from Form2. Before I discuss what is really happening here, let's implement and run the code.

The code required for Form1 is shown in Figure 2.5. The code required for Form2 is shown in Figure 2.6. You can type it all in if you like, or if you prefer to load the source code from disk, the name of the project is Sample1 in the WinSock directory on the CD-ROM.

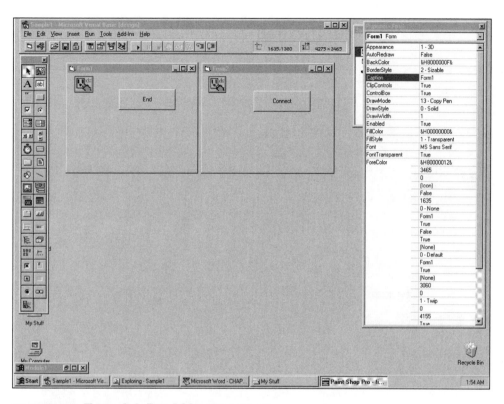

▬▬▬▬▬ **Figure 2.4** Two DSSocket controls.

Run the program. The two forms appear, with Form1's caption reading "Listening to port 2700" and Form2's caption reading "Not Connected." Press the Connect button on Form2. If everything works, you should see the word "Connected" in both the client and the server application and the Connect button should now read "Close." Press the Close button and the program should look exactly as it did at startup, with Form1's caption reading "Listening to port 2700" and Form2's caption reading "Not Connected."

Repeat the process as many times as you like, connecting and disconnecting the socket. When you are satisfied that it's actually working, click the End button on Form1 to exit the program. Do not click VB's Stop button to end the program. You will see why in a minute.

■■■■■■■ **Figure 2.5** Code for Form1 in the Sample1 application.

```
Option Explicit


Private Sub Form_Load()


    '-- Show the client form
    Form2.Show


    '-- Set the local port number to 2700 (arbitrary)
    DSSocket1.LocalPort = 2700


    '-- Open a server socket to Listen to port 2700
    On Error Resume Next    '-- Trap errors
    DSSocket1.Action = SOCK_ACTION_LISTEN


    If Err Then
        '-- An Error occurred, display the error
        MsgBox Error, vbExclamation, "Listen Error"
    End If


    '-- If there was no error, the DSSocket1_Listen event
    '   should fire, indicating that DSSocket1 is listening
    '   to port 2700.


End Sub


Private Sub DSSocket1_Listen()


    '-- We are now monitoring port 2700 on this machine.
    '   When a client connects, the DSSocket1_Accept event will fire.


    Caption = "Listening to port 2700"
```

```
End Sub


Private Sub DSSocket1_Accept(SocketID As Integer)


    '-- A client is attempting to connect. We must complete
    '   the connection by setting the Socket property of
    '   *any* DSSOCK control to SocketID. In this case, we
    '   will use the second DSSOCK control.


    On Error Resume Next    '-- Trap errors
    DSSocket2.Socket = SocketID


    If Err Then
        '-- An Error occurred, display the error
        MsgBox Error, vbExclamation, "Accept Error"
    Else
        '-- No errors. We are connected!
        Caption = "Connected!"
    End If


End Sub


Private Sub DSSocket2_Close(ErrorCode As Integer, ErrorDesc As String)


    '-- The client closed the connection.
    Caption = "Listening to Port 2700"


End Sub


Private Sub btnEnd_Click()


    '-- When the "End" button is pressed, unload the client
    '   form, which closes the connection, and then unload this
```

```
    '   form, which closes all connections and sockets and ends.
    Unload Form2
    Unload Me


End Sub


Private Sub Form_Unload(Cancel As Integer)

    '— Make sure the socket is closed
    On Error Resume Next    '-- Trap errors
    DSSocket1.Action = SOCK_ACTION_CLOSE


    End


End Sub
```

■■■■■

■■■■■ **Figure 2.6** Code for Form2 in the Sample1 application.

```
Option Explicit


Private Sub Form_Load()

    '-- Tell everyone we are not connected to anything.
    Caption = "Not Connected"


End Sub


Private Sub btnAction_Click()

    If btnAction.Caption = "Connect" Then
        '-- Only proceed if we are not already connected.
```

```
      If DSSocket1.State > 1 Then
          MsgBox "Already Connected", vbInformation, "Sample1"
          Exit Sub
      End If


      '-- Set the port of the server socket
      DSSocket1.RemotePort = 2700


      '-- Set the address of the server computer.
      '   In this case it is the same as the client.
      DSSocket1.RemoteDotAddr = DSSocket1.LocalDotAddr


      '-- Try and connect.
      On Error Resume Next    '-- Trap error
      DSSocket1.Action = SOCK_ACTION_CONNECT


      If Err Then
          '-- An Error occurred, display the error
          MsgBox Error, vbExclamation, "Connect Error"
      End If


      '-- If there was no error, than the
      '   DSSocket1_Connect event will fire, indicating
      '   that we've connected to the server.
Else
      '-- Close the connection (if there is one)
      On Error Resume Next
      DSSocket1.Action = SOCK_ACTION_CLOSE


      '-- Reset the button and form captions
      btnAction.Caption = "Connect"
      Me.Caption = "Not Connected"
```

```
      End If

End Sub

Private Sub DSSocket1_Connect()

    '-- We have connected to the server!
    Caption = "Connected!"

    '-- Reset the functionality of the command
    '   button to closing the port.
    btnAction.Caption = "Close"

End Sub

Private Sub Form_Unload(Cancel As Integer)

    '-- Make sure the socket is closed
    On Error Resume Next    '-- Trap errors
    DSSocket1.Action = SOCK_ACTION_CLOSE

End Sub
```

What's Going On Here?

The two controls on the server form serve two different purposes. The first control acts as an *answering socket*. Its job is to answer the port, if you will. The second control is the *data socket*. The data socket takes over the connection, leaving the answering socket ready to answer the next connection request. All socket activity between client and server occurs with the data socket.

Take a look at the Form_Load event of Form1 in Figure 2.5. The first thing that happens is that Form2 is displayed, after which a socket is opened on port 2700.

2700 is an arbitrary number, and you can change it to whatever you like, as long as there isn't already an application using it. Port numbers are 16-bit, so they can be as high as 32767 in Visual Basic (actually you can use negative numbers for values greater than 32767). If you plan on using an arbitrary port number for an application, use a number above 1024. The reason for this is that all reserved ports fall below 1024, so it just makes good sense to use higher numbers.

The socket is set to port 2700 via the LocalPort property. Then, DSSOCK is told to listen to that port, or become a server when the Action property is set to the constant, SOCK_ACTION_LISTEN. By using On Error Resume Next, we can trap any error that occurs. In this case, the typical error is that the local port is already being used. This can happen if you do not close the connection before the program is exited.

The Form_Unload event procedure, which is run right before the form is unloaded from memory, closes the connection. Again, by using On Error Resume Next, we can discard any error, such as "Socket not connected," that might occur. You should not end the program by clicking Visual Basic's Stop button because doing so does not allow the Unload event procedure of each form a chance to run. The Form_Unload event is where open sockets are usually closed. If you do not close any open sockets, they will remain open until you reboot your machine. In the words of NOMAD, "Error!, sterilize!"

If there is no error when you attempt to listen, then the DSSocket1_Listen event will fire, indicating that a server socket has been opened on port 2700. Check out the DSSocket1_Listen event procedure. In this procedure, we set the form's caption to "Listening to port 2700." If you do not see this in the caption when you run this program, then the socket was not opened properly. But, if this were the case, you would get an error message, so the fact that the form comes up without an error means that it is listening on port 2700.

Now, let's jump over to Figure 2.6 to the btnAction_Click event. When you click this button, an attempt to connect to the server on port 2700 is made.

In order to connect a client to a server, you must set the RemotePort property and either the RemoteDotAddr or RemoteName property. If you specify the RemoteName property and the name exists outside of your domain, your DNS service will kick in and resolve the IP address (see Chapter 1, Name Resolution). If you specify the IP address, the connection will be made without the need for resolving a name. In this case, the server machine is the same as the client machine, so we just specify the RemoteDotAddr property to be the LocalDotAddr property, our IP address.

If an error occurs here, it will most likely be that either the connection is already open or the connection failed because the server is either not running or out of connections. There is no defined limit to the number of connections a server application can handle. Basically, you must decide on a limit based on performance. For example, if your server application is file intensive and running on an Intel P-60 or lower, you may want to limit the number of active connections to 30 or 40. Only your observations can determine how many connections to allow. I will talk more about handling connections later, but I wanted to bring it up here in context for your benefit.

SocketID and the Socket Property

At this point, the client (Form2) has attempted to connect to the server (Form1). Let's jump back to Figure 2.5, the server application, to the DSSocket1_Accept event procedure. This occurs on the server when a connection attempt is made. The argument SocketID is passed to the Accept event. This is the Socket Identifier number. Think of it as a token, or a handle, that identifies one side of a socket connection. You are free to assign this connection to any DSSOCK control. Typically this is done by loading a new instance of an array of DSSOCK controls, and assigning the SocketID to the new instance, which keeps the original control (in this case DSSocket1) open to accept more connections.

I will show you how to handle multiple connections shortly, but for our example, we are going to accept only one connection. The second DSSOCK control on Form1, called DSSocket2, is used in the communication. DSSocket1 is used to accept only incoming connections. This is typical of TCP/IP server applications. In our example, we pass the connection to DSSocket2 by setting its Socket property to the SocketID. If no error occurs, the caption displays the word "Connected."

At this point Form2.DSSocket1 is connected to Form1.DSSocket2. If these two forms were inside of two applications anywhere in the world, they could send data back and forth to each other, the speed of the transmission limited only by the speed of one's Internet connection, which can range from a 2400-baud modem connection to a multi-gigabit direct connection. Think of it; There is some extremely cool software to be written here!

Closing the Connection

When you click the btnAction button at this point, as the caption "Close" indicates, the client will close the connection. Take a look again at Figure 2.6 at the btnAction_Click event procedure. If the caption of the button is "Close," then the second piece of code in this procedure is executed. The Action property is set to the constant SOCK_ACTION_CLOSE, inside a local error handler of course, and the button and form captions are reset.

The server detects that the connection was closed and fires the DSSocket2_Close event (shown in Figure 2.5). In this event, the server form's caption is reset to "Listening to port 2700" and the whole process is ready to happen again.

The Close event only occurs when the other side closes the connection. It does not fire when you close the connection by setting Action to SOCK_ACTION_CLOSE.

Two properties, Timeout and Linger, determine what happens when you close a connection yourself. When the Linger property is True and the Timeout is greater than zero, then when you close the connection the connection isn't closed until either all data in the send buffer is sent, or Timeout number of seconds have elapsed.

If Linger is True and Timeout is false, DSSOCK closes immediately without waiting for data to be sent. If Linger is false, and Timeout is greater than zero, then DSSOCK waits Timeout number of seconds before closing, and does not close prematurely even if all data has been sent.

The only thing left to talk about for this example is what happens when the End button is clicked. What happens is important. Instead of just executing a Visual Basic End statement, the forms are unloaded. In each form's Unload event, any and all socket controls on that form are told to close their connections, whether or not there are any connections. Using On Error Resume Next prevents any "The connection is already closed" errors from rearing their ugly heads. In the main form's Unload event procedure, after all the other forms are unloaded, an End statement can safely end the program.

Visual Basic's End statement, like the Stop button, does not allow forms' Unload event to fire, which means that data can be lost and connections stranded. Can you imagine if you were running a web server, which absolutely *must* listen and respond to connections on port 80, and an error brought the application down? You would have to reboot. Oops!

Handling Multiple Connections on the Server Side

This sample we've been looking at is fine for demonstration purposes, but you and I both know that in the real world a server has to handle multiple connections at the same time. Fortunately, with a little smart code you can handle as many connections as your server can handle.

The main idea behind multiple connections is that one instance of a DSSOCK control equals one connection. So, for every incoming connection you must have an available DSSOCK control loaded in memory to act as a data socket. Therefore, you must have at least one socket control as a control array (Index Property set to 0) so that new instances can be loaded as needed. You still use only one listen control to act as an answer agent.

Assuming that dssData is a control array, here is how you would load a new instance:

```
Load dssData(Index)
```

where Index is the control index that you want to load. You must keep track of this index. Every time you load a new instance, you have to keep track of its instance. For example:

```
Global nNumSockets As Integer

nNumSockets = nNumSockets + 1

Load dssData(nNumSockets)
```

Since nNumSockets keeps track of how many Socket controls are being used, the index will always be correct. If dssData(1) is not loaded, you can load dssData(3), but if you have already loaded dssData(3) and you try and load it again, you will get an error.

Right now you might be thinking that you could just keep loading new instances of the DSSOCK control for each new connection. Although this will work up to the point where you run out of memory, it is not a good idea. Every time you get a connection you have to first look at each of the loaded controls and use the first one that is not already in use.

Take a look at the code in Figure 2.7. This code makes use of a global Socket user-defined Type array that holds information about the sockets used in the project. Every time a new DSSOCK control is loaded, the Socket array grows so that the new control's index is the same as the highest index in the Socket array. Therefore, for a given index the following is always true: Socket(Index) holds information about DSSock1(Index).

▬▬▬▬▬▬ **Figure 2.7** Handling multiple connections.

```
Private Sub dssAnswer_Accept(SocketID As Integer)
'-- Assign a DSSOCK control instance to this connection.


    Dim nIndex As Integer


    For nIndex = 1 To gnNumSockets
        If Socket(nIndex).Connected = False Then
            '-- This socket control is not in use. Use it.
            Socket(nIndex).Connected = True
            dsSocket1(nIndex).Socket = SocketID
            Exit Sub
        End If
    Next


    '-- All loaded socket controls are in use. Load a new one.
    gnNumSockets = gnNumSockets + 1
    Load dsSocket1(gnNumSockets)


    '-- Grow the Socket array
    ReDim Preserve Socket(1 To gnNumSockets) As SockStatusType
```

```
        Socket(gnNumSockets) = True


    '-- Assign the socket connection
    dsSocket1(gnNumSockets).Socket = SocketID

End Sub



Private Sub dsSocket1_Close(Index As Integer, ErrorCode As Integer, _
ErrorDesc As String)


    '-- Default SendReady to False
    Socket(Index).Connected = False

End Sub



Private Sub dss_Exception(Index As Integer, ErrorCode As Integer, ErrorDesc _
As String)


    '-- Did the socket close?
    If ErrorCode = SOCK_ERR_CLOSED Then
        '-- Default SendReady to False
        Socket(Index).Connected = False
    End If

End Sub



Private Sub SendData (Index As Integer, szData As String)


    '-- Default SendReady to False
    Socket(Index).SendReady = False
```

```
    '-- Capture the error
    On Error Resume Next
    dsSocket1(Index).Send = szData


    '-- Did we get an "operation would block" error?
    If Err = SOCK_ERR_OPERATIONWOULDBLOCK Then
        '-- Wait until the SendReady event has fired
        Do
            DoEvents
        Loop Until Socket(Index).SendReady
        dsSocket1(Index).Send = szData
    End If

End Sub



Private Sub dsSocket1_SendReady (Index As Integer)

    Socket(Index).SendReady = True

End Sub
```

DSSOCK has a property called State. It is used to determine whether or not the socket is connected. I choose not to use it because the documentation states that if an exception has occurred, the State property may not be accurate. Instead, my code sets the Socket(Index)Connected array member to True when the socket is initially connected, and to False if and when either the Close event is fired or the Exception event with a close error is fired.

When a new connection attempt is made in the Accept event, the code walks through the Socket array looking to see if one of the controls already loaded is available. It does this by checking the Socket(Index).Connected value. If one is available, the SocketID is assigned to it, and its corresponding Connected value is set True.

If the loop completes indicating that no free socket controls were found, a new one is loaded, gnNumSockets, the number of sockets variable is incremented by one, the SocketID is assigned, and its corresponding Connected value is set True. Using this technique, there are only as many controls in memory as the highest number of simultaneous connections.

Sending Data

What could be easier than sending data? DSSocket1.Send = <string>. Well, yes, it is that easy, but a problem can occur that you should be aware of. If you send data to WinSock faster than it can send it down the stack, it will return an error. The error is WinSock 1.1 error 21035, or "Operation Would Block." This occurs when the underlying network is busy sending other data, and cannot send your data right away. *Blocking* is what happens when an application goes into a tight loop waiting for the availability of some other process, and in doing so it locks up the system.

DSSOCK.BAS includes a SendData routine, which accepts a DSSock control and a string of data and makes sure it is sent to the server.

```
Sub SendData(DSSock As Control, szData As String)

    gnSendReady = False


    On Error Resume Next
    DSSock.Send = szData
    If Err = SOCK_ERR_OPERATIONWOULDBLOCK Then
        Do
            DoEvents
        Loop Until gnSendReady
        DSSock.Send = szData
    End If


End Sub
```

In this routine, if an Operation Would Block error occurs when trying to send the data (szData), the code goes into a loose loop (for lack of a better word), calling DoEvents so the system doesn't lock up. The loop is broken when the gnSendReady global integer variable is set to True, which only occurs when DSSock's SendReady event is fired after an Operation Would Block error is resolved. For this reason, you must put the line gnSendReady = True in the client DSSOCK control's SendReady event.

Receiving Data

The smooth operation of your WinSock program depends almost entirely on how you handle received data. There are many different ways to do this, and you will have to make the final decision as to how you are going to approach it.

The DSSOCK WinSock custom control fires a Receive event when data is received:

```
Private Sub DSSocket1_Receive (ReceiveData As String)


End Sub
```

Anytime data is received by DSSOCK, this event fires. The Receive event will not fire if your code is in a tight loop, or a loop in which DoEvents is not called. *If the Receive event does not fire when it has to, you will lose your data!*

How important is it that you not write code with tight loops? Extremely; read on.

LineMode, EOLChar, and DataSize

There are two ways to tell DSSOCK to receive data, in line mode or binary mode. When DSSOCK is in line mode then the Receive event is fired for every line of text received. A line of text usually ends with a line feed (ASCII 10) but you can tell DSSOCK which character to recognize as an *end-of-line* character. When DSSOCK is in binary mode (the default), the Receive event is fired after every block of data is received by WinSock.

To set DSSOCK into line mode, set the LineMode property to True. Define the end-of-line character by setting the EOLChar property to the ASCII value of the character. The default value is 10 (line feed).

When LineMode is False, indicating binary mode, the DataSize property defines the maximum size of the ReceiveData variable, or the largest amount of data DSSOCK will receive before firing the Receive event.

The Simple Approach

The first and easiest method for handling received data is to write the data process-ing code right in the Receive event itself. For example, let's say you connect to a server application, and the server application sends you one line command that you must respond to. It would be very easy to write it like the code shown in Figure 2.8.

■■■■■■■ **Figure 2.8** Simple example of handling received data.

```
Private Sub DSSocket1_Receive (ReceiveData As String)

 '-- A one-line command was received from the server.

    Dim szCmd as String

    '-- The leftmost two characters define the command.
    szCmd = Left$(ReceiveData, 2)

    '-- Everything from the third character on is data.
    ReceiveData = Mid$(ReceiveData, 3)

    '-- What does the server want us to do?
    Select Case szCmd

        Case "GD"  '-- GetDate command.
            Call GetDate(ReceiveData)

        Case "SD"  '-- SetDate command.
            Call SetDate(ReceiveData)

    End Select

End Sub
```

A New Twist

Since DSSOCK is in line mode, and every line consists of a command and data, you can parse the data easily with a Select Case statement. What if the server sent two lines per command, the first line being the command and the second line being data? How would you discern the command from the data? Is the command a fixed length? If so, then you can test the length of ReceiveData to determine whether you are receiving a command or data. The code in Figure 2.9 shows how to handle this scenario.

▰▰▰▰▰▰ **Figure 2.9** A slightly more sophisticated example of handling received data.

```
Private Sub DSSocket1_Receive (ReceiveData As String)

    '-- Save the value of szCmd between events.
    Static szCmd as String


    '-- Is this a command?
    If Len(ReceiveData) = 4 Then
        '-- Yes. The leftmost two characters define the command.
        szCmd = Left$(ReceiveData, 2)
    Else
        '-- What was the last command we received?
        Select Case szCmd


            Case "GD"   '-- GetDate command.
                Call GetDate(ReceiveData)


            Case "SD"   '-- SetDate command.
                Call SetDate(ReceiveData)


        End Select


        '-- Reset the command to an empty string because
```

```
          '    we are done with it.
          szCmd = ""


     End If


End Sub
```

If the data received is four bytes (characters) long, then we have received a command. The Static keyword tells VB to preserve the value of this variable. When a
command is received, it is saved into the szCmd string variable, and saved for the
next time the Receive event is fired. When that happens, if ReceiveData is not a
command, then the last command received is processed, the data associated with
the command being the current ReceiveData variable. The only problem with this
approach occurs when the data is exactly four bytes, the same size as a command.

Splitting Up the Process with Flags

Sometimes your program executes a series of commands, each of which must be
handled differently. Many times, the data cannot be identified simply by its length
or its content. It is for this reason I like to use flags. A flag is a variable that is set
in one part of the program and read in another part of the program to help your
program communicate with itself across its functions and subroutines.

Many people have a dislike for flags because they can be easily abused and you feel
you have lost control. I disagree. Ever since the days of assembler programming
flags have played an important part in determining states of code and data. If you
are careless in how you use flag variables they can make your life miserable.
However, the problem isn't the use of flags, but simply knowing when and when
not to use them.

Consider the following scenario. You are requesting to download a file from a server,
but first you need to know how many files there are. The protocol dictates that first
you must send a DIR command to get a list of files. The server then sends one filename per line followed by a period on a line by itself to indicate the end of the list.

Let's also say that you want to write a routine to handle the whole process. The routine sends the DIR command to the server. How is your routine going to know when the list of files has been completely received? Consider the code in Figure 2.10.

■■■■■■■■■ **Figure 2.10** Receiving data with flags—example 1.

```
Option Explicit

Dim nNumLinesReceived As Integer   '-- Number of lines received.
Dim nComplete As Integer           '-- Flag set True when data has
                                   '   been completely received.
Dim szData() As String             '-- String array that holds
                                   '   received data.


Private Sub DSSocket1_Receive (ReceiveData As String)

    '-- A new line has been received. Up the count
    nNumLinesReceived = nNumLinesReceived + 1


    '-- Grow the szData array by one element
    Redim Preserve szData(nNumLinesReceived) As String


    '-- Set the data into the new array element
    szData(nNumLinesReceived) = ReceiveData


    '-- Is this data a period on a line by itself?
    If ReceiveData = "." & vbCrLf Then
        '-- Yes. Tell the app we've received all the data.
        nComplete = True
    End If


End Sub


Private Sub Command1_Click ()
```

```
'-- We are assuming the DSSocket1 control
'       already connected to the server.

Dim nIndex As Integer

'-- Initialize
Command1.Enabled = False
nComplete = False
Redim szData(0) As String
nNumLinesReceived = 0

'-- Send the command to get the list of files.
DSSocket1.Send = "DIR" & vbCrLf

'-- Wait for flag to clear
Do Until nComplete
     DoEvents
Loop

'-- Fill a list box with the file names.

ListBox1.Clear '-- clear the contents first.

'-- Indexes 1 through nNumLinesReceived - 1 hold
'     the list of files. The last line is the period.
For nIndex = 1 To nNumLinesReceived - 1
     ListBox1.AddItem szData(nIndex)
Next

Command1.Enabled = True

End Sub
```

This code shows the interaction between an initiating process (Command1_Click) and the Receive event where data is received. The code assumes that you have a list box and a DSSOCK control on the form, and that the DSSOCK control is already connected to its host. Also, it is assumed that the DSSOCK control's LineMode property is set to True, and that the EOLChar property is set to 10 (linefeed). The goal is to receive an array of filenames from the server by issuing a DIR command. The server responds by sending a list of files, one per line, ending with a period on a line by itself.

The nNumLinesReceived variable, nComplete variable, and the szData string array are shared between all subs and functions in the form because they are defined in the form's General Declarations section. Every time a new line is received, the nNumLinesReceived integer is incremented by one, a new element is added to the szData array, and the received data is copied to the new array element. If the received data is a period on a line by itself, then the nComplete flag is set to True.

In Command1_Click, the DIR command is sent to the server, which prompts the server to send the list of filenames. After the command is sent, the code waits in a DoEvents loop until the nComplete flag is set, indicating that all the filenames have been received. It is imperative that you use DoEvents in this loop; otherwise your application will appear to hang as it executes the loop over and over again without allowing other processes to occur. People will begin to think you are a terrible programmer. You'll be fired, and you'll lose all your friends. You think I'm kidding?

A Slight Variation

OK, what if your commands elicit short, one- or two-line responses from the server, with no period on a line by itself to indicate the end of the server's responses? What if all you have to go by is the number of lines that should be received? Simple: Just wait in your loop until x number of lines have been received. Skip the nComplete flag altogether. Consider the code in Figure 2.11, a modification to Command_Click in Figure 2.10. The difference is that instead of waiting for a period to be received signifying the end of transmission, simply wait until the appropriate number of lines have been received. If the server is supposed to send back two lines of text, wait until two lines are received. Also, in the Receive event, increment the nNumLinesReceived variable last so that the loop will not exit until the routine has completed.

Figure 2.11 A slight modification to the code in Figure 2.10.

Figure 2.11 A slight modification to the code in Figure 2.10.

```
Private Sub Command1_Click ()
    '-- We are assuming the DSSocket1 control
    '     already connected to the server.

    '-- Initialize
    Command1.Enabled = False
    Redim szData(0) As String
    nNumLinesReceived = 0

    '-- Send some command that elicits a two-line response
    DSSocket1.Send = "FOO"

    '-- Wait to receive two lines
    Do
        DoEvents
    Loop Until nNumLinesReceived >= 2

        '-- At this point the data has been received. Process it here.

    Command1.Enabled = True

End Sub
```

Event Driven = No Loops

What if you don't want to use DoEvents in your code? You've heard that excessive use of DoEvents can cause recursion (see recursion). This is both true and not true. It could cause problems in this case only if the user could press the Command button again while your loop is executing. Fortunately, though, setting the Enabled property of the button to False at the top of the code and reenabling it at the bottom of the code prevents this from happening, so you are safe.

It does bring up a good point, however. What if you don't want to sit in a loop for any particular reason? You could instead have the Receive event call a particular routine when it has completely received the data. Imagine now that the server responds to two commands: DIR and GET. DIR is the same as before, but a new command, GET, tells the server to send a file. In your client application you want to let the user pick a filename from the list box we filled in Figure 2.10, and then once the file has been received you want it to show up on the Windows 95 desktop.

The code in Figure 2.12 does this by introducing nCommandNumber, a new variable that will identify the last command sent to the server. Clicking the command button sets nCommandNumber to COMMAND_DIR, or 1, sends the DIR command, and exits. No loops are necessary in this case.

▬▬▬▬▬ **Figure 2.12** Receiving data with flags—example 2.

```
Option Explicit


Dim nNumLinesReceived As Integer    '-- Number of lines received.
Dim szData() As String              '-- String array that holds
                                    '      received data.
Dim nCommandNumber As Integer       '-- Holds the command last issued.


Const COMMAND_DIR = 1               '-- Command number constants.
Const COMMAND_GET = 2


#If Win32 Then
    Private Declare Function GetWindowsDirectory Lib "kernel32" Alias _
        "GetWindowsDirectoryA" (ByVal lpBuffer As String, _
        ByVal nSize As Long) As Long
#ElseIf Win16 Then
    Private Declare Function GetWindowsDirectory Lib "Kernel" _
        (ByVal lpBuffer As String, ByVal nSize As Integer) As Integer
```

```
#End If


Private Sub DSSocket1_Receive (ReceiveData As String)


    '-- A new line has been received. Up the count
    nNumLinesReceived = nNumLinesReceived + 1


    '-- Grow the szData array by one element
    Redim Preserve szData(nNumLinesReceived) As String


    '-- Set the data into the new array element
    szData(nNumLinesReceived) = ReceiveData


    '-- Is this data a period on a line by itself?
    If ReceiveData = "." & vbCrLf Then
        '-- Yes. Call the appropriate procedure
        Select Case nCommandNumber
            Case COMMAND_DIR
                Call FillListBox
            Case COMMAND_GET
                Call SaveFileToDesktop
        End Select
    End If


End Sub


Private Sub Command1_Click ()
    '-- We are assuming the DSSocket1 control
    '       already connected to the server.


    '-- Initialize
```

```
        Command1.Enabled = False
        Redim szData(0) As String
        nNumLinesReceived = 0


        '-- Set the nCommandNumber
        nCommandNumber = COMMAND_DIR


        '-- Send the command to get the list of files.
        DSSocket1.Send = "DIR" & vbCrLf


        Command1.Enabled = True

End Sub


Private Sub ListBox1_Click ()
        '-- We are assuming the DSSocket1 control
        '     already connected to the server.

        '-- Initialize
        Command1.Enabled = False
        Redim szData(0) As String
        nNumLinesReceived = 0


        '-- Set the nCommandNumber
        nCommandNumber = COMMAND_GET


        '-- Send the command to receive the currently selected file.
        DSSocket1.Send = "GET " & ListBox1.List(ListBox1.ListIndex) & vbCrLf


        Command1.Enabled = True


End Sub
```

```
Private Sub FillListBox ()

    Dim nIndex As Integer
    '-- Fill a list box with the file names.

    ListBox1.Clear '-- clear the contents first.

    '-- Indexes 1 through nNumLinesReceived - 1 hold
    '   the list of files. The last line is the period.
    For nIndex = 1 To nNumLinesReceived - 1
        ListBox1.AddItem szData(nIndex)
    Next

End Sub

Private Sub SaveFileToDesktop ()

    Dim nFileNum As Integer
    Dim nIndex As Integer
    Dim szBuffer As String
    Dim lLenBuffer As Long
    Dim szWindowsDir as String

    '-- Get the Windows directory name
    szBuffer = Space$(255)
    lLenBuffer = GetWindowsDirectory(szBuffer, Len(szBuffer))
    szWindowsDir = Left$(szBuffer, lLenBuffer)

    nFileNum = FreeFile

    '-- Index 1 holds the name of the file.
    Open szWindowsDir & "\DESKTOP\" & szData(1) For Output As nFileNum
```

```
'-- Indexes 2 through nNumLinesReceived - 1 hold
'   the file data. The last line is the period.
For nIndex = 1 To nNumLinesReceived - 1
    Print #nFileNum, szData(nIndex);
Next


Close nFileNum


End Sub
```

The Receive event receives all the data, and just like in Figure 2.10, determines if the data is complete by looking for a period on a line by itself. When complete, it calls the appropriate routine, based on the value of nCommandNumber. In the case of COMMAND_DIR, the FillListBox routine is called, which fills the list box with the names of the files, just as in Figure 2.10.

When the user clicks on a filename in the list box, nCommandNumber is set to COMMAND_GET, or 2, the GET command is sent to the server, and the routine exits. Again, no looping is necessary. Let's assume that the server will send the name of the file on the first line, then the file data itself line by line, and ending, of course, with a period on a line by itself. Once the file has been completely received in the Receive event the SaveFileToDesktop routine is called, which gets the desktop directory name and saves the file right on the Windows 95 desktop. The user sees the file just *appear.* This approach to receiving data makes the most sense in an event-driven language, such as Visual Basic, because the code is never polling or sitting in a loop waiting for something.

Which Approach Is Better?

Use whatever is appropriate for the task at hand. If you are processing only a few commands, and you know the requirements will not grow, then you are extremely naive. No! You should use whatever approach fits the requirements.

There is no best approach for all situations across the board. If you are going to have lots of different types of transactions that all require different processing then use the event-driven method. If there is lots of conversation between the client and server for a particular transaction, use the polling method, where you wait in a loop until x number of lines have been received. As long as you know what options are available to you, you can use the best method for the job.

Error Handling

Error handling is an essential part of communications programming. Communications applications are among the hardest to debug because they happen in real time. It is absolutely vital that you implement some method of error handling. In this section I'll show you a few techniques that you can use to help you write the perfect application.

WinSock Errors

DSSOCK catches all of the WinSock errors and reports them via the Exception event. Figure 2.13 shows a list of all the possible WinSock errors. If you are confused about what they mean, don't worry. There are only two people on the planet who actually do. If it sounds like I'm brushing off an opportunity for some extended research, you're right. I am doing exactly that. The fact is that you are an applications programmer and you don't care why your WinSock isn't working. All you need to know is that it doesn't work. There are plenty of diagnostic tools available for network administrators that help pinpoint problems with the network. Besides, your users don't want to see seven consecutive dialog boxes that say stuff like "Address family not supported by protocol family" or some other wacky message. When I write WinSock apps, I usually just throw up a dialog box saying that the connection has been broken when it breaks because of an error. The only time I will attempt to reconnect is if the application is in the middle of transferring a file or some other valuable information.

Even though you should shield the user from these errors when they occur, you should monitor them while you are writing and debugging your code. There are times when you go to open a socket and its already open because you stopped the program in the middle somewhere before it had a chance to close.

Figure 2.13 WinSock error codes and descriptions.

Error Variable	Number	Explanation
WSAEINTR	21004	Interrupted system call
WSAEBADF	21009	Bad file number
WSAEACCES	21013	Permission denied
WSAEFAULT	21014	Bad address
WSAEINVAL	21022	Invalid argument
WSAEMFILE	21024	Too many open files
WSAEWOULDBLOCK	21035	Operation would block
WSAEINPROGRESS	21036	Operation now in progress
WSAEALREADY	21037	Operation already in progress
WSAENOTSOCK	21038	Socket operation on non-socket
WSAEDESTADDRREQ	21039	Destination address required
WSAEMSGSIZE	21040	Message too long
WSAEPROTOTYPE	21041	Protocol wrong type for socket
WSAENOPROTOOPT	21042	Bad protocol option
WSAEPROTONOSUPPORT	21043	Protocol not supported
WSAESOCKTNOSUPPORT	21044	Socket type not supported
WSAEOPNOTSUPP	21045	Operation not supported on socket
WSAEPFNOSUPPORT	21046	Protocol family not supported
WSAEAFNOSUPPORT	21047	Address family not supported by protocol family
WSAEADDRINUSE	21048	Address already in use
WSAEADDRNOTAVAIL	21049	Can't assign requested address
WSAENETDOWN	21050	Network is down
WSAENETUNREACH	21051	Network is unreachable
WSAENETRESET	21052	Net dropped connection or reset
WSAECONNABORTED	21053	Software caused connection abort
WSAECONNRESET	21054	Connection reset by peer
WSAENOBUFS	21055	No buffer space available
WSAEISCONN	21056	Socket is already connected

WSAENOTCONN	21057	Socket is not connected
WSAESHUTDOWN	21058	Can't send after socket shutdown
WSAETOOMANYREFS	21059	Too many references, can't splice
WSAETIMEDOUT	21060	Connection timed out
WSAECONNREFUSED	21061	Connection refused
WSAELOOP	21062	Too many levels of symbolic links
WSAENAMETOOLONG	21063	File name too long
WSAEHOSTDOWN	21064	Host is down
WSAEHOSTUNREACH	21065	No Route to Host
WSAENOTEMPTY	21066	Directory not empty
WSAEPROCLIM	21067	Too many processes
WSAEUSERS	21068	Too many users
WSAEDQUOT	21069	Disc Quota Exceeded
WSAESTALE	21070	Stale NFS file handle
WSAEREMOTE	21071	Too many levels of remote in path
WSASYSNOTREADY	21091	Network SubSystem is unavailable
WSAVERNOTSUPPORTED	21092	WINSOCK DLL Version out of range
WSANOTINITIALISED	21093	Successful WSASTARTUP not yet performed
WSAHOST_NOT_FOUND	22001	Host not found
WSATRY_AGAIN	22002	Non-Authoritative Host not found
WSANO_RECOVERY	22003	Non-Recoverable errors: FORMERR, REFUSED, NOTIMP
WSANO_DATA	22004	Valid name, no data record of requested type

For the final version the only exception you need to be concerned with (other than Operation Would Block) is the close error SOCK_ERR_CLOSED. If the connection is lost due to an error, you have a decision to make. Do you attempt to reconnect, do you do nothing, or do you ask the users if they want to attempt to reconnect? It totally depends on the design of your application.

Error-Handling Techniques

I have a few general error-handling techniques up my sleeve that lend themselves very nicely to communications programming and let me tell you, they itch! The most valuable technique for debugging is using error-handling options, which can be controlled by the user via the command line. I like to give my applications a command line switch that tells me whether or not to catch errors and whether or not to display them.

Visual Basic's Command$ function returns the entire command line, or everything after the executable name that is used to launch your program. For example, say that your application's name is NETZAP.EXE and the command used to start it is defined like so:

```
C:\NETZAP\NETZAP.EXE /D
```

In this case, Command returns /D. Anywhere in your program you can use the Command$ function as a string variable that contains /D, or whatever the command line consists of.

You might want to establish a command line option /D that stands for *debug mode*. Immediately following the /D the user enters a number to indicate the mode, for example, /D1, /D2, and so on.

Minimal Error Trapping

When your application is not in debug mode, that is, no command line switch, it is best to present only those errors that the user can do something about. For example, if your WinSock connection is unexpectedly broken because of a network error you will first get an Exception event indicating the network error, then you will get another Exception event with the close error, indicating that the connection is closed.

Don't just pop up a MsgBox in the Exception event. Ignore the first error. When the close error (via the Exception event) occurs, inform the user that the connection was unexpectedly broken and that she might want to wait a few minutes before reconnecting in case there is a problem at the other end. You might want to explain that this kind of thing happens from time to time and that she can still save her data, or whatever. The more you make the user feel at ease, the more enjoyable the experience of using your software. I can't tell you how invaluable that advice has proven itself to be in my part of the world.

Every time an error occurs, you could save the description, date, and time in module-level variables. If an error causes the connection to be lost, display a message box with the last error that occurred and when it occurred, if at all. This is a nice level of error handling to give the user. You might also want to display any helpful tips at this time to restore the user's confidence.

Debug.Print Error Trapping

The Visual Basic Debug window is a nice way to monitor your application during development. You can display any string with the Debug.Print method like so:

```
Debug.Print "This is what I'm displaying in the debug window"
```

Since you can print any string, you can comprise your own error and status messages from variables that you wish to monitor. For example, let's say you want to monitor the number of lines of text received. With LineMode set to True, you could use the following code in the Receive event:

```
Sub dsSocket1_Receive(ReceiveData As String)

    Static nLineCount As Integer

    nLineCount = nLineCount + 1
    Debug.Print Str$(nLineCount) & " lines received"

    '-- Process data here

End Sub
```

Message Dialog Reporting

This is the most widely used and abused method of reporting errors. Most programmers don't realize that reporting errors during development and reporting errors to the user are *two totally different globs of petroleum.* When you are developing you want errors to be short and to the point. The user, however, is probably not a developer and has not spent half as much time using the program as you have developing it. Therefore, it is absolutely vital that you clean up error messages for the user before you ship your product. Did I mention that this was important?

Error Log Reporting

This is my favorite method of debugging. You can write errors and data to a log file in real time as you are sending and receiving data. A little extra code is required to implement this, but when you need it, it will save your behind.

Error-Handling Code in DSSOCK.BAS

DSSOCK.BAS contains code for helping you handle errors in your application. Take a look at the code in Figure 2.14. Call GetDebugMode from your startup form or procedure. GetDebugMode checks the Command line for a /D debug mode option and sets the global integer gnDebugMode. If a command line option is not specified then the default option applies.

■■■■■■■■ **Figure 2.14** Error handling code in DSSOCK.BAS.

```
'-- Error log file name. Change if desired
Global Const gszLogFileName = "ERRORLOG.TXT"


'-- File handle for the log file (if used)
Global gnLogFileNum As Integer


'-- Which debug option is used
Global gnDebugMode As Integer


Global Const DEBUG_MODE_MINIMAL = 0
Global Const DEBUG_MODE_DESIGNTIME = 1
Global Const DEBUG_MODE_DIALOG = 2
Global Const DEBUG_MODE_WRITELOG = 3


Sub GetDebugMode()


    Dim szCmd As String
    Dim nPos As Integer
```

```
        szCmd = Trim$(UCase$(Command$))

        '-- Are there any command line options?

        If Len(Command) = 0 Then

            '-- No. Exit

            Exit Sub

        Else

            nPos = InStr(Command, "/D")

            If nPos Then

                gnDebugMode = Val(Mid$(Command$, nPos + 2, 1))

            End If

        End If


    End Sub



Sub WriteLogFile(szData As String)


        '-- Is the file not open yet?

        If gnLogFileNum = 0 Then

            '-- Open it

            gnLogFileNum = FreeFile

            Open App.Path & "\" & gszLogFileName For Binary As gnLogFileNum

            Seek #gnLogFileNum, LOF(gnLogFileNum) + 1

        End If


        '-- Write the string

        szData = Str$(Now) & Chr$(9) & szData & vbCrLf

        Put #gnLogFileNum, , szData


    End Sub
```

When an error occurs in your program you can check the gnDebugMode value (see Figure 2.15). Depending on the debug mode set via the command line, one of the four actions will occur. Take a look at the last case, DEBUG_MODE_WRITELOG. The WriteLogFile function writes a string to a log file. It's a fairly simple function, but I'd like to point it out anyway.

▬▬▬▬ **Figure 2.15** Intelligent error handling.

```
Sub dsSocket1_Exception(ErrorCode As Integer, ErrorDesc As String)

    Static szLastError As String
    Static szLastTime As String
    Dim szMsg As String
    Dim szErrorMsg As String

    szErrorMsg = "Error" & Str$(ErrorCode) & " " & ErrorDesc

    Select Case gnDebugMode
        Case DEBUG_MODE_MINIMAL
            If ErrorCode = SOCK_ERR_CLOSED Then
                szMsg = "The connection has been unexpectedly broken."
                If Len(szLastTime) Then
                    szMsg = szMsg & vbCrLf & _
                        "The Last error to occur was " & _
                        Chr$(34) & szLastError & Chr$(34) & _
                        " which occurred at " & szLastTime
                End If
                MsgBox szMsg, vbInformation
            End If
        Case DEBUG_MODE_DESIGNTIME
            Debug.Print szErrorMsg
```

```
        Case DEBUG_MODE_DIALOG
            MsgBox szErrorMsg
        Case DEBUG_MODE_WRITELOG
            WriteLogFile szErrorMsg
    End Select


    szLastError = szErrorMsg
    szLastTime = Now


End Sub
```

If you look at the WriteLogFile function, you will notice that the file is opened in Binary mode. Why is that? Speed: Binary mode is absolutely the fastest way to access a disk file in Visual Basic. The global gnLogFileNum integer variable holds the file number of the log file. If this number is zero then the log file has not been accessed yet and is opened in binary mode.

After being opened, the Seek command moves the file pointer to the end of the file, so that everything written to the file is appended to the end. The only problem that might occur with the code like this is if your application crashes and the program is ended abnormally, in which case the contents of the log file might get hosed. To avoid this, you can modify the code to simply open and close the file every time within the WriteLogFile routine, as shown in Figure 2.16.

UDP—User Datagram Protocol

UDP, or User Datagram Protocol, is a Transport layer protocol like TCP that can be used to move data. Since UDP is part of the TCP/IP protocol suite, it is readily available. In fact, DSSOCK is among the available WinSock controls that support UDP in addition to TCP.

The main difference with UDP is that it is connectionless and unreliable. Connectionless means that a handshake is not required before data can be sent, and

Figure 2.16 A more intelligent WriteLogFile routine.

```
Sub WriteLogFile(szData As String)

    Dim nLogFileNum As Integer

    '-- Open the log file
    nLogFileNum = FreeFile
    Open App.Path & "\" & gszLogFileName For Binary As nLogFileNum
    Seek #nLogFileNum, LOF(nLogFileNum) + 1

    '-- Write the string
    szData = Str$(Now) & Chr$(9) & szData & vbCrLf
    Put #nLogFileNum, , szData

    '-- Close the file
    Close nLogFileNum

End Sub
```

unreliable means that no error checking is performed on the data to insure that it arrived intact at its destination.

Since UDP does not have to do so much work to send data, it is faster than TCP. Since there is no error checking, however, UDP is not always used over TCP. Remember my motto, "Use the right tool for the job." Sometimes UDP is the right tool for the job and sometimes TCP is. You might not be able to think of a situation in which reliability is not an issue; however there are many different situations where UDP is very desirable.

One such situation is the broadcasting of digital audio and/or video over the Internet. Most all of the high-tech Internet audio and video systems out there use UDP over TCP because it is fast and error checking is not necessary. What happens if you are listening to digital audio in real time and you miss a few bytes? Considering that you are probably listening to eight thousand or more bytes per second, you won't even notice it. CU-SeeMe is a very popular Internet videoconferencing program that uses UDP. For more information on CU-SeeMe, check out the Yahoo database list of CU-SeeMe links at the following URL:

```
http://www.yahoo.com/Computers_and_Internet/Multimedia/Videoconferencing/CU_seeme/
```

Another good application of UDP is the U.S. Naval Observatory's Time server, which gives you an accurate time of day via UDP by connecting to their server. For more information on the U.S. Naval Observatory's Network Time Services, check out their home page at the following URL:

```
http://tycho.usno.navy.mil/ntp.html
```

Because of the lack of error handling there are risks that go along with using UDP. One risk is that you may receive packets out of sequence. One of the things TCP does very well is the resequencing of packets. Every TCP packet is numbered, and TCP guarantees that the packets are moved up the stack at the destination in the correct order. UDP does not employ such a method. UDP does no processing at all to the data except to tack a source address and a destination address onto each packet. If a router between the source and destination went down in midtransmission of your packets, and then came back on again before the transmission was complete, you might receive your packets out of order. This can be helpful, however, if the application using UDP wishes to handle packet sequencing itself and doesn't want the added overhead of TCP. Because of the sequencing issue, UDP is used mostly when sending either small and complete pieces of data or broadcasting streams of data, the idea being that if one packet misses the boat there are plenty more chances for successful transmission.

Another risk is that the data may not get to the destination at all. If a TCP packet fails to reach the destination, TCP reattempts to send the data until it is received. UDP packets are not so lucky. Therefore, UDP is well suited for query-response systems in which a response is required for each transmission. If a response is not received, then another query is sent until a response is delivered.

Yet another risk associated with UDP is that some routers filter out UDP packets entirely. The Network File System (NFS) is a file-sharing system that allows users to mount drives, like the Windows 95 Explorer or Windows 3.1 File Manager allow you to "attach" or "connect" other users' drives and directories to your machine. Well, NFS uses UDP. Therefore, many firewalls block UDP packets so that outsiders can't mount local directories and access the network unlawfully (as if there are actual laws to protect us from such crimes).

Since UDP is fast, it is desirable to use as an interprocess communication system on a local area network. Use it like you would use NetDDE (*gasp*) to send messages between applications on a network. Notify all the clients attached to the same server database that you've just changed the data they are viewing, and to refresh their display, and so on. DSSOCK has a property called SocketType. When set to 0 (default), WinSock is used. When set to 1, however, DSSOCK uses UDP if it is available. Since no connection is necessary, simply set the RemotePort and RemoteDotAddr properties, and send data with the send property.

Terminal—A WinSock Terminal Program

The Terminal program that comes with this book (TERMINAL.VBP) will help you determine the input and output requirements of any WinSock application you write. Terminal simply lets you connect to any machine on any port, lets you send data, and displays received data in a window.

Figure 2.17 shows the main screen of Terminal. You can open a connection by either clicking the Open button, or selecting Open from the Connection menu. Doing so displays the dialog box shown in Figure 2.18.

Enter the address and port number you wish to connect to. The Host Name can be either a name or IP address. If you check off the Line Mode Character option, the ASCII value given will be interpreted as the end of a line. If Line Mode is not checked off, the ASCII value given will not be used. Clicking the Cancel button cancels the operation of connecting.

Once connected, you will see received data displayed in the window as it is received. Sending data requires a bit more explanation, however. Typically

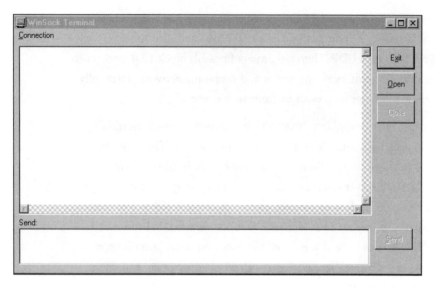

■■■■■■ **Figure 2.17** Main terminal screen.

when talking to servers on the Internet, you will be required to send single-line commands and parameters. Enter the text you want to send in the *send window* below the display window. To send, either press Enter or click the Send button. You can optionally append the text you send with a carriage return, a linefeed, or both. Typically a server will require a carriage return/linefeed (CR/LF) pair at the end of each line. This is not always the case, however; hence the option.

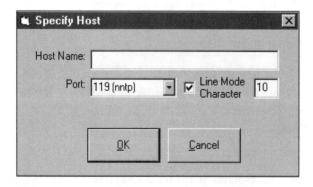

■■■■■■ **Figure 2.18** Connection dialog box.

I originally wrote Terminal to help me visualize how the protocols I write about in this book work. It's a lot of fun to connect to an NNTP server, for example, and browse Usenet articles with the raw protocol. It really gives you an idea of how things work.

Epilogue

By now you should have a good understanding of some of the most efficient techniques for communications programming, and you should have a working knowledge of the DSSOCK custom control. The chapters that follow use these techniques to access the more popular resources on the Internet: Gopher, Usenet, email, FTP, and the World Wide Web.

I feel it is wise to keep your protocols in Visual Basic so that they may be changed or updated easily and quickly as changes in technology advance. It is not necessary to spend a lot of money on tools that basically manipulate text through a high-level network connection. By using Visual Basic, you are leveraging VB's greatest strength, short development time, and at the same time keeping the size and requirements of your application to a minimum.

As you read these next chapters, try to think of ways that you can integrate the protocols into your own real-world problems and opportunities. The time is now for the creative spark to completely redifine how computers are used in the twenty-first century and beyond.

3

THE GOPHER

PROTOCOL

What Is Gopher?

Gopher is a protocol originally developed at the University of Minnesota in 1991. Minnesota is known as the "Gopher State," hence the origin of the name *Gopher*. The Gopher Protocol was designed as a means to standardize and simplify search and retrieval of documents and files on the Internet. Originally, it was a means for different universities and campuses to publish documents, making them globally available through the Internet. I hope this settles the raging debate once and for all. Fred Grandy had *nothing* to do with the Gopher protocol!

With a Gopher client program, you can connect to a Gopher server and browse hierarchical menus which point you to files and other menus. Gopher lets you download files, and other related utilities like Veronica let you perform searches for menu items and documents that exist on Gopher servers all over the world. The collection of Gopher servers and all their files available on the Internet is called Gopherspace.

In my opinion, Gopher is the precursor to the World Wide Web, which is the most popular form of Internet access. Before the web, you could still surf the net looking for files on Gopher servers, the main difference being that Gopher is text only, and the web has multimedia capabilities. According to the Internet Index, which is compiled by Win Treese (treese@OpenMarket.com), as of April 1994 there were 6958 Gopher servers on the Internet. This number has gone up since then, but surprisingly not much. The use of Gopher servers is dwindling due to the rapid success of the World Wide Web.

There are many more File Transfer Protocol (FTP) sites than there are Gopher sites on the Internet. However, I can tell you from a programmer's point of view, Gopher is a much easier protocol than FTP for simply downloading a file. FTP is really an OS shell, in which you can get directory listings, move and copy files, and assign permissions (attributes) of files and directories. Gopher is a much simpler protocol, although it does not have so many features. That, however, can work to your benefit if you are faced with the relatively easy task of simply connecting to a host and downloading a file.

You may think that the process for downloading a file from a Gopher server is a complex task. It isn't. As a matter of fact, the real strength of the Gopher Protocol is its simplicity. In a nutshell, the Gopher client connects to a Gopher server and sends a string that tells the server to send a file. The Gopher server then immediately sends the file and closes the connection. There is no external protocol such as Xmodem or Zmodem that you as a VB programmer have to use or implement. The data comes into your application through Windows Sockets, and you save it to disk. The underlying protocol takes care of all the data validation and packet sequencing, letting you concentrate on the application.

But before I go into how the Gopher protocol works and how to program it, I'm going to show you what using a Windows-based Gopher client is like. The program I use is called HGopher (by Martyn Hampson), a shareware Winsock-based Gopher client that we've included on the CD-ROM.

The HGopher main screen is shown in Figure 3.1. Each item in this list contains all the information needed to connect to its associated Gopher server and retrieve the item, which could be text, graphics, a file, or another list of menu items. You can view this information by clicking the info button, which is located to the left of a

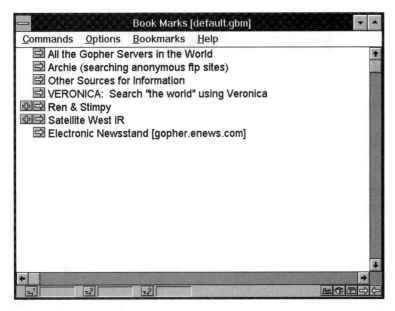

Figure 3.1 HGopher, a shareware Gopher client application.

particular item in the list. Click the info button for Electronic Newsstand [gopher.enews.com]. Figure 3.2 shows a dialog box that pops up containing connection information for the Electronic Newsstand Gopher. The dialog indicates that to access the Electronic Newsstand Gopher server, you must connect to gopher.enews.com on port 70.

Figure 3.3 shows a magazine article from *Alaska* Magazine that I retrieved by navigating the gopher menus.

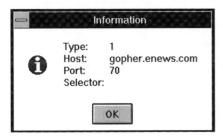

Figure 3.2 Information dialog box.

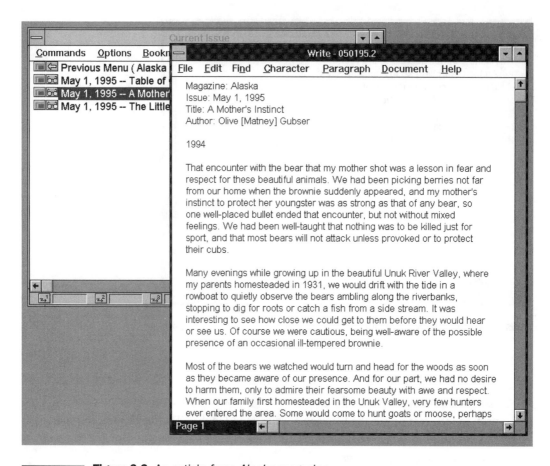

■■■■■■ **Figure 3.3** An article from *Alaska* magazine.

The Gopher Protocol— Behind the Scenes

It all starts with the items in the main menu of HGopher, or the items that are available when you first run the program. These items are saved in a local file, and they are called *bookmarks*. Basically, bookmarks are a starting point for you to find your way to other servers.

Note that bookmark is a general term used with many Internet client applications to describe the addresses of Internet hosts that you can save to a list and use to connect to those hosts at a later time. Bookmarks have nothing to do specifically with the Gopher protocol.

The information dialog box for the Electronic Newsstand shows us that we need to connect to gopher.enews.com on port 70, and that's exactly what HGopher does. Once connected, the client sends an empty line consisting of a carriage return and line feed (CR/LF). The Electronic Newsstand gopher sends back a list of menu items in a special format. Each item is separated by a CR/LF, and contains the following data separated by tabs, or ASCII character 9. Everything after the port number can be ignored. In this case, the Electronic Newsstand returns a plus sign after every line. Ignore it. You do not need this information. Figure 3.4 shows the format and an example of data returned by a Gopher server upon connection. After sending all the items, the Gopher server sends a period on a line by itself and closes the connection.

■■■■■■■ **Figure 3.4** Format and example of data returned by a Gopher server upon connection.

FORMAT:

[Item Type][Display Text][**TAB**][Selector][**TAB**][Host Name][**TAB**][Port][CRLF]

EXAMPLE:

```
0Visit our WWW site:
http://www.enews.com/{TAB}0/www{TAB}gopher.enews.com{TAB}70{TAB}+{CRLF}
1Introduction to The Electronic
Newsstand{TAB}1/Introduction{TAB}gopher.enews.com{TAB}70{TAB}+{CRLF}
0Notice of Copyright and General Disclaimer — Please
Read{TAB}0/Copyright{TAB}gopher.enews.com{TAB}70{TAB}+{CRLF}
1Magazines, Periodicals, and Journals (all
titles){TAB}1/magazines{TAB}gopher.enews.com{TAB}70{TAB}+{CRLF}
1Electronic
Bookstore{TAB}1/bookstore{TAB}gopher.enews.com{TAB}70{TAB}+{CRLF}
1Electronic Car Showroom(tm) (Toyota U.S.A. and more!)
{TAB}1/showroom{TAB}gopher.enews.com{TAB}70{TAB}+{CRLF}
1Business and Finance
```

```
Center{TAB}1/business{TAB}gopher.enews.com{TAB}70{TAB}+{CRLF}

1Computer and Technology

Resources{TAB}1/computers{TAB}gopher.enews.com{TAB}70{TAB}+{CRLF}

1Entertainment

Area{TAB}1/entertainment{TAB}gopher.enews.com{TAB}70{TAB}+{CRLF}

1Health and Medical

Center{TAB}1/health{TAB}gopher.enews.com{TAB}70{TAB}+{CRLF}

1The Renaissance Room{TAB}1/ren-room{TAB}gopher.enews.com{TAB}70{TAB}+{CRLF}

1Sports, Recreation and Leisure
Center{TAB}1/sports{TAB}gopher.enews.com{TAB}70{TAB}+{CRLF}

1Travel Resources{TAB}1/travel{TAB}gopher.enews.com{TAB}70{TAB}+{CRLF}

1News Services{TAB}1/news_services gopher.enews.com{TAB}70{TAB}+{CRLF}

1Search All Electronic Newsstand Articles by
Keyword{TAB}1/search{TAB}gopher.enews.com{TAB}70{TAB}+{CRLF}

.{CRLF}
```

In the example in Figure 3.4, the very first character in each line identifies the type of Gopher item for that line. The different Gopher Item types are shown in Figure 3.5. The first item is a text file, as indicated by a zero (0). The text displayed for this item is: Visit our WWW site: http://www.enews.com/. To retrieve this text file, we are instructed to connect to gopher.enews.com on port 70 and send the selector string, 0/www followed

Figure 3.5 Gopher item types. This information was taken from RFC (Request For Comments) file #1436 dated March, 1993. If you are confused by any of these item types, don't worry. You don't need to know all this stuff right away. Our VB Gopher client only deals with item types 0, 1, 3, 9, and g (text, menu, error, binary, and GIF files). It's nice to know that you could write Telnet support into a Gopher client, though.

Gopher Item Types:

0   Text File
1   Menu Item

2	CSO Phone Book Entity[1]
3	Error
4	Macintosh BINHEX encoded file
5	PC-DOS binary file of some type
6	UUEncoded file
7	Information applies to an Index Server[2]
8	Telnet session[3]
9	Binary file of any type
+	Information applies to a duplicate server[4]
g	GIF graphics file
I	Some type of image file
T	tn3270 based telnet session[3]

1. The client should talk CSO protocol.

2. The client should use a FullText Search transaction.

3. The client should connect to the given host at the given port. The name to log in at this host is in the selector string.

4. The information contained within is a duplicate of a primary server. The primary server is defined as the last DirEntity that has a non-plus "Type" field The client should use a transaction as defined by the primary server type field.

by a line feed (ASCII character 10). I know it doesn't say to use a line feed; however, you must. Whenever you send a selector string to a Gopher server, always end it with a linefeed or a CR/LF pair. A selector string is a string of text that you send to a Gopher server to retrieve an item, be it a menu, text file, graphic, or other file.

Accessing Gopher Servers in Visual Basic

Now that you have an idea of how Gopher works, how do you access a Gopher item in Visual Basic? Seeing that this is the first hands-on chapter, your chances are good that it's so easy you'll wonder why your VB guru friend down the hall doesn't know. You can actually write this sample code as you read, it's so easy. I promise.

The first thing you need to do is get all the data you need to access an item by Gopher. This consists of the Host Name, Port number, and selector. You can find this information by accessing the Gopher item with HGopher and clicking the Info button for the item whose information you wish to view. For our example, we will use the data for the first item in the Electronic Newsstand's main menu to retrieve a text file describing the Newsstand's World Wide Web server:

```
Host Name:      gopher.enews.com
Port:           70
Selector:       0/www
```

Start a new project in Visual Basic and load DSSOCK.VBX. Place a DSSOCK control onto your form and name it dssGopher. As well, create a command button on the form and name it btnGo. Next, add the DSSOCK constant file (DSSOCK.BAS) to your project. This file contains constants used by DSSOCK, such as:

```
Global Const SOCK_ACTION_CONNECT = 2
```

Use Option Explicit for this exercise. You can do this by selecting Environment from Visual Basic's Options menu and enabling syntax checking from the Environment Options window. This effectively enters the line Option Explicit in every module's declarations section.

DSSOCK has two ways in which it returns data to you, line mode or normal (not line mode). In line mode, the Receive event is fired every time a line is received. You can tell DSSOCK which character to recognize as the end-of-line character with the EOLChar property. For this example, set the LineMode property to True to enable line mode, and set EOLChar to 10 (line feed). You can either set these properties in the Form_Load procedure or at design time in the property window.

If you do not use LineMode, data is passed to the Receive event in chunks. This is good for receiving binary files, which we will cover later on.

There are four logical steps to receiving data from the Gopher server. The first step is to connect to the host computer. For this you must set DSSOCK's RemoteHost property to the name of the host, set the RemotePort property to the port number, and attempt a connection by setting the Action property to SOCK_ACTION_CON-NECT. Figure 3.6 shows the code to enter in the btnGo_Click event to make the

■■■■■■ **Figure 3.6** Connecting to a Gopher server.

```
Sub btnGo_Click ()

    dssGopher.RemotePort = 70
    dssGopher.RemoteHost = "gopher.enews.com"
    On Error Resume Next
    dssGopher.Action = SOCK_ACTION_CONNECT
    If Err Then
        MsgBox Error, 48
    End If

End Sub
```

■■■■■■

connection. Enter the code in Figure 3.6 now. When DSSOCK attempts a connection and there is a problem, an error is returned. For this reason, you need to trap any error that may occur with On Error Resume Next.

The second step is to send the selector upon connection to retrieve the desired item. When DSSOCK connects, it fires the Connect event. Send the selector string followed by a linefeed in the dssGopher_Connect event. This code is shown in Figure 3.7.

Step three is to process the received data. Once you send the selector, data will start pouring in. How you handle that data is totally up to you. In this case, we need to write all the received data to a file. In the Receive event, open the file for Output when the first line is received, and write the data to the file. In order to keep track of the file number, we need to create a module-level integer variable to hold it. Define this integer variable in the declarations section of your form:

```
Dim nFileNum As Integer
```

Figure 3.7 Sending a selector string to a Gopher server upon connection.

```
Sub dssGopher_Connect ()

    dssGopher.Send = "0/www" & vbCrLf

End Sub
```

In the Receive event procedure, if the file has not been opened yet, open it. The FreeFile function returns the next available file number. We know it will be 1 in this case, but it's good practice to always use it. Write the received data to the file whether or not the file was just opened. Figure 3.8 shows this code in the DSSOCK's Receive event.

Figure 3.8 Saving received data to a file.

```
Sub dssGopher_Receive (ReceiveData As String)

    '-- nFileNum is a form-level declared integer variable.
    If nFileNum = 0 Then
        nFileNum = FreeFile
        Open "TEMP.FIL" For Output As nFileNum
    End If

    '-- Write the data to the file.
    Print #nFileNum, ReceiveData;

End Sub
```

The final step is to close the file. When the file has been completely received, close it and display it with NOTEPAD.EXE. When the Gopher server has completed sending the file, it will close the connection. You can trap this with DSSOCK's Close event procedure. In the Close event procedure, first see if the file is still open, and then close it. If there is data in the file (checked via the LOF() function) then display it with NOTEPAD.EXE. Figure 3.9 shows the code for the Close event.

Of course, for demonstration purposes the code assumes that NOTEPAD.EXE is in C:\WINDOWS. If your windows directory is on another drive, specify the correct path to your windows directory instead of C:\WINDOWS. If you're not sure, then you probably installed Windows with the default options, in which case the code will work.

That's all there is to retrieving a known text file via Gopher! Don't you feel proud of yourself? This stuff is simple, isn't it? If you think some of the other chapters in this book are really difficult, think again. Using Winsock is the same from application to

▬▬▬▬ **Figure 3.9** Closing and displaying the file with NOTEPAD.

```
Sub dssGopher_Close ()

    Dim hTask As Long

    If nFileNum Then
        If LOF(nFileNum) Then
            Close nFileNum
            hTask = Shell("C:\WINDOWS\NOTEPAD.EXE TEMP.FIL", 1)
        End If
        nFileNum = 0
    End If

End Sub
```

application. Think about what you already know how to do. Connect to any computer on the Internet and transfer data between the host and your machine. The basic connection process is the same no matter what type of Internet program you are writing.

GETFILE: A Simple Routine to Download a File from a Gopher Server

Now that you know how to download a text file from a Gopher server, let's look at the GetFile function, which downloads a file from a Gopher server in binary mode, and wraps it all in a Visual Basic function that returns a success value. (*It figures, doesn't it? The guy makes me go through the arduous and painful process of writing a code to download a file, and now he tells me that I can just use a VB routine? Sheesh!*)

The GetFile function is pretty neat because it communicates with the DSSOCK control with flag variables, and even updates a status bar as the download takes place. Let's take a look at it. Open the GETFILE example project from the GETFILE sample directory. The GETFILE example is already set up to connect to the University of Illinois Department of Atmospheric Sciences Weather Machine Gopher Server and download the latest infrared satellite photo taken over the western United States, which is updated hourly. Figure 3.10 shows the GETFILE example program running under Windows 95.

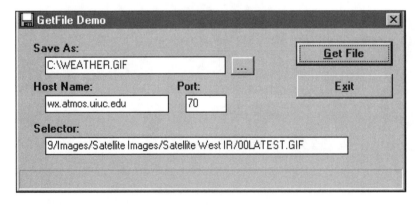

■■■■■■■ **Figure 3.10** GetFile Demo.

This is an extremely cool Gopher site, and perfect for demonstration purposes, because every hour at this site a file called 00LATEST.GIF is updated with a current photo. Therefore, no code ever has to change. You can run this program once an hour to get the latest photo. Figure 3.11 shows a satellite weather photo from the UIUC Weather Machine.

I first wrote about accessing the Internet with Visual Basic in the April 1995 *Visual Basic Programmer's Journal*. In that issue, I wrote a small application that connects to the UIUC Weather Machine hourly, converts the GIF file to a BMP file, and makes it your desktop's Wallpaper bitmap. You can get the source code that I wrote for that article from CompuServe in the VBPJFO forum, Magazine Library. The filename is INTER.ZIP. You can also download the file from Carl & Gary's VB Home Page, in the FTP section. The URL for the file on the VB home page is

Univ of Illinois, Urbana/Champaign – Dept of Atmospheric Sciences   Tue, May 23, 04 AM CDT 95052309Z

▮▮▮▮▮▮ **Figure 3.11** Weather map from the University of Illinois Department of Atmospheric Sciences Weather Machine Gopher Server.

http://www.apexsc.com/vb/ftp/misc/inter.zip. Also, the Netpaper sample program on the CD-ROM is an enhanced version of this application.

Figure 3.12 shows the calling syntax for GetFile. The return value is True if the file was successfully downloaded, or False if the file was either interrupted or an error occurred while downloading.

Let me talk briefly about the last parameter, picStatus. This is a picture control whose name you pass to GetFile. It will be used as a status field to display the number of bytes received and other status messages while the file is being downloaded. If you do not want this feature, simply remove all references to it from the code.

■■■■■■■■ **Figure 3.12** Call syntax for GetFile, a function that retrieves a file from a Gopher server.

Syntax:

```
Dim nResult As Integer


Result = GetFile(szFileName, szHostName, lPort, szSelector, picStatus)
```

Where:

- szFileName is a string containing the full path and filename that you want the file to be saved as.
- szHostName is a string containing the name of the remote host, for example: wx.atmos.uiuc.edu.
- lPort is a long integer that specifies the remote port, which is 70 for most Gopher servers.
- szSelector is a string containing the selector to retrieve the file.
- picStatus is the name of a picture control that will be used to display status information.

GetFile Event Summary

Here is a summary of the events that occur when you call GetFile:

1. The GetFile routine is called by your program and passed the remote host name, remote port, save filename, and Gopher selector string for retrieving the file.

2. The client (you) connects to the specified Gopher server at the specified port.

3. The client waits in a loop until connected to the Gopher server, or until a timeout has occurred. The user can also cancel the transfer at this or any point.

4. The client sends the server the specified selector, or Gopher command, to retrieve the file.

5. The client waits in a loop until the file has been received, indicated by the value of a global flag variable.

6. The client receives the file in chunks via the ReceiveData event.

7. On the first received chunk, the specified file is opened.

8. The client saves each chunk to the open file in the ReceiveData event.

9. After sending the entire file, the server closes the connection, which fires the Close event.

10. In the Close event, the file is closed, and status flags are set to indicate that the file has been sent.

11. The GetFile routine returns True if the file was received completely.

12. The GetFile routine returns False if an error occurs during transmission or the user cancels the transmission.

Diving into the GetFile Code

Figure 3.13 shows the GetFile function. GetFile requires that GETFILE.FRM be loaded. GETFILE.FRM is used in conjunction with GetFile. It contains a DSSOCK control, and more importantly, the code to process the file as it is received. You may be asking yourself *why, then do we need a routine at all? Why can't you just use GETFILE.FRM?* The answer is simple. If you were to use just GETFILE.FRM, you'd have to write code every time you use it to make it fit your application. With GetFile, the entire process is encapsulated in a routine, which returns True if the file was received. It makes things easier in the long run.

Figure 3.13 The GetFile function downloads a file from any Gopher server.

```
Function GetFile (szFileName As String, szHostName As String, lPort As Long,_
szSelector As String, picStatus As Control)
'-- This function interacts with frmGetFile (GETFILE.FRM) to
'   download a file from an Internet Host.

    Dim lLastByteCount As Long

    '-- Initialize flags and variables
    gnGetFile_Downloading = True
    gnGetFile_ReceivedFile = False
    glBytes_Received = 0

    picStatus.Cls
    picStatus.Print " Connecting"

    '-- Make sure we are not connected
    On Error Resume Next
    frmGetFile.dssGetFile.Action = SOCK_ACTION_CLOSE

    '-- Set the global filename used by GETFILE.FRM
    gszGetFile_FileName = szFileName

    '-- Set connection data
    frmGetFile.dssGetFile.RemoteHost = szHostName
    frmGetFile.dssGetFile.RemotePort = lPort

    '-- Attempt a connect
    On Error Resume Next
    frmGetFile.dssGetFile.Action = SOCK_ACTION_CONNECT
    If Err Then
        picStatus.Cls
        picStatus.Print " Could not connect"
```

```
        gnGetFile_Downloading = False
        Exit Function
End If
On Error GoTo 0

'-- Wait until we've connected
Do Until gnGetFile_Connected
    DoEvents
    '-- Were we cancelled?
    If gnGetFile_Downloading = False Then
        picStatus.Cls
        picStatus.Print " Cancelled"
        Exit Function
    End If
Loop

'-- Update the status
picStatus.Cls
picStatus.Print " CONNECT"

'-- Send the selector to retrieve the file.
frmGetFile.dssGetFile.Send = szSelector & vbCrLf

'-- Wait until its all over (either an error, or the connection was closed by the host)
Do Until gnGetFile_Connected = False
    '-- Do we have a new byte count?
    If lLastByteCount <> glBytes_Received Then
        '-- Display the byte count
        picStatus.Cls
        picStatus.Print Str$(glBytes_Received)
        lLastByteCount = glBytes_Received
    End If
    DoEvents
```

```
    Loop

    '-- Reset gnGetFile_Downloading
    gnGetFile_Downloading = False

    picStatus.Cls
    If gnGetFile_ReceivedFile Then
        '-- Display "Done"
        picStatus.Print " Done"
    Else
        picStatus.Print " Error"
    End If

    '-- Return the status (boolean)
    GetFile = gnGetFile_ReceivedFile

End Function
```

■■■■■■

At the top of the routine GetFile initializes three variables, gnGetFile_Downloading, gnGetFile_ReceivedFile, and glBytes_Received. gnGetFile_Downloading is a global numeric variable (hence the "gn" prefix), which identifies the status of the download. It is set to True when downloading and False when not downloading. However, if your program sets gnGetFile_Downloading to False, the download aborts. The GETFILE sample program sets gnGetFile_Downloading to False when the user presses the escape key during a download. gnGetFile_ReceivedFile is a global integer that gets set to True by the code behind the socket control on GET-FILE.FRM if the file was successfully received. This lets GetFile know the status of the transfer. glBytes_Received is a global long integer that holds the number of bytes received as data is coming in. This variable is monitored by GetFile while the file is being downloaded.

The next piece of code sets the global filename variable, gszGetFile_FileName, specifies the remote host name and port, and attempts a connection. The RemoteHost property is set to the name passed to GetFile, the RemotePort property is set to the specified port number, and the Action property is set to SOCK_ACTION_CONNECT. The error handling traps any error that would occur while trying to make the connection, such as the host name not existing, a bad port number, or just general connectivity problems. The Exception event does not fire at this stage because the connection has not yet been established.

Next, GetFile sits in a loop, waiting for the socket control to connect to the remote host. Note the use of DoEvents. Whenever your code enters a loop and no DoEvents is used, your whole system will lock up, except if you are running Windows NT 3.51, in which case it won't lock up. It may just *appear* to be locked up because of the speed at which things happen under Windows NT. (Just kidding, Mr. Gates. Please don't send me a nastygram). Actually, Windows NT is the best environment for development. The reason it is not as fast as Windows for Workgroups or Windows 95 is that it's always doing a lot more stuff, if you will pardon my scientific jargon. In fact, Windows NT 4.0 is downright zippy, especially at the Network layer.

There are two flags being checked in this loop: gnGetFile_Downloading and gnGetFile_Connected. The gnGetFile_Downloading flag can be set by your program if you want to cancel the file transfer. If gnGetFile_Downloading is set False during this loop execution, GetFile returns with a value of zero, indicating failure. The gnGetFile_Connected flag is set in the dssGetFile_Connect event. The Connected event is fired when a connection is made. So if a connection is made, the gnGetFile_Connected flag is set true, and the code exits the loop. Simple.

Once connected, the selector string is sent by setting the socket control's Send property to the selector string followed by a CR/LF pair. After the selector string is sent, data will start to be received. We now jump over to GETFILE.FRM to the dssGetFile_Receive event, which processes the received data. Let's take a look at it. Figure 3.14 shows the code in the Receive event.

dssGetFile_Receive uses a form-level integer, nGetFile_FileNumber, to hold the VB File Number for the file being saved. The first time data is received, this number is zero, in which case we need to open the file specified by gszGetFile_FileName. The FreeFile function returns the next available VB File Number, so the code will not

■■■■■■■■■ **Figure 3.14** The code in the dssGetFile_Receive event from GETFILE.FRM saves received data to disk using Visual Basic's binary file mode, the fastest way to save data to disk in Visual Basic.

```
Sub dssGetFile_Receive (ReceiveData As String)
'-- Data was received. Save to the specified file


    '-- Update the number of bytes received.
    glBytes_Received = glBytes_Received + Len(ReceiveData)


    '-- Were we canceled?
    If gnGetFile_Downloading = False Then
        On Error Resume Next
        dssGetFile.Action = SOCK_ACTION_CLOSE
        '-- Close the file
        If nGetFile_FileNumber Then
            Close nGetFile_FileNumber
            nGetFile_FileNumber = 0
        End If
        '-- We did not receive the file successfully
        gnGetFile_ReceivedFile = False
        '-- We are not downloading
        gnGetFile_Downloading = False
        '-- We are no longer connected
        gnGetFile_Connected = False
        Exit Sub
    End If


    '-- Is this a new file?
    If nGetFile_FileNumber = 0 Then
        '-- Yes. Open it.
        nGetFile_FileNumber = FreeFile
        Open gszGetFile_FileName For Binary As nGetFile_FileNumber
    End If
```

```
'-- Append the data to the end of the open file.
Put #nGetFile_FileNumber, , ReceiveData


End Sub
```

accidentally assign a file number that is in use. The file is opened in binary mode. Why? Because using binary mode is the fastest method of reading and writing data to disk with Visual Basic, and fast is the name of the game. No matter if this is the first block of received data, or any other block; the data is written to disk with the Put command.

If gnGetFile_Downloading has been set False, then the transfer is aborted by closing the connection with the Action property, closing the file if it's open, and setting all the global flags to false, indicating that the download was not successful. Note: Closing the file and setting the globals is necessary only because the Close event does not fire when you close the connection, only when the other side closes the connection.

When the Gopher server is done sending the file, it closes the connection. When this happens, the Close event will fire. Figure 3.15 shows the code in the Close event from GETFILE.FRM to close the file and set the global variables.

Before we can say that the file was received, three conditions must be true:

1. The file is open.
2. We have not been canceled.
3. We have received data.

These conditions are tested right off the bat. If they are met, gnGetFile_ReceivedFile is set to True.

Next, if the file is open, it is closed. The nGetFile_FileNumber variable is set back to zero to indicate that a file is not being transferred, and the gnGetFile_Connected flag is set to false, indicating that the connection has been broken.

Figure 3.15 The code in the dssGetFile_Close event from GETFILE.FRM closes the file when the Gopher server closes the connection.

```
Sub dssGetFile_Close (ErrorCode As Integer, ErrorDesc As String)
'-- The connection was closed by the remote host


    '-- Is there a file pending?
    If nGetFile_FileNumber Then
        '-- Yes. Were we NOT canceled?
        If gnGetFile_Downloading Then
            '-- Have we received any data?
            If LOF(nGetFile_FileNumber) Then
                '-- Yes. Set this flag so GetFile will know.
                gnGetFile_ReceivedFile = True
            End If
        End If


        '-- Close the file and reset the file number to zero.
        Close nGetFile_FileNumber

        nGetFile_FileNumber = 0
    End If

    '-- We are not downloading
    gnGetFile_Downloading = False

    '-- We are no longer connected
    gnGetFile_Connected = False


End Sub
```

Back in the GetFile routine, our code is in a loop waiting for the connection to close. As soon as the gnGetFile_Connected flag is set to false, this loop exits. The gnGetFile_Downloading flag is reset and the return value of GetFile is set to gnGetFile_ReceivedFile, which could be False if the user canceled the transfer, or if an error occurred.

The only code we did not talk about is the error-handling code in DSSOCK.VBX, the Exception event. Figure 3.16 shows the code in the dssGetFile_Exception event on GETFILE.FRM. The file is closed (if indeed it was open) and the global flags are set to False to indicate the transfer was not successful and that the connection is closed.

The Exception event occurs right before a connection is closed because of an error, such as your dog tripping over your phone or network cable and yanking it out of the wall. Although Winsock deals with complicated networking protocols and there are

Figure 3.16 The code in the dssGetFile_Exception event from GETFILE.FRM closes the file and clears all global flags.

```
Sub dssGetFile_Exception (ErrorCode As Integer, ErrorDesc As String)
'-- An error occurred in communications

    '-- Close the file
    If nGetFile_FileNumber Then
        Close nGetFile_FileNumber
        nGetFile_FileNumber = 0
    End If
    '-- We did not receive the file successfully
    gnGetFile_ReceivedFile = False
    '-- We are not downloading
    gnGetFile_Downloading = False
    '-- We are no longer connected
    gnGetFile_Connected = False


End Sub
```

lots of high-tech things that can go wrong, you need not concern yourself with handling every single error that occurs, because you can't do anything about them. The connection is going to close every time. You do not have a choice. The ErrorCode and ErrorDesc arguments describe the error for you, but you do not need to bother the user with Sockets error descriptions. If you want to say anything, say "The connection has been unexpectedly broken." If you want to test the Exception event, start receiving the file, and shut your modem off, or kill the connection however you can.

Don't get me wrong about error handling. Errors should not be ignored. Error codes and descriptions are useful to developers and network administrators who need to pinpoint bugs or anomalies in their systems. My advice if you want to write a top-notch, think-of-everything kind of app is to write any errors to a log file, which can be handed over to the appropriate people. If you decide to write to a log file, don't forget to write a date/time stamp to the file. For more information on error handling techniques, see Chapter 2.

Sample Application: GOPHCLNT.VBP

GOPHCLNT (Gopher client) is a simple client application that lets you browse through Gopherspace viewing text and downloading binaries and using indexed searches. With a little code and some third-party graphics tools you could turn it into a complete Gopher client, including bookmarks and helper applications.

Figure 3.17 shows the GOPHCLNT application. The Port field lets you specify the port, the Host field lets you specify the Gopher server, and the Selector field lets you enter the selector. Clicking the GO button connects to the host on the given port and sends the selector.

It works just like HGopher in that you just click on an item to retrieve it. Figure 3.18 shows the Electronic Newsstand Gopher (the default selector). Notice that the directories have folder icons and the files have leaf icons.

Figure 3.19 shows the display window that appears when you double-click on the item "Copyright and General Disclaimer—Please Read." When you click on any text item this window appears to display the text.

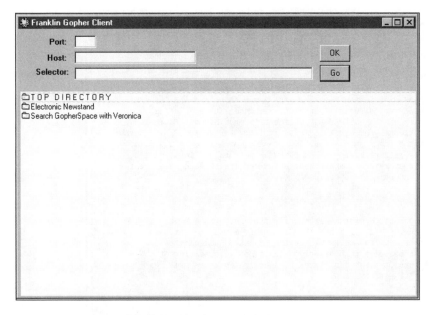

Figure 3.17 Gopher Client.

Figure 3.18 Gopher Client connecting.

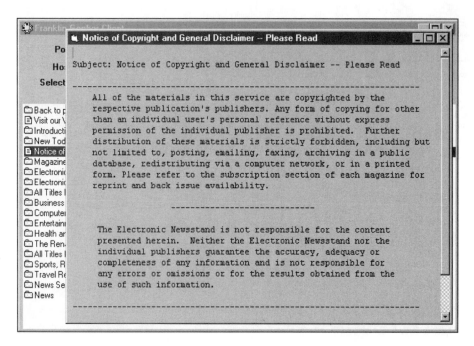

■■■■■■■ **Figure 3.19** Viewing a text file in Gopherspace.

GOPHCLNT Under the Hood

Figure 3.20 shows the contents of GOPHCLNT.BAS, the globals and type definitions for this application. Let me briefly discuss the important items.

The SelectorType user-defined type is for storing information about a Gopher item.
Each item that appears in the list has an associated host name, port, Gopher resource
type, and selector. Since a list box or outline control can't store all this information,
we keep a separate array, called Selectors(), that holds all the details for each item in
the outline control. The indexes relate one to one with the outline control. In other
words, Selectors(2).Selector is the selector string of olGopher.List(2) (the item in the
third row of the outline control).

The History array is of the same type, but holds the selectors that produce the lists
you browse. When you click on a directory folder, that item's details are copied to a
new History element. This is so that you can click on the Go Back item at the top
of each list to get back to the previous menu.

Figure 3.20 GOPHCLNT.BAS—Globals and user-defined Types.

```
Option Explicit
'-- Stores info about a Gopher selector
Type SelectorType
    GopherType    As Integer
    Port          As Integer
    HostName      As String
    Selector      As String
End Type


'-- The current list of selectors is stored here
Global Selectors()      As SelectorType

'-- This is a history of single selectors that produce
'   each list, so you can go backwards from whence you
'   came.
Global History()        As SelectorType

'-- Number of selectors in the current list
Global gnGopherItems    As Integer

'-- The number of levels that you've advanced
Global gnNumLevels      As Integer

'-- The current level from the top
Global gnCurLevel       As Integer

'-- VB File Handle for saved files
Global gnFileNum        As Integer

'-- Flag that tels us if we've received the first line
```

```
'   of a list yet.
Global gnFirstLine       As Integer

'-- The type of the current selector
Global gnCurrentType     As Integer

'-- Selector types
Global Const TYPE_FILE = 0
Global Const TYPE_DIRECTORY = 1
Global Const TYPE_ERROR = 3
Global Const TYPE_SEARCH = 7
Global Const TYPE_BINARY = 9
Global Const TYPE_GIF = 10
```

There are several other variables listed here that are well documented by the comments, but take a look at the Selector type constants. Although this code handles only types 0, 2, and 7 (files, directories, and search indexes), you can easily extend it to support more types.

Retrieving a Directory

Figure 3.21 shows the olGopher_DblClick routine, which occurs when you double-click on an item in the outline control.

If the user selected an item other than the top item (the Go Back item), the connection information is taken from the Selectors array. After making sure the data is valid, the code calls SocketConnect to connect to the host. After connection, the selector is sent.

If the user does select the top item, the gnCurLevel variable is decremented by one. gnCurLevel is the current index into the History array, which holds the selectors that return the menus the user selects while using the program. The gnCurrentType is set to TYPE_DIRECTORY, because we want to get the last directory listing.

▰▰▰▰▰▰ **Figure 3.21** This code executes when you double-click on an item in the outline control.

```
Private Sub olGopher_DblClick()

    Dim nLI         As Integer
    Dim szSelector  As String
    Dim szSearch    As String


    nLI = olGopher.ListIndex


    '-- Is this not the "Go back" item?
    If nLI > 0 Then
        '-- Are there items here?
        If gnGopherItems >= nLI Then


            '-- Make sure the port is not zero
            If Selectors(nLI).Port = 0 Then
                Exit Sub
            End If


            '-- Make sure the host name is not null
            If Len(Selectors(nLI).HostName) = 0 Then
                Exit Sub
            End If


            '-- Set the gopher type
            gnCurrentType = Selectors(nLI).GopherType


            '-- Is this an Index search?
            If gnCurrentType = TYPE_SEARCH Then
                '-- Ask for a search string
                szSearch = InputBox$("Enter Search Terms")
```

```
             If Len(szSearch) = 0 Then Exit Sub
        End If


        '-- Connect
        If SocketConnect(DSSocket1, (Selectors(nLI).Port), _
           (Selectors(nLI).HostName), 20) Then
             MsgBox Error, vbExclamation
             Exit Sub
        End If


        '-- Is this an Index search?
        If gnCurrentType = TYPE_SEARCH Then
             '-- Send the selector, a tab, and the search string
             SendData DSSocket1, Selectors(olGopher.ListIndex).Selector & _
                 vbTab & szSearch & vbCrLf
        Else
             '-- Send the selector
             SendData DSSocket1, Selectors(olGopher.ListIndex)_
             .Selector & vbCrLf
        End If


        Screen.MousePointer = vbHourglass
        Me.Enabled = False


    End If
Else
    If gnCurLevel > 1 Then
        '-- Go back one level
        gnCurLevel = gnCurLevel - 1
        gnCurrentType = History(gnCurLevel).GopherType


        '-- Connect
```

```
        If SocketConnect(DSSocket1, _
            (History(gnCurLevel).Port), (History(gnCurLevel)_
            .HostName), 20) Then
                MsgBox Error, vbExclamation
                Exit Sub
        End If


        '-- Send the history selector
        SendData DSSocket1, History(gnCurLevel).Selector & vbCrLf
        Screen.MousePointer = vbHourglass
        Me.Enabled = False
    Else
        InitailizeOutline
    End If
End If


End Sub
```

A connection is made using the History array data, and once connected, the selector from the history array is sent. The server then sends back a list of Gopher strings, each terminated with a CR/LF, and all ending with a period on a line by itself. The Gopher server closes the connection after sending all the data.

Jump now to DSSocket_Receive, shown in Figure 3.22. If we are receiving a file (gnCurrentType) then a temporary file (TEMP.FIL) is opened, and written to. If we are receiving a directory listing, the line must be parsed. (Figure 3.4 shows the format of the data that is received for a directory listing.)

If this is the first menu item we've received, then a couple of things happen. First the gnCurLevel variable is upped by one. This keeps track of where we are in the History array. If necessary, the array is grown by one, then the current selector details are added to the array. Also on the first menu option received, the outline control is cleared and the Go Back string is added as the top item.

Figure 3.22 The DSSocket1_Receive event occurs when a line of text is received from a Gopher server.

```
Private Sub DSSocket1_Receive(ReceiveData As String)


    Dim nLI     As Integer


    Select Case gnCurrentType


        Case TYPE_FILE   '-- File
            '-- Open the file if its not open yet.
            If gnFileNum = 0 Then
                gnFileNum = FreeFile
                Open "TEMP.FIL" For Output As gnFileNum
            End If


            '-- Write this line to the file.
            Print #gnFileNum, ReceiveData;


        Case TYPE_DIRECTORY, TYPE_SEARCH   '-- Directory/Search


            '-- Make sure this is not the last line.
            If Trim$(ReceiveData) = "." & vbCrLf Then
                Exit Sub
            End If


            '-- Have we not received the first line yet?
            If gnFirstLine = False Then
                '-- No. This is the first line.
                nLI = olGopher.ListIndex


                '-- nFirstRecieved is False if this is our first time
                '    receiving anything (app just started).
```

```
        If nLI > 0 Then


            '-- Add one to the current level
            gnCurLevel = gnCurLevel + 1


            '-- Do we need to grow the History array?
            If gnCurLevel > gnNumLevels Then
                gnNumLevels = gnNumLevels + 1
                ReDim Preserve History(1 To gnNumLevels) As _
                SelectorType
            End If


            '-- Save the current selector info to the History array.
            History(gnCurLevel).GopherType = _
            Selectors(nLI).GopherType
            History(gnCurLevel).Selector = Selectors(nLI).Selector
            History(gnCurLevel).HostName = Selectors(nLI).HostName
            History(gnCurLevel).Port = Selectors(nLI).Port
        End If


        '-- Since this is the first item, clear the list box and add
        '   the "Go back" item.
        olGopher.Clear
        olGopher.AddItem "Back to previous gopher menu"
        gnFirstLine = True
        gnGopherItems = 0
    End If


ReceiveData = Trim$(ReceiveData)


'-- Add one to the number of items received (for this list)
```

```
gnGopherItems = gnGopherItems + 1

'-- Grow the selector list array (for this list only).
ReDim Preserve Selectors(1 To gnGopherItems) As SelectorType

'-- Retrieve the Gopher Type
Selectors(gnGopherItems).GopherType = Val(Left$(ReceiveData, 1))
ReceiveData = Mid$(ReceiveData, 2)

olGopher.AddItem SuperTrim$(szParseString(ReceiveData, vbTab, 1))

'-- Is this a file or a directory?
Select Case Selectors(gnGopherItems).GopherType
    Case TYPE_DIRECTORY
        olGopher.PictureType(olGopher.ListCount - 1) = 0
    Case TYPE_SEARCH
        olGopher.PictureType(olGopher.ListCount - 1) = 1
    Case TYPE_FILE
        olGopher.PictureType(olGopher.ListCount - 1) = 2
End Select

'-- Retrieve the selector
Selectors(gnGopherItems).Selector = szParseString(ReceiveData, _
   vbTab, 2)

'-- Retrieve the host name
Selectors(gnGopherItems).HostName = szParseString(ReceiveData, _
   vbTab, 3)

'-- Retrieve the port
Selectors(gnGopherItems).Port = Val(szParseString(ReceiveData, _
   vbTab, 4))
```

```
    End Select

    '-- Done!


End Sub
```

GnGopherItems keeps track of how many items have been received, and which one we are currently receiving. The Selector array holds the details of each item, and the szParseString routine is used to parse out the sections of the received string.

This string consists of four sections separated by tabs. The first section consists of a number that specifies the type of Gopher resource immediately followed by the text to display as a menu option to the user. Next is the selector string followed by the host name and finally the port.

The display text is added to the outline control. Note that the PictureType property of the outline control is set to a folder or a leaf bitmap depending on the type of Gopher resource.

Going Back One Level

The information for all previously viewed menus is saved in the History array. If you double-click on the top row of the outline control to go back one level, the program connects to the machine and port in the History array for the previous list, and sends the selector for that same list.

Beyond the point where the selector is sent, the code executes the exact same way; the only difference is in the olGopher_DblClick() procedure, shown in Figure 3.21.

gnCurLevel holds the current index into the History array, or where the selector for the current menu of items is in the History array. gnCurLevel is always the last item in the History array when moving forward. However, as you move back, gnCurLevel is decremented by one each time, and the selector information from the History array is used to retrieve the previous directory listings.

Performing an Index Search

The Gopher type 7 (Index search) lets you enter a string and perform a search against a resource on the server. Index search items are displayed with a question mark. Figure 3.23 shows a Veronica search menu, which you can view by clicking the third item in the list when the program starts up.

When the olGopher_DblClick() procedure fires, and the Gopher type is TYPE_SEARCH, an InputBox pops up and asks for a search string. When you send this type of selector, the format is this:

```
Selector String + Tab + Search String + CRLF
```

A simple if/then clause sends the selector string in this format if it is indeed a search Gopher type.

■■■■■■ **TIP**

A Word about Veronica: A Veronica server exists for the purpose of keeping a list of Gopher menus and items throughout the world. A user can send a search string to a Veronica server, and it returns a list of Gopher items that match the string. A similar resource called Archie exists for FTP sites. With Archie, you can search for a file across all the anonymous FTP servers known to the Archie server. Veronica and Archie are free services.

■■■■■■

Retrieving a File

If you click on an item with a leaf icon (a text file) the selector is sent just as if it was for a directory. The only difference here is in the DSSocket1_Receive event (see Figure 3.22) and in the DSSocket1_Close event (see Figure 3.24).

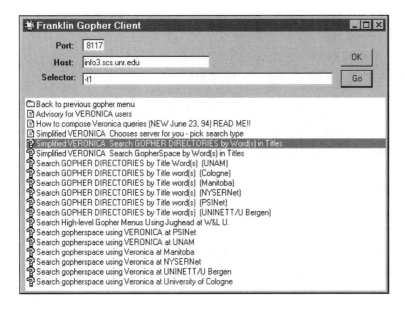

▬▬▬▬▬ **Figure 3.23** Veronica search menu.

▬▬▬▬▬ **Figure 3.24** The DSSocket1_Close event occurs after the Gopher server
sends either a directory listing or a text file.

```
Private Sub DSSocket1_Close(ErrorCode As Integer, ErrorDesc As String)


    Dim nFileNum    As Integer
    Dim lInst       As Long
    Dim szBuffer    As String


    Select Case gnCurrentType
        Case TYPE_FILE   '-- We just received a text file
            If gnFileNum Then
                '-- Close the file
                Close gnFileNum
```

```
'-- Open the file in binary mode
nFileNum = FreeFile
Open "TEMP.FIL" For Binary As nFileNum

'-- Is it too big to display?
If LOF(nFileNum) > 50000 Then
   MsgBox "There is too much information to show in a VB _
      Text Box. Displaying only the first _
      50,000 bytes", vbInformation
      szBuffer = Space$(50000)
Else
      szBuffer = Space$(LOF(nFileNum))
End If

'-- Read the file in
Get #nFileNum, , szBuffer
Close #nFileNum

'-- Force "Garbage Collection"
szBuffer = ""

'-- Display the contents
frmDisplay.Caption = olGopher.List(olGopher.ListIndex)
frmDisplay.txtDisplay = szBuffer
frmDisplay.Show 1
Unload frmDisplay
Set frmDisplay = Nothing

'-- Reset globals
gnCurrentType = 1
gnFileNum = 0
End If
```

```
      Case TYPE_DIRECTORY


    Case Else
        MsgBox "File Received"


  End Select


  gnFirstLine = False


  Me.Enabled = True
  Screen.MousePointer = vbNormal


End Sub
```

In the Receive event, if nGopherType indicates we are receiving a file, first the code tests to see if the file is already open. If not, it is opened. The received string is then appended to the file.

After the server has finished sending the file, it closes the connection. The file must be closed in the DSSocket1_Close event.

After closing the file, it is reopened in binary mode, and read in for display. This program uses a Visual Basic Text Box control to display the received file.

▬▬▬ **TIP**

Note that the Visual Basic line continuation character does not support separation in the middle of a quoted string, but the string was too long to print on one line.

Epilogue

Gopher is an extremely versatile and simple protocol because of its menulike interface. This lends itself rather nicely to Visual Basic and the MS Outline control. I encourage you to extend the client application as an exercise in communications programming. For an exercise you can add the means to configure a helper application to display .GIF files, and one for .JPG files as well.

Now that you've had a taste of programming the Internet, let me show you how easy it is to retrieve Usenet news from an NNTP server using only the DSSock control and some simple Visual Basic code. I promise, no Fred Grandy jokes.

4

USENET NEWS

Introduction

Next to electronic mail and the World Wide Web, Usenet news is the most widely utilized service on the Internet. The ARPANet and Internet community have always been big on the idea of news. In the beginnings of the Internet, scientists and researchers needed a way to distribute memos throughout the Internet to keep everyone up to date on research and other projects. Usenet provides a way for news messages (called articles) to spread throughout the Internet community at a fair speed.

Usenet is a network of news servers within the Internet that propagate messages spanning a huge number of discussion groups (called *newsgroups*). There are thousands of newsgroups with topics ranging from software bug fixes to recipes to fan clubs to diaper fetishes (I'm not making this up). If you are familiar with messaging on electronic Bulletin Board Systems (BBS) you may be familiar with FIDONet, a network similar to Usenet that operates within the BBS community. Usenet is similar except that the messages are propagated throughout the entire Internet. Your Internet access provider should offer Usenet service via an NNTP server at their network site.

The first Usenet software used UUCP (Unix-to-Unix Copy Protocol) as a data transport mechanism. UUCP is a somewhat outdated protocol for moving data, being replaced by TCP/IP. However, it is still used in some places for dialup access to Usenet.

Usenet actually preceded the Internet. It started in 1979 at Duke University and the University of North Carolina, Chapel Hill. Graduate students from both universities created the Usenet rules and wrote the first programs to handle the flow of news articles. They had over fifty sites signed up after the first year. Once TCP/IP hit the streets, Usenet news took the Internet by storm.

News articles bounce around from news server to news server via the NNTP (Network News Transfer Protocol), a text-based protocol that you will have no trouble utilizing in Visual Basic. Like most mainstream Internet protocols, NNTP is line-based, employing a command and response system that we have come to know and love.

Once you learn how to use NNTP in Visual Basic you can do many powerful things. How would you like to write a program that monitors your favorite Usenet newsgroups, searches for several key words, and based on the existence of those words, emails the articles to you or archives them in a database? Looking for a job? Monitor the bc.jobs or the biz.jobs.offered newsgroup. Be quick to respond to posted articles thanks to your special program that's constantly scanning the newsgroups for you. Interested in a specific topic? Start archiving articles in a database. When you have a question that people in the newsgroup might have an answer to, search your database. There are hundreds of vertical applications waiting to be written that involve Usenet news.

In this chapter I'll show you how to log onto an NNTP server, get lists of articles (new and old), retrieve specific articles, and post new articles. You won't believe how easy it really is.

NNTP

NNTP is a text-based protocol used to send and receive Usenet news articles between a newsreader client and an NNTP server, and also between two NNTP servers. If your Internet Access Provider gives you the ability to read Usenet news, then it probably has an NNTP server on site. Request For Comments (RFC) 977 states that "NNTP specifies a protocol for the distribution, inquiry, retrieval, and posting of news articles using a reliable stream-based transmission of news among the ARPA-Internet community. NNTP is designed so that news articles are stored in a central database allowing a subscriber to select only those items he wishes to read. Indexing, cross-referencing, and expiration of aged messages are also provided."

While it sounds like all the news is in one central repository, this is not true. Unlike popular online services such as CompuServe, America Online, or the Microsoft Network, Usenet news articles are instantly replicated throughout the Internet by connected servers. Servers must subscribe to specific newsgroups in order to be able to send and receive articles on a given topic.

NNTP servers maintain 24-hour socket-connections to each other. Any one server may be connected to three or four (or many more) other servers. There are commands that ask questions such as "Do you have message number 11233 in alt.winsock.programming?" to which the other side says yea or nay. This should give you some idea of the intricate network that is Usenet.

NNTP servers accept connections on port 119, which are maintained throughout the entire session until either the client or server closes it. If you wish you can use the Winsock Terminal included with this book to connect to an NNTP server and actually navigate through newsgroups and articles by using NNTP manually as you are reading and learning about NNTP.

MessageIDs vs. Message Numbers

First of all, a message number is a number and a MessageID is a combination of alphanumeric characters. Here is a typical MessageID:

```
<1995Nov1.133231@apexsc.com>
```

A message number is relative to the server, and a MessageID is relative to the Internet. A message number is simply a number that identifies an article on a server. Think of a newsgroup as a table in a database, and each article in that newsgroup is a separate record. The MessageID is the primary key of the table. It's a means for local identification.

A MessageID is a string that identifies a single Usenet article throughout the entire Internet. For this reason, servers have to make sure to assign MessageIDs carefully, so that there is no chance of creating a duplicate. Typically, a MessageID consists of some extraction of the system time, an @ sign, and the domain that assigned it.

Some of the NNTP commands accept both message numbers and MessageIDs as ways to specify a particular article. You can't go wrong if you follow this rule: If you are a news client use message numbers. If you are a server, use MessageIDs.

NNTP Versions

As with all public protocols, NNTP is constantly changing. At the time of this writing, the current NNTP standard is defined by RFC 977 by Brian Kantor (U.C. San Diego) and Phil Lapsley (U.C. Berkeley), dated February 1986.

Although this is the most current RFC regarding NNTP, today's NNTP servers support extended NNTP commands that are not defined in RFC 977. These commands were derived from an Internet Draft Document called draft-barber-nntp-imp-01.txt, which was released June 26, 1995. Internet Drafts have a life span of 6 months and are not meant to be reference material, but since almost all of Usenet operates with the commands set forth in this document I am choosing to ignore this. After all, why let a little thing like reality spoil our fun?

To learn the current status of any Internet Draft, you can download the file, 1id-abstracts.txt listing contained in the Internet Drafts Shadow Directory on the following FTP servers:

ftp.is.co.za (Africa)
nic.nordu.net (Europe)
munnari.oz.au (Pacific Rim)
ds.internic.net (US East Coast)
ftp.isi.edu (US West Coast)

This file contains the current filenames and versions of all Internet Drafts.

NNTP Commands

Command Structure

NNTP is a text protocol. All commands are single words, some of which require parameters. Parameters are always separated by a space *Chr$(32)* or a tab

Chr$(9). Commands are always terminated with a carriage return and a linefeed (vbCrLf).

For example, the GROUP command selects a Usenet Newsgroup. Here are two examples of an assembled GROUP command string ready to be sent to the NNTP server:

```
Cmd$ = "GROUP alt.winsock.programming" & vbCrLf
```

or

```
Cmd$ = "GROUP rec.audio.pro & vbCrLf
```

Sample Conversation

Figure 4.1 shows a typical conversation between a newsreader and an NNTP server. <T> stands for the Tab character (ASCII 9). Note the periods between the header and body as well as to specify the end of a list. Lines starting with an apostrophe are comments.

■■■■■■■ **Figure 4.1** A typical conversation between an NNTP client and server.

```
[CONNECT]

'-- This line is the first thing received. It identifies the server and
'   indicates whether or not posting is allowed.
[RECV] 200 joes.net InterNetNews NNRP server INN 1.4 22-Dec-93 ready
(posting ok).


'-- The LIST command returns a detailed list of newsgroups available on the
'   server. The first field is the name of the newsgroup. Second is the
'   first known article number. Third is the last known article number.
'   The last field is y or n to indicate whether the article is currently
'   available.
[SEND] LIST<CRLF>


'-- The first line should be 215 to indicate that the server is sending
'   the list.
[RECV] 215 list of newsgroups follows<CRLF>
```

```
'-- The server then sends a listing of newsgroups followed by a period on a
'   line by itself.
alt.1d 0000001252 000000459 y<CRLF>
alt.0d 0000001257 000000364 y<CRLF>
alt.2600 0000024553 000001183 y<CRLF>
. <CRLF>


'-- The GROUP command selects a newsgroup
[SEND] GROUP comp.lang.basic.visual.misc<CRLF>


'-- The server sends back a 211 reply indicating the number of articles,
'   first article number, last article number, and the name of the newsgroup.
[RECV] 211 61 14614 14674 comp.lang.basic.visual.misc<CRLF>


'-- The XOVER command receives the Subject, From address, Date, ArticleID,
'   Byte Size, and number of lines for each article in the specified range.
[SEND] XOVER 14614-14616<CRLF>


'-- The server sends a 224 reply to indicate that the list of messages follows.
[RECV] 224 data follows<CRLF>


'-- The server then sends the selected header information for each article
'   followed by a period on a line by itself
14614 <Subj><T><From><T><Date><T><ArticleID><T><Size><T><Lines><CRLF>
14615 <Subj><T><From><T><Date><T><ArticleID><T><Size><T><Lines><CRLF>
14616 <Subj><T><From><T><Date><T><ArticleID><T><Size><T><Lines><CRLF>
.


'-- The ARTICLE command tells the server to send the header and message body
'   of a specified article (by article number or ID)
[SEND] ARTICLE 14615<CRLF>
'-- The server sends a 220 reply indicating that it is sending the article.
'   Also included in this line is the poster's email address.
[RECV] 220 14615 <From Address> article<CRLF>
```

```
'-- The server then sends the header followed by a period on a line by
'   itself. This is immediately followed by the article body ending with a
'   period on a line by itself.
<HEADER TEXT>
.
<BODY TEXT>
.


'-- The quit command ends a session
[SEND] QUIT<CRLF>


'-- The server acknowledges the QUIT command by sending a 205 reply, and
'   drops the connection.
[RECV] 205<CRLF>


[SERVER DISCONNECTS]
```

The WILDMAT format

WILDMAT is a format for specifying a search pattern. Some NNTP commands use the Wildmat format for text arguments such as a newsgroup pattern like comp.lang.basic.visual.* Here is a definition of this format taken from the Internet Draft file draft-barber-nntp-imp-01.txt by S. Barber, June 1995:

> The WILDMAT format was first developed by Rich Salz to provide a uniform mechanism for matching patterns in the same manner that the UNIX shell matches filenames. There are five pattern matching operations other than a strict one-to-one match between the pattern and the source to be checked for a match. The first is an asterisk (*) to match any sequence of zero or more characters. The second is a question mark (?) to match any single character. The third specifies a specific set of characters. The set is specified as a list of characters, or as a range of characters where the beginning and end of the range are separated by a minus (or dash) character, or as any combination of lists and ranges. The dash can also be included in

the range as a character if it is the beginning or end of the range. This set is enclosed in square brackets. The close square bracket (]) may be used in a range if it is the first character in the set. The fourth operation is the same as the logical not of the third operation and is specified the same way as the third with the addition of a caret character (^) at the beginning of the test string just inside the open square bracket. The final operation uses the backslash character to invalidate the special meaning of the open square bracket ([), the asterisk, or the question mark.

Examples

[^]-]

Matches any character other than a close square bracket or a minus sign/dash.

*bdc

Matches any string that ends with the string bdc including the string bdc (without quotes).

bdc

Matches any string that contains the string bdc including the string bdc (without quotes).

[0-9a-zA-Z]

Matches any alphanumeric string.

a??d

Matches any four-character string which begins with a and ends with d.

Server Responses

Server responses consist of a three-digit number and a space *Chr$(32)* usually followed by one or more parameters (also separated by spaces) and ending with a carriage return and a linefeed (vbCrLf).

For example, the appropriate positive response from the aforementioned GROUP command is the number 201 followed by the number of messages in the newsgroup, the first article number, the last article number, and then a message indicating the group is selected:

```
"201 112 43211 43323 alt.winsock.programming group selected" & vbCrLf
```

The above response from the GROUP command indicates that the alt.winsock.programming group has been selected, that there are 112 articles available, and that the first article number is 43211 and the last is 43323. "Being selected" means that any ARTICLE or HEAD commands (or any other commands that refer to article numbers) are to be acted upon within the selected newsgroup.

I know this is not really the place to discuss the 201 response, but you cannot always count on the first argument (number of articles) to be accurate. Sometimes the value may be zero, sometimes it may be incorrect. You also cannot count on getting the number of articles by subtracting the first article number from the last. Don't ask me why, it's just the way it is. My feeling is that you should check both and when in doubt go with the second method (subtracting the first number from the last number). Besides, who cares if the number is off by a couple messages? The point is that you should never assume anything in your application, except that the user has not paid for his or her copy of your software.

Figure 4.2 shows what each digit of the response code represents, and Figure 4.3 shows a summary of NNTP server responses. The first number identifies the message to your program, and the text describes the reply.

Figure 4.2 The response code's first two digits classifies it according to these general rules.

The first digit indicates broad success or failure:

1xx - Informative message. You can generally ignore these.

2xx - Command OK.

3xx - Command OK so far, send the rest of it.

4xx - Command was correct, but couldn't be performed for some reason.

5xx - Command unimplemented, or incorrect, or a serious program error occurred.

The second digit indicates the response's category:

x0x - Connection, setup, and miscellaneous messages

x1x - Newsgroup selection

x2x - Article selection

x3x - Distribution functions

x4x - Posting

x8x - Nonstandard (private implementation) extensions

x9x - Debugging output

Figure 4.3 Summary of NNTP server responses.

100 help text follows

190-199 debug output

200 server ready - posting allowed

201 server ready - no posting allowed

202 slave status noted

205 closing connection - goodbye!

211 n f l s group selected

        n = estimated number of articles in group,

        f = first article number in the group,

        l = last article number in the group,

        s = name of the group.

215 list of newsgroups follows

220 <article number> <message-id> article retrieved - head and body follow

221 <article number> <message-id> article retrieved - head follows

222 <article number> <message-id> article retrieved - body follows

223 <article number> <message-id> article retrieved - request text separately

230 list of new articles by message-id follows

235 article transferred ok

240 article posted ok

282 XOVER data follows.

335 send article to be transferred. End with <CR-LF>.<CR-LF>

340 send article to be posted. End with <CR-LF>.<CR-LF>

400 service discontinued

411 no such news group

412 no newsgroup has been selected

420 no current article has been selected

421 no next article in this group

422 no previous article in this group

423 no such article number in this group

430 no such article found

435 article not wanted - do not send it

436 transfer failed - try again later

437 article rejected - do not try again

440 posting not allowed

441 posting failed

480 Transfer permission denied

500 command not recognized

501 command syntax error

502 access restriction or permission denied

503 program fault - command not performed

Usenet Article Format

A Usenet article is comprised of a header and the text body.

Figure 4.4 shows a sample of a Usenet article header. The article format is essentially the widely accepted ARPANET mail message format with a few extensions required by Usenet. For a complete description of the Usenet message format see RFC 850 entitled "Standard for Interchange of USENET Messages," by Mark R. Horton.

■■■■■■ **Figure 4.4** Sample Usenet article header.

Path: mindport.net!newsfeed.internetmci.com!news
From: mnguyen@clark.net (CDSI)
Newsgroups: alt.winsock.programming
Subject: Q : winsock programming server
Date: 4 Sep 1995 13:58:32 GMT
Organization: Clark Internet Services, Inc., Ellicott City, MD USA
Lines: 14
Message-ID: <42f0m8$9ho@clarknet.clark.net>
NNTP-Posting-Host: clark.net
Mime-Version: 1.0
Content-Type: TEXT/PLAIN; charset=ISO-8859-1
Content-Transfer-Encoding: 8bit
X-Newsreader: TIN [UNIX 1.3 950726BETA PL0]

Relay-Version: version B 2.10 2/13/83; site cbosgd.UUCP
Posting-Version: version B 2.10 2/13/83; site eagle.UUCP
Path: cbosgd!mhuxj!mhuxt!eagle!jerry
From: jerry@eagle.uucp (Jerry Schwarz)
Newsgroups: net.general
Subject: Usenet Etiquette -- Please Read
Message-ID: <642@eagle.UUCP>
Date: Friday, 19-Nov-82 16:14:55 EST
Followup-To: net.news
Expires: Saturday, 1-Jan-83 00:00:00 EST
Date-Received: Friday, 19-Nov-82 16:59:30 EST
Organization: Bell Labs, Murray Hill

■■■■■

Sometimes an article header can have the following older format:

From: cbosgd!mhuxj!mhuxt!eagle!jerry (Jerry Schwarz)
Newsgroups: net.general

Title: Usenet Etiquette — Please Read

Article-I.D.: eagle.642

Posted: Fri Nov 19 16:14:55 1982

Received: Fri Nov 19 16:59:30 1982

Expires: Mon Jan 1 00:00:00 1990

Either way, you will be able to retrieve specific header lines with NNTP, so if there is no Subject header, you can get the Title header instead.

VB Programming Technique

I have found that the best way to write for this type of protocol is by writing a response handler in the Receive event or within the event or subroutine that receives incoming data. You must use LineMode with DSSOCK. If you are using another tool, make sure it fires a Receive event for each line of text it receives. Chapter 2 covers programming with DSSOCK, and you should refer to it if you have any questions specific to DSSOCK as you read the rest of this chapter.

Fortunately, I have already done the dirty work of writing the response code handler in Visual Basic, and for the most part you can drop it right into your application. I have put comments in the code for each of the responses so you can step through the handler code for each response and modify it if need be. Of course, I will discuss this code in detail in the pages that follow.

NNTP commands can be sent anywhere from within your program, such as from a command button, menu option, or list box double-click. Unlike some of the other code in this book, it is not necessary to wait for a response in a loop after sending a command. The client code is state-oriented, meaning a command is sent and a state is entered, the state of waiting for a response. Once the response has been received, the state changes back to idle. The response handling code operates on the response codes differently depending on the state when the code was received. This will become more obvious when we start looking at the code.

Take a look at the sample code in Figure 4.5, which simply sends the server a GROUP command to specify the alt.winsock.programming newsgroup, and retrieves the number of articles and their number range. This code clip assumes that you are already connected to the NNTP server on port 119. When the Command1 button is clicked, the GROUP command is sent, which tells the server to select the alt.winsock.programming newsgroup. The application is at that time waiting for a response from the server, which could be either a 211 indicating success, or a 411 indicating that there is no such newsgroup.

■■■■■■■ **Figure 4.5** This code sends the server a GROUP command to specify the alt.winsock.programming newsgroup, and retrieves the number of articles and their number range.

```
Sub Command1_Click ()

    SendData "GROUP alt.winsock.programming" & vbCrLf

End Sub



Sub DSSocket1_Receive(ReceiveData As String)

    Dim nPos As Integer
    Dim nCode As Integer

    Dim lNumArticles As Long
    Dim lFirstArticle As Long
    Dim lLastArticle As Long

    If Len(ReceiveData) > 3 Then

        '-- Determine the reply code
        nCode = Val(Left$(ReceiveData, 3))
```

```
Select Case nCode

    Case 211 '-- Article information for selected newsgroup

        '-- Trim the reply code off the left of the string
        nPos = InStr(ReceiveData, " ")
        ReceiveData = Mid$(ReceiveData, nPos + 1)


        '-- Get the number of articles
        nPos = InStr(ReceiveData, " ")
        lNumArticles = Val(Left$(ReceiveData, nPos - 1))
        ReceiveData = Mid$(ReceiveData, nPos + 1)


        '-- Get the first article number
        nPos = InStr(ReceiveData, " ")
        lFirstArticle = Val(Left$(ReceiveData, nPos - 1))
        ReceiveData = Mid$(ReceiveData, nPos + 1)


        '-- Get the last article number
        nPos = InStr(ReceiveData, " ")
        lLastArticle = Val(Left$(ReceiveData, nPos - 1))



    Case 411

        MsgBox "No Such Newsgroup Exists"


    End Select
End Sub
```

If the 211 reply string is received via the Receive event then the number of articles, the first article number, and the last article number are parsed out of the reply string. If the 411 reply string is received, a message box pops up to tell the user that the specified newsgroup does not exist on the server.

String Parsing

The string parsing code is fairly common for this type of programming. Let me explain the first four lines of code following the "Case 211" line. These four lines (actually the first, third, and fourth lines) are all you need to parse values from a string.

Step 1 is to identify the position of the next space within the string. The Instr function returns the position of one string within another string:

```
'-- Suppose ReceiveData = "211 100 1200 1300"
nPos = InStr(ReceiveData, " ")
'-- nPos equals 4 because the space after "211" is the fourth character.
```

Step 2 is to trim the 211 and the space from the left of the string. The Mid$ function returns the portion of the string (first argument) starting with the character position (second argument):

```
'-- ReceiveData = "211 100 1200 1300" and nPos = 4
ReceiveData = Mid$(ReceiveData, nPos + 1)
'-- ReceiveData now equals "100 1200 1300"
```

Step 3 is a repeat of Step 1 which returns the position of the next space within ReceiveData using the Instr function.

```
'-- Suppose ReceiveData = "100 1200 1300"
nPos = InStr(ReceiveData, " ")
'-- nPos equals 4 because the space after "100" is the fourth character.
```

Step 4 is to retrieve the value of the string up to but not including the space. The Left$ function returns the leftmost number of characters (second parameter) of the string (first parameter). The Val function returns the value of the string returned by the Left$ function:

```
'-- ReceiveData = "100 1200 1300" and nPos = 4

lNumArticles = Val(Left$(ReceiveData, nPos - 1))

'-- lNumArticles = 100
```

The szParseString Function

While it is important to understand how to parse strings using VB, it is not always desirable to do it manually. That's why I wrote szParseString for returning portions of a string. szParseString is a routine in DSSOCK.BAS that will return a portion of a string given the string, a delimiter character, and the segment number. For example, say we have the following string:

```
szText = "The Quick Brown Fox"
```

The following code will return "The":

```
Print szParseString(szText, " ", 1)
```

The following code will return "Brown":

```
Print szParseString(szText, " ", 3)
```

Sample Program—NNTP.VBP

Figure 4.6 shows NNTP, a simple newsreader application. You can use it to browse and view news in any newsgroup and post new articles (if posting is allowed). The code snippets discussed here are all taken from this sample application.

Enter the news server name or address in the NNTP Server Name text box and click the Connect button. The client connects to the NNTP server on port 119. After a successful connection, you can view a newsgroup by entering its name in the Newsgroup Name text box and pressing the Retrieve button. The client then logs onto the specified newsgroup and sends you a list of articles, as shown in Figure 4.7. You can view any article by double-clicking on it. The client downloads the article and displays it, as in Figure 4.8.

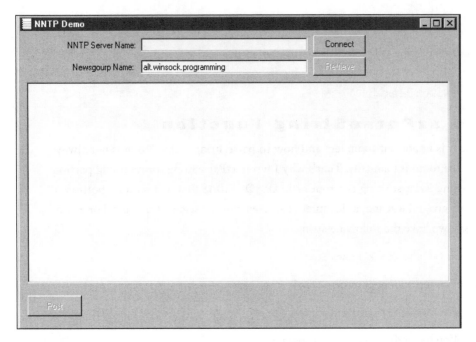

■■■■■■■ **Figure 4.6** The NNTP sample newsreader program.

If you want to post to any newsgroup, hit the Post button. The post form, shown in Figure 4.9, pops up. Fill in the newsgroup, your email address, the subject, and the article text and hit the Post button to post the message. When the client receives a positive reply it shows a confirmation dialog box, shown in Figure 4.10.

Connecting to an NNTP Server

Connect to your NNTP server the same way you'd connect to any Internet server. NNTP listens to port 119. Therefore, the following syntax will do nicely:

```
If SocketConnect (DSSocket1, 119, "your.nntp.server", 30) Then
    MsgBox "Error Connecting to server", vbInformation
Else
    MsgBox "Connected!"
End If
```

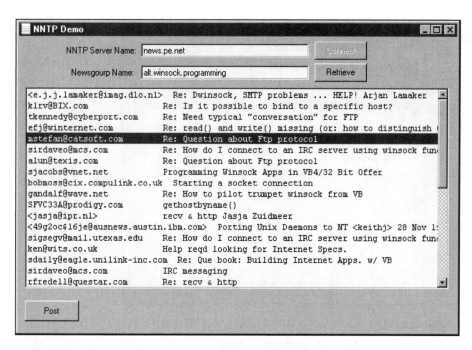

Figure 4.7 NNTP displays a list of articles when you enter a newsgroup name and press the Retrieve button.

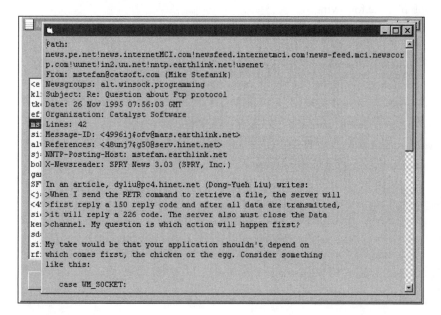

Figure 4.8 View an article by double-clicking on it in the list.

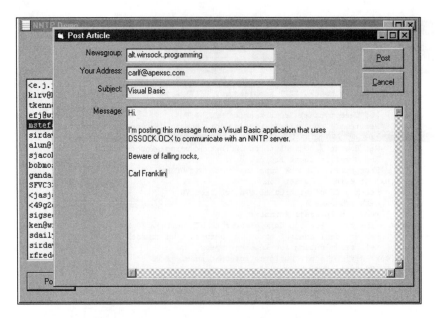

Figure 4.9 Click the Post button to pop up the Post form. Enter a message and press the Post button on the Post form.

Upon connection you will receive either a 200 or a 201 reply and a welcome line that might look like the following:

```
200 mindport.net InterNetNews NNRP server INN 1.4 22-Dec-93 ready (posting ok).
```

The 200 reply indicates that posting is allowed, while a 201 reply indicates that it isn't. The reply number is followed by the domain name, the version of NNTP software, and sometimes a textual indication of posting being allowed or not. After receiving this line, you should send the command, "MODE READER" to tell the server that you are a newsreader. The server sends back another 200 reply. At this point you are ready to converse with the server.

Figure 4.10 The client gives you confirmation following a successful post.

Retrieving an Article Header

Now that you know how it works, let's add some complexity to the above example. When the number of articles and first and last article numbers are received, the code should send the HEAD command to retrieve the header for the first article in the newsgroup and display the date, subject, and sender's name in the debug window.

Now there must be two states, or *modes* if you will. State 1 is when we are receiving reply strings, and state 2 is when we are receiving text (the article's header).

The header is sent as individual lines of text terminated by a period on a line by itself (with a CR/LF on either side of it). The HEAD command is fairly simple. The format is "HEAD" followed by a space and the article number, and terminated with a CR/LF.

The example in Figure 4.11 adds onto the ReceiveData subroutine from the previous example with code to return and parse the header of the first article in the archive. There are some fundamental differences between this example and the first one. Besides using szParseString to return the different portions of ReceiveData, the nCode variable is among several variables declared Static. Static variables hold their values for the life of the program. When the subroutine runs, the Static variables will be whatever their values were when the sub was previously exited. nCode is Static so that the last reply code received is always available.

Also static are string variables szSubject, szDate, and szSender. These will hold the values extracted from the article header until the header has been completely received, at which point they are displayed in a message box.

nCommandMode is a flag that indicates whether we are receiving reply strings or header data. If nCommandMode is False (the default value) then we are receiving reply strings. When nCommandMode is True, then we are receiving header text.

After sending the HEAD command you should receive a 221 message indicating that the header is being sent to you. The next several lines will be the text of the header ending with a period on a line by itself. Remember that every line ends with a CR/LF.

If the code received is 221, then nCommandMode is set to True. When a line of header data is received, then the nCode value is tested, indicating the last reply code received. If this code is 221, then ReceiveData is a line of header text.

```
Sub DSSocket1_Receive(ReceiveData As String)

    Dim nPos As Integer         '-- Used with Instr
    Const chrSpace = " "        '-- Used with Instr"
    Const szPeriod = "."        '-- Used to determine the end of x-mission.

    Static lNumArticles As Long   '-- Number of articles in group
    Static lFirstArticle As Long  '-- First Article Number
    Static lLastArticle As Long   '-- Last Article Number

    Static szSubject As String    '-- Article Subject
    Static szDate As String       '-- Creation Date
    Static szSender As String     '-- Who posted the article
    Static szArticleText As String

    Static nTextMode As Integer   '-- When True, we are receiving data
                                  '   When False, reply codes.
    Static nCode As Integer       '-- The last reply code received.


'-----------------------------------------------------------------------------


    If nTextMode = False Then
        '-- Receiving reply codes

        nCode = Val(Left$(ReceiveData, 3))

        Select Case nCode
            Case 211 '-- Article information for selected newsgroup

                '-- Get the number of articles
```

```
                    lNumArticles = Val(szParseString(ReceiveData, chrSpace, 2))


                    '-- Get the first article number
                    lFirstArticle = Val(szParseString(ReceiveData, chrSpace, 3))


                    '-- Get the first article number
                    lLastArticle = Val(szParseString(ReceiveData, chrSpace, 4))



                    '-- Retrieve the Header for the first article
                    SendData DSSocket1, "HEAD" & Str$(lFirstArticle) & vbCrLf


            Case 220, 221, 222
                    '-- 220 Header and Body follows
                    '-- 221 Header follows
                    '-- 222 Body follows


                    '-- Prepare to receive data
                    nTextMode = True


            Case Is > 399  '-- An error occurred
                    MsgBox szParseString(ReceiveData, 2), vbInformation


        End Select
    Else
        '-- Transmission complete?
        If SuperTrim$(ReceiveData) = szPeriod & vbCrLf Then
            '-- What was the last code received?
            Select Case nCode
                Case 220 '-- Header and body follows
                    '-- szArticleText holds the complete article text.
                    Debug.Print szArticleText
                Case 221 '-- Header follows
```

```
                            Debug.Print szSubject
                            Debug.Print szDate
                            Debug.Print szSender
                    End Select
                    '-- Done receiving text. Ready for another code.
                    nTextMode = False
            Else
                    '-- What was the last code received?
                    Select Case nCode
                        Case 220 '-- Header and body follow
                            szArticleText = szArticleText & ReceiveData & vbCrLf
                        Case 221 '-- Header follows
                            If Left$(UCase$(ReceiveData), 8) = "SUBJECT:" Then
                                szSubject = ReceiveData
                            ElseIf Left$(UCase$(ReceiveData), 5) = "DATE:" Then
                                szDate = ReceiveData
                            ElseIf Left$(UCase$(ReceiveData), 5) = "FROM:" Then
                                szSender = ReceiveData
                            End If
                    End Select
            End If
        End If

End Sub
```

Retrieving a Complete Article

With just a slight modification of the above code, we can tell the NNTP
server to send us a specific article. The code is exactly the same, except that
you send the ARTICLE command instead of the HEAD command. Where
HEAD retrieves the header for an article, ARTICLE retrieves the entire article.
To return just the body text of the article, send the BODY command.

Instead of this:

```
'-- Retrieve the Header for the first article
SendData DSSocket1, "HEAD" & Str$(lFirstArticle) & vbCrlf
```

specify this command:

```
'-- Retrieve the whole article
SendData DSSocket1, "ARTICLE" & Str$(lFirstArticle) & vbCrlf
```

Retrieving Article Information

When you use a newsreader program, such as the shareware WinVN application, to browse a newsgroup you are usually presented with a one-line description of each article. This line may include the date, subject, sender's email address, number of lines, and so on. Where does this information come from? The answer is the XOVER command. Here is the syntax for this command:

```
XOVER <article number range. ex: 200-400> <CRLF>
```

See the XOVER command definition at the end of this chapter for range options.

XOVER returns the following information on a line for each article in the specified range, ending with a CR/LF on a line by itself:

```
<Article Number> <Subject> <Date> <Article ID> <Size in bytes> <Number of Lines>
```

Example: Displaying Article Descriptions in a List Box

The following example shows how to ask for a list of all articles in a newsgroup using the XOVER command, and displays the result in a list box (it is assumed that you are already connected).

```
'-- Send the XOVER command to retrieve all messages.
DSSocket1.Send "XOVER 1-" & vbCrLf
```

The server sends back a 211 reply, indicating the number of messages in the group, and the first and last MessageIDs. At that point the XOVER command is sent to retrieve the descriptions of all messages in the entire group.

The server then sends back a 224 reply, indicating that the list is about to be sent. At that point a flag is set to indicate that we are receiving the list. Each line received after that is parsed and the data displayed in a list box. At the end of the list, the server sends a period on a line by itself. When this is received, the connection is closed.

Posting an Article

In order to post an article, you should have received the words "posting ok" in the first line received when you connect to the server. If you don't receive this string there's a good chance the server is not accepting posts.

To initiate a posting, send the POST command like so:

```
DSSocket1.Send = "POST" & vbCrLf
```

You will receive back either a 340 reply indicating that you can go ahead and send the article, or a 440 reply indicating that posting is not allowed. If you get a 340, you can immediately start sending the article text.

To post a message, you need to create at least a minimal header. In NNTP land the following fields are considered required:

1. From   Name and email address of the sender having the following format:

    ```
    Carl Franklin <carlf@apexsc.com>
    ```

2. Newsgroups   List of groups to post to separated by comma
3. Subject   Subject of your message

Here is a perfect example of a header that you will create when posting a new article:

```
From: Carl Franklin <carlf@apexsc.com>
Newsgroups: test.newsgroup
Subject: This is a test post
```

The NNTP server fills in all the detail header fields, such as the Message-ID, Date, and so on.

The message body follows the header, from which it is separated by a blank line. The body ends with a period on a line by itself. Figure 4.12 shows an example of a complete article ready to be posted. All lines are terminated with a CR/LF.

After sending the POST command and receiving a 340 reply, you can execute the sample code shown in Figure 4.13 to post a message. Of course, you would want to let your user specify the actual article data, but this is a good example from a programmer's perspective.

▬▬▬ TIP

It is not efficient to send your text one line at a time; I wrote the example this way to bring attention to the different lines that make up the sent text. It would be better to concatenate the entire message together into one string, and then send that string.

After executing this code, you will either receive a 240 indicating success, or a 4xx series error, indicating a wide variety of errors all meaning that the post was rejected for one reason or another. Figure 4.14 shows the actual errors you could receive.

▬▬▬ Figure 4.12 A complete Usenet article ready to be posted.

From: Carl Franklin <carlf@apexsc.com>
Newsgroups: test.newsgroup
Subject: This is a test post

This is a test post from a Visual Basic Application.
Want to know how it's done?
Just ask the master (heh heh heh).

Carl Franklin

Figure 4.13 Example: Posting an article.

```
DSSocket1.Send = "From: Carl Franklin <carlf@apexsc.com>" & vbCrlf

DSSocket1.Send = "Newsgroups: test.newsgroup" & vbCrlf

DSSocket1.Send = "Subject: This is a test post" & vbCrlf

DSSocket1.Send = vbCrlf

DSSocket1.Send = "This is a test post from a Visual Basic Application!" &_
                 vbCrlf

DSSocket1.Send = "Want to know how its done?" & vbCrlf

DSSocket1.Send = "Just ask the master (heh heh heh)." & vbCrlf

DSSocket1.Send = vbCrlf

DSSocket1.Send = "Carl Franklin" & vbCrlf

DSSocket1.Send = "." & vbCrlf
```

Figure 4.14 Possible errors resulting from posting an article.

```
400 service discontinued
435 article not wanted - do not send it
437 article rejected - do not try again
440 posting not allowed
441 posting failed

500 command not recognized
501 command syntax error
502 access restriction or permission denied
503 program fault - command not performed
```

Assuming that you receive a 240 reply back from the server, you can immediately retrieve the article with the ARTICLE command, although you will need to get the article number. There is a good chance that it will be the last article posted to the group, although this is not 100 percent guaranteed because someone else could be posting at the exact same moment as you. It's best to do an XOVER on the last ten or so articles to find your article number. Figure 4.15 shows what the article might look like when read with a newsreader.

Posting a Reply to a Previous Message

When posting a reply, you need to fill in just one other header, the Reply-To header. For example, Figure 4.16 shows the same message posted as a reply to an article

Figure 4.15 What the sample article might look like when read with a newsreader.

Path: mindport.net!news
From: Carl Franklin <carlf@apexsc.com>
Newsgroups: test.newsgroup
Subject: This is yet another test post
Date: 30 Oct 1995 14:39:07 GMT
Organization: Mindport Internet Services
Lines: 5
Message-ID: <472o2b$98c@draco.mindport.net>
NNTP-Posting-Host: 199.35.240.135

This is a test post from a Visual Basic Application.
Want to know how it's done?
Just ask the master (heh heh heh).

Carl Franklin

■■■■■■■■ **Figure 4.16** Posting a reply to a previous message.

```
DSSocket1.Send = "From: Carl Franklin <carlf@apexsc.com>" & vbCrlf
DSSocket1.Send = "Newsgroups: rec.audio.pro" & vbCrlf
DSSocket1.Send = "Subject: Re: Why should I get a sampler?" & vbCrlf
DSSocket1.Send = "Reply-To: Jon Smith <jons@somewhere.net>" & vbCrlf
DSSocket1.Send = vbCrlf
DSSocket1.Send = "> Why would one buy a sampler?" & vbCrlf
DSSocket1.Send = "> What is a sampler, anyway?" & vbCrlf
DSSocket1.Send = "> Just Curious," & vbCrlf
DSSocket1.Send = "> " & vbCrlf
DSSocket1.Send = "> Jon Smith" & vbCrlf
DSSocket1.Send = vbCrlf
DSSocket1.Send = "Jon," & vbCrlf
DSSocket1.Send = "A sampler lets you record small digital clips" & vbCrlf
DSSocket1.Send = "of your favorite instruments and them reproduce them" & vbCrlf
DSSocket1.Send = "with a MIDI controller. They are great for drums." & vbCrlf
DSSocket1.Send = vbCrlf
DSSocket1.Send = "Carl Franklin" & vbCrlf
DSSocket1.Send = "." & vbCrlf
```

■■■■■■

posted by Jon Smith. The original message is enclosed in quotes as is the common practice when replying to an article.

Retrieving a List of Newsgroups

LIST Returns a List of Newsgroups

By sending the LIST command you are really asking for trouble in that the server will return the monster list of all newsgroups. The server sends a 215 reply followed by each newsgroup's information on separate lines and ending with a period on a line by itself. Each line has the following format:

```
<newsgroup> <last article number> <first article number> <posting allowed (y or n)>
```

For example, the following command:

```
DSSocket1.Send = "LIST" & vbCrLf
```

would return the following:

```
215 List Follows
alt.barney.dinosaur.die.die.die 1100 1000 y
alt.barney.dinosaur.why.why.why 320 297 y
<and so on>
```

If you are writing a newsreader, it would be best to save the output of the list command to a database or some other file and give the user the option of retrieving it every time.

LIST ACTIVE Returns Selective Newsgroups

LIST ACTIVE returns a listing of active newsgroups, and perhaps more importantly, lets you limit the range of groups for which information is returned. The server returns a 215 reply followed by a list of newsgroups. For example, the following command:

```
DSSocket1.Send = "LIST ACTIVE comp.lang.basic.visual.*" & vbCrLf
```

could return the following data:

```
215 list follows
comp.lang.basic.visual.3rdparty 2200 1923 y
comp.lang.basic.visual.announce 240 237 y
comp.lang.basic.visual.database 11293 11245 y
comp.lang.basic.visual.misc 23098 22432 y
.
```

TIP

It has been my experience that LIST ACTIVE does not always accept an argument, and will only return a complete list of active newsgroups.

XGTITLE Returns
Newsgroup Descriptions

The XGTITLE command returns a list of newsgroups that fit the specified WILDMAT search mask. The server returns a 282 reply followed by a list of newsgroups. On each line is returned the name of the newsgroup and a short description. For example:

```
DSSocket1.Send = "XGTITLE comp.lang.basic.visual.*" & vbCrLf
```

would return the following:

```
282 list follows
comp.lang.basic.visual.3rdparty   Add-ins for Visual Basic.
comp.lang.basic.visual.announce   Official information on Visual Basic. (Moderated)
comp.lang.basic.visual.database   Database aspects of Visual Basic.
comp.lang.basic.visual.misc       Visual Basic in general.
  .
```

You could return the description of just one newsgroup by specifying it without any wildcards. For example:

```
DSSocket1.Send = "XGTITLE comp.lang.basic.visual.misc" & vbCrLf
```

would return this:

```
282 list follows
comp.lang.basic.visual.misc       Visual Basic in general.
  .
```

LIST NEWSGROUPS Also Returns
Newsgroup Descriptions

The LIST NEWSGROUPS command does essentially the same thing as XGTITLE, but it returns a 215 result code. For example, this command:

```
DSSocket1.Send = "LIST NEWSGROUPS comp.lang.basic.visual.*" & vbCrLf
```

would return the following:

```
215 Descriptions in form "group description".
comp.lang.basic.visual.3rdparty  Add-ins for Visual Basic.
comp.lang.basic.visual.announce  Official information on Visual Basic.
(Moderated)
```

```
comp.lang.basic.visual.database   Database aspects of Visual Basic.
comp.lang.basic.visual.misc       Visual Basic in general.
```

▰▰▰▰ **TIP**

> It has been my experience that LIST NEWSGROUPS does not always accept
> an argument, and will only return a complete list of newsgroups.

▰▰▰▰

Retrieving a List
of Article Numbers

You can retrieve a list of just the valid article numbers for a newsgroup with the
LISTGROUP command. LISTGROUP takes as an argument the name of a newsgroup. Here is the syntax:

```
LISTGROUP <newsgroup name> <CRLF>
```

After receiving a LISTGROUP command the server sends a 211 reply followed by a
list of article numbers, each on a line by itself and ending with a period. For example, the following command:

```
DSSocket1.Send = "LISTGROUP comp.lang.basic.visual.announce" & vbCrLf
```

would return the following output:

```
211 List follows
11143
11145
11146
    .
```

Retrieving a Specific
Header Field

The XHDR command lets you retrieve a specific header field for a given article.
Here is the command syntax:

```
XHDR <Field Name> <Article Number> <CRLF>
```

The server returns a 221 reply followed by a line containing the article number and header information and a period on a line by itself. For example, the following command:

```
DSSocket1.Send = "XHDR Subject 14619" & vbCrLf
```

could return the following server output:

```
221 Subject fields follow
14619 Re:VB Decompiler
.
```

This is very handy when you want only specific pieces of the header. For example, if you were to write an application that routes certain newsgroup articles by email, you would not need all the distribution headers, and whatnot. You just want the sender's name, email address, and the date and subject of the message.

Searching for Articles by Header

The XPAT Command

XPAT lets you retrieve a list of articles in the current newsgroup given a range of articles, a header field, and a match pattern. XPAT returns the article number and the specified header field for all articles where the header field matches the pattern. Here is the syntax:

```
XPAT <Header> <Range|Message-ID> <Wildmat String> [<Wildmat String>] <CRLF>
```

Here is some example code that searches for all articles where "VB4" appears in the subject for the comp.lang.basic.visual.misc newsgroup:

```
DSSocket1.Send = "XPAT Subject 1- *VB4*" & vbCrLf
```

Here is an example that returns all messages posted by Carl Franklin:

```
DSSocket1.Send = "XPAT From 1- *carlf@apexsc.com*" & vbCrLf
```

The server returns a 221 reply followed by a list of articles ending with a period on a line by itself. For example, consider the output of XPAT From 1- *carlf@apexsc.com*:

```
221 From matches follow.
10894 Carl Franklin <carlf@apexsc.com>
.
```

There are many great practical uses for this type of search. Are you having trouble finding someone who you know is active on Usenet? Pick out a list of newsgroups that he or she frequents and search them on a daily basis for any articles with your friend's name in the From header field.

Is someone you know looking for a job? Search biz.jobs.offered headers for keywords like "Engineer" or "Sacramento." Just for kicks, email all the desired articles to yourself, or throw them into an Access database.

You see, programming the Internet is not about accessing the Internet, it's about disseminating the information available for real-world practical reasons.

Server-to-Server Communication

NNTP is much more than a protocol for news clients, it's also how NNTP servers communicate with each other. An NNTP server will have at least one other server connected to it at all times, although it is not uncommon for it to be linked to three or four other servers. Whenever your site receives a post from a local user it is quickly passed on to the other servers using the IHAVE command. Your server is constantly receiving news from the other servers with the IHAVE command also. IHAVE is the way news is replicated throughout the Internet.

Here is a conversation that takes place between two servers to successfully replicate an article:

```
RECV: IHAVE <krwaosRREdf3.342@netcom.com> <CRLF>
SEND: 335 send article to be transferred.  End with <CR-LF>.<CR-LF>
RECV:  [Server sends the article ending with a period on a line by itself]
SEND: 235 article transferred OK <CR-LF>
```

Here is a conversation that takes place between two servers when the receiver already has the article:

```
RECV: IHAVE <krwaosRREdf3.342@netcom.com> <CRLF>
SEND: 435 article not wanted - do not send it <CR-LF>
```

Epilogue

NNTP may seem at first like it wouldn't fit well into an existing framework. However, you can use NNTP to supplement an information system by tapping the largest source of subject-oriented material the Internet can offer.

One practical (and profitable) use of Usenet is archiving. Write an application to archive news articles for one or more newsgroups and then provide search capabilities either on the subject line or on the articles themselves. I know that on Carl & Gary's Visual Basic Home Page our news archive database is a real crowd pleaser. We receive a steady stream of compliments on it. Although it was originally written with Perl scripts in UNIX, the same thing could easily be written in Visual Basic. You can store the articles in any database format from Access to MS SQL Server.

What about an NNTP server? No problem. You can write one in 32-bit Visual Basic 4.0 that runs on Windows NT storing articles in a SQL Server. Yeah, that should be fast. There are lots of ways you can use NNTP for any kind of project. I know you'll think of something.

CHAPTER 5

ELECTRONIC MAIL

Introduction

Electronic mail, or email, is the most widely used resource on the Internet. Many modern companies, large and small, rely on email as their primary source of communication. The world of electronic mail seems mysterious when you first approach it. There are all these computers whizzing your messages around the world at the speed of light. How do they work? What happens when you send mail? What's the difference between email and CompuServe or America Online mail messages?

After reading this chapter, you'll understand how email systems work, and you will know how to use the SMTP and POP3 protocols to send and receive email messages and files using Visual Basic 4.0.

Electronic mail is a kind of catchall phrase that describes any transfer of textual (and binary) data from one computer user to another via some sort of communications network. For me, as for many of us, my first encounter with electronic mail was CompuServe. I went nuts when I saw CompuServe for the first time. I could send mail to people. I could get into the CB simulator and talk in real time (almost) with other people all over the world.

CompuServe uses its internal network and software to move messages around from mailbox to mailbox. This includes pieces of the Internet at certain points of transmission, but the whole process is managed by CompuServe. America Online, Prodigy, and the Microsoft Network are other examples of commercial networks that offer electronic mail.

But there is another type of electronic mail which is much broader in scope and definition. Its roots are in the academic institutions of the world. Internet mail can be set up and accessed by anyone, not just a CompuServe or an AOL. In fact, there are probably a few Internet Access Providers in your neighborhood that offer connectivity to the Internet including email for a nominal monthly charge. These "small shops" are increasing daily all over America, and are really representative of the open architecture of Internet protocols. A local access provider will have a mail server that speaks SMTP and POP3. You can access email from this server with one of many shareware or commercial email applications like Pegasus or Eudora, which do exactly what the sample code in this chapter does.

If you couldn't wait and have already looked at the sample code for this chapter, you may be struck by how simple it is. The truth is that these and other Internet protocols are so easy that the main marketing focus of big commercial networks is convincing the masses that using their system is better than using just the public Internet systems, which in reality are some of the biggest reasons for the Internet's incredible popularity. In most cases commercial online services add an unnecessary layer between you and the mail gateway.

I'm not saying that commercial networks are not excellent sources of information and Internet services, I'm merely trying to help you understand that there is a difference between CompuServe mail and Internet mail. This difference really becomes apparent when you try to write programs to access email on a commercial network versus an Internet server. To access email on CompuServe you need either a high-level system such as Microsoft Exchange or you need to write a serial communications program to access CompuServe with a modem, coding your way to the email section and sending the right strings to send or get your mail. Each commercial network has a different protocol (or set of rules) for sending and receiving mail. Some networks may not even offer a way for you to write code to get your mail, instead making you use their own applications. This is why it's very important that there be some sort of standard protocols for sending and receiving mail with a mail server. Enter SMTP (for sending) and POP3 (for receiving).

If you access the Internet through a local provider, you need to find out the name of your mail server. Call them up and ask them if they have an SMTP/POP3 mail server, and could you please have the address. With only the address of the server and your name and password, you are ready to use some very simple Visual Basic code to send and receive email.

The SMTP Protocol

The Simple Mail Transport Protocol (SMTP) is used to send mail messages. SMTP uses port 25. That is, to send a message to a mail server with SMTP you must first connect to that server on port 25. Once connected, there is an exchange of commands and responses back and forth between you (the client) and the mail server. Every line you send must end with a carriage return/linefeed pair.

Take a look at the sample session in Figure 5.1, which sends an email message to an SMTP server taken from RFC 821. The letter *S* stands for Send and the letter *R* for Receive.

The first line sent tells the server who the mail is from, to which the server responds with a 250 OK reply. The number 250 is a code which means OK. Other numbers mean other things, but we'll get to that in a minute.

The next line sent to the server identifies the receiver. The server responds with OK. This can be repeated for as many recipients as required. The third line sent in this example shows what happens if the specified receiver does not exist at the domain. The server will send back the number 550 followed by an error message.

Jumping down to the fourth block, this is where the message itself is sent. If the server accepts the DATA command indicating it is ready to receive data, it will send back the number 354, at which point the client sends the message followed by carriage return/linefeed pair, a period, and another carriage return/linefeed. If the message was sent successfully the server sends back 250 OK.

■■■■■■■ **Figure 5.1** Sample session between an SMTP client and server.

```
S: MAIL FROM:<Smith@Alpha.ARPA>

R: 250 OK


S: RCPT TO:<Jones@Beta.ARPA>

R: 250 OK


S: RCPT TO:<Green@Beta.ARPA>

R: 550 No such user here


S: RCPT TO:<Brown@Beta.ARPA>

R: 250 OK


S: DATA

R: 354 Start mail input; end with <CRLF>.<CRLF>

S: Blah blah blah...

S: ...etc. etc. etc.

S: <CRLF>.<CRLF>

R: 250 OK
```

SMTP Commands

SMTP uses a series of simple four-character commands such as MAIL and QUIT that perform the various tasks required to send an email message. These commands are listed in the SMTP Reference Appendix at the back of this book. SMTP commands are always followed with a CR/LF pair.

Server Responses

After sending an SMTP command, you will receive a reply which consists of a three-digit number followed by a space and a text message. Figure 5.2 shows a list of reply codes in numeric order. The full descriptions of these codes can be found in RFC 821.

▰▰▰▰ **Figure 5.2** SMTP reply codes.

- 211 System status, or system help reply
- 214 Help message

  [Information on how to use the receiver or the meaning of a particular non-standard command; this reply is useful only to the human user]

- 220 <domain> Service ready
- 221 <domain> Service closing transmission channel
- 250 Requested mail action okay, completed
- 251 User not local; will forward to <forward-path>
- 354 Start mail input; end with <CRLF>.<CRLF>
- 421 <domain> Service not available, closing transmission channel

  [This may be a reply to any command if the service knows it must shut down]

- 450 Requested mail action not taken: mailbox unavailable

  [E.g., mailbox busy]

- 451 Requested action aborted: error in processing

- 452 Requested action not taken: insufficient system storage
- 500 Syntax error, command unrecognized

  [This may include errors such as command line too long]
- 501 Syntax error in parameters or arguments
- 502 Command not implemented
- 503 Bad sequence of commands
- 504 Command parameter not implemented
- 550 Requested action not taken: mailbox unavailable

  [E.g., mailbox not found, no access]
- 551 User not local; please try <forward-path>
- 552 Requested mail action aborted: exceeded storage allocation
- 553 Requested action not taken: mailbox name not allowed

  [E.g., mailbox syntax incorrect]
- 554 Transaction failed

Reply Code Categories

Each digit of the reply code has a specific meaning. There are five values for the first digit of the reply code: 1 is not used in SMTP, 2 indicates a positive reply, 3 indicates a positive intermediate reply in which case the server is waiting for more information, 4 indicates that the command was not accepted and the requested action did not occur yet the condition is temporary, and 5 indicates absolute failure.

The second digit indicates the category of the reply: 0 indicates a syntax error, 1 indicates informational content, 2 indicates a message concerning the transmission channel, 3 and 4 are not used, and 5 indicates a message concerning the status of the mail system. The third digit merely specifies the level of granularity of messages in a particular category.

Figure 5.3 shows a quick summary of how to interpret SMTP reply codes. You should consult RFC 821 for a complete discussion of these.

▬▬▬▬ **Figure 5.3** How to interpret SMTP reply codes.

2xx   Positive Reply

3xx   Positive Intermediate Reply

4xx   Transitive Negative Completion Reply

5xx   Permanent Negative Completion Reply

x0x   Syntax Error

x1x   Information

x2x   Connections

x3x   Unspecified as yet

x4x   Unspecified as yet

x5x   Mail system

▬▬▬▬

VB Programming Technique

SMTP is a command/reply protocol. That is, for every SMTP command, the server will respond with one or more reply codes. In Visual Basic, this is all handled in the Receive event of DSSOCK.

Brain-Dead SMTP

Don't laugh, it works most of the time. I'm talking about Brain-Dead SMTP, or sending blind without listening to the server. You can just ignore all the servers responses if you are so sure of yourself, but I don't recommend shipping product with Brain-Dead SMTP. Still, it's good for demonstration purposes, so here's how to do it.

Figure 5.4 shows the Visual Basic routine, SendBrainDead, which accepts a DSSOCK control connected to a mail server on port 25, a "from" string, a "to" string, a subject string, and a string containing the message, and sends it blindly, in true brain-dead fashion.

The szCompleteMsg string is made up of a header, which is simply the date, from address, to address, and the subject on four lines, and the message itself, with a blank line in between the header and the message. Notice that every line ends with a carriage return/linefeed pair and that the whole message ends with a period on a blank line by itself.

Do you want to try it? Go ahead: Load the project called BRAINDED from the SMTP subdirectory. BRAINDED uses this routine to send a mail message.

■■■■■■ **Figure 5.4** SendBrainDead sends an email message with no error checking.

```
Sub SendBrainDead(dsSock As Control, szFrom As String, szTo As String, _
    szSubject As String, szMsg As String)
    Dim szCompleteMsg As String
    szCompleteMsg = "MAIL FROM: <" & szFrom & ">" & vbCrlf _
        & "RCPT TO: <" & szTo & ">" & vbCrlf _
        & "DATA" & vbCrlf _
        & "DATE: " & Format$(Now, "dd mmm yy ttttt") & vbCrlf _
        & "FROM: " & szFrom & vbCrlf _
        & "TO: " & szTo & vbCrlf _
        & "SUBJECT: " & szSubject & vbCrlf & vbCrlf _
        & szMsg & vbCrlf & "." & vbCrlf

    dsSock.Send = szCompleteMsg

End Sub
```

True SMTP

The cool thing about Brain-Dead SMTP is that you can write it quickly and use it right away. The obvious downside is that there is no error handling. What happens if the recipient doesn't exist? Your program should know if it sends mail with a bad recipient address so the user can fix it. The server sends reply codes after every command it receives. For example, if you specify a bad recipient address the server will send a 550 reply code, which means "mailbox not available."

In order to have a true SMTP service, you must interact with the other machine on a command/reply basis. The basic idea behind command/reply programming is that you set up a reply code handler in the Receive event and take action based on the reply code that you've received as well as on the last command that you issued. You must react to reply codes accordingly. Fortunately, SMTP is fairly simple.

Connecting and Disconnecting

When you connect to an SMTP server you will receive a 220 reply, at which time you should send a HELO command with the following format:

```
HELO <SP> <domain> <CRLF>
```

where <domain> is the domain portion of your email address. For example, if your email address is santa@northpole.com, your domain is northpole.com.

When disconnecting, send the QUIT command. It is considered rude to simply disconnect the socket, although it is perfectly acceptable in most cases because SMTP servers are fairly thick-skinned and do not insult easily. Anyway, here is the format of the QUIT command:

```
QUIT <CRLF>
```

After sending the QUIT command, you will receive a 221 reply and then the socket will disconnect. When using DSSOCK, the Close event will fire.

Sample Application: SMTP.VBP

Figure 5.5 shows the main screen of the SMTP sample application. Figure 5.6 shows the code. It is important that you keep track of the last command you sent the server so that you will know how to interpret the reply codes you receive. The SendSMTPCommand procedure sends a specified command string, and assigns the command portion to a global string (gszCommand). At any time you can determine the last command sent by looking at gszCommand.

Check out the DSSocket1_Receive event procedure. The first thing that happens is the reply code is determined. Since this code is always the first three digits of a received string, we can simply use the Left$ function to return the three leftmost characters, and convert this to an integer with the Val function like so:

```
nCode = Val(Left$(ReceiveData, 3))
```

Next, a Select Case structure defines the reply handler. The first code you will receive after connecting is a 220 (Connect OK or Command OK). Receiving this code is the true indication that you've successfully connected to the SMTP server. Therefore, the sample code sets the gnConnected variable to True upon receiving this code, rather than in the Connect event.

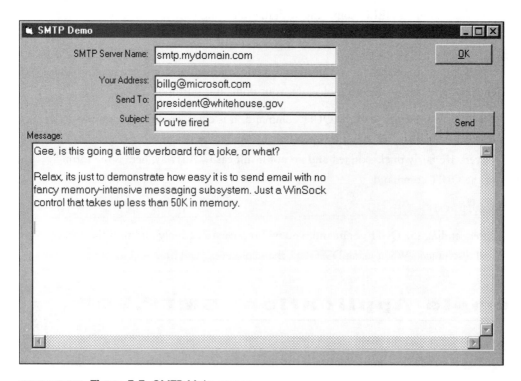

■■■■ **Figure 5.5** SMTP Main screen.

▬▬▬▬ **Figure 5.6** SMTP listings.

SMTP.BAS Listing

```
Option Explicit


'-- Holds the last command issued
Global gszCommand    As String


'-- These variables hold fields of the
'   message to be sent.
Global gszTo         As String
Global gszFrom       As String
Global gszSubject    As String
Global gszMsg        As String


Sub SendSMTPCommand(DSSock As Control, szCmd As String)


    '-- Save the last command sent
    gszCommand = szParseString(szCmd, " ", 1)


    '-- Send the command
    SendData DSSock, szCmd & vbCrlf


End Sub
```

SMTP.FRM Listing

```
Option Explicit


Sub CheckFields()


    '-- Enables the send button only
    '   if all the fields are filled in.
    If Len(txtHost) Then
        If Len(txtFrom) Then
```

```
                    If Len(txtTo) Then
                        If Len(txtSubject) Then
                            If Len(txtMsg) Then
                                btnSend.Enabled = True
                                Exit Sub
                            End If
                        End If
                    End If
                End If
            End If


            btnSend.Enabled = False


End Sub


Private Sub btnOK_Click()


    Unload Me


End Sub


Sub btnSend_Click()
'-- Send an Email message. All we have to do here is
'    fill in the global strings that make up the message
'    from the text controls, and connect. The protocol does
'    the rest.

    '-- Disable the buttons
    btnSend.Enabled = False
    btnOK.Enabled = False
    Screen.MousePointer = vbHourglass

    '-- Fill in the global strings
```

```
    gszFrom = txtFrom
    gszTo = txtTo
    gszSubject = txtSubject
    gszMsg = txtMsg


    '-- Connect to the host
    If SocketConnect(DSSocket1, 25, (txtHost), 30) Then
        '-- An error occurred.
        MsgBox "Could not connect", vbInformation, "SMTP Client"
        btnSend.Enabled = True
        btnOK.Enabled = True
        Screen.MousePointer = vbNormal
    End If


    '-- The protocol takes over from here (DSSocket1_Receive)


End Sub


Sub DSSocket1_Close(ErrorCode As Integer, ErrorDesc As String)


    gnConnected = False


End Sub


Private Sub DSSocket1_Connect()


    gnConnected = True


End Sub



Sub DSSocket1_Receive(ReceiveData As String)
'-- SMTP Client Protocol in action!
```

```
Dim nPos          As Integer        '-- Used with Instr

Dim nIndex        As Integer
Dim szFullMsg     As String

Const chrSpace = " "               '-- Used with Instr
Const szPeriod = "."               '-- Used to determine the end of x-mission.

Static nTextMode As Integer        '-- When True, we are receiving data
                                   '   When False, reply codes.
Static nCode As Integer            '-- The last reply code received.

Static bReceived220 As Integer     '-- Set true after receiving the first
                                   '   220, indicating a connection.


'-----------------------------------------------------------------------------


'-- Grab the reply code.
nCode = Val(Left$(ReceiveData, 3))

'-- What is it?
Select Case nCode

    Case 220    '-- Connect and/or Command OK.
        '-- Is this the first 220?
        If Not bReceived220 Then
            '-- Yep. Flip the flag.
            bReceived220 = True

            '-- This means we're connected. At this
            '   point SocketConnect will exit.
            '-- Send the MAIL command to initiate the send
```

```
'   process.
SendSMTPCommand DSSocket1, "HELO <" & _
    Mid$(gszFrom, Instr(gszFrom, "@")) & ">"


gnConnected = True

    End If


Case 250    '-- Command OK
    '-- What was the last command?
    Select Case gszCommand$
        Case "HELO"
            '-- Send the MAIL command to initiate the send
            '   process.
            SendSMTPCommand DSSocket1, "MAIL FROM: <" & gszFrom & ">"
        Case "MAIL"
            '-- After MAIL, send the RCPT command to
            '   establish the final destination
            SendSMTPCommand DSSocket1, "RCPT TO: <" & gszTo & ">"
        Case "RCPT"
            '-- After RCPT, send the DATA command
            '   to request permission to send the mail message.
            '   This should yield a 354 reply.
            SendSMTPCommand DSSocket1, "DATA"
        Case "DATA"
            '-- This is the second time we get 250... after the
            '   mail has been sent. We actually get a 354
            '   after sending the DATA command (see below)


            '-- Confirmation that the message was delivered.
            MsgBox "Message Delivered", vbInformation, "SMTP Client"
            btnSend.Enabled = True
```

```
                    btnOK.Enabled = True
                    Screen.MousePointer = vbNormal
                    bReceived220 = False


            End Select


    Case 354
        '-- There should only be one command... DATA
        Select Case gszCommand$
            Case "DATA"
                '-- Now we have permission to send the message.
                '    Compose the complete message. Note the date format.
                '    This is very important.
                szFullMsg = "DATE: " & Format$(Now, "dd mmm yy ttttt") & vbCrlf _
                    & "FROM: " & gszFrom & vbCrlf _
                    & "TO: " & gszTo & vbCrlf _
                    & "SUBJECT: " & gszSubject & vbCrlf & vbCrlf _
                    & gszMsg & vbCrlf & "." & vbCrlf

                '-- Don't use SendSMTP command, so the
                '    last command will still be "DATA"
                SendData DSSocket1, szFullMsg


        End Select


    Case Is >= 400


        '-- An error of some sort occurred. Display to the user and
        '    reset everything.

        MsgBox Mid$(ReceiveData, 4), vbInformation, "Error From Server"
        btnSend.Enabled = True
```

```
            btnOK.Enabled = True
            Screen.MousePointer = vbNormal
            bReceived220 = False


        Case Else
            '-- Something we weren't expecting
            Debug.Print ReceiveData


    End Select

End Sub

Sub DSSocket1_SendReady()

    gnSendReady = True

End Sub

Sub Form_Load()

    DSSocket1.LineMode = True

End Sub


Sub Form_Unload(Cancel As Integer)

    SocketDisconnect DSSocket1
    End

End Sub
Private Sub txtFrom_Change()
```

```
        CheckFields

End Sub


Private Sub txtHost_Change()

        CheckFields

End Sub

Private Sub txtMsg_Change()

        CheckFields

End Sub


Private Sub txtSubject_Change()

        CheckFields

End Sub


Private Sub txtTo_Change()

        CheckFields

End Sub
```

Sending Mail

After receiving a 220 code for the first time the SMTP project code initiates a transaction by sending a MAIL command. At this point you could substitute SEND, SAML, or SOML for the MAIL command depending on how you want the message to be delivered. More on this shortly.

You will receive a 220 code more than once, so in order to send at the appropriate time you must set a flag after receiving 220 the first time. Then, simply check to see that the flag is not set before sending the MAIL command. The bReceived220 variable is used for this purpose. Figure 5.7 shows how this static variable is used.

▬▬▬▬▬ **Figure 5.7** Using static variables.

```
'-- What is it?
Select Case nCode


    Case 220     '-- Connect and/or Command OK.
        '-- Is this the first 220?
        If Not bReceived220 Then
            '-- Yep. Flip the flag.
            bReceived220 = True


            '-- This means we're connected. At this
            '   point SocketConnect will exit.
            gnConnected = True


            '-- Send the MAIL command to initiate the send
            '   process.
            SendSMTPCommand DSSocket1, "MAIL FROM: <" & gszFrom & ">"
        End If
```

The MAIL command specifies the sender's email address. The correct syntax is as follows:

```
MAIL FROM: <email_address>
```

After receiving the MAIL command the server will send back a 250 reply if it can accept email. If you do not get a 250 then you cannot send mail. Figure 5.8 shows

■■■■■ **Figure 5.8** Handling a 250 reply.

```
Case 250, 251    '-- Command OK
    '-- What was the last command?
    Select Case gszCommand$
        Case "MAIL"
            '-- After MAIL, send the RCPT command to
            '   establish the final destination
            SendSMTPCommand DSSocket1, "RCPT TO: <" & gszTo & ">"
        Case "RCPT"
            '-- After RCPT, send the DATA command
            '   to request permission to send the mail message.
            '   This should yield a 354 reply.
            SendSMTPCommand DSSocket1, "DATA"
        Case "DATA"
            '-- This occurs after successfully sending an
            '   email message.

            '-- Confirmation that the message was delivered.
            MsgBox "Message Delivered", vbInformation, "SMTP Client"

            btnSend.Enabled = True
            btnOK.Enabled = True
            Screen.MousePointer = vbNormal
            bReceived220 = False
    End Select
```

how the code handles a 250 reply. The code response will depend on the last command sent. In this case, the last command was "MAIL" so the RCPT command is sent:

```
'-- After MAIL, send the RCPT command to
'   establish the final destination
SendSMTPCommand DSSocket1, "RCPT TO: <" & gszTo & ">"
```

RCPT tells the SMTP server who the recipient is. The correct syntax for RCPT is as follows:

```
RCPT TO: <email_address>
```

If the SMTP server has no problem with the RCPT command, you will again get a 250 reply. When a 250 is received after sending a RCPT command, the DATA command is issued:

```
Case "RCPT"
        '-- After RCPT, send the DATA command
        '   to request permission to send the mail message.
        '   This should yield a 354 reply.
        SendSMTPCommand DSSocket1, "DATA"
```

DATA is just sent as is. This tells the server that you are about to send the message header and body. When the server is ready for you to send the message it sends a 354 reply, which means "go ahead and send your message." When you send the message you are not sending a command, you are sending data. Therefore, you should just use the SendData routine and not SendSMTPCommand.

What happens here is a little tricky to code. After receiving the 354 you send the message and then you receive a 250 when the server has successfully received it. Using our current programming technique, after receiving the 250 the last command sent will be DATA. Figure 5.9 shows the code for handling the 354 reply. The format of the message is the most important factor here. If it's not perfect it will be refused. Figure 5.10 shows a sample message. Assume that every line ends with a CR/LF.

OK, now you've sent the message. You will now receive a 250 from the server. Here is what happens when you receive this:

```
Case "DATA"
        '-- This occurs after successfully sending an
```

```
'    email message.

'-- Confirmation that the message was delivered.
MsgBox "Message Delivered", vbInformation, "SMTP Client"

btnSend.Enabled = True
btnOK.Enabled = True
Screen.MousePointer = vbNormal
bReceived220 = False
```

Figure 5.9 Handling a 354 reply.

```
'-- What is it?
Select Case nCode


    Case 354
        '-- There should only be one command... DATA
        Select Case gszCommand$ '-- what was the last command sent?
            Case "DATA"
                '-- Now we have permission to send the message.
                '   Compose the complete message. Note the date format.
                '   This is very important.
                szFullMsg = "DATE: " & Format$(Now, "dd mmm yy ttttt") & vbCrlf _
                    & "FROM: " & gszFrom & vbCrlf _
                    & "TO: " & gszTo & vbCrlf _
                    & "SUBJECT: " & gszSubject & vbCrlf & vbCrlf _
                    & gszMsg & vbCrlf & "." & vbCrlf


                '-- Don't use SendSMTP command, so the
                '   last command will still be "DATA"
                SendData DSSocket1, szFullMsg


        End Select
```

■■■■■■ **Figure 5.10** Sample SMTP message.

DATE: 23 Nov 95 0800
FROM: me@mydomain.com
TO: someone@somedomain.com
SUBJECT: This is a test

Hello. This is the first line of an Email message
This is the second line

Above is a blank line. That's perfectly acceptable.
There MUST be a blank line between the SUBJECT
line and the first line of the message.

You can include UUEncoded data (files) anywhere in this
message body.

The message ends with a period on a line by itself.

Sincerely,

Nathan, the goofy one (gotcha, Nonzo)

■■■■■■

This is where you tell the user that the message has been sent. It's important that you set the bReceived220 flag back to false here, and do any other reset procedures that your app may need.

Sending vs. Mailing

When you SEND (as opposed to MAIL) a message, the message is delivered directly to the user's terminal if the user indeed *has* a terminal and is logged on. SENDing is really only appropriate for terminal-based UNIX shell systems and does not apply throughout the enterprise.

There are four commands for delivering a mail message. MAIL, the standard command for sending mail, sends a message to a user's mailbox. SEND sends the message directly to the user's terminal. SAML (Send And Mail) sends to the user's terminal if available and also MAILs the message to the user's mailbox. Finally, SOML (Send Or Mail) sends directly to the user and only MAILs to the mailbox if there is a problem SENDing.

In today's world, if you are going to write routines to send email, you should stick to the MAIL command.

Replying to Mail

Sending a reply uses the exact same mechanism as sending a standard message. The only difference is really the subject line, which should start with "Re:" (but this is not necessary for delivery) and you may want to quote the original document in the body of the code. In short, sending a reply is sending a message. The content of the subject and body are the only differences, and those differences are optional.

Forwarding Mail

Sometimes when you attempt to send a message, the recipient no longer has an account at the post office you are sending to. The server notifies you after you send the RCPT command if forwarding is necessary. If you receive a 251 reply, then the server will forward the mail for you in which case you don't have to do any special processing. Just tack 251 as a criterion onto the 250 reply handler because 251 is a specific reply that occurs only under this condition. For example:

```
251 User not local; will forward to <Postel@USC-ISIF.ARPA>
```

This can be handled by the same code that handles 250:

```
Case 250, 251
```

However, if the server cannot (or will not) forward the mail, you will receive a 551 reply like so:

```
551 User not local; please try <Mockapetris@USC-ISIF.ARPA>
```

If you receive a 551 you should automatically substitute the new address for the current one, and resend the RCPT command. Figure 5.11 shows how this is handled.

Verifying an SMTP address

The VRFY command lets you verify that a user does in fact have an account on the post office. The argument is the first part of the user's email address (up to the at sign) or the first or last name of the user. For example, my email address is carlf@apexsc.com. If you were to connect to Apex software's SMTP gateway and send a VRFY command it would be as follows:

```
SendSMTPCommand DSSocket1, "VRFY carlf"
```

■■■■■■ **Figure 5.11** Handling email redirection.

```
Select Case nCode



    . . .

    . . .



    Case 551
        '-- What was the last command?
        Select Case gszCommand$
            Case "RCPT"
                '-- The specified recipient does not exist here but there is
                '   a forwarding address. Parse it and resend the RCPT command
                gszTo = szParseString(ReceiveData, "<", 2)
                nPos = InStr(gszTo, ">")
                If nPos Then
                    gszTo = Left$(gszTo, nPos - 1)
                    SendSMTPCommand DSSocket1, "RCPT TO: <" & gszTo & ">"
                End If
        End Select
```

There are four possible responses to a VRFY command. A 250 command returns the full email address of anyone matching the last name specified. For example:

```
250 carlf<carlf@apexsc.com>
```

If the user does not exist, you will receive a 550 reply like so:

```
550 String does not match anything
```

If the string you specify applies to more than one user you will get a 553 reply like so:

```
553 User ambiguous
```

If the user is not local, the server sends back a 551 reply with the forwarding address:

```
551 User not local; please try <carlf@somewhere.else.com>
```

Figure 5.12 shows how to handle the successful completion of a VRFY command. In this scenario a VRFY command has been sent and a 250 code has been received. If upon receiving a 250 the last command sent was VRFY, a message box simply shows the user the verification message. You might want to use the VRFY command before sending a message to absolutely make sure that mail goes through.

Error Handling

Any code over 400 is considered an error and should at least be reported to the user, if not written to a log.

There may be times when a particular error received after sending a particular command would require some specific action (how's that for mumbo-jumbo?). In this case, you can handle the error the same way positive replies are handled, with a Select Case block.

So far we have discussed how to send email using SMTP. The rest of this chapter deals with how to retrieve your email using the Post Office Protocol (POP3).

Post Office Protocol 3 (POP3)

POP3 is the protocol by which email messages are retrieved from an Internet server. Like SMTP, the client sends commands to the server to which the server replies with coded responses. You may think that POP3 has more commands and codes than SMTP but actually this is not the case. POP3 is extremely simple.

■■■■■■ **Figure 5.12** Verifying an email address.

```
    Case 250, 251      '-- Command OK
        '-- What was the last command?
        Select Case gszCommand$
            Case "MAIL"
                '-- After MAIL, send the RCPT command to
                '    establish the final destination
                SendSMTPCommand DSSocket1, "RCPT TO: <" & gszTo & ">"
            Case "RCPT"
                '-- After RCPT, send the DATA command
                '    to request permission to send the mail message.
                '    This should yield a 354 reply.
                SendSMTPCommand DSSocket1, "DATA"
            Case "DATA"
                '-- We have just sent the message successfully.

                '-- Confirmation that the message was delivered.
                MsgBox "Message Delivered", vbInformation, "SMTP Client"

                btnSend.Enabled = True
                btnOK.Enabled = True
                Screen.MousePointer = vbNormal
                bReceived220 = False
            Case "VRFY"
                MsgBox Mid$(ReceiveData, 4), vbInformation, "User Verified"
```

■■■■■■

POP3 Commands

POP3 uses a series of simple four-character commands such as RETR and LIST that perform the various tasks required to retrieve email messages. These commands are listed in the POP3 Reference Appendix at the back of this book. POP3 Commands are always followed with a CR/LF pair.

Server Responses

After sending a POP3 command, you will receive a reply that begins with either a plus sign (+) to indicate success or a minus sign (–) to indicate failure. These commands begin with either +OK or –ERR. Immediately following either of these responses on the same line is an informative message for the user. Here are a couple of sample replies:

```
+OK message 2 deleted
-ERR message not found
```

Figure 5.13 shows a sample POP3 session modified from RFC 1725. *S* stands for "server" and *C* stands for "client," indicating who is doing or sending what. As you can see, it's pretty straightforward. After the client connects, the server sends either a +OK message indicating that the server is available, or a –ERR message if the server is not available. Actually, every command response from the POP3 server either begins with +OK or –ERR.

Figure 5.13 Sample POP3 conversation.

```
S:   <wait for connection on TCP port 110>


C:   <opens a connection>
S:   +OK POP3 server ready <popserver@somewhere.com>


C:   USER santaclaus
S:   +OK Password required for santaclaus


C:   PASS hohoho
S:   +OK santaclaus has 2 message(s) (320 octets).


C:   TOP 1, 0
S:   +OK 120 octets
```

S: <the POP3 server sends the header for message 1>
S: .

C: RETR 1
S: +OK 120 octets
S: <the POP3 server sends message 1>
S: .

C: DELE 1
S: +OK message 1 deleted

C: TOP 2, 0
S: +OK 200 octets
S: <the POP3 server sends the header for message 1>
S: .

C: RETR 2
S: +OK 200 octets
S: <the POP3 server sends message 2>
S: .

C: DELE 2
S: +OK message 2 deleted

C: QUIT
S: +OK POP3 server signing off (maildrop empty)
S: <closes connection>
S: <wait for next connection>

The client then sends the username and password: First the USER command, then the PASS command. If either the user or password are invalid, the server returns a –ERR message. The server sends a +OK after receiving the USER command, and again after the PASS command.

The STAT command returns the number of messages in the mailbox and the total number of bytes used by the messages. In the example above there are two messages that, combined, total 320 bytes, or octets.

Note that the STAT command is being phased out in lieu of the server sending the STAT information in the reply to the PASS command (after the user has successfully logged on). This is really the current state of POP3, but I wanted you to see the example from the RFC untouched.

■■■■■■■ **TIP**

> By the way, an *octet* is a byte. More specifically, it is eight bits. The word
> only exists to distinguish eight bits from a byte, which in the world of the
> Internet can mean a basic data unit containing more than eight bits on
> some systems.

■■■■■

The LIST command returns the number of bytes for each message. You can optionally specify a message number to get its size. Generally, you won't need this information because you will most likely be receiving data in carriage return/linefeed–delineated lines.

Another command shown in this example, TOP, returns the header information (From:, Subject:, Date:, etc.) from a specified message. This is used to create a string to present to the user in a list box, say, to identify a message. More on this later.

The RETR command retrieves the text of a specific message. The first line is an +OK response followed by the size of the message. The text of the message is sent with every line ending in a carriage return/linefeed pair. A period on the last line indicates the end of the message.

Finally, the DELE command deletes a message from the server's mailbox, and the QUIT command ends the session by instructing the POP3 server to close the socket connection.

POP3 States

The POP3 client and server enter into three different states during a session. These are as follows:

1. *Authorization*. The client must identify itself to the POP3 server.
2. *Transaction*. The client requests actions on the part of the POP3 server.
3. *Update*. The POP3 server releases any resources acquired during the transaction state and says goodbye.

Authorization State

The authorization state is the first state and exists between the time of initial connection up until the point where the client has successfully logged on. The following commands are legal in the authorization state:

PASS

USER

QUIT

As soon as a connection is established the server sends back a +OK reply indicating that a clean connection has been made. At this point you must send the USER command with your username. The server sends back a +OK reply to the USER command, at which point you must send the PASS command followed by your password.

▰▰▰▰ **TIP**

The user name and password are the ones you use to log in to your POP3 server. If you only have one user name and password for all Internet access, then use this information.

▰▰▰▰

Once the server validates you then it sends back a +OK reply indicating the number of messages you have like so:

```
+OK <username> has 2 message(s) (320 octets)
```

The number of messages is always preceded by the word HAS and followed by the word MESSAGE. In parentheses at the end of the line is the total number of bytes in your mailbox, or the total size of all your messages added together.

After receiving the previous line, you are now in the transaction state and can exchange transaction commands with the server.

Transaction State

The transaction state begins after the client has logged on and ends when the client sends a QUIT command to end the session. The following commands are legal in the transaction state:

DELE

NOOP

LIST

RETR

RSET

STAT

There are two main ways in which you can go about downloading messages. One way is to first ask for the headers of each message, display the header information on a line in a list box (or equivalent), and then only retrieve the whole message when the user double-clicks on it in the list. The other method is what most implementations do, and that is to download all of the messages and immediately delete them from the post office, keeping them in a local database instead. This way the user only has to wait until all the new mail is downloaded. The other way, the user has to wait every time he or she wants to read a message.

Update State

The update state exists between the time that the server receives the QUIT command and when the client is disconnected. When in the update state, the server removes all messages marked as deleted and removes all locks on the mailbox.

VB Programming Technique

The programming technique I recommend for POP3 access is exactly the same as with SMTP. All logic resides inside the Receive event. Since there are only two types of replies (+OK and –ERR) the first test is for a +OK reply. If you get a positive reply then we look to see what the last command sent was. Action is then taken based on the last command.

Sample Program: POP3

The POP3 sample application connects you to a POP3 mail server, downloads descriptions of your mail and displays them in a list box, and lets you view any message by double-clicking on a message in the list.

Take a look at Figure 5.14, which shows the Receive event for a simple POP3 mail viewer. Just like the SMTP example, there are two modes for receiving data: Command Mode and Data Mode. The nCommandMode variable is True when receiving commands, its default state. Any time you send a command that returns data, such as TOP or RETR, the flag is switched off so that the program can collect the data in another part of the code.

■■■■■■■ **Figure 5.14** Simple POP3 handler.

```
Private Sub DSSocket1_Receive(ReceiveData As String)

    Static nBeenHere       As Integer
    Static nCurMessage     As Integer
    Static nNumMessages    As Integer
    Static szReceived      As String
    Static szDate          As String
    Static szFrom          As String
    Static szSubject       As String

    Dim nPos               As Integer
    Dim nPos2              As Integer
    Dim szTemp1            As String
    Dim szTemp2            As String
    Dim szTemp3            As String
```

```
'-- nCommandMode is True when we are receiving commands
If nCommandMode Then
    '-- Is this a positive reply?
    If UCase$(Left$(ReceiveData, 3)) = "+OK" Then
        '-- Yes. Is this the first line we've received?
        If nBeenHere = False Then
            '-- Yes. Send the USER command (user's name)
            SendPOP3Command DSSocket1, "USER " & mszUser
        Else
            '-- Nope, we've been here before.

            '-- What is the last command sent?
            Select Case mszCommand
                Case "DEL"   '-- DELE
                    MsgBox "Message Deleted", vbInformation

                Case "LIS"   '-- LIST
                    nCommandMode = False

                Case "NOO"   '-- NOOP
                    '-- You can set a flag here if you want to
                    '   use the NOOP command.

                Case "PAS"   '-- PASS
                    '-- Logged in! Get the messages.
                    szTemp1 = UCase$(ReceiveData)
                    szTemp2 = UCase$(mszUser) & " HAS"
                    szTemp3 = "MESSAGE"

                    nPos = InStr(szTemp1, szTemp2)
                    If nPos Then
                        nPos2 = InStr(szTemp1, szTemp3)
                        If nPos2 Then
```

```
                        nNumMessages = Val(Mid$(szTemp1, _
                            nPos + Len(szTemp2), nPos2 - _
                            (nPos + Len(szTemp2)))))

                        frmMain.Caption = Str$(nNumMessages) & _
                            " New Messages"
                        '-- Once we have the number of messages
                        '   send the TOP command to retrieve the
                        '   header (once for each message).
                        '   nCurMessage keeps track of the message
                        '   we're currently reading the header of.
                        nCurMessage = 1
                        Screen.MousePointer = vbHourglass
                        SendPOP3Command DSSocket1, "TOP 1 0"
                End If
            End If


        Case "QUI"  '-- QUIT
            '-- Reset the last command
            mszCommand = ""


        Case "RET"  '-- RETR
            '-- Here comes the message
            nCommandMode = False
            Screen.MousePointer = vbHourglass


        Case "RSE"  '-- RSET
            mszCommand = ""


        Case "STA"  '-- STAT


        Case "TOP"  '-- TOP
            '-- Here comes the header data
```

```
                    nCommandMode = False


            Case "UID"    '-- UIDL


            Case "USE"    '-- USER
                SendPOP3Command DSSocket1, "PASS " & mszPassword


            Case ""        '-- First command
        End Select
      End If
    Else
        '-- This is an error reply. Display the error portion
        '   in a message box.
        Screen.MousePointer = vbNormal
        MsgBox SuperTrim$(Mid$(ReceiveData, InStr(ReceiveData, " ") + _
            1)), vbInformation


        '-- Reset the last command sent to nothing.
        mszCommand = ""
    End If
Else
    '-- Not in command mode. We are instead receiving data. either a list
    '   of messages or a message itself


    '-- Is this the end of the data transmission?
    If ReceiveData = "." & vbCrLf Then
        '-- Yes.


        '-- What was the last command sent?
        Select Case mszCommand
            Case "RET"  '-- RETR (retrieves a message)
                Screen.MousePointer = vbNormal
                '-- Display the message
```

```
                    frmDisplay.txtText = szReceived
                    frmDisplay.Show vbModal
                    Unload frmDisplay
                    Set frmDisplay = Nothing
                    '-- Go back to Command mode
                    nCommandMode = True
                Case "TOP"
                    '-- Display the header
                    If Len(szFrom) > 19 Then
                        szFrom = Left$(szFrom, 19)
                    End If
                    If Len(szSubject) > 24 Then
                        szSubject = Left$(szSubject, 24)
                    End If
                    lbMessages.AddItem Format$(szFrom, "!" & String$(23, "@")) & _
                        Format$(szSubject, "!" & String$(27, "@")) & _
                        szDate
                    If nCurMessage < nNumMessages Then
                        nCurMessage = nCurMessage + 1
                        SendPOP3Command DSSocket1, "TOP" & _
                                Str$(nCurMessage) & ", 0"
                    Else
                        Screen.MousePointer = vbNormal
                        lbMessages.Enabled = True
                    End If
            End Select
            '-- Flush the receive buffer
            szReceived = ""
            '-- Go back to Command mode
            nCommandMode = True
        Else
            '-- No. We are still receiving data.
```

```
                  '-- What was the last command received?
                  Select Case mszCommand
                      Case "LIS"  '-- LIST
                            lbMessages.AddItem szTrimCRLF(ReceiveData)
                      Case "RET"  '-- RETR (Retrieve a message)
                          szReceived = szReceived & ReceiveData
                      Case "TOP"  '-- Retrieves the header
                          szReceived = szReceived & ReceiveData
                          Select Case UCase$(szParseString(ReceiveData, ":", 1))
                              Case "SUBJECT"
                                  szSubject = szTrimCRLF(Trim$(Mid$(ReceiveData, 9)))
                              Case "DATE"
                                  szDate = szTrimCRLF(Trim$(Mid$(ReceiveData, 6)))
                              Case "FROM"
                                  szFrom = szTrimCRLF(Trim$(Mid$(ReceiveData, 6)))
                          End Select
                  End Select
              End If
          End If


      '-- Make sure we know we've been here before.
      nBeenHere = True


  End Sub
```

Let me first explain the code at the top of the routine, and then I'll get into the signal flow issues. The first thing that happens when a string is received is a test for Command Mode. If indeed we are accepting commands, then we check to see if this reply is positive (+OK) or negative (–ERR).

If the reply is negative, the error message is displayed to the user and the variables are reset. If the reply is positive, then another flag (nBeenHere) is tested. This flag is set at the bottom of the subroutine and merely provides a way to determine if this is the first string being received for a particular session. If it IS the first line received, the code automatically begins the log-in process by sending the USER command and exiting the routine.

Just like with SMTP, it is absolutely necessary to keep track of the last command issued so that the code can determine how to respond to a given command reply. The SendPOP3Command performs this service. Shown in Figure 5.15, it simply sets the module-level mszCommand variable to the first three letters of the command issued (three characters is enough to identify a POP3 command).

Logging into the Server

To log into a POP3 server you first send a USER command (with your username), wait for a +OK, and then send the PASS command (with your password).

Let's say that the last command we sent was USER. We now know that we've sent the server our user name and it replied positively. Now it's waiting for the password. So, send the PASS command.

The next time the Receive event fires, it should fall into the block where PASS is the last command issued. In this block, we determine how many messages the user has based on the reply from the server, and begin to retrieve the headers for these

■■■■■■ **Figure 5.15** Keeping track of the last command sent.

```
Sub SendPOP3Command(DSSock As Control, szCmd As String)

    mszCommand = Left$(szCmd, 3)

    SendData DSSock, szCmd & vbCrLf

End Sub
```

messages. Figure 5.16 shows the code that occurs when a +OK is received after sending the password.

The server sends back a string like so:

```
+OK carlf has 3 message(s).
```

■■■■■■■■ **Figure 5.16** After sending the password to log in.

```
Case "PAS"   '-- PASS
    '-- Logged in! Get the messages.
    szTemp1 = UCase$(ReceiveData)
    szTemp2 = UCase$(mszUser) & " HAS"
    szTemp3 = "MESSAGE"

    nPos = InStr(szTemp1, szTemp2)
    If nPos Then
        nPos2 = InStr(szTemp1, szTemp3)
        If nPos2 Then
            nNumMessages = Val(Mid$(szTemp1, nPos + _
                Len(szTemp2), nPos2 - (nPos + Len(szTemp2))))

            frmMain.Caption = Str$(nNumMessages) & " New Messages"
            '-- Once we have the number of messages send the TOP
            '   command to retrieve the header (once for each
            '   message). nCurMessage keeps track of the message
            '   we're currently reading the header of.
            nCurMessage = 1
            Screen.MousePointer = vbHourglass
            SendPOP3Command DSSocket1, "TOP 1 0"
        End If
    End If
```

In order to get the number of messages out of this string, the code does a bit of manual string parsing. First the word "HAS" is found in the string (all Instr's are done in uppercase). Then the word "MESSAGE" is located. The number of messages lies between these two words, and is saved into the nNumMessages variable.

Retrieving Message Headers

The next task is to retrieve header information for each of the messages so that they can be displayed in a list box for the user to select. At this point a few things happen. The number of messages is displayed in the caption of the form. The nCurMessage variable, which keeps track of which message's header we are currently retrieving, is initialized to 1. The cursor changes to an hourglass (until the last header has been received), and finally, the TOP command is sent to retrieve the header of the first message. Here is the syntax of the TOP command:

```
TOP 1, 0
```

This tells the server, "give me the header lines for message 1 and zero lines of the message body." The TOP command takes two arguments. First is the message number. Message numbers always start at one and go up from there. You do not have to return a wacky message number for each message. Specifying message number 1 means "for the first message."

After receiving the TOP command, the server returns a +OK reply followed by all the header lines ending with a period on a line by itself. Here is an example header:

```
Received: by upsmot02.msn.com id AA24082; Sat, 25 Nov 95 22:57:32 -0800
Date: Sun, 26 Nov 95 06:49:31 UT
X-UIDL: 817369062.000
From: "Carl Franklin" <CarlFranklin@msn.com>
Message-Id: <UPMAIL02.199511260658180351@msn.com>
To: "'carlf@apexsc.com'" <carlf@apexsc.com>
Subject: Hello
Status: RO
```

The header is received one line at a time, giving our code to look for specific header lines like Subject, From, and Date. These header lines are sufficient for creating a string to present to the user to identify a message.

Follow the code down to where we are *not* in command mode, and it is not the end of the data transmission. Figure 5.17 shows that block of code. Once again, knowing the last command issued is critical in determining actions. Look at where the last command is TOP. We know that this is data. We know that this is a header line. All we need to do is look at the first word up to but not including the colon. In this manner the subject, from address, and date are all kept in static string variables.

Now jump up to where this *is* the end of data transmission and the last command given was TOP. Figure 5.18 shows this code. If TOP was the last command issued,

■■■■■■■ **Figure 5.17** Parsing a POP3 mail header.

```
'-- No. We are still receiving data.

'-- What was the last command sent?
Select Case mszCommand
    Case "LIS"  '-- LIST
        lbMessages.AddItem szTrimCRLF(ReceiveData)
    Case "RET"  '-- RETR (Retrieve a message)
        szReceived = szReceived & ReceiveData
    Case "TOP"  '-- Retrieves the header
        szReceived = szReceived & ReceiveData
        Select Case UCase$(szParseString(ReceiveData, ":", 1))
            Case "SUBJECT"
                szSubject = szTrimCRLF(Trim$(Mid$(ReceiveData, 9)))
            Case "DATE"
                szDate = szTrimCRLF(Trim$(Mid$(ReceiveData, 6)))
            Case "FROM"
                szFrom = szTrimCRLF(Trim$(Mid$(ReceiveData, 6)))
        End Select
End Select
```

then we have just received a complete header for one of the messages. The code
then concatenates the from address, subject, and date into a complete string and
adds it to the list box (lbMessages) on the main screen.

▬▬▬▬▬▬ **Figure 5.18** Displaying the received POP3 mail header.

```
Case "TOP"
    '-- Display the header
    If Len(szFrom) > 19 Then
        szFrom = Left$(szFrom, 19)
    End If
    If Len(szSubject) > 24 Then
        szSubject = Left$(szSubject, 24)
    End If
    lbMessages.AddItem Format$(szFrom, "!" & String$(23, "@")) & _
        Format$(szSubject, "!" & String$(27, "@")) & _
        szDate

    If nCurMessage < nNumMessages Then
        nCurMessage = nCurMessage + 1
        SendPOP3Command DSSocket1, "TOP" & Str$(nCurMessage) & ", 0"
    Else
        Screen.MousePointer = vbNormal
        lbMessages.Enabled = True
    End If

'-- Flush the receive buffer
szReceived = ""
'-- Go back to Command mode
nCommandMode = True
```

Next, we check to see if the current message is less than the total number of messages. If so, then we have another TOP command to issue (at least one more). The nCurMessage variable is increased, and the TOP command is issued to receive the next header. If this was a TOP command for the *last* message, the mouse pointer is restored to normal.

After the successful receiving of a complete block of data (not commands) the szReceived variable is zeroed and Command Mode is set back to True so we can process the next command.

Retrieving Messages

To retrieve a specific message, send the RETR command (with the message number). In our application this is initiated in the list box's double-click event like so:

```
Private Sub lbMessages_DblClick()
    Screen.MousePointer = vbHourglass
    SendPOP3Command DSSocket1, "RETR" & Str$(lbMessages.ListIndex + 1)
End Sub
```

Jumping back now to our Receive code, take a look at the block of code that executes when a positive reply is received after sending the RETR command:

```
Case "RET"   '-- RETR
    '-- Here comes the message
    nCommandMode = False
    Screen.MousePointer = vbHourglass
```

The only thing we need to do is turn the cursor to an hourglass and flip Command Mode off. The next line to be received is the first line of the message:

```
Case "RET"   '-- RETR (Retrieve a message)
    szReceived = szReceived & ReceiveData
```

All we are doing is adding the new line to szReceived, a static string variable that will contain the whole of the message when it has been completely received.

The server will send a period on a line by itself after completely sending the message. The code snippet in Figure 5.19 shows what happens next. After a message has been received in full, szReceived will contain the entire thing. The sample application simply throws it in a read-only text box and displays it. As always, the code then goes back to Command Mode.

Sending and Receiving Binary Files

Before a binary file can be sent via email, it must be encoded such that all the characters that represent the file's data are printable and viewable with any ASCII editor. A process called UU encoding converts binary data into printable ASCII. The reciprocal process is called UU decoding. There are many simple utilities available for free on the Internet that encode and decode files; however, I could not find any BASIC or Visual Basic source code to do the deed.

■■■■■ **Figure 5.19** Displaying an email message.

```
'-- What was the last command sent?
Select Case mszCommand
    Case "RET"  '-- RETR (retrieves a message)
        Screen.MousePointer = vbNormal
        '-- Display the message (with a definite lack of imaginative UI)
        frmDisplay.txtText = szReceived
        frmDisplay.Show vbModal
        Unload frmDisplay
        Set frmDisplay = Nothing
        '-- Go back to Command mode
        nCommandMode = True
```

After acquiring the C source for UU encoding and decoding from my friend Tory Toupin (ttoupin@du.edu) and figuring out how it would work in VB, I wrote some routines with a little help from Steve Cramp of Dolphin Systems (stephenc@idirect.com) to make it easy to encode and decode on the fly in your Visual Basic apps. The routines are included in UUCode.bas on the CD-ROM, and we will discuss them here.

How UU Encoding Works

The basic idea behind UU encoding is that for every three characters or bytes of data, you must convert into four 6-byte characters which are offset by the space character, or 32. In other words, three 8-bit characters is 24 bits. Four 6-bit characters is also 24 bits. A value of 32 is added to each 6-bit character, to insure that the character is printable, or greater than a space character. Here is another way to visualize the two ways to interpret 24 bits of data:

```
1 2 3 4 5 6 7 8 1 2 3 4 5 6 7 8 1 2 3 4 5 6 7 8


1 2 3 4 5 6 1 2 3 4 5 6 1 2 3 4 5 6 1 2 3 4 5 6
```

You may already be thinking there is no easy way to access 6-bit characters in Visual Basic, and you are right. There is not. The process requires the use of the bitwise And operator, and division to coerce the right values out of the 8-bit characters we use exclusively in Visual Basic.

Let me show you how it works. Let's say we have a file in which the first three bytes are GSU. The UU encoding process works on three ASCII characters at a time, converting them into four printable ASCII characters. Here is the Visual Basic code to retrieve a UU-encoded character from the first of three bytes:

```
szA_1 = "G"
szUU_1 = Chr$(((Asc(szA_1) And 252) \ 4) + 32)
```

Here is the same logic using binary arithmetic:

```
71              =           1000111    (ASCII 71 = "G")
252             =          11111100
4               =               100
```

```
71 AND 252      =       1000100     =       68
\ 4             =         10001     =       17
+ 32            =        110001     =       49
```

UU encoded Character 1 = Chr$(49) = "1"

Notice how in order to get 6 bits, you have to AND the 8-bit value with a binary number where all the desired bits are true. Then, dividing by 4 shifts the bits to the right by two places, resulting in a 6-bit value. Adding 32 to this value gives us a UU-encoded character.

There are four characters, however, to every three bytes. So the two unused bits on the right side of the first ASCII character make up the first two bits of the second UU character. The first four bits of the second ASCII character make up the right-most four bits of the second UU character. Got it? This is the kind of stuff that turns a mild-mannered VB programmer into "Code-zilla."

To accomplish this in VB, you must multiply the remaining bits from the first ASCII character by 16 to shift them left four bit positions, and then add this value to the first four bits of the second ASCII character, which have been shifted to the right four places using the same method as the first character. The only difference is, you AND the second ASCII character by 240 and divide by 16 instead of ANDing with 252 and dividing by 4. Add 32 to the result to get the UU-encoded value. Here is the VB Code to get the remainder from the first character and create the second UU-encoded character:

```
szA_2 = "S"


nRemainder = (Asc(szA_1) And 3) * 16
szUU_2 = Chr$(nRemainder + ((Asc(szA_2) And 240) \ 16) + 32)
```

Figure 5.20 shows how the binary arithmetic works. Retrieving the third UU-encoded character from the three 8-bit characters uses the same logic. The last four bits of the second ASCII character make up the first four bits of the third UU character. The first two bits of the third ASCII character are the last two bits of the third UU character.

■■■■■■■ Figure 5.20 Encoding the first of three characters.

```
Acquiring the Remainder:
========================


71              =         1000111   (ASCII 71 = "G")
3               =              11
16              =           10000


71 AND 3        =              11    =    3
* 16            =          110000    =    48




Acquiring the rightmost four bits:
==================================


83              =         1010011   (ASCII 83= "S")
240             =        11110000
32              =          100000
16              =           10000


83 AND 240      =         1010000    =    80
\ 16            =             101    =    5
+ 32            =          100101    =    37
+ 48 (rem)      =         1111010    =    122


UU encoded Character 2 = Chr$(122) = "z"
```

The first four bits must be shifted left two places, which is done by ANDing the ASCII character with 15 and multiplying by 4. The next two bits, which come from the third ASCII character, must be shifted right by six positions. This is done by ANDing the character with 192 and then dividing by 64. As before, adding 32 to the result renders the UU-encoded character value. Here is the VB code to retrieve the third character:

```
szA_3 = "U"


nRemainder = (Asc(szA_2)) And 15) * 4
szUU_3 = Chr$(nRemainder + ((Asc(szA_3) And 192) \ 64) + 32)
```

Figure 5.21 shows the binary arithmetic, which illustrates the method clearly.

▬▬▬▬▬ **Figure 5.21** Encoding the second of three characters.

```
Acquiring the Remainder:
========================


83              =         1010011    (ASCII 83= "S")
15              =            1111
4               =             100


83 AND 15       =              11      =        3
* 4             =            1100      =       12




Acquiring the rightmost two bits:
=================================


85              =         1010101    (ASCII 85 "U")
192             =        11111100
64              =         1000000


85 AND 192      =         1000000      =       64
```

```
\ 64            =            1        =    1
+ 32            =            100001   =    33
+ 12 (rem)      =            101101   =    45


UU encoded Character 3 = Chr$(45) = "-"
```

Finally, the last UU character is equal to the remaining six bits of the third ASCII character. To get the UU-encoded value, AND it with 63 and add 32. Here is the VB code:

```
szUU_4 = Chr$((Asc(szA_3)) And 63) + 32)
```

Figure 5.22 shows the binary arithmetic. Therefore, the ASCII values GSU become UU encoded into 1z-5.

UUCODE.BAS—Encoding and Decoding Routines

The UUCODE.BAS file contains two routines, UUEncode and UUDecode, which accept a source file and a destination file, and produce an encoded ASCII file and a decoded binary, respectively.

Figure 5.22 Encoding the third of three characters.

```
85              =            1010101  (ASCII 85 "U")
63              =            111111


85 AND 63       =            10101    =    21
+ 32            =            110101   =    53


UU encoded Character 4 = Chr$(53) = "5"
```

UUEncode

Here is the prototype for UUEncode:

```
Function UUEncode(szFileIn As String, szFileOut As String, _
    nAppend As Integer) As Integer
```

It accepts an input file and an output file and a flag that tells UUEncode to append the new data to the output file. The input file is the fully qualified path and name of any binary file, and the output file is the encoded ASCII file to be created. You can specify a full path for the output file as well, so that you can save your encoded file anywhere. If nAppend is False, the output file is overwritten, otherwise it is appended.

UUEncode returns zero if no error occurs, or the error number if an error occurs while encoding. The error number represents a standard Visual Basic error. If an error occurs you can retrieve a descriptive error message by using the Error$ function. Here is an example of how you would call UUEncode:

```
Dim nErrCode    As Integer
nErrCode = UUEncode("C:\MYFILE.EXE", "C:\MYFILE.UUE", False)
If nErrCode Then
    MsgBox Error$(nErrCode), vbInformation
End If
```

UUDecode

Here is the prototype for UUDecode:

```
Function UUDecode(szFileIn As String, szFileOut As String) As Integer
```

Just as with UUEncode, UUDecode accepts two filenames, one for input and one for output. The input file is the full path- and filename of an encoded ASCII file, and the output file is the name of the binary file which will be created. You can specify a full path for the output file as well, so that you can save your decoded file anywhere.

UUDecode returns zero if no error occurs, or the error number if an error occurs while decoding. The error number represents a standard Visual Basic error. If an error occurs you can retrieve a descriptive error message by using the Error$ function. Here is an example of how you would call UUDecode:

```
Dim nErrCode      As Integer

nErrCode = UUDecode("C:\MYFILE.UUE", "C:\MYFILE.EXE")

If nErrCode Then
    MsgBox Error$(nErrCode), vbInformation
End If
```

Sending an Encoded File with SMTP

To embed an encoded file into an email message, simply tack on the encoded data to the end of your email message. To do this, you should first create the complete message including all encoded files (you can send more than one) using the nAppend flag of UUEncode, and then send the file as your message. Now, I know that probably involves some code, but you're going to have to write it yourself. Ha! Just kidding. I already wrote it for you.

nSendFileAsMsg

Shown in Figure 5.23, this is a function in SMTP.BAS that sends a file via email. The file can contain one or more encoded files and text. Here is a list of the parameters:

szFileName—the full path and filename of your encoded file (e.g., c:\myfile.txt)

DSSocket—the sockets control being used

lBlockSize—the maximum size of each chunk of data sent

szFrom—the sender's email address

szTo—the recipient's email address

szSubject—the subject of the message

szText—the textual portion of the message (if not already contained in the file)

nSendFileAsMsg returns an error code if an error occurs, otherwise it returns zero.

▇▇▇▇▇ **Figure 5.23** The sSendFileAsMsg function sends a file via SMTP. The file can contain one or more encoded files.

```
Function nSendFileAsMsg(szFileName As String, DSSocket As Control, _
    lBlockSize As Long, szFrom As String, szTo As String, _
    szSubject As String, szText As String)


'*************************************************************
'   nSendFileAsMsg (by Carl Franklin)
'
'   This function sends a file via email.
'   If you want to send binary files you must
'   first UUEncode them. Use the function
'   nMakeMsgWithFiles (in UUCODE.BAS) to create
'   a file that has a text message and one or
'   more binary files embedded in it.
'
'   Parameters: szFileName  Full path and filename
'               DSSocket     Sockets control
'               lBlockSize   The maximum size of each block
'                             (default is 8192)
'               szFrom       Sender's email address
'               szTo         Recipient's email address
'               szSubject    Subject of the message
'               szText       Any text you want to tag on
'                             to the top of the message.
'*************************************************************

    Dim nMsgFile    As Integer
    Dim szLine      As String
    Dim szBuffer    As String

    On Error GoTo nSendFileAsMsg_Error
```

```
'-- Default block size = 8K
If lBlockSize = 0 Then
    lBlockSize = 8192
End If


'-- Open the message file
nMsgFile = FreeFile
Open szFileName For Binary As nMsgFile


'-- szBuffer holds up to <blocksize> number of bytes
'    and is sent when it becomes full.


'-- Send the header first
szBuffer = "DATE: " & Format$(Now, "dd mmm yy ttttt") & vbCRLF _
    & "FROM: " & szFrom & vbCRLF _
    & "TO: " & szTo & vbCRLF _
    & "SUBJECT: " & szSubject & vbCRLF & vbCRLF _
    & szText & vbCRLF
SendData DSSocket, szBuffer


'-- Send the file in chunks
Do Until EOF(nMsgFile)
    szBuffer = Space$(lBlockSize)
    Get #nMsgFile, , szBuffer
    SendData DSSocket, szBuffer
Loop


Close nMsgFile


'-- Send the final period.
SendData DSSocket, vbCRLF & "." & vbCRLF


Exit Function
```

```
nSendFileAsMsg_Error:


     nSendFileAsMsg = Err
     On Error Resume Next
     Close nMsgFile
     Exit Function


End Function
```

▬▬▬▬

Epilogue

Email is a powerful medium for moving data from one person to another anywhere in the world. By now you know my mantra: Apply this technology to your own real-world problems and opportunities. You can use SMTP and POP3 to integrate nicely into any enterprise. Do you need the results of some computer-based research? Email them. Do you need to supply up-to-date product information to your customers? Email them.

How about this? You have a team of beta testers hammering on your program. They are all connected to the Internet. Install an error handler in your application. Anytime someone has an error, email yourself important information about the state of your program and the machine. You'll have a report in your hands before the tester has time to pick up the phone and call you (well, maybe not that fast). The point is that email is a medium. How you use it is completely up to you.

FILE TRANSFER

PROTOCOL

Introduction

Up until 1994, when the World Wide Web took over the Internet, File Transfer Protocol (FTP) was the most widely used Internet client application besides email. It is used as a remote shell for file access on an Internet host. Using an FTP application, you can connect to an FTP server, navigate through the available directories, and transfer files.

An FTP site can be public, private, or both. With a private account, you can be given access to the entire network's directory structure, or just specific areas. For the longest time I used a private FTP account to manage the files on Carl & Gary's Visual Basic Home Page.

The Internet is also home to thousands of public access FTP servers that allow anyone to connect and transfer files to and from specific directories regardless of whether they have an account on the host. This is called *anonymous FTP*. When you connect to an anonymous FTP site, you usually specify "anonymous" as your user name and "guest" or your email address as your password. Anonymous FTP sites are used, for example, to publish a large listing of public domain and/or shareware files. One of the most famous public FTP sites for shareware is ftp.cica.indiana.edu, which has mirror sites all over the world for its famous CICA shareware library.

FTP was designed mainly for use by programs, but the FTP application itself has turned out to be a critical part of any TCP/IP implementation. FTP.EXE is also an application that is installed when you use Microsoft TCP/IP drivers in Windows for Workgroups 3.11, Windows 95 or Windows NT.

In fact, FTP is built into Netscape and other World Wide Web browsers so you can browse FTP servers with the same program that you use to browse the Web.

As stated in RFC 959, there were four objectives in the design of the FTP protocol:

1. To promote sharing of files (computer programs and/or data)
2. To encourage indirect or implicit (via programs) use of remote computers
3. To shield a user from variations in file storage systems among hosts
4. To transfer data reliably and efficiently

When Should You Use FTP?

If you are writing an app that does a fair amount of file transfer and are considering using FTP as your primary means of transferring files, you should know a few things. First of all, FTP is a client/server protocol. Using FTP to transfer files from one application to another is not practical. You should consider FTP only if you have to transfer files with a known FTP server, or if you are writing a general-use FTP client program.

Sometimes it's a good idea to use an FTP server as a repository for files shared by all the users of your application. It completely depends on what your project goals are. If you want to give your users access to a bunch of shared files, FTP is a good tool for the job.

FTP does not have file control commands such as VB's Open, Input # and Print # commands. If your project requires that you open a file remotely and have file-level access to it then FTP will not work. FTP is used primarily for getting directory listings and transferring files.

This chapter includes code that lets you connect to, navigate, and transfer files to and from any FTP server. I will show you how to use these routines in your VB applications, as well as how they work.

The FTP Program

FTP refers to both the FTP protocol and an FTP application. The FTP protocol defines a series of commands that the client sends the server, and how the client and server transfer data. An FTP application is usually a character-based terminal-type application in which you connect to an FTP server. The purpose for the FTP application is to provide Englishlike commands and help/error messages, as well as higher-level functionality than just a terminal could provide.

If you are using Microsoft's TCP/IP drivers then you should have a file in your Windows directory called FTP.EXE. This is an FTP client application. I have noticed that many Windows users are not hip to FTP at all. I feel that knowing how to use FTP ranks right up there with knowing how to use the Windows File Manager or Explorer. Given that, I feel I should educate you on how to use it.

Figure 6.1 shows the FTP window. You may notice that it looks like a DOS window. It is a character-based terminal program. You can view it either in a window or full screen, just like any DOS text-mode application. If you are using Windows NT you can enjoy some nicer features such as scrolling back through your commands with the up-arrow.

Connecting and Logging In

When you first run FTP you are presented with the following prompt:

```
ftp> _
```

You can connect to any ftp site with the OPEN command. Type OPEN followed by the name of the FTP server. For example, to connect to Microsoft's public FTP site type the following:

```
ftp> open ftp.microsoft.com <enter>
```

At this time the program attempts to connect to the server on port 21. Once connected, you will receive a 220 reply followed by a welcome message. Here's the welcome message at ftp.microsoft.com:

```
Connected to ftp.microsoft.com.
220 ftp Microsoft FTP Service (Version 1.0).
```

Next, you get a prompt to enter your user name. If you have an account on the server you can enter your user name, but for public access (anonymous ftp) just type anonymous:

```
User (ftp.microsoft.com:(none)): anonymous
331 Anonymous access allowed, send identity (e-mail name) as password.
```

Next you are asked for a password. Again, if you have an account you can enter your password here, but if you are connecting for public access, just enter your email address. Note that your password is not echoed to the screen.

```
Password:
```

The server then grants you access with another welcome message, and you finally get the ftp prompt again. Think of this like a DOS prompt. There are a fixed set of commands that you can use to navigate through the directories on the server and download files.

■■■■■■ **Figure 6.1** FTP window. FTP.EXE is a simple FTP client that comes with Windows 95, Windows NT, and MS TCP/IP drivers for WFW 3.11.

```
230-This is ftp.microsoft.com.  See the index.txt file
  in the root directory for more information
230 Anonymous user logged in as anonymous.
```

Listing Directories

One of the commands you can use to navigate through directories is DIR. In reality there is no DIR command in the FTP protocol spec. However, the standard user interface for accessing FTP servers has brought this command forward from the operating system because it's more user friendly (as if typing a bunch of commands into a terminal is at all user friendly).

Figure 6.2 shows what you get when you type DIR at an ftp prompt. Note that there's a lot more information here than you were probably expecting. In the right-most column is the file or directory name. To the right of that is the file date and size. All the way to the left is a field of ten bits. These are attributes. In DOS there are a limited number of attributes for files and directories such as Hidden, Read-Only, and Archive. However, UNIX has a much more extensible set of attributes. You can create masks that give access to certain groups of users or prevent other users from gaining access. You can tell which is a file and which is a directory by the "d" attribute, which is displayed in the far left attribute field. If there is a "d" then it's a directory.

Changing Directories

You can change directories with the CD command. CD works exactly like it does in DOS but using forward slashes instead of backslashes. Here is the command to change to the /developr/vb directory:

```
ftp> cd developr/vb
250 CWD command successful.
```

Once again, typing DIR gives you a list of files and directories. Figure 6.3 shows the result of typing DIR in the /developr/vb directory on ftp.microsoft.com.

Downloading

Downloading a file is simple and straight ahead. Before you download, however, you must make sure you are in *binary* mode. There are two modes, ASCII and binary. To change to binary mode just type BIN:

```
ftp> bin
200 Type set to I.
```

■■■■ **Figure 6.2** The DIR command displays a directory listing.

```
ftp>dir
200 PORT command successful.
150 Opening ASCII mode data connection for /bin/ls.
d---------   1 owner     group              0 Jul  3 13:52 bussys
d---------   1 owner     group              0 Aug  9  3:00 deskapps
d---------   1 owner     group              0 Oct 27  7:35 developr
----------   1 owner     group           7905 Oct  5  8:53 dirmap.htm
----------   1 owner     group           4510 Oct  5  8:52 dirmap.txt
----------   1 owner     group            712 Aug 25  1994 disclaimer.txt
----------   1 owner     group            860 Oct  5  1994 index.txt
d---------   1 owner     group              0 Aug 31 12:17 KBHelp
----------   1 owner     group        7393252 Nov 28  4:04 ls-lR.txt
----------   1 owner     group         914179 Nov 28  4:05 ls-lR.Z
----------   1 owner     group         766409 Nov 28  4:04 LS-LR.ZIP
d---------   1 owner     group              0 Oct 20  9:27 MSCorp
----------   1 owner     group          28160 Nov 28  1994 MSNBRO.DOC
----------   1 owner     group          22641 Feb  8  1994 MSNBRO.TXT
d---------   1 owner     group              0 Oct 11  3:00 peropsys
d---------   1 owner     group              0 Aug 23 21:55 Products
d---------   1 owner     group              0 Oct  5  8:46 Services
d---------   1 owner     group              0 Nov 22 14:38 Softlib
----------   1 owner     group           5095 Oct 20  1993 support-phones.txt
----------   1 owner     group            802 Aug 25  1994 WhatHappened.txt
226 Transfer complete.
1407 bytes received in 0.99 seconds (1.42 Kbytes/sec)
```

■■■■

To change back to ASCII mode type ASC. You do not have to change back and forth. In fact, I usually leave FTP in binary mode all the time so I don't forget and download a file in ASCII mode. (Don't run that .EXE! I used ASCII mode! Yikes!)

■■■■■■■ **Figure 6.3** Listing of the /developr/vb directory of Microsoft.

```
ftp> dir
200 PORT command successful.
150 Opening ASCII mode data connection for /bin/ls.
d---------    1 owner     group            0 Oct 25   6:39 kb
d---------    1 owner     group            0 Feb 24 11:35 public
----------    1 owner     group         1571 Aug 24   1994 README.TXT
d---------    1 owner     group            0 Aug 24   1994 unsup-ed
226 Transfer complete.
270 bytes received in 0.22 seconds (1.23 Kbytes/sec)
```

■■■■■■

The GET command is used to retrieve a file. If you want to download with its original filename in the default directory, just type GET <filename> <enter>. Figure 6.4 shows this interaction.

You can also just type GET, after which you are prompted for the file you want to download, and then again for the name of the file (and path) on your system. This makes it easier to move files from a UNIX or Win32 system (where filenames are long) to a Windows for Workgroups machine, or just to download to a directory other than where your FTP.EXE app is.

■■■■■■■ **Figure 6.4** The Get command retrieves a file from the server.

```
ftp> get readme.txt
200 PORT command successful.
150 Opening BINARY mode data connection for readme.txt(1571 bytes).
226 Transfer complete.
1571 bytes received in 3.46 seconds (0.45 Kbytes/sec)
```

■■■■■■

Uploading

You can upload a file in much the same way with the SEND command. You must be in a public area that allows uploads, of course. Figure 6.5 shows an example of uploading a file to Carl & Gary's VB file upload area (ftp.apexsc.com/pub/cgvb/uploads).

Supported Commands

If you want to view a list of supported commands, just type HELP. Figure 6.6 shows what you get on ftp.microsoft.com when you type HELP.

Ending the Session

You can end your FTP session at any time by typing BYE at any FTP prompt.

```
ftp> bye
<the server disconnects the client>
```

Using a Web Browser to Download Files

There is a much easier way to download files from an anonymous FTP site. Use a web browser. With a web browser you can download any file by either making a link to it in an HTML document and clicking the link, or simply entering an FTP URL in the location edit window (which most web browsers display at the top of

■■■■■■ **Figure 6.5** The SEND command sends a file to the server.

```
ftp> send
(local-file) myfile.zip
(remote-file) myfile.zip
200 PORT command successful.
150 Opening BINARY mode data connection for myfile.zip.
226 Transfer complete.
3018 bytes sent in 0.06 seconds (50.30 Kbytes/sec)
```

▄▄▄▄▄▄ **Figure 6.6** The Help command returns a list of supported commands.

```
ftp>help
Commands may be abbreviated.  Commands are:

!             delete       literal      prompt       send
?             debug        ls           put          status
append        dir          mdelete      pwd          trace
ascii         disconnect   mdir         quit         type
bell          get          mget         quote        user
binary        glob         mkdir        recv         verbose
bye           hash         mls          remotehelp
cd            help         mput         rename
close         lcd          open         rmdir
ftp>
```

▄▄▄▄▄▄

the window directly under the menu section). Using a web browser for FTP access is good and fast, but it is limited in what you can access. For example, you cannot send files. But for downloading files from public sites, you can't beat it.

Here is an example URL that downloads the Visual Basic FAQ (Frequently Asked Questions) document from Carl & Gary's VB Home Page FTP server:

```
ftp://ftp.apexsc.com/pub/cgvb/vbfaq/vbfaqwin.txt
```

If you enter the URL directly from the browser make sure you turn on the "save to disk" option. If you create an HTML file with a link, the file should look like this:

```
<a href="ftp://ftp.apexsc.com/pub/cgvb/vbfaq/vbfaqwin.txt">FAQ</a>
```

Using Netscape you can click on the link while holding down the Shift key to save to disk.

The FTP Protocol

The commands you give to an FTP application are a bit different from the commands that an FTP application gives to an FTP server. For example, to get a directory listing with an FTP application you would use the DIR command. However, the FTP application uses the LIST command. When I refer to FTP from now on, I am referring to the protocol, unless otherwise noted.

If there is any one big difference between FTP and the protocols that we've covered up to this point, it is that FTP uses more than one port. Port 21, the control connection, is used for transferring commands, and another port, the data connection, is used for transferring data. The default port for the data connection is 20, but any other port can be used also. This makes FTP a wee bit more difficult to code than, say, SMTP or POP3.

FTP Errata

Yes, there is plenty of weirdness concerning FTP, and why not? FTP has long been the staple file transfer mechanism of the Internet community. Because it is so popular, everyone has a way to improve on it. Therefore, there are more addenda, comments, and additions to FTP than to almost any other protocol. This has yielded some inconsistencies in FTP commands between servers. For that reason you must exercise a bit of caution when extending the power of FTP to your users.

For example, if your client only connects to your server and you have tested the connection then you needn't worry. On the other hand, if you incorporate FTP as a means to grab any file from any FTP server, and extend that functionality to the user, you may be in for a headache. Most third-party FTP tools maintain a list of server types and the different commands that the server may or may not understand. Using the FTP protocol, if you send the SYST command, the FTP server will send you back the FTP server name and version. It is beyond the scope of this book to list all of the different inconsistencies among FTP servers. You will have to glean this information from experience.

I am not trying to make it sound like FTP is not a standard. For the most part, FTP server implementations stick to the standard commands. The commands in this chapter were taken from RFC 959, which is the standard FTP protocol definition. Any deviation from this standard is a risk, and software shops should know this.

Connections

The FTP server accepts initial connections on port 21. Unlike HTTP and GOPHER which reconnect on every command, FTP keeps the connection open. This connection is for the processing of FTP commands only. A separate connection is used for data transfer. These two connections are called the control connection and the data connection, respectively.

For example, when retrieving a file the client usually sends the PORT command, accepts a connection on port 20 and then tells the server to send the file using the RETR command. The server then sends the data, and closes the connection. The reason this method is used and not the familiar *send data ending with a period on a line by itself* method, is because FTP sends binary data. There is no practical way to interpret an end-of-line character when every possible character could be interpreted as data.

Another option is for the client to tell the server to listen to a particular port with the PASV command (indicating passive mode), and then connect to that port for the data connection. I like to use passive mode because you don't have to accept a connection, which isn't always possible.

If you are going to use the PORT method, it is best to open either port 20 or the next available port over 1024 and then send a PORT command to the server. That way, if the user is already transferring a file with a standalone FTP application, there is no chance of interfering with it. (I say to use ports over 1024 because ports 1–1024 are reserved for TCP/IP and standard protocols.)

FTP Commands

FTP uses a series of simple commands such as LIST and RETR that perform the various tasks of navigating directories and transferring files with an FTP server. These commands are listed in the FTP Reference in Appendix D at the back of this book. FTP commands are always followed with a CR/LF pair.

Server Responses

After sending an FTP command, you will receive a reply which consists of a three-digit number followed by a space and a text message. Figure 6.7 shows a list of reply codes in numeric order. The full descriptions of these codes can be found in RFC 959.

Reply Code Categories

Each digit of the reply code has a specific meaning. There are five values for the first digit of the reply code: 1 indicates a positive preliminary reply (the command was accepted, and this is the first of more than one positive reply from the server); 2 indicates a permanent positive reply; 3 indicates a positive intermediate reply, in which case the server is waiting for more information; 4 indicates that the command was not accepted and the requested action did not occur, yet the condition may be temporary; 5 indicates absolute failure.

■■■■■■ **Figure 6.7** Reply codes.

- 110 Restart marker reply.

  In this case, the text is exact and not left to the
  particular implementation; it must read:
  MARK yyyy = mmmm

  Where yyyy is User-process data stream marker, and mmmm
  server's equivalent marker (note the spaces between markers
  and "=").

- 120 Service ready in nnn minutes.
- 125 Data connection already open; transfer starting.
- 150 File status okay; about to open data connection.

- 200 Command okay.
- 202 Command not implemented, superfluous at this site.

- 211 System status, or system help reply.
- 212 Directory status.
- 213 File status.
- 214 Help message.

  On how to use the server or the meaning of a particular non-standard command. This reply is useful only to the human user.

- 215 NAME system type.

  Where NAME is an official system name from the list in the Assigned Numbers document.

- 220 Service ready for new user.
- 221 Service closing control connection.

  Logged out if appropriate.

- 225 Data connection open; no transfer in progress.
- 226 Closing data connection.

  Requested file action successful (for example, file transfer or file abort).

- 227 Entering Passive Mode (h1,h2,h3,h4,p1,p2).
- 230 User logged in, proceed.
- 250 Requested file action okay, completed.
- 257 "PATHNAME" created.

- 331 User name okay, need password.
- 332 Need account for login.
- 350 Requested file action pending further information.

- 421 Service not available, closing control connection.

  This may be a reply to any command if the service knows it must shut down.

- 425 Can't open data connection.
- 426 Connection closed; transfer aborted.
- 450 Requested file action not taken.

  File unavailable (e.g., file busy).

- 451 Requested action aborted: local error in processing.
- 452 Requested action not taken.

  Insufficient storage space in system.

- 500 Syntax error, command unrecognized.

  This may include errors such as command line too long.

- 501 Syntax error in parameters or arguments.
- 502 Command not implemented.
- 503 Bad sequence of commands.
- 504 Command not implemented for that parameter.
- 530 Not logged in.
- 532 Need account for storing files.

- 550 Requested action not taken.

  File unavailable (e.g., file not found, no access).

- 551 Requested action aborted: page type unknown.
- 552 Requested file action aborted.

  Exceeded storage allocation (for current directory or dataset).

- 553 Requested action not taken.

  Filename not allowed.

▬▬▬▬

The second digit indicates the category of the reply: 0 indicates a syntax error; 1 indicates informational content; 2 indicates a message concerning the transmission channel; 3 refers to authentication or accounting messages; 4 is not used; and 5 indicates a message regarding the file system status. The third digit merely specifies the level of granularity of messages in a particular category.

Figure 6.8 shows a quick summary of how to interpret FTP reply codes. You should consult RFC 959 for a complete discussion.

Visual Basic Code

The project FTPDEMO.VBP is an FTP client application. With it, you can connect to any FTP server, navigate and list directories, and send and receive files. Figure 6.9 shows the FTPDemo program. FTPDemo does not have a command parser, such as does the FTP.EXE application. Instead, it has a series of command buttons for FTP actions. FTPDemo is a modular program, meaning that you can "take out" the FTP code and plunk it into your own projects easily.

Figure 6.8 Interpreting FTP reply codes.

1xx   Positive Preliminary Reply

2xx   Positive Reply

3xx   Positive Intermediate Reply

4xx   Transient Negative Completion Reply

5xx   Permanent Negative Completion Reply

x0x   Syntax error

x1x   Information

x2x   Connections

x3x   Authentication and accounting

x4x   Unspecified as yet

x5x   File system

I tried to make adding FTP to your applications as painless as possible, so I made a form (FTP.FRM: frmFTP) that has three DSSock controls on it; one for the control connection (dsSocket1), one to accept a data connection, and the third for the data connection itself. The module FTP.BAS then has FTP routines such as FTPLogon that log you into the FTP server. FTP.BAS requires FTP.FRM and vice versa. First, I'll show you how to use the FTP routines, and then we'll get into how they work.

Using a Display Terminal

The FTP code has a provision for using a list box or a text box to display messages and directory listings from the FTP server. If you want to use this feature, you need

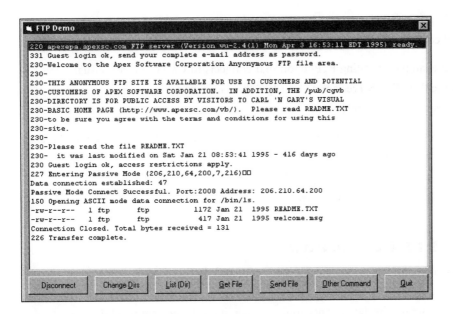

```
220 apexepa.apexsc.com FTP server (Version wu-2.4(1) Mon Apr 3 16:53:11 EDT 1995) ready.
331 Guest login ok, send your complete e-mail address as password.
230-Welcome to the Apex Software Corporation Anyonymous FTP file area.
230-
230-THIS ANONYMOUS FTP SITE IS AVAILABLE FOR USE TO CUSTOMERS AND POTENTIAL
230-CUSTOMERS OF APEX SOFTWARE CORPORATION.  IN ADDITION, THE /pub/cgvb
230-DIRECTORY IS FOR PUBLIC ACCESS BY VISITORS TO CARL 'N GARY'S VISUAL
230-BASIC HOME PAGE (http://www.apexsc.com/vb/).  Please read README.TXT
230-to be sure you agree with the terms and conditions for using this
230-site.
230-
230-Please read the file README.TXT
230-  it was last modified on Sat Jan 21 08:53:41 1995 - 416 days ago
230 Guest login ok, access restrictions apply.
227 Entering Passive Mode (206,210,64,200,7,216)□□
Data connection established: 47
Passive Mode Connect Successful. Port:2008 Address: 206.210.64.200
150 Opening ASCII mode data connection for /bin/ls.
-rw-r--r--   1 ftp      ftp          1172 Jan 21  1995 README.TXT
-rw-r--r--   1 ftp      ftp           417 Jan 21  1995 welcome.msg
Connection Closed. Total bytes received = 131
226 Transfer complete.
```

| Disconnect | Change Dirs | List (Dir) | Get File | Send File | Other Command | Quit |

████████ **Figure 6.9** FTPDemo program.

to modify one line of code in FTP.BAS. Specifically, the DisplayMessage routine has a line that sets a local object called Display to a list box or a text box. Simply change this line to point to your list box or text box on any form:

```
'-- Set your control name here (Text Box or List Box)
Set Display = frmMain.List1
```

You can, of course, modify this routine to display text in any type of display control. The Demo project (FTPDemo) uses a list box as a display window.

FTPLogon

The first thing you need to do is connect to an FTP server. Use the FTPLogon Function for this. Here is the syntax:

Success% = FTPLogon (ServerName$, UserName$, Password$, Timeout%)

The return value is True if successfully connected and authorized, and False if there was any problem either connecting or logging in. ServerName$, UserName$, and

Password$ are self-explanatory. Timeout% is the number of seconds to wait for a successful connection.

Here is an example of calling FTPLogon that connects to Carl & Gary's Visual Basic Home Page FTP Server anonymously as santaclaus@northpole.com, and waits up to 30 seconds for a connection:

```
If FTPLogon ("ftp.apexsc.com", "anonymous", "santaclaus@northpole.comt", 30) Then
    MsgBox "Connected!"
Else
    MsgBox "There was a problem connecting or logging in"
End If
```

SendFTPCommand

SendFTPCommand has provisions for any command that requires a data connection, such as RETR and STOR. If a data connection is required, it first sends the command to set up the data connection, and then it sends the command. Here is the syntax:

```
SendFTPCommand FTPCommand$, BinaryMode%, FileName$
```

FTPCommand$ is any valid FTP command.

FileName$ is an optional argument that specifies a FileName when sending a file with STOR or STOU, or retrieving a file with RETR.

When retrieving a file using the RETR command, FileName$ is the local name that the file will be saved to. When sending a file using STOR or STOU, FileName$ specifies the name of file on the server that will be created.

BinaryMode indicates whether or not the output from the server is sent in binary mode or ASCII mode. Setting BinaryMode to True indicates binary mode. In general you should send and receive all files using BinaryMode True. When retrieving directory listings with LIST, you should specify BinaryMode False.

Here is an example in which MYFILE.ZIP is downloaded:

```
SendFTPCommand "RETR", True, "MYFILE.ZIP"
```

Retrieving a Directory Listing

To retrieve a directory listing of the current directory on the FTP server, use the RETR command with the following syntax:

```
SendFTPCommand "LIST", False
```

Note that you do not have to specify a filename if it is not required. SendFTPCommand uses the Visual Basic 4.0 Optional keyword for the FileName argument, so it is not required.

You can also return a listing of files that match a particular spec. For example, the following command returns all files with an extension .zip:

```
SendFTPCommand "LIST *.zip", False
```

If you are using a display terminal then the directory listing will be displayed. If not, then you will have to intercept the data in the frmFTP.DSSocket2_Receive event, which is where all data received via the data connection enters your application.

Changing Directories

To change to a new directory, send the CWD (Change Working Directory) command specifying the directory name. For example, to change to /pub/cdrom:

```
SendFTPCommand "CWD /pub/cdrom", False
```

Downloading a File

To download a file, send the RETR command with the name of the file. The FileName$ argument is the name to which the downloaded file will be saved. When sending RETR, make sure you specify nBinaryMode as True. Here is an example that downloads a file in the current FTP server directory called MYFILE.ZIP and saves it locally to C:\FILES\MYFILE.ZIP:

```
SendFTPCommand "RETR MYFILE.ZIP", True, "C:\FILES\MYFILE.ZIP"
```

GetFileFromURL

You can also use the GetFileFromURL to connect to an anonymous FTP server, download a file, and disconnect all in one shot. This is similar to using a web browser to download a file from an anonymous FTP site. Here is the syntax:

```
Success% = GetFileFromURL%(URL$, DestPath$, Email$, Timeout%)
```

The return value is True if the file was downloaded and False if there was a problem with either connecting or downloading. URL$ is a URL pointing to an anonymous FTP file. It can either start with file:// or ftp://. DestPath$ is a local directory name where the file will be saved. Email$ is your email address (used to connect anonymously). If you leave this blank, then "guest" is used as an email address (some sites don't allow this). Timeout% is the number of seconds to wait for a connection before the function returns False.

Here is an example that downloads the file sleigh.zip from ftp.northpole.com in the directory /pub/games and saves it to the local C:\ directory. The user's email address is specified as me@here.com, and the routine will wait up to 30 seconds for a connection.

```
If GetFileFromURL("file://ftp.northpole.com/pub/games/sleigh.zip", _
  "c:\", "me@here.com", 30) Then
    MsgBox "Success!"
Else
    MsgBox "Failure"
End If
```

The GetFileFromURL function does not return to your code until it has either successfully downloaded the file or determined that there was an error.

Uploading a File

To send a file to an FTP Server you can either use SendFTPCommand or the SendFile routine. SendFile is a wrapper for SendFTPCommand, and adds the benefit of automatically setting the transfer mode to binary, and waiting until your file is sent before it returns. Here is the syntax for SendFile:

```
ErrCode% = SendFile%(SourceFileName$, DestFileName$, ErrorMessage$)
```

SendFile% returns zero if all goes well; otherwise it returns the FTP reply that represents an error that occurred. In order to use SendFile you must already be connected to the FTP server (See FTPLogon).

SourceFileName$ is the name of a local file to be sent. DestFileName$ is the path and filename of the file that will be written on the server. The path uses forward slashes (/) not backslashes (/) and must not contain wildcard characters. ErrorMessage$ returns with an error message if an error occurs.

Here is an example that sends the file c:\myfile.zip to /pub/uploads on the server:

```
Dim szErrMsg As String

If SendFile("c:\myfile.zip", "/pub/uploads/myfile.zip", szErrMsg) Then
    MsgBox szErrMsg, vbInformation
End If
```

Debugging

My FTP code (in fact, all the code) comes with an excellent debugging tool for those times when you just want to know what's going on in the code. Stepping through the code is impossible during an FTP session, so the only way to see the flow of data is to write a log file.

The WriteLogFile function is a routine that writes a string to a file in the current directory called ERRORLOG.TXT. It writes the date and time, and the string to the file. If the file is not open it is opened. The string is automatically appended to the file. WriteLogFile only writes to the log file if you use /D on the command line of your application.

Even if you are not having trouble with the code, chances are that sooner or later someone is going to have trouble. You can tell them to start your app with /D and then send you the LOG file. That way you can trace what happens; the last line written to the log indicates the last successful action that the program took before the error occurred.

Figure 6.10 shows the WriteLogFile routine, contained in DSSOCK.BAS. The file number is kept completely within this routine, so there is no problem with other file I/O stepping on you. The second line checks the command line for /D. Only if it has been specified is the string written to the file. Notice that the file is opened in binary mode. This is the fastest way to perform file I/O in Visual Basic (or in any BASIC language).

The SEEK command positions the file pointer at the end of the file, and the PUT command writes the string that consists of the date and time (Now), a tab character, and the data string (plus a CR/LF).

Figure 6.10 WriteLogFile writes error messages to a file.

```
Sub WriteLogFile(szData As String)

    '-- File handle for the log file (if used)
    Static nLogFileNum As Integer

    If InStr(UCase$(Command$), "/D") Then
        '-- Is the file not open yet?
        If nLogFileNum = 0 Then
            '-- Open it
            nLogFileNum = FreeFile
            Open App.Path & "\" & szLogFileName For Binary As nLogFileNum
            Seek #nLogFileNum, LOF(nLogFileNum) + 1
        End If

        '-- Write the string
        szData = Str$(Now) & Chr$(9) & szData & vbCrLf
        Put #nLogFileNum, , szData
    End If

End Sub
```

You can use WriteLogFile in any of the applications (or any of your own for that matter). I find it an invaluable little debugging tool for real-time communications.

WriteLogFile is called at every critical point in the FTP code. Here is the list of where it is called in the FTP code:

Routine	Description
SendData	Sending data to a server (writes the data)
dsSocket1_Close	When the control connection is closed by the server

dsSocket1_Connect	When the control connection is made between you and the server
dsSocket1_Exception	When a WinSock error occurs in the control connection (writes the error)
dsSocket1_Receive	When data is received on the control connection (writes the data)
dsSocket1_SendReady	When the control connection becomes ready to send data
dsSocket2_Accept	When a data connection has been established with the server by means of the server connecting to you (PORT)
dsSocket2_Close	When the data connection is closed by the server
dsSocket2_Connect	When a data connection has been established with the server by means of you connecting to the server (PASV)
dsSocket2_Exception	When a WinSock error occurs in the data connection (writes the error)
dsSocket2_Receive	When data is received on the data connection (writes the data)
dsSocket2_SendReady	When the data connection becomes ready to send data
CloseDataConnection	When the code closes the data connection (even if it's not open)

As you can see, using /D will create quite a nice little error log for you to study. I used it several times in debugging the FTP code.

Inside the FTP Code

The FTP Code is a bit complex because of the flags and globals that help bridge the gap between the routines and the FTP form, where all the data transfer occurs. Instead of going over the code line by line, I will instead walk through the data flow using the typical example uses of FTP, connecting to a server, getting a directory, and transferring files. If you are the curious type, you can read the well-commented code.

Take a look at the FTP Form. There are two DSSocket controls. The first one (DSSocket1) is used for the control connection. The second (DSSocket2) is used for the data connection. Because there can be more than one data connection, this control is an array, having an index of zero.

Connecting to the Server

This is done with FTPLogon. FTPLogon does more than just connect you to the server, it logs you into the server and waits for the server to say you are logged in. Figure 6.11 shows the FTPLogin function.

The first thing this routine does is make sure that DSSocket1 (the control connection) is in Line mode (not binary) and that the end-of-line character is a linefeed.

Next it sets two globals (gszUserName and gszPassword) to the user name and password passed to FTPLogin. These will be used in the DSSocket1_Receive event to answer the server's request for the user name and password.

Also, the flag gnFTPReady is initialized to False. This is set True when we have received login confirmation from the server.

Next, SocketConnect is called to connect to the FTP server. If you remember back in Chapter 2 on WinSock programming, SocketConnect is the generic connect routine for any type of Internet host.

■■■■■■■■■■ **Figure 6.11** The FTPLogon routine connects and logs into an FTP server.

```
Function FTPLogon(szHostAddress As String, szUserName As String, _
    szPassword As String, nTimeout As Integer)


    Dim EndTime


    Screen.MousePointer = vbHourglass


    '-- Set Line Mode and EolChar (Linefeed)
    frmFTP.dsSocket1.LineMode = True
    frmFTP.dsSocket1.EOLChar = 10
```

```
'-- Set the username and password
gszUserName = szUserName
gszPassword = szPassword
gnFTPReady = False


'-- Connect (with a timer)
If SocketConnect(frmFTP.dsSocket1, 21, szHostAddress, nTimeout) = 0 Then
    '-- Use the same timer value to wait for gnFTPReady
    '   which is set in DSSocket1_Receive

    EndTime = DateAdd("s", nTimeout, Now)
    Do
        DoEvents
            If Now >= EndTime Then
                Exit Do
            End If
    Loop Until gnFTPReady


    '-- Success?
    If gnFTPReady Then
        '-- Yes! We be connected
        FTPLogon = True
    Else
        '-- Error. disconnect
        SocketDisconnect frmFTP.dsSocket1
    End If
End If


Screen.MousePointer = vbNormal

End Function
```

Check out the next block of code:

```
EndTime = DateAdd("s", nTimeout, Now)
Do
    DoEvents
        If Now >= EndTime Then
            Exit Do
        End If
Loop Until gnFTPReady
```

This code waits for gnFTPReady to be set True, indicating a successful FTP login, but exits after nTimeout number of seconds has expired.

The timing code uses the Now function, which returns a date/time value of the exact moment when it is called. The DateAdd function adds nTimeout number of seconds to Now, and returns a value that represents nTimeout number of seconds in the future. Inside the loop, Now is tested against EndTime and exits if the number of seconds has elapsed.

If indeed the loop exits because of a timeout then gnFTPReady will be false. If this is so, then we did not connect; otherwise FTPLogin returns True to indicate success.

Let's look at the data flow that actually happens when you connect. Immediately after connection, the FTP Server sends a 220 reply with a welcome string. For example:

```
220 apexepa.apexsc.com FTP server (Version wu-2.4(1) Mon Apr 3 16:53:11 EDT

1995) ready.
```

In the DSSocket1_Receive event, a Select Case statement is set up on the value of the reply code (the value of the leftmost three digits of ReceiveData). If the code is 220, then we have just logged into the server and should send the USER command with the user name. Here is the code to handle this precise moment:

```
Case 220    '-- Service ready for new user.

    SendData dsSocket1, "USER " & gszUserName & vbCrLF
```

Now the USER command (specifying the user name) has been sent and we should get back a 331 reply indicating that the user name requires a password. Here is the code to handle this (also in dsSocket1_Receive):

```
Case 331    '-- User name okay, need password.

      SendData dsSocket1, "PASS " & gszPassword & vbCrLf
```

Now, if the password is accepted, then we will get back a 230 command. If this occurs, then gnFTPReady is set to True in the following clause:

```
Case 230    '-- User logged in, proceed.

   '-- This flag tells FTPLogin that we're actually logged in.
   gnFTPReady = True
```

Once the gnFTPReady flag is set to True, then the loop in FTPLogin exits, FTPLogin is set to True, and we're in!

Reality Break

About this time is where most people want to put the book down and use a custom control to do all this. Believe me, it's not as complex as you think, and you should avoid using controls whenever possible. Remember, I am showing you the innards of the code which you can access at a high level. The dirty work is done. You have the added benefit of being able to tinker with the code, which you don't get with an FTP control.

So take a few deep breaths, count to 11,239, pour a cup of coffee, put on your fuzzy slippers and forge ahead. Just think of all the boneheads you'll impress with just the buzzwords alone, let alone the fact that you'll be able to communicate with FTP servers in Visual Basic, something that my cats can't even do (and they're not stupid!).

Inside SendFTPCommand

Figure 6.12 shows the SendFTPCommand routine. I want to bring to your attention right off the bat to the block of code that begins with:

```
If gszLastCmdSent <> "TYPE" Then
```

This code determines if the user has specified a change of transfer mode (binary to ASCII or vice-versa). If so, the command string passed in to SendFTPCommand is saved in the global gszDataCommand variable, the TYPE command is sent to change the mode, and the routine is exited. When the OK reply (200) is received after sending the TYPE command, the original command (gszDataCommand) is then issued.

```
Sub SendFTPCommand(szCommand As String, szFileName As String, _
    nBinaryMode As Integer)

'-- This function sends any command that requires a data connection.
'   These commands are "RETR", "APPE", "LIST", "NLST", "STOR", and "STOU".
'   Add more as they become necessary.

    Dim nPos1       As Integer
    Dim nPos2       As Integer
    Dim nPos3       As Integer
    Dim nSpace      As Integer

    Dim szAddr      As String
    Dim szPort      As String

    '-- Set up an error handler
    On Error GoTo ERR_SendDataCommand

    WriteLogFile "SendFTPCommand: " & szCommand & ", " _
        & szFileName & "," & Str$(nBinaryMode)

    '-- Save the command internally
    gszLastCmdSent = UCase$(Left$(szCommand, 4))
    gnFileOK = False

    If gszLastCmdSent <> "TYPE" Then
        '-- Handle the data mode (binary or ASCII)
        If gnLastMode <> nBinaryMode Then
            gnLastMode = nBinaryMode
```

```
        gszDataCommand = szCommand
        gszLastCmdSent = "TYPE"
        gszFileName = szFileName
        If nBinaryMode Then
            SendData frmFTP.dsSocket1, "TYPE I" & gszCRLF
        Else
            SendData frmFTP.dsSocket1, "TYPE A" & gszCRLF
        End If
        Exit Sub
    End If
End If


gszFileName = szFileName


Select Case gszLastCmdSent

    Case "RETR", "APPE", "LIST", "NLST", "STOR", "STOU"
        '-- These commands require setting up a data connection.
        gnBinaryMode = nBinaryMode

        '-- Make sure the data connections are closed
        CloseDataConnection

        '-- Close the data file if open.
        If gnFileNum Then
            Close gnFileNum
        End If
        gnFileNum = 0

        '-- Save this command
        gszDataCommand = szCommand
```

```
'-- If gnPassiveMode is True, then we connect to the
'   FTP server, otherwise it connects to us (for a
'   data connection).

If gnPassiveMode Then
    gszLastCmdSent = "PASV"

    '-- Send the PASV command
    SendData frmFTP.dsSocket1, "PASV" & gszCRLF

Else
    On Error Resume Next
    frmFTP.dsSocket2(0).Action = SOCK_ACTION_CLOSE
    On Error GoTo ERR_SendDataCommand

    '-- Tell the data connection socket to listen to
    '   the next available port.
    frmFTP.dsSocket2(0).LocalPort = 0
    frmFTP.dsSocket2(0).LocalDotAddr = ""
    frmFTP.dsSocket2(0).ServiceName = ""
    frmFTP.dsSocket2(0).Action = SOCK_ACTION_LISTEN

    '-- Devise a PORT command to tell the FTP server where
    '   to connect.
    szAddr = frmFTP.dsSocket2(0).LocalDotAddr
    nPos1 = InStr(szAddr, ".")
    nPos2 = InStr(nPos1 + 1, szAddr, ".")
    nPos3 = InStr(nPos2 + 1, szAddr, ".")

    szPort = "PORT " & Left(szAddr, nPos1 - 1) & ","
    szPort = szPort & Mid(szAddr, nPos1 + 1, nPos2 - nPos1 - 1) & ","
```

```
            szPort = szPort & Mid(szAddr, nPos2 + 1, nPos3 - nPos2 - 1) & ","
            szPort = szPort & Mid(szAddr, nPos3 + 1, _
                Len(szAddr) - nPos3) & ","


            szPort = szPort & frmFTP.dsSocket2(0).LocalPort \ 256 & ","
            szPort = szPort & frmFTP.dsSocket2(0).LocalPort Mod 256


            gszLastCmdSent = "PORT"


            '-- Send the port command
            SendData frmFTP.dsSocket1, szPort & gszCRLF


        End If


    Case Else
        '-- Send the specified command
        SendData frmFTP.dsSocket1, szCommand & gszCRLF


    End Select



    Exit Sub


ERR_SendDataCommand:

    Debug.Print "Error" & Str$(Err) & ": " & Error
    On Error Resume Next
    Exit Sub


End Sub
```

This intermediate step takes the burden off you as the programmer of constantly sending a TYPE command before every single command.

At the top of the routine the leftmost four characters of the command are saved as the global gszLastCmdSent. This variable always contains the last command sent via SendFTPCommand, and is necessary for determining action to be taken based on the codes received.

Changing Directories

The CWD command is extremely simple. Use the following example as a model for syntax:

```
SendFTPCommand "CWD /pub/cdrom/win3", False
```

When you send this command, the server will change directories and send back a 250 reply to notify success. There is no special handling for the CWD command in the code, but you can add it by simply looking at gszLastCmdSend. If it's CWD, then you have yourself a handler.

Creating a Data Connection

The next thing the code does is determine if the command requires a data connection. There are two basic types of FTP commands: those that require a data connection and those that don't. For example, the CWD command does not require a data connection. The commands RETR, APPE, LIST, NLST, STOR, and STOU all require a data connection.

```
Select Case gszLastCmdSent
```

```
    Case "RETR", "APPE", "LIST", "NLST", "STOR", "STOU"
```

A data connection can be created one of two ways. You can either connect to the FTP server on a port that the server gives you, or you can tell the server to connect to you on a port you give it. The PORT command tells the server to connect to you, while the PASV (passive) command asks the server for a port to connect to for the data connection.

Usually the PORT command is used, but there are situations when you want to connect to the server for a data connection, such as when you are behind a firewall that does not allow incoming connections. It is for this reason, that I use PASV in the demo code as the default method of creating a data connection.

The gnPassiveMode variable determines who connects to whom for the data connection. Set gnPassiveMode to False if you want to accept the data connection, otherwise leave it set to True (the default).

If gnPassiveMode is True, then the PASV command is sent, otherwise a connection is created with DSSocket2(1). In the case that gnPassiveMode is False, the code that begins with the following comment devises a string to be sent to the server that defines the IP address and port that DSSocket2(0) is listening on:

```
'-- Devise a PORT command to tell the FTP server where
'   to connect.
```

Once the new control is listening, the PORT command is sent with the aforementioned string that defines the IP address and port for the data connection, and the routine exits.

At this point we've sent the PORT command and are waiting for a reply. When DSSocket2(0) answers the connection, it passes the socket to DSSocket2(1) and the data connection is established, and the FTP server sends an OK reply (200). If, when this is received, the last command sent was PORT, then the original command (gszDataCommand) is sent. Figure 6.13 shows the code in DSSocket1_Receive that handles this precise moment.

If the last command was PORT, that means that the data connection is made (or is in the process of being made) and the server is ready to accept the original command that required a data connection. At this time, the original command is sent, and the results are returned via the data connection. When the sending side of the connection has finished sending, it closes the connection.

Retrieving a Directory Listing

A directory listing involves the use of a display terminal. (See Using a Display Terminal.) All you need to do to get a directory is send the LIST command.

LIST takes a filespec parameter just like DOS's DIR command. Here is an example that asks for a directory listing of all the ZIP files in /pub/cgvb/misc:

```
SendFTPCommand "LIST /pub/cgvb/misc/*.zip", False
```

■■■■■■■■ **Figure 6.13** After receiving a PORT command, the server sends a 200 reply, at which point you send the original commands such as RETR or STOR.

```
Case 200    '-- Command okay.


        '-- What was the last command sent?
        Select Case gszLastCmdSent
            Case "TYPE" '-- Type toggles between Binary and Ascii
                        '   modes too.
                '-- Set the binary mode flag accordingly
                If InStr(UCase$(ReceiveData), "SET TO A") > 0 Then
                    gnBinaryMode = False
                ElseIf InStr(UCase$(ReceiveData), "SET TO I") > 0 Then
                    gnBinaryMode = True
                End If
                gnLastMode = gnBinaryMode
                If Len(gszDataCommand) Then
                    SendFTPCommand gszDataCommand, gszFileName, gnBinaryMode
                End If


            Case "PORT"
                '-- Send the actual command that the PORT command
                '   was sent to prepare for.
                DisplayMessage "Sending command: " & gszDataCommand
                SendData dsSocket1, gszDataCommand & gszCRLF
        End Select
```

Unix Wildcards

FTP uses UNIX wildcards in filespecs. Here are a few of the most commonly used UNIX wildcards:

?   matches a single character. Unlike DOS, "hell?" will match "hell" but not "hello".

*   matches any sequence (including a period).

[xxx]   where 'xxx' is a collection of letters or a range of letters (like A–Z). "hello.[A-Za-z]" matches "hello.z" but not "hello.9".

The LIST command requires the use of the data connection. The data connection must be created on the fly before sending the actual LIST command or any other command that requires it. (See Creating a Data Connection.)

When you call SendFTPCommand with LIST as the command, first a data connection is made using either PORT or PASV, depending on gnPassiveMode. Once the data connection is made, then the LIST command gets sent. The server immediately sends the directory information and the DSSocket2_Receive event fires upon receiving the data. Figure 6.14 shows the code in this event.

■■■■■■■ **Figure 6.14** Receiving data via the data connection.

```
Sub dsSocket2_Receive(Index As Integer, ReceiveData As String)

    WriteLogFile "RD: " & Str$(Len(ReceiveData)) _
        & " bytes. First 10 = " & Left$(ReceiveData, 10)


    '-- What was the last command sent?
    Select Case UCase$(Left$(gszDataCommand, 4))
        Case "RETR" '-- The retrieve command is the same as a
                    '   Download command, the purpose is to
                    '   retrieve a file. If we are here then
                    '   we are receiving file data.
```

```
        '-- Is the file not open?
    If gnFileNum = 0 Then
        '-- Was a file specified?
        If Len(gszFileName) Then
            '-- Yes. Open the file in binary mode (always)
            gnFileNum = FreeFile
            Open gszFileName For Binary As gnFileNum
        End If
    End If


    '-- If the file is open, write the data.
    If gnFileNum Then
        Put gnFileNum, , ReceiveData
    End If

Case "LIST"

    '-- This is a line of a directory listing. If you wish to parse
    '    it to determine the properties of the files, you should do
    '    so here, but be warned... The format of this listing may
    '    change from server to server.

    DisplayMessage ReceiveData



Case Else
    '-- We are not retrieving a file, so display the
    '    received data. Of course, you can modify this
    '    logic to also display retrieved file data (if
    '    in text mode, or something like that) or to save
    '    all received data to a file.
    DisplayMessage ReceiveData
```

```
    End Select


    '-- Update the number of bytes received.
    glBytesReceived = glBytesReceived + Len(ReceiveData)


End Sub
```

Look at the statement "Case LIST." This is where the code arrives after sending the LIST command. By default the code simply calls DisplayMessage, which displays the text in either a list box or a text box, depending on which you want to use. The demo program uses a list box.

Uploading a File

When you call the SendFile Routine (shown in Figure 6.15) the first thing that happens is the STOR command is sent with SendFTPCommand. The data connection is created using either the PASV command or the PORT command, and the STOR (or STOU) command string is temporarily stored in the gszDataCommand variable. Now, the server sends either a 125 or a 150 code indicating that the transfer is starting. Figure 6.16 shows the code in the DSSocket1_Receive event that handles this precise moment.

Simply put, the file is opened in Binary mode and sent in chunks. The chunk size is set with the variable gnSendBlockSize, which you can set in the Form_Load event of frmFTP. The default is 32000. The basic rule is that there is more overhead in sending two blocks of n bytes than sending one block of $2n$ bytes. In other words, the bigger the buffer, the better. So, try to avoid bagging bugs by barking with big buffers. Once the file has been sent, the data connection is closed.

SendFile makes use of another handy routine, called WaitForFileResponse. This routine waits in a loop for the gnFileOK global integer variable to be set, and returns the value of gnFileOK. gnFileOK is set to any 200 completion code or error

Figure 6.15 The SendFile routine sends a file to the server.

```
Function SendFile(szSourceFile As String, szDestFile As String, _
    szErrorMessage As String) As Integer

    Dim nRetVal As Integer

    SendFTPCommand "STOR " & szDestFile, szSourceFile, True
    nRetVal = WaitForFileResponse()
    If nRetVal = 226 Then
        nRetVal = False
    Else
        szErrorMessage = gszErrMsg
    End If
    SendFile = nRetVal

End Function
```

code. It is not set by interim codes such as 200, but is set only after a command has been completely carried out. Using WaitForFileResponse is an easy way to return control to your program after a command has been carried out. I use it in the FTPdemo project to temporarily disable the form until a command is complete. This prevents the user from stacking up commands on top of each other, which could yield unpredictable results.

Downloading a File

The RETR (Retrieve) command downloads (receives) a file from the FTP server. The file can be anywhere on the server (that's available to you, of course) and you can specify a full server-side path with the filename.

Here is the syntax to download a file:

```
SendFTPCommand "RETR MYFILE.ZIP", True, "C:\FILES\MYFILE.ZIP"
```

■■■■■ **Figure 6.16** The dsSocket2_Close event occurs when the server closes the data connection.

```
Sub dsSocket2_Close(Index As Integer, ErrorCode As Integer, ErrorDesc As String)

    WriteLogFile "dsSocket2(" & Trim$(Str$(Index)) & ")_Close"

    DisplayMessage "Connection Closed. Total bytes received = " _
        & glBytesReceived & gszCRLF

    '-- Close the file if its open
    If gnFileNum Then
        Close gnFileNum
        gnFileNum = 0
    End If

    '-- You cannot unload dsSocket2(0)
    If Index = 1 Then
        Unload dsSocket2(Index)
    End If

    gszDataCommand = ""
    glBytesReceived = -1

End Sub
```

■■■■■

When you send this command, just like with LIST, SendFTPCommand saves the RETR command to gszDataCommand and sends the PORT command (or the PASV command) to initiate a data connection. Once the data connection is made, the original command (RETR) is sent. The server responds positively with a 150 reply to indicate that it's OK to start the transfer, or a 125 if the data connection is already open.

At this time you are ready to start receiving the file. Look at Figure 6.14 again, which shows the DSSocket2_Receive event. If the last command sent was RETR then you are receiving binary file data. The code opens the file if it is not open and writes the received data to the file.

When the server has finished sending the data, it closes the data connection. Figure 6.17 shows the DSSocket2_Close event that occurs when the server closes the data connection. gnFileNum, the VB file handle of the received file, is closed when the data connection is closed. Also, the data connection control DSSocket2(Index) is unloaded from memory. To clean up, gszDataCommand is zeroed and the number of bytes received is set to –1 to indicate an end of file to the code in DSSocket1_Receive.

Epilogue

The FTP protocol isn't difficult on paper, but it requires a sort of state-machine mentality to write in Visual Basic, hence all the gszLastCommand variables and what-not. In all honesty, because of this, the FTP code took me the longest to write. Fortunately for you, you can just drop this code in your project and be sending and receiving files in no time. Please be sure and stop by the Visual Basic Internet 4.0 Programming site (http://www.apexsc.com/vb/vbip) for code updates and utilities.

ACCESSING THE

WORLD WIDE WEB

The World Wide Web

Just since early 1994, the World Wide Web has brought the elusive world of the Internet into homes all over America. Once the sole realm of universities and research firms, the Internet is now a household word. This is all due to the growing popularity of the World Wide Web.

The World Wide Web is the Internet. It is a term for the huge collection of web servers out there on the Internet. The reason it is called a "web" is because of how it is accessed. With the click of a mouse, you can connect to any web server anywhere in the world. Once you've connected, you can view documents that have hypertext jumps, or "links," to other web servers anywhere else in the world. The act of jumping around from server to server is called *surfing the net*.

I know you've either read the above paragraph somewhere before, or you've probably heard Bryant Gumble repeat it on the *Today* show, or maybe you heard it on the radio or saw that episode of *Beyond 2000*. It seems like everyone is talking about the World Wide Web, and why shouldn't they? This is the future. That's why you are reading this book, because you want to know how to be a part of the future in a big way.

Let's forget about the hype for a minute and take a look at what's really going on under the hood of the web, so to speak. First, a couple of definitions.

HTTP—Hypertext Transfer Protocol

HTTP is the protocol by which web clients, such as Netscape and MS Internet Explorer, communicate with web servers, such as WebSite. In this chapter I make references to HTTP servers and web servers. The two are the same. HTTP is the protocol of the World Wide Web.

Like all protocols, there is a set of rules. I am not going to go into the innermost workings of HTTP, but you will undoubtedly pick up on some of them as you read this chapter and implement the code.

HTML—Hypertext Markup Language

HTML stands for Hypertext Markup Language. It is in the same category as RTF (Rich Text Format). HTML is the source code of the World Wide Web. Using any good web browser, you can connect to any site and view the HTML source for the page you are looking at.

In a nutshell, HTML is an enhanced text format. Certain commands, or "tags" as they are called, are embedded in the text that tell the HTML display program what to display. To display a GIF file, you use the <IMG> tag like so:

```
<IMG SRC=PICTURE.GIF>
```

To display text in bold, you would do this:

```
<B>This is some bold text</B>
```

and so on. There are tags for creating lists, displaying text input fields, buttons, horizontal ruler lines, and many other things.

Do not confuse HTML with HTTP. HTTP is the protocol, or the set of rules, by which HTML and other data is transmitted between web clients and web servers.

HTML is a markup language the specific purpose of which is the display of text, graphics, and hypertext jumps.

If you want to know more about HTML and writing it, there are lots of places on the web that have tutorial and reference documents. The best source of these documents can be found at the Yahoo database (Stamford University). Here is the link for that list:

```
http://www.yahoo.com/Computers_and_Internet/Software/Data_Formats/HTML/
```

I also recommend the *HTML Sourcebook* by Ian S. Graham (John Wiley & Sons, 1995).

Understanding the World Wide Web

Basically, an HTTP server is a sockets application that listens to port 80. When a blind connection is made, it sends an HTML file (usually INDEX.HTML) from its default document directory to the client using the HTTP protocol, and immediately closes the connection. The client is now viewing the index page complete with text and graphics. On that page, there are links to other pages, which may be anywhere in the world. In HTML, a link is defined as follows:

```
<A HREF="http://some.server.somewhere.com/">This is the link text</A>
```

The A stands for *anchor*. An anchor is a reference to another HTML page (or program) running on an HTTP server somewhere in the world. When the user clicks on that anchor, the client makes a new connection to the HTTP server defined in the anchor. In this case, the server name is some.server.somewhere.com. Since the port is already defined as 80, there is no need to specify the port.

An anchor can also contain the name of a specific HTML file, for example:

```
<A HREF="http://www.apexsc.com/users/carlf/index.html">Carl's Page</A>
```

This anchor points to my personal page on the machine www.apexsc.com. The name of the file is /users/carlf/index.html. The root directory is defined by the HTTP server.

You may have been wondering why files and directories are defined with forward slashes as opposed to backslashes. The reason is UNIX. Since the web started with

UNIX machines, it naturally follows that HTTP and HTML separate files and directories the same way UNIX does, with forward slashes. It does not matter what platform you run your HTTP server on, HTML and HTTP will always use forward slashes, even when the operating system does not, as is the case with Windows NT.

It is easy to see why the problem of "dead links" exists on the web. There is no referential integrity. Any web site has the right to change its paths and HTML filenames if it wants to. When this happens, any existing outside references to the page are considered dead. It is for that reason that most people leave a page that proclaims "This site has moved to the following address" at the old site.

This chapter shows you how to use the Hypertext Transfer Protocol, or HTTP, the protocol of the World Wide Web. The primary focus is on how to connect to and manipulate web pages programmatically, and interpret the data that comes back from the web site. There is nothing in this chapter about writing back-end server CGI applications. That topic is covered in Chapters 8 and 9. In this chapter we write several interesting programs. One program retrieves a text file from Carl & Gary's Visual Basic Home Page, and another downloads ad-hoc street-level maps of anywhere in the United States.

I must preface this chapter with a hideous invention of the legal profession called a disclaimer. It is sometimes unlawful to extract and present data that exists on web pages for your own purposes. Before setting out to write any kind of application that uses data gleaned from somebody's web page, or any existing Internet host for that matter, make sure you have permission. John Wiley and Sons, Inc. and myself (Carl Franklin) will in no way be held responsible by your actions. There, that wasn't so bad was it?

I learned about this legal issue the old fashioned way. I wrote a VB program that connects daily to a stock quote server, retrieves several quotes, and logs them to an Access database. I was debugging the application when all of a sudden it stopped working. The message that was coming back from the web page was that I had asked for more than 100 quotes in one day, which was not allowed. In the same message, they explained that it was unlawful to run automated scripts against their server, and they would prosecute those who did. Whoops! I never get to have any fun!

Another point I'd like to make is that the sites listed here in this chapter, as elsewhere in this book, existed at the time I wrote the book. Since the Internet has a tendency to change, I cannot guarantee that they are still in existence. You should use the code set forth as a guide for creating your own little demons of death and destruction. Heck, for all I know by the time you read this, Microsoft may have bought the rights to the Internet and this book may be banned!

How to Read a URL

URL stands for Universal Resource Locator. A URL identifies an object (HTML page, document or a file) that exists on any web site anywhere in the world. Using Netscape or some other web browser you can enter a URL at the top of the screen in the location field, and you will soon be downloading (and with a little luck, viewing) the object defined by the URL. Everything you need to know to retrieve a document or file on the web is contained in the URL. Consider this URL for Carl & Gary's Visual Basic Home Page: http://www.apexsc.com:80/vb/index.html.

Figure 7.1 shows the different portions of a URL. The first portion (http://) identifies the protocol used to retrieve the resource. The second part is the machine name or IP address (www.apexsc.com). The third part of the URL identifies the port of the web site (:80). This is usually not used unless the port is other than 80. Port 80 is the default port for all HTTP servers. Next comes the full path and filename of the resource (/vb/index.html).

If you simply specify a directory name with no filename, then the default file will be sent. Usually this is called index.html but webmasters can set the default file to any file, not just index.html. It just so happens that the following URL is exactly the same as the above URL: http://www.apexsc.com/vb.

No port is specified so 80 is assumed, and no file is specified so index.html is sent.

The best way to learn how HTTP works is to look at the data that flows between client and server during a session. You can do this with the Listen utility written by Ian S. Graham, author of the *HTML Sourcebook* (John Wiley & Sons, 1995), an excellent book on HTML with quite a bit of information on HTTP. The Listen utility that comes with Graham's book displays all data that is sent from the web client to the server. Getting the server's response data is a bit trickier. You have to use the

■■■■ **Figure 7.1** Portions of a URL.

```
Portion              Examples
----------------------------------------------------


Protocol             http://


Machine Name         www.apexsc.com
                     192.204.192.200


Port Number          :80
                     <none>


Full Path Of File    /vb/whatsnew.html
                     /vb/index.html
                     <none> (implies default file)
```

Terminal program (see Chapter 2) to connect to the web server on port 80 and manually type in or paste in the exact data that the client sends the server. The server will send you the data exactly as your web client receives it.

Let's take a look at what really happens when you click on a URL in Netscape or any other web client. This is exactly what gets sent to Carl & Gary's VB Home Page when you enter the URL to read the Suggestion Box Page, http://www.apexsc.com/vb/suggest.html:

```
GET /vb/suggest.html HTTP/1.0
User-Agent: Mozilla/1.1N (Windows; I; 32bit)
Accept: */*
Accept: image/gif
Accept: image/x-xbitmap
Accept: image/jpeg
 <CRLF>
```

All HTTP messages end with a carriage return/linefeed on a line by itself. That is how the receiver identifies the end of the message.

HTTP Message Headers

All HTTP messages contain a header that serves several purposes. First and foremost, the header is for identification. The message sent to the server is called a *request message*, and consists entirely of an HTTP *request header*. The request header has several fields, a field being a line ending with a carriage return/linefeed. The first field is called the *method field*, which is followed by several *request fields*. The method field has the following format:

```
<HTTP method> <identifier> <HTTP version>
```

In this case, the HTTP method is GET, which retrieves a document from the server. There are several other methods defined by HTTP, which are shown in Figure 7.2. The request fields provide additional information about the client (or server).

▄▄▄▄▄ **Figure 7.2** Methods of accessing a web page.

Method	Description
GET	Retrieves the indicated URL (document or otherwise).
HEAD	Retrieves the HTTP Header information for the indicated URL.
TEXTSEARCH	Sends a query to the URL using a GET method against a URL that contains query data.
LINK	Links one object (file or executable) to another.
UNLINK	Removes the link between two objects.
POST	Sends data to a URL. The URL must already exist.
PUT	Replaces data sent by a POST method to a URL. The URL must already exist.

For example, several Accept: fields are sent to tell the server which types of data the client can view. If your web client can decode inline GIF images, it will send the following request field:

```
Accept: image/gif
```

Otherwise, it won't. The client usually identifies itself to the server with the User-Agent request header:

```
User-Agent: Mozilla/1.1N (Windows; I; 32bit)
```

This could be useful, for example, if a client-of-tomorrow connects to a server-of-tomorrow, which supports neural communication via ESP. The server could detect that the client is "one of its kind" and send it special commands. This type of built-in intelligence is part of the reason why web browsers work so well on many different platforms.

The request fields are optional. If you know what you are getting back from the server, there is no need to go crazy with the request fields. This method field itself is usually enough to return a text or HTML file from any server.

Interpreting the Server's Response

When the server receives the request message it performs the requested method on the object specified and returns a result message back to the client. Figure 7.3 shows the server's response to the above request message from the client.

The first line of the header, like the request header, is a status line which usually follows this format:

```
<HTTP Version> <Status Code> <Explanation>
```

The status code is a three-digit number that tells the client exactly what the response is. As defined in the HTTP 1.0 draft document, Figure 7.4 shows the possible status codes that the server sends the client.

In this case, the status is 200, or OK. As a general rule, codes between 200 and 299 indicate success. Codes 300 to 399 indicate a redirection to another object (more on this later). Codes from 400 to 599 indicate error messages.

▆▆▆▆▆▆▆ **Figure 7.3** Sample response from Carl & Gary's Visual Basic Home Page.

```
HTTP/1.0 200 Document follows
Date: Tue, 12 Sep 1995 10:51:53 GMT
Server: NCSA/1.4.1
Content-type: text/html
Last-modified: Wed, 05 Jul 1995 07:45:44 GMT
Content-length: 1183


<html>
<title>Carl 'n Gary's Suggestion Box</TITLE>
<body background=lyellow.gif>
<head>
<img src=vbicon.gif align=left border=0 hspace=20>
<h1>VB Home Page Suggestion Box</h1>
</Head>
Tell us what you think.  Praise, suggestions, flames, or funny stories
if you have any.
<p>
We're committed to providing a great page, and any ideas you have could
easily show up sometime soon.  Just fill in your suggestion or comment
below and click Send or Cancel.  If you have any problems submitting
suggestions using this interface, you can send mail directly to
<i><a href="mailto:vb-admin@apexsc.com>vb-admin@apexsc.com</a></i> as well.<p>
<br clear=right>
<hr>
<FORM METHOD="POST" ACTION="vb-bin/post-sug.pl">
<p>Please provide an e-mail address if we need to get back to you.
You don't need to include one if you don't want any replies from us.
<p>
E-mail address:
```

```
<input name="email" size="50"><br>
Your suggestion, comment, or criticism:
<p>
<textarea name="comments" rows=15 cols=60></textarea>
<p>
<input type=submit value="Send"> <input type=reset value="Clear Form">
</form>
<hr>
If you have specific services to offer beyond your suggestions,
please use the <a href="register.html">registration form</a> provided.
<p>
<A HREF="index.html">Back To Carl & Gary's VB Home Page</A>
</body>
</html>
```

Figure 7.4 Status codes returned by the HTTP server.

```
"200"   ; OK
"201"   ; Created
"202"   ; Accepted
"204"   ; No Content
"301"   ; Moved Permanently
"302"   ; Moved Temporarily
"304"   ; Not Modified
"400"   ; Bad Request
"401"   ; Unauthorized
"403"   ; Forbidden
"404"   ; Not Found
"500"   ; Internal Server Error
```

```
"501"    ; Not Implemented
"502"    ; Bad Gateway
"503"    ; Service Unavailable
```

The explanation is a short description of the status code. Unlike status codes, however, the explanation can vary from server to server. The main benefit of the explanation is for the human user.

Every line below the status line is some sort of response header information field. The *Date* field sends the date and time of the transmission in Greenwich Mean Time (GMT). The *Server* field identifies the name and version of the HTTP server software, with the name and version separated by a forward slash. The *Content-type* field tells the client the MIME data-type of the object. Sometimes you will also receive a *MIME-version* field, which identifies the version of the MIME protocol. Finally, the *Last-modified* field gives the date and time of the last modification to the object being sent, and the *Content-length* field gives the object's size in bytes. HTTP headers always end with a carriage return/linefeed on a line by itself (an empty line).

Accessing HTTP Servers in Visual Basic

The WebDemo sample project shown in Figure 7.5 and listed in Figure 7.6 shows how to connect to Carl & Gary's VB Home Page and retrieve a text file. You can change the name of the document in the GET command to any publicly accessible file that exists on the server.

Take a look at the code in Figure 7.6. In the Form_Load event, the program connects to www.apexsc.com on port 80, after which the command GET /vb/greeting.txt HTTP 1.0 is sent followed by two carriage return/linefeed pairs. As the text file is received from the server, it is appended to the text in the txtText text box (whew!, that's a mouthful!). It's really a very simple program.

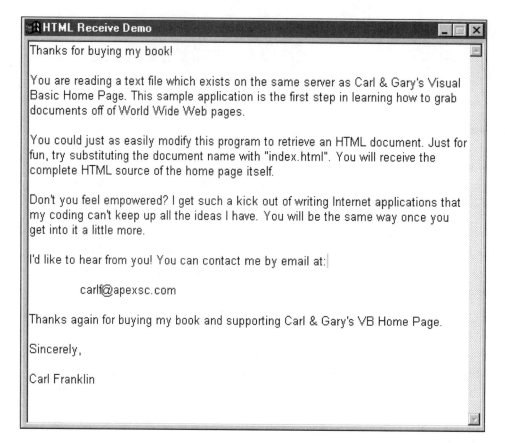

Figure 7.5 The WebDemo program retrieves a text file from Carl & Gary's Visual Basic Home Page.

Figure 7.6 The HHTP command GET tells a web server to send you the contents of a file. In this case it is a personal greeting from the author.

```
DSSOCK.BAS (included in project)


Option Explicit


Dim szReceived As String
```

```
Private Sub Form_Load()
    '-- Use Line Mode
    DSSocket1.LineMode = True
    DSSocket1.EOLChar = 10

    '-- Temporarily disable the form and set the hourglass cursor
    Enabled = False
    Screen.MousePointer = vbHourglass

    '-- Show the form
    Show

    If SocketConnect(DSSocket1, 80, "www.apexsc.com", 20) Then
        '-- There was an error. Re-enable the form
        '   and reset the mouse pointer
        Screen.MousePointer = vbDefault
        Enabled = True

        '-- Display the error
        MsgBox "Error connecting: " & Error
        Exit Sub
    Else
        '-- Send the command to get a file from the server
        SendData DSSocket1, "GET /vb/greeting.txt" & vbCrLf & vbCrLf
        'SendData DSSocket1, "GET /vb/index.html" & vbCrLf & vbCrLf
    End If

End Sub

Private Sub DSSocket1_Close(ErrorCode As Integer, ErrorDesc As String)

    '-- Before you add a received line to a text box, you must make
```

```
'    sure it ends with a CRLF and not just a LF
szReceived = szStripHTML(szLFToCRLF(szReceived))


'-- Append the line to the Text Box
Me.txtText.SelStart = Len(Me.txtText) + 1
Me.txtText.SelText = szReceived


szReceived = False


'-- Re-enable the form and reset the mouse
'    pointer
Screen.MousePointer = vbDefault
Enabled = True
gnConnected = False

End Sub


Private Sub DSSocket1_Connect()


'-- Set this flag indicating we've connected
gnConnected = True

End Sub


Private Sub DSSocket1_Receive(ReceiveData As String)


'-- Append the received data to szReceived
szReceived = szReceived & ReceiveData

End Sub
```

```
Private Sub DSSocket1_SendReady()

    gnSendReady = True

End Sub
```

▬▬▬

Comment out the line in btnGo_Click that retrieves welcome.txt and uncomment the line that retrieves index.html and run the program again. Looks a bit different, doesn't it? You are looking at the source code of the *what's new* page. The function of a web client program like MS Internet Explorer or Netscape is to take this raw HTML text and make it look like a web page.

Now go to the Receive event and uncomment the line that calls szStripHTML. This function removes the HTML codes from the text, making it a bit more readable. Figure 7.7 shows the szStripHTML routine.

▬▬▬▬▬ **Figure 7.7** szStripHTML removes HTML codes from a string and does some simple reformatting with CRLFs and horizontal rulers. It is not intended to be a complete HTML parser.

```
Function szStripHTML(szString As String) As String
'-- szStripHTML by Carl Franklin
'   This function strips HTML codes from a string
'   and attempts to reformat with CRLFs.


    Dim szTemp As String
    Dim szResult As String
    Dim nPos As Integer
    Dim nMarker As Integer


    '-- Copy the argument into a local
```

```
'    string so the original does not
'    get whacked.
szTemp = szString


'-- Remove HTML codes
Do
    nPos = InStr(szTemp, "<")
    If nPos = False Then
        Exit Do
    Else
        '-- szResult contains the final
        '    product of this routine.
        szResult = szResult & _
            Left$(szTemp, nPos - 1)
        '-- szTemp is the working string,
        '    which is continuously
        '    shortened as new codes
        '    are found
        szTemp = Mid$(szTemp, nPos + 1)
        nPos = InStr(szTemp, ">")
        If nPos = False Then
            '-- No complimentary arrow
            '    was found.
            Exit Do
        Else
            '-- What was the code?
            Select Case szParseString(UCase$(Left$(szTemp, nPos - 1)), " ", 1)
                Case "P", "/H1", "/H2", "/H3", "/H4", "/H5", "DL"
                    szResult = szResult & vbCrLf & vbCrLf
                Case "BR"
                    szResult = szResult & vbCrLf
                Case "HR"
```

```
                  szResult = szResult & vbCrLf & String$(50, "-") & vbCrLf
            End Select



            '-- Shorten the working
            '   string
            szTemp = Mid$(szTemp, _
                nPos + 1)
        End If
    End If
Loop


'-- Find a marker byte by looking for
'   a char that does not already exist
'   in the string.
For nMarker = 255 To 1 Step -1
    If InStr(szResult, Chr$(nMarker)) = 0 Then
        Exit For
    End If
Next


'-- Remove carriage returns
Do
    nPos = InStr(szResult, vbCr)
    If nPos Then
        szResult = Left$(szResult, _
            nPos - 1) & Mid$(szResult, _
            nPos + 1)
    Else
        Exit Do
    End If
```

```
    Loop


    '-- Replace linefeeds with Marker bytes
    Do
        nPos = InStr(szResult, vbLf)
        If nPos Then
            szResult = Left$(szResult, _
                nPos - 1) & Chr$(nMarker) _
                & Mid$(szResult, nPos + 1)
        Else
            Exit Do
        End If
    Loop


    '-- Replace marker bytes with CR/LF pairs
    Do
        nPos = InStr(szResult, Chr$(nMarker))
        If nPos Then
            szResult = Left$(szResult, _
                nPos - 1) & vbCrLf _
                & Trim$(Mid$(szResult, nPos + 1))
        Else
            Exit Do
        End If
    Loop


    '-- Thats all for this routine!
    szStripHTML = szResult

End Function
```

■■■■■

You can use this technique to write applications that retrieve news or other timely documents from any web page and use it in your personal applications. Someday, I'd like to write myself an application that goes and gets news from a variety of sources (web sites, Usenet groups, etc.), picks out stories of interest, and creates one big document that I can then view in the morning when I get up.

Accessing Forms

The coolest part of accessing the World Wide Web has to be manipulating forms. With some simple code and HTTP savvy you can connect to a form page, enter values into the text boxes or select options, and press buttons. This is all done programmatically, of course. There are no "virtual buttons" you have to press. Your code bypasses the user interface, talking directly to the web site in HTTP.

There are two ways in which you can send data to a web site: The POST method and the PUT method. POST is the most common command used to send data to a web site. You have probably come across many web forms in your time. A form is a page that has input fields that you fill in and a button that lets you send the data.

A Brief Overview of the Common Gateway Interface (CGI)

A form assigns names to each of the input fields. When you fill out these fields and press a Submit button on the form, the client sends a POST method message to the server along with all the values for each of the field names.

The server then runs a program (called a *gateway* program) at the web site and passes it the data that you have entered into the form. The interface between the HTTP server and the gateway program is called the Common Gateway Interface, or CGI.

The gateway program does its thing (whatever it does) and returns HTML text to the HTTP server, which passes it through to the client.

In Chapter 8, I show you how to create your own gateway programs in Visual Basic using Windows CGI, a special version of CGI made specifically for Visual Basic programmers. In Chapter 9 I show you how to use OLE DLLs written in VB as CGI programs with Microsoft's Internet Information Server.

As I said before, every input field on a form has a name. Take a look at the form section of Carl & Gary's Suggestion Box HTML page in Figure 7.8. All form definitions start with the <FORM> tag and end with the </FORM> tag. Every form has a method associated with it. The method is sent when the Submit button is pressed. A Submit button is a button whose job it is to execute the form's method. In the case of our suggestion box, the form uses the POST method to send the data in the fields to the server application, which is defined in the ACTION portion of the FORM tag as vb-bin/post-sug.pl. This is a UNIX script written in the Perl scripting language.

Yes, I know, Carl & Gary's runs on a UNIX machine! How are we supposed to promote Microsoft with an attitude like that? Well, the fact is that when we started all the really good web software (and most Internet software in general) ran on UNIX, but that is changing. Windows NT is the future of operating systems. NT does take up much more memory than SunOS or any other UNIX flavor, but it does so many great things. (Well, that's another book, isn't it?) Anyway, Carl & Gary's uses MS Internet Information Server for some of the pages. Which, of course, run on an NT box.

◾◾◾◾ **Figure 7.8** An HTML snippet from Carl & Gary's Visual Basic Home Page Suggestion Box.

```
<FORM METHOD="POST" ACTION="vb-bin/post-sug.pl">


<P>
Please provide an e-mail address if we need to get back to you.
You don't need to include one if you don't want any replies from us.
<P>


E-mail address:


<INPUT NAME="email" SIZE="50"><br>


Your suggestion, comment, or criticism:
<P>
```

```
<TEXTAREA NAME="comments" ROWS=15 COLS=60></ TEXTAREA >

<P>

<INPUT TYPE=SUBMIT VALUE="Send"> <INPUT TYPE=RESET VALUE="Clear Form">

</FORM>
```

The input fields are defined with the INPUT and TEXTAREA tags. You can create a Submit button by setting VALUE=SUBMIT. The VALUE parameter identifies the text on the button.

Let's say for the sake of argument that you connect to this suggestion box page with your web browser and enter your email address as reader@myhouse.com, and enter a suggestion that reads, "Carl & Gary are the coolest VB programmers I know!" When the Submit button is pressed, the data in Figure 7.9 is sent to the server.

▬▬▬▬ **Figure 7.9** A sample of data sent to a server when a Submit button is pressed.

```
POST vb-bin/post-sug.pl HTTP/1.0
Accept: */*
Accept: image/gif
Accept: image/x-xbitmap
Accept: image/jpeg
User-Agent: Mozilla/1.1N (Windows; I; 32bit)
Content-type: application/x-www-form-urlencoded
Content-length: 90
 <CRLF>
&email=reader@library.com&comments=Carl+%26+Gary+are+the+coolest+VB+programmers+I+know%21
 <CRLF>
```

There are two sections to the POST command, a header section and a data section. The header section contains the Content-type and other HTTP headers. Like the GET request message, the header section begins with a status line. The command is POST, the identifier is the CGI script post-sug.pl located in the vb-bin directory on the server, and the protocol is HTTP version 1.0.

Notice the Content-type field. When sending data to an HTTP 1.0 server, there is only one content type and that is application/x-www-form-urlencoded. There is no other option. Also, the Content-length field is used in the request method because data is being sent in the message body. The content length is the length of this data.

By the way, that's not a typo. Urlencoded is the word, not uuencoded. URL = Universal Resource Locator, hence urlencoded.

The data section is comprised of a string of "variable=data" equations like so:

&variable1=data1&variable2=data2

These variables are defined by the server in the HTML that defines the form.

You might have noticed that spaces are replaced with the plus character (+). As well, there are some strange numbers in the place of the ampersand and the exclamation point. Those numbers are the hexadecimal values of the characters. As a general rule, if a character in your data is being used by the protocol and has special meaning, encode it as a percent sign followed by its hex value (26 is the hex value of the ampersand, and 21 is the hex value of the exclamation point).

You can encode any character using Visual Basic with the following code:

```
Encoded$ = "%" & Hex$(Asc(Character$))
```

Mapping with the TIGER Map Service

While in the last official month of writing this book, I stumbled on a most interesting web site, the TIGER Map Service (TMS). This page is operated by the U.S. Bureau of the Census. The goal of the service is to provide a public resource for

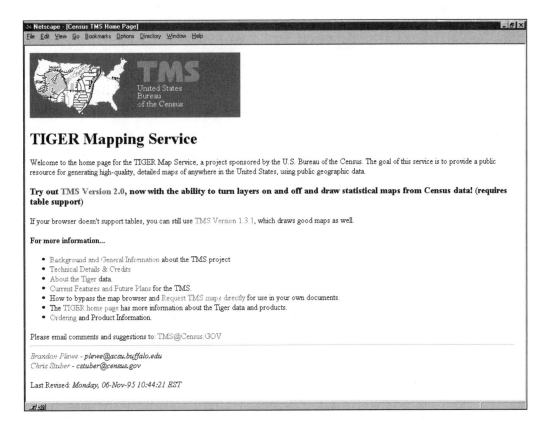

■■■■■■■ **Figure 7.10** TIGER Mapping Service.

generating high-quality, low-detail maps of anywhere in the United States using public geographic data. In short, you can send a query to this page specifying an exact location in the United States using longitude and latitude values, and the picture size, and it returns to you a GIF file of a map. The URL of the TIGER Mapping Service (shown in Figure 7.10) is http://tiger.census.gov/

There is an interactive page, where you can generate maps and look at them, and then there is a page that tells you how to send queries.

Basically, you connect on port 80 to tiger.census.gov and send a POST command with the coordinate data tagged on at the end. Here is a list of some of the variables you can specify:

lon=number The longitude, in decimal degrees, of the center of the map. Remember that longitudes for the Western Hemisphere are negative numbers. Longitudes for the contiguous United States range between about −67 and −125 degrees.

lat=number The latitude, in decimal degrees, of the center of the map. Latitudes for the contiguous United States range between about 24 and 49 degrees.

wid=number The desired width, in decimal degrees of longitude, of the coverage of the map. The actual coverage of the map may vary slightly from this number, due to fitting the requested coverage to the shape of the image.

ht=number The desired height, in decimal degrees of latitude, of the coverage of the map. It may turn out slightly different, for the reason given above.

iwd=number The image width, in pixels. If none is specified, the default is 512.

iht=number The image height, in pixels. If none is specified, the default is 256.

legend=on If included, the legend graphic is returned rather than the map.

To get an idea of what these maps look like, check out Figure 7.11. This is a map of the mall in Washington, DC. Since you can specify the image's pixel width and height, you can render a graphic suitable for printing. Granted, there are no street names, but the streets are shown! Not bad.

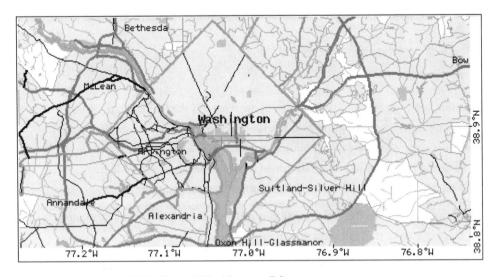

■■■■■■■■■ **Figure 7.11** Map of Washington, DC.

The page has some sample URLs that generate maps. One example is a shot of Lower Manhattan. Here is the URL:

```
http://tiger.census.gov/cgi-bin/mapgen/.gif?lat=40.739& _
        lon=-73.99&wid=0.06&ht=0.08&iht=500&iwd=240
```

From this we can extrapolate that this is a POST command with the following variables:

lat = 40.739

lon = 73.99

wid = 0.06

ht = 0.08

iht = 500

iwd = 240

Figure 7.12 shows the data you should send once you've connected to tiger.census.gov on port 80. Now, wouldn't it be cool if you had a program that let you enter coordinates and displayed a map in a Visual Basic picture or image control? Well, bust my buttons! I wrote one for you.

Figure 7.12 Sending this text to tiger.census.gov on port 80 will return a map of Washington, DC.

```
POST /cgi-bin/mapgen/.gif HTTP/1.0
Accept: image/gif
Content-type: application/x-www-form-urlencoded
Content-length: 57
 <CRLF>
?lat=38.89&lon=-77.028&wid=.06&ht=.01&iht=300&iwd=400&mark=-77.03
64,38.8973,redpin,White+House;-77.01,38.8895,blueball,Capitol
<CRLF>
```

Sample Application—MAP

MAP (shown in Figure 7.13) is a sample program that lets the user retrieve a map from TIGER Map Service from specified coordinates. Figure 7.14 shows the source code for this project. When you press the Generate button, MAP first connects to the server with the SocketConnect routine, and then calls the GetMap routine with

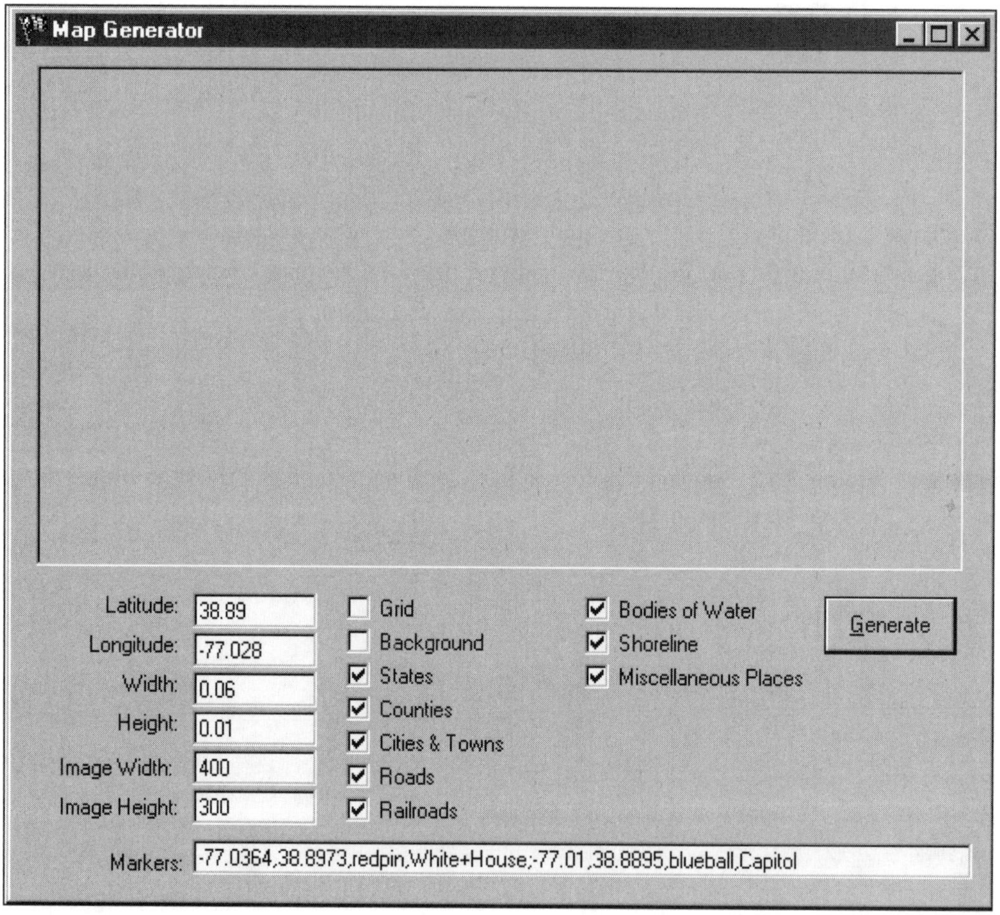

Figure 7.13 TIGER retrieval program.

all the user-defined data and options. GetMap is the heart of the program. It accepts the following data for parameters:

    longitude
    latitude
    width
    height
    image width (in pixels)
    image height (in pixels)
    marker string
    grid
    background
    states
    counties
    places (cities and towns)
    roads
    railroads
    water (Bodies of water)
    shoreline
    miscellaneous places (like parks and schools)

Figure 7.14 The GetMap routine, which uses the specified coordinates and options and sends a query to the TIGER Map Service, which then sends back the map as a GIF file and closes the connection.

```
Sub GetMap(szLat As String, szLon As String, szWid As String, _
    szHgt As String, sziWid As String, sziHgt As String, _
    szMark As String, nGrid As Integer, nBack As Integer, _
    nStates As Integer, nCounties As Integer, nPlaces As Integer, _
    nRoads As Integer, nRailroads As Integer, nWater As Integer, _
    nShoreline As Integer, nMisc As Integer)


    Dim szSendMe    As String
    Dim szData      As String
    Dim szOn        As String
```

```
Dim szOff        As String

If nGrid Then
    szOn = szOn & "GRID,"
Else
    szOff = szOff & "GRID,"
End If


If nBack Then
    szOn = szOn & "BACK,"
Else
    szOff = szOff & "BACK,"
End If


If nRoads Then
    szOn = szOn & "roads,majroads,"
Else
    szOff = szOff & "roads,majroads,"
End If


If nStates Then
    szOn = szOn & "states,"
Else
    szOff = szOff & "states,"
End If


If nCounties Then
    szOn = szOn & "counties,"
Else
    szOff = szOff & "counties,"
End If
```

```
If nPlaces Then
    szOn = szOn & "places,CITIES,"
Else
    szOff = szOff & "places,CITIES,"
End If


If nRailroads Then
    szOn = szOn & "railroads,"
Else
    szOff = szOff & "railroads,"
End If


If nWater Then
    szOn = szOn & "water,"
Else
    szOff = szOff & "water,"
End If


If nShoreline Then
    szOn = szOn & "shorelin,"
Else
    szOff = szOff & "shorelin,"
End If


If nMisc Then
    szOn = szOn & "miscell"
Else
    szOff = szOff & "miscell"
End If


szData = "lat=" & szLat & "&lon=" & szLon _
  & "&wid=" & szWid & "&ht=" & szHgt _
```

```
        & "&iht=" & sziHgt & "&iwd=" & sziWid _
        & "&mark=" & szMark _
        & "&on=" & szOn _
        & "&off=" & szOff


    szSendMe = "POST /cgi-bin/mapgen/.gif HTTP/1.0" & vbCrLf

    szSendMe = szSendMe & "Accept: text/plain" & vbCrLf

    szSendMe = szSendMe & "Content-type: application/x-www-form-urlencoded" & vbCrLf

    szSendMe = szSendMe & "Content-length:" & Str$(Len(szData)) & vbCrLf

    szSendMe = szSendMe & vbCrLf

    szSendMe = szSendMe & szData & vbCrLf


    SendData DSSocket1, szSendMe


End Sub
```

■■■■■■■

Complete documentation of the accepted parameters for the TIGER Map Service are listed at the following URL: http://tiger.census.gov/instruct.html.

Once the POST command is sent, the map service whips up a GIF file and starts sending it. The code in DSSocket1_Receive writes the data to a local file named MAP.GIF. When the file has been completely sent, the server closes the connection, and the DSSocket1_Close event fires. Here the file is converted to a BMP file with Dolphin System's freeware GIFBMP32.DLL, a DLL that converts 256 color GIF files into BMP files. Thanks go out to Steve Cramp at Dolphin Systems for whipping up this little gem for us. Once converted to a BMP, it is displayed in the picture control. You can opt to leave it as a GIF and display it with some other tool, or anything else you want to do with it.

Figure 7.15 shows a detail map of my hometown, Mystic, CT. If you ever saw the movie *Mystic Pizza*, this is where I spent the first 20 years of my life. To answer your question, yes there really is a Mystic Pizza. I used to go there every summer on the last day of school when I was a kid.

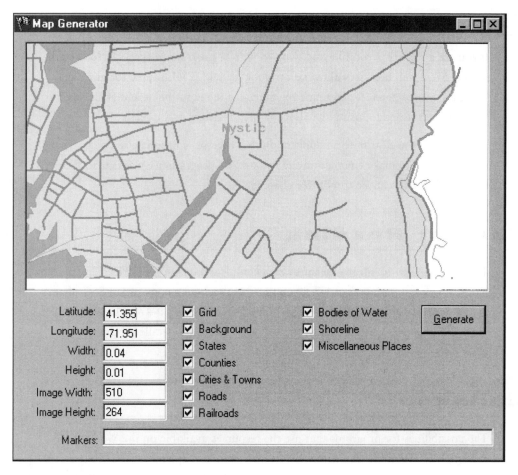

▬▬▬▬▬ **Figure 7.15** Map of Mystic, CT.

NetPaper

NetPaper is a program that I wrote to download weather maps or other timely GIF and BMP files from both Web and Gopher sites, and displays them on the desktop as wallpaper. For images on web sites, it simply uses the GET command just as WebDemo does. For images on Gopher sites it simply sends a Gopher selector as the code in Chapter 3 does. The files are downloaded on a timer, and you can tell NetPaper to download a different image from the list each time, one after another.

Tips for HTTP Programming

If you see a page that you like and want to write a program to access it, look at the source. Most web browsers allow you to look at the HTML source for any page. Using the source you can determine the names of the input fields and construct the string of data to send it using the above HTTP messages as a model.

Think before you distribute an application that accesses someone else's page. That is an easy way to make enemies on the net, and no programmer wants that. (See the ugly disclaimer at the top of this chapter.)

Further Reading

This chapter is by no means meant to be a complete discussion of HTTP. For a more complete description of HTTP and HTML, pick up a copy of Ian S. Graham's *HTTP Sourcebook*, published by John Wiley & Sons (ISBN: 0-471-11849-4). I highly recommend it. Also, read the HTTP 1.0 Draft for a detailed technical description of HTTP.

Epilogue

The possibilities for programs that use the resources available on the World Wide Web go way beyond what I can possibly cover in this chapter. Hopefully, these sample applications have sparked your curiosity and have given your imagination a jump start. I'd like to hear about any really cool ways in which you've used these techniques yourself. Please send any comments to me at carlf@apexsc.com.

WINDOWS CGI:

SERVER-SIDE

PROGRAMMING

The Common Gateway Interface (CGI)

What Is the CGI?

The CGI is an interface between an HTTP server and an application. CGI is what allows users of the World Wide Web to access data and processes that do not specifically exist within the realm of the HTTP server and HTML documents. Have you ever connected to a web-searching page, such as WebCrawler (http://webcrawler.com/) or the World Wide Web Worm (http://www.cs.colorado.edu/home/mcbryan/WWWW.html) that finds web pages from keywords that you specify? Where does the information come from? The answer is a database. Since today's sophisticated databases cannot be accessed directly by the HTTP protocol, some other application must be accessing the database. The tasks, then, are (1) to give the application that accesses the database the user's input data (the search terms), and (2) to return the output of the application to the HTTP server, which in turn presents it to the user.

CGI is implemented differently on different platforms. A CGI application, or one that interacts with an HTTP server, is sometimes called a *script* because it is written in a scripting language, or what us DOS people call batch language. Under the UNIX platform CGI scripts are typically written in either the Perl, TCI, or UNIX shell, all of which are UNIX-based scripting languages. Perl is the language of choice for UNIX because of its high-level control and low-level speed.

Windows CGI and WebSite

Enter Windows CGI. Windows CGI is a Windows implementation of CGI developed by Bob Denny, the creator of one of the more popular NT-based HTTP server applications, WebSite. Denny needed a clean implementation of CGI to handle the requirements of Windows applications, so he created Windows CGI. WinCGI, as it is referred to, uses INI files to pass data to and from the CGI app. Any Windows application can be a CGI app, as long as you follow the guidelines. In particular, WinCGI was written with Visual Basic programmers in mind. The WebSite product I spoke about comes not only with a VB module for interfacing with WinCGI, but sample applications, and devotes an entire chapter in the manual to using WinCGI with Visual Basic.

Before Mr. Denny authored WebSite, he created a shareware HTTP server that runs only on 16-bit Windows, called HTTPD. This version also uses Windows CGI, and is in fact included on the CD-ROM, so you can get started right away experimenting with creating your own web pages and CGI applications.

There are currently several Windows NT-based HTTP servers available. They range from free to up to many thousands of dollars. I can assure you that paying a lot of money for a web server is a thing of the past since the market is booming. Anyway, here are five inexpensive HTTP servers that exist at the time of this writing:

- Microsoft Internet Information Server (MIIS). This is Microsoft's Web/Gopher/FTP Server application for Windows NT. It is included with Windows NT 4.0 Server and MSDN (Microsoft Developer Network) level III. It was available for downloading on Microsoft's Web Site at the time this book was written. See Chapter 9 for a detailed look at MIIS.

- The European Microsoft Windows NT Academic Center (EMWAC) in the Czech Republic distributes a freeware Windows NT-based HTTP server. It does not support Windows CGI at the time of this writing, so writing Visual Basic applications for it is out of the question. However, in the interest of fair play I have included it on the CD-ROM in case you want to check it out.

- HTTPD is not shareware, but you get to evaluate it free for 30 days, and then it costs $99.00. This is the 16-bit version of WebSite, a more complete and professionally done HTTP server that supports WinCGI. Like WebSite, HTTPD also supports WinCGI. At the time of this writing it supports CGI 1.1, but you can get the latest and greatest version on the Web at the following address: http://www.city.net/win-httpd/. Version 1.4C is included on the CD-ROM.

- A very nice commercial Windows NT HTTP server is WebSite. At the time of this writing, WebSite was going for $499.00 US. Since its creator also defined Windows CGI, you can bet this server will always be state of the art. I have used WebSite, and I can offer you my honest opinion. I think it's very slick. The user interface is simple enough for anyone to use, and the security is entirely adequate. You can get the latest info on WebSite at the following URL: http://website.ora.com.

- Netscape offers a couple of excellent servers starting at around $500.00. You can check them out at http://home.mcom.com/comprod/server_central/index.html. Netscape servers do not support Windows CGI at this time, but using WebLink for Visual Basic you can use Visual Basic as a CGI platform. See Other CGI Options for more information on WebLink.

Windows CGI Speed Issues

I am not going to pretend that Windows CGI is perfect, because it is not. The only real problem I can find with it is speed. The speed at which a VB program loads can be very slow, depending on the server configuration and the size of the application. It is for this reason that you must keep custom controls and excessive code in your Windows CGI apps to a minimum. For best results, use a single module. The more forms and controls you have in your project, the slower it will load. If your site starts getting hundreds of requests per minute, your system could really slow down.

Carl & Gary's Visual Basic Home Page (http://www.apexsc.com/vb) runs partially on a Sun Sparc 2 UNIX workstation. We use Perl to write our UNIX CGI scripts.

In this configuration, about 35–50 Perl scripts can run per second. That's pretty fast, but that kind of performance is required for high-traffic sites like ours. If we were to use Windows CGI on an equivalent NT server, it might take two to ten seconds to load and run a simple Visual Basic 4.0 application that opens a database and writes data. Assuming that the VB app was stripped down to one or two modules, this kind of performance is adequate for a small to medium-traffic web site, but would be unbearably slow when traffic gets high. See the section entitled Optimizing for Speed for some more tips on how to make your Windows CGI applications perform as fast as possible.

HTML Forms and the ACME.HTM Sample Form

An HTML form is a special type of web page that has input fields to let the user enter data. Usually, forms have a Submit button that tells the HTTP server to run a CGI application and pass the data that the user entered to it. The form user interface is all defined with HTML.

There are some excellent books on the subject of writing HTML forms, so I won't go into a lot of detail on the subject. Instead, I will discuss some of the features of our sample form, a request form for Product Information sponsored by the Acme company (and my mother used to tell me that watching the Road Runner was a waste of time!). Figure 8.1 shows the form as it looks in Netscape Navigator, and Figure 8.2 shows the HTML source.

Form Definition

The Acme form has several interesting features. One feature that I'd like to point out is the background. When the form is displayed, this defined bitmap (BACK.GIF) is sent and displayed in a pattern. The dimensions of BACK.GIF are 1 pixel high and 1024 pixels wide. Since it is so small, it gets sent and displayed rather quickly. The smart thing is that it is only one pixel high. That's as high as it has to be to give the form the classic look of stationery. The background is defined in the <BODY> statement at the top of the form like so:

```
<BODY BACKGROUND=BACK.GIF>
```

Acme Product Information

DON'T CLICK!

Thank you for your interest in Acme products. We want to know more about you, so please take just a minute to fill out this information form. We will send you our current catalog which showcases all of our products and prices. Please email direct inquiries to the Acme staff at staff@acme.com. Thank you and have a nice day.

Demographic Information:

First Name: [   ]
Last Name: [   ]
Email Address: [   ]
Address Line 1: [   ]
Address Line 2: [   ]
Address Line 3: [   ]
City, State & Zip: [   ] , [   ] [   ]
Home Phone: [   ]
Work Phone: [   ]

Professional Information:

Operating System: [Windows 16-Bit ▼]

Primary Language: [Visual Basic ▼]

Years in Development: [This is my first year ▼]

Clicking this button will transfer your information to our database, and you will be sent a catalog as soon as possible.

[Register]

Figure 8.1 Acme production information. A sample HTML form.

■■■■■■ **Figure 8.2** The Acme form's HTML source.

```
<HTML>
<HEAD>
<TITLE>Acme Product Information</TITLE>
<BODY BACKGROUND=BACK.GIF>
<A HREF="SLMONK.WAV"><IMG SRC=DONT.GIF BORDER=0 ALIGN=LEFT HSPACE=20></A>

<H1>Acme Product Information</H1>

Thank you for your interest in Acme products. We want to know more about you, so
please take just a minute to fill out this information form. We will send you our
current catalog which showcases all of our products and prices. Please email
direct inquiries to the Acme staff at <A HREF="MAILTO:staff@acme.com">staff@acme.com</A>.
Thank you and have a nice day.

<BR CLEAR=LEFT>
</HEAD>
</CENTER>
<FORM ACTION="/cgi-win/acme.exe" METHOD="POST">
<IMG SRC=BACK2.GIF>
<P>

<CENTER><FONT SIZE=4><I>Demographic Information:</FONT SIZE=4></I></CENTER>
<PRE>
              First Name: <INPUT SIZE=25 NAME="FirstName">
               Last Name: <INPUT SIZE=25 NAME="LastName">
           Email Address: <INPUT SIZE=40 NAME="Email">
         Address Line 1: <INPUT SIZE=40 NAME="Address1">
         Address Line 2: <INPUT SIZE=40 NAME="Address2">
         Address Line 3: <INPUT SIZE=40 NAME="Address3">
        City, State & Zip: <INPUT SIZE=20 NAME="City">, <INPUT SIZE=2
NAME="State">  <INPUT SIZE=12 NAME="Zip">
```

```
                        Home Phone: <INPUT SIZE=12 NAME="HomePhone">
                        Work Phone: <INPUT SIZE=12 NAME="WorkPhone">


</PRE>


<IMG SRC=BACK2.GIF>
<P>


<CENTER><FONT SIZE=4><I>Professional Information:</FONT SIZE=4></I></CENTER>
<PRE>
                        Operating System: <SELECT NAME="OperatingSystem">
        <OPTION>Windows NT
        <OPTION>Windows 95
        <OPTION>OS/2 Warp
        <OPTION SELECTED>Windows 16-Bit
        <OPTION>UNIX
        <OPTION>Mac
        <OPTION>DOS
        <OPTION>Other
        </SELECT>


                        Primary Language: <SELECT NAME="PrimaryLanguage">
        <OPTION SELECTED>Visual Basic
        <OPTION>Visual C++
        <OPTION>C
        <OPTION>Delphi
        <OPTION>Other Pascal
        <OPTION>Smalltalk
        <OPTION>Other
        </SELECT>


                Years in Development: <SELECT NAME="Years">
```

```
        <OPTION SELECTED>This is my first year
        <OPTION>2
        <OPTION>3
        <OPTION>4
        <OPTION>5
        <OPTION>6-9
        <OPTION>10+
        </SELECT>


<IMG SRC=BACK2.GIF>

                        Clicking this button will transfer your
                        information to our database, and you will
                        be sent a catalog as soon as possible.

                        <INPUT TYPE="submit" VALUE="Register">

</PRE>


<P>


<IMG SRC=BACK2.GIF>


<FONT SIZE=1>
<BR>
<I>
<BLOCKQUOTE>
<BLOCKQUOTE>
<BLOCKQUOTE>
<BLOCKQUOTE>
Copyright 1995, 1996 Acme Software Inc<BR>
All rights reserved<BR>
```

```
</BLOCKQUOTE>
</BLOCKQUOTE>
</BLOCKQUOTE>
</BLOCKQUOTE>
</I>
</FONT SIZE=1>
<P>
</FORM>
</BODY>

</HTML>
```

Another feature is the image that displays "Don't Click," which is Latin for "Click Me Now!" When the user clicks the image, a WAV file is sent. In this case, it is of my favorite cartoon duo, Ren and Stimpy. This is just an example, of course, and you wouldn't really want to subject your users to the disgusting and tasteless sounds of Ren and Stimpy. Or would you?

Notice how the GIF file is transparent. This is done with a public domain command-line GIF utility called GIFTOOL, which is included on the CD-ROM. There isn't any real documentation for this utility but if you type "GIFTOOL -help" at the command line, it will display the command syntax and options.

The image is made into an anchor by incorporating the <IMG> tag within the anchor <A> tag, as follows:

```
<A HREF="SLMONK.WAV"><IMG SRC=DONT.GIF BORDER=0 ALIGN=LEFT HSPACE=20></A>
```

The file SLMONK.WAV is sent when the image is clicked. The SRC=DONT.GIF command in the <IMG> tag defines the image file. The BORDER=0 command defines the image with no border, or no box around the image (this is critical to giving the transparent illusion). The ALIGN=LEFT command places the image on the left-hand side of the form. Finally, the HSPACE=20 command places a little bit of horizontal space between the image and the surrounding text.

All HTML forms start with a <FORM> tag (and end with a </FORM> tag). Here is our <FORM> tag:

```
<FORM ACTION="/cgi-win/acme.exe" METHOD="POST">
```

The ACTION command defines what happens after the form has been completed. In this case we want to run our CGI program, acme.exe. The second command, METHOD="POST", defines a method performed on the CGI application. This can be either GET, which requests data from the CGI application; or POST, which sends data to the CGI application. In the case of our example, we are sending data to the application, so POST is used.

Field Definitions

The input fields may look complex, but they really are not. The fields themselves are all part of HTML, and are created graphically by the HTTP client. The HTML text just defines the fields; the client actually manages the input.

The ACME.HTM form has 11 text entry fields, and three option (multiple-choice) fields. Defining a field is easy. For example, look at the definition of the first text field:

```
First Name: <INPUT SIZE=25 NAME="FirstName">
```

The <INPUT> tag defines the field. There are two parameters: SIZE=25, which defines the length of the field; and NAME="FirstName", which defines the name of the field. Your Visual Basic WinCGI application will reference these fields by name.

HTML has a dropdown list input type called SELECT. Select fields are a bit different from text fields, in that there are several selectable options and a default option. Figure 8.3 shows the definition for the first select field. The select field is defined by the <SELECT> tag. Between the <SELECT> tag and its trailer tag, </SELECT>, you can have one or more options, defined with the <OPTION> tag. Whichever option you desire to be the default option you can specify as such with the <OPTION SELECTED> tag. As with the <INPUT> tag, the NAME parameter specifies the name of the field.

The Submit Button

When all the fields are filled in, the user presses the button that says "Register." This button is defined as follows:

```
<INPUT TYPE="submit" VALUE="Register">
```

■■■■■■ **Figure 8.3** Definition for the first select field in the Acme demonstration.

```
Operating System: <SELECT NAME="OperatingSystem">
<OPTION>Windows NT
<OPTION>Windows 95
<OPTION>OS/2 Warp
<OPTION SELECTED>Windows 16-Bit
<OPTION>UNIX
<OPTION>Mac
<OPTION>DOS
<OPTION>Other
</SELECT>
```

■■■■■■

Just like a text field, the button is defined with an <INPUT> tag. The TYPE="submit" defines the field as a Submit button. When a Submit button is pressed, the action defined in the <FORM> tag is executed, and the CGI application is run. In the case of our Acme form, the application is run with the POST method defined.

Once the CGI application is run, the HTTP server is no longer communicating directly with the client. The CGI application sends any thank-you or error messages to the client from this point on. Now, let's take a look at the ACME sample CGI application, which takes the user's data and saves it to an Access database.

Hands-On Windows CGI

What follows is a dissection of the elements of the Windows CGI Visual Basic interface. Along the way, we will discuss the sample WinCGI program ACME.VBP.

CGI32.BAS

The only thing you need to add to a VB project to create a CGI application is CGI32.BAS, or CGI.BAS for 16-bit VB. The only difference is the declaration of GetPrivateProfileString. CGI32.BAS contains all the constants, declares, and routines for CGI access.

Windows CGI uses files to pass data back and forth. Yes, writing to the disk can be slow, but it works. See the section entitled Optimizing for Speed for more information on how to get the best performance out of WinCGI. Data is passed from the client to the server to your app via a Windows INI file. The Windows API call used to retrieve data from an INI file is a function called GetPrivateProfileString.

Data is sent back to the server from your CGI app via a sequential file. The WinCGI interface handles all of this for you. All you really have to do is get the data from the form, process it, and send back HTML text, which will be displayed to the client.

ACME.BAS: CGI_Main and Inter_Main

The ACME.BAS module contains the code that interacts with the server at the highest level. This is where you process the GET and/or POST methods. Whenever you create a WinCGI app, you must have two static subroutines, CGI_Main, and Inter_Main. CGI_Main is called whenever a GET or POST method is performed on your application. This is where you do your magic, which we will demonstrate in a minute. Inter_Main is called when your application is executed directly by a user, as from the File Manager or Explorer, or an icon in a program group. This is where you can simply put up a dialog or a message box describing the application. No more than that is necessary.

Dissecting Sub Main in CGI32.BAS

CGI32.BAS has a Sub Main, which is to be the startup form (or in this case procedure) for the project. This is the first code that executes. Take a look at Figure 8.4, which shows the code in Sub Main. If the app is executed without any command line arguments, that means that it was probably started directly by the user, in which case the Inter_Main sub is called and the program ends.

If command line parameters are specified, the sub InitializeCGI is called (see Figure 8.5), which grabs all of the CGI variables out of the INI file, the name of which is passed on the command line. The CGI variables are global variables that contain information such as the user-defined field data (from our form's <INPUT> and <SELECT> tags), information about the user and the browser that she is using, the EXE file path, security information, and some other stuff.

▬▬▬▬ **Figure 8.4** CGI32.BAS—Sub Main listing.

```
'--------------------------------------------------------------------
'
'   main() - CGI script back-end main procedure
'
' This is the main() for the VB back end. Note carefully how the error
' handling is set up, and how program cleanup is done. If no command
' line args are present, call Inter_Main() and exit.
'--------------------------------------------------------------------
Sub Main()
    On Error GoTo ErrorHandler

    If Trim$(Command$) = "" Then      ' Interactive start
        Inter_Main                     ' Call interactive main
        Exit Sub                       ' Exit the program
    End If


    InitializeCGI          ' Create the CGI environment


    '===========
    CGI_Main               ' Execute the actual "script"
    '===========


Cleanup:
    Close #CGI_OutputFN
    Exit Sub                           ' End the program
'------------
ErrorHandler:
    Select Case Err                    ' Decode our "user defined" errors
        Case ERR_NO_FIELD:
            ErrorString = "Unknown form field"
        Case Else:
```

```
          ErrorString = Error$      ' Must be VB error
    End Select


    ErrorString = ErrorString & " (error #" & Err & ")"
    On Error GoTo 0                  ' Prevent recursion
    ErrorHandler (Err)               ' Generate HTTP error result
    Resume Cleanup
'------------

End Sub
```

■■■■■■■

■■■■■■■ **Figure 8.5** CGI32.BAS Sub InitializeCGI.

```
'----------------------------------------------------------------------------
'
'   InitializeCGI() - Fill in all of the CGI variables, etc.
'
' Read the profile file name from the command line, then fill in
' the CGI globals, the Accept type list and the Extra headers list.
' Then open the input and output files.
'
' Returns True if OK, False if some sort of error. See ReturnError()
' for info on how errors are handled.
'
' NOTE: Assumes that the CGI error handler has been armed with On Error
'----------------------------------------------------------------------------
Sub InitializeCGI()
    Dim sect As String
    Dim argc As Integer
    Static argv(MAX_CMDARGS) As String
    Dim buf As String
```

```
CGI_DebugMode = True      ' Initialization errors are very bad

'

' Parse the command line. We need the profile file name (duh!)

' and the output file name NOW, so we can return any errors we

' trap. The error handler writes to the output file.

'

argc = GetArgs(argv())

CGI_ProfileFile = argv(0)


sect = "CGI"

CGI_ServerSoftware = GetProfile(sect, "Server Software")

CGI_ServerName = GetProfile(sect, "Server Name")

CGI_RequestProtocol = GetProfile(sect, "Request Protocol")

CGI_ServerAdmin = GetProfile(sect, "Server Admin")

CGI_Version = GetProfile(sect, "CGI Version")

CGI_RequestMethod = GetProfile(sect, "Request Method")

CGI_LogicalPath = GetProfile(sect, "Logical Path")

CGI_PhysicalPath = GetProfile(sect, "Physical Path")

CGI_ExecutablePath = GetProfile(sect, "Executable Path")

CGI_QueryString = GetProfile(sect, "Query String")

CGI_RemoteHost = GetProfile(sect, "Remote Host")

CGI_RemoteAddr = GetProfile(sect, "Remote Address")

CGI_Referer = GetProfile(sect, "Referer")

CGI_From = GetProfile(sect, "From")

CGI_AuthUser = GetProfile(sect, "Authenticated Username")

CGI_AuthPass = GetProfile(sect, "Authenticated Password")

CGI_AuthRealm = GetProfile(sect, "Authentication Realm")

CGI_AuthType = GetProfile(sect, "Authentication Method")

CGI_ContentType = GetProfile(sect, "Content Type")

buf = GetProfile(sect, "Content Length")

If buf = "" Then

    CGI_ContentLength = 0
```

```
    Else
        CGI_ContentLength = CLng(buf)
    End If
    buf = GetProfile(sect, "Server Port")
    If buf = "" Then
        CGI_ServerPort = -1
    Else
        CGI_ServerPort = CInt(buf)
    End If


    sect = "System"
    CGI_ContentFile = GetProfile(sect, "Content File")
    CGI_OutputFile = argv(2)
    CGI_OutputFN = FreeFile
    Open CGI_OutputFile For Output Access Write As #CGI_OutputFN
    buf = GetProfile(sect, "GMT Offset")
    CGI_GMTOffset = CVDate(CDbl(buf) / 86400#) ' Timeserial offset
    buf = GetProfile(sect, "Debug Mode")          ' Y or N
    If (Left$(buf, 1) = "Y") Then                  ' Must start with Y
        CGI_DebugMode = True
    Else
        CGI_DebugMode = False
    End If


    GetAcceptTypes          ' Enumerate Accept: types into tuples
    GetExtraHeaders         ' Enumerate extra headers into tuples
    GetFormTuples           ' Decode any POST form input into tuples


End Sub
```

■■■■■

Let's move on to WinCGI's Error Handler. The implementation is pretty good. If an error occurs anywhere in the app, the error handler in Sub Main will display the error to the web client and the application will exit. The statement On Error Goto ErrorHandler installs the error handler.

CGI_Main: Where the Magic Happens

Once this data is loaded, the CGI_Main subroutine (in your module) is called. This is where you process the user's input data and display a report in HTML format to the user. This is the real power of Windows CGI, leveraging the world of Visual Basic on the Internet. In this case, we are going to open an access database (ACME.MDB) using the Jet Database Access Objects in Visual Basic 4.0 and, using an append query, save the user's data.

ACME.MDB should reside in the same directory as the ACME.EXE program. It has one table, CustomerInfo, which has several text fields that are exactly the same size as the fields defined in the form, ACME.HTM.

Retrieving and Saving the Data

Figure 8.6 shows the CGI_Main subroutine. The first thing that happens is a test to see whether the method used to send data is GET or POST. We want to respond only to the POST method. If a POST method was invoked, then we proceed with retrieving the data field values. This is done with the GetSmallField() function. GetSmallField returns the data in a field given the name of the field.

Figure 8.6 Sub CGI_Main listing.

```
Sub CGI_Main()

    Dim szFirstName As String
    Dim szLastName As String
    Dim szEmail As String
    Dim szAddress1 As String
    Dim szAddress2 As String
    Dim szAddress3 As String
    Dim szCity As String
```

```
Dim szState As String

Dim szZip As String

Dim szHomePhone As String

Dim szWorkPhone As String

Dim szOperatingSystem As String

Dim szPrimaryLanguage As String

Dim szYears As String


Dim dbAcme As DATABASE

Dim szSQL As String

Dim lRows As Long

Dim szQuote As String


szQuote = Chr$(34)


Select Case CGI_RequestMethod
    Case "POST" '-- A POST method was executed.


        '-- Retrieve the user data
        szFirstName = GetSmallField("FirstName")
        szLastName = GetSmallField("LastName")
        szEmail = GetSmallField("Email")
        szAddress1 = GetSmallField("Address1")
        szAddress2 = GetSmallField("Address2")
        szAddress3 = GetSmallField("Address3")
        szCity = GetSmallField("City")
        szState = GetSmallField("State")
        szZip = GetSmallField("Zip")
        szHomePhone = GetSmallField("HomePhone")
        szWorkPhone = GetSmallField("WorkPhone")
        szOperatingSystem = GetSmallField("OperatingSystem")
        szPrimaryLanguage = GetSmallField("PrimaryLanguage")
```

```
szYears = GetSmallField("Years")

    '-- Open the Access database
    Set dbAcme = OpenDatabase(App.Path & "\ACME.MDB")

    '-- Create an append query to insert a record.
    szSQL = "INSERT INTO CustomerInfo (FirstName, LastName, Email, "
    szSQL = szSQL & "Address1, Address2, Address3, City, State, Zip, "
    szSQL = szSQL & "HomePhone, WorkPhone, OperatingSystem, "
    szSQL = szSQL & "PrimaryLanguage, Years) "
    szSQL = szSQL & "VALUES (" & szQuote & szFirstName & szQuote
    szSQL = szSQL & ", " & szQuote & szLastName & szQuote & ", "
    szSQL = szSQL & szQuote & szEmail & szQuote & ", " & szQuote
    szSQL = szSQL & szAddress1 & szQuote & ", " & szQuote & szAddress2
    szSQL = szSQL & szQuote & ", " & szQuote & szAddress3 & szQuote
    szSQL = szSQL & ", " & szQuote & szCity & szQuote & ", " & szQuote
    szSQL = szSQL & szState & szQuote & ", " & szQuote & szZip & szQuote
    szSQL = szSQL & ", " & szQuote & szHomePhone & szQuote & ", "
    szSQL = szSQL & szQuote & szWorkPhone & szQuote & ", " & szQuote
    szSQL = szSQL & szOperatingSystem & szQuote & ", " & szQuote
    szSQL = szSQL & szPrimaryLanguage & szQuote & ", " & szQuote
    szSQL = szSQL & szYears & szQuote & ")"
    '-- Insert the data
    On Error Resume Next
    dbAcme.Execute szSQL, dbFailOnError
    If Err = 0 Then
        '-- The append query worked.
        Send "Content-type: text/html"
        Send ""
        Send "<TITLE>Thank You!</TITLE>"
        Send "<HEAD><CENTER><H1>Thank you for completing our form!</H1></CENTER>"
        Send "</HEAD><P><HR SIZE=7><P>"
```

```
          Send "The following information was saved in our database:"
          Send "<P>"
          Send "<PRE>"
          Send "<B>                    Name: </B>" & szFirstName & " " & szLastName
          Send "<B>                   Email: </B>" & szEmail
          Send "<B>                 Address: </B>" & szAddress1
          If Len(szAddress2) Then
              Send "<B>                         </B>" & szAddress2
          End If
          If Len(szAddress3) Then
              Send "<B>                         </B>" & szAddress3
          End If
          Send "<B>                         </B>" & szCity & ", " & szState & " " & szZip
          Send "<B>              Home Phone: </B>" & szHomePhone
          Send "<B>              Work Phone: </B>" & szWorkPhone
          Send "<P>"
          Send "<B>  Operating System: </B>" & szOperatingSystem
          Send "<B>  Primary Language: </B>" & szPrimaryLanguage
          Send "<B>  Years experience: </B>" & szYears
          Send "</PRE><P><P><HR SIZE=7><P>"
      Else
          '-- The append query didn't work for some reason.
          Send "Status: 500 Internal Server Error"
          Send "Content-type: text/html"
          Send ""
          Send "<TITLE>Error saving data</TITLE>"
          Send "<HEAD><CENTER><H1>Error saving data</H1></CENTER>"
          Send "</HEAD><P>"
          Send "There was a problem saving your data to the Acme database. "
          Send "Error Text: " & Error
          Send "Contact the system administrator at <A HREF=" & "mailto:"
          Send CGI_ServerAdmin & ">" & CGI_ServerAdmin & "</A><P>"
```

```
        End If

        '-- Close the database.
        dbAcme.Close

    End Select

End Sub
```

For example, let's say the user entered his first and last name as "John Smith". The following lines of code retrieve the first name and last name from the form:

```
szFirstName = GetSmallField("FirstName")
szLastName = GetSmallField("LastName")
```

In this case, szFirstName returns "John" and szLastName is "Smith."

Once we have the raw data from the user, the next step is to open the ACME.MDB database and enter a new record. The OpenDatabase command opens the MDB. *Remember, if there is an error, it will be handled by the universal error handler in Sub Main.* Once the database is open, an append query is defined in the szSQL string variable. I know it looks complex, but it is not. I broke down the creation of this long query into several statements for readability. Basically, an append query has the following format:

```
INSERT INTO TableName (Field1, Field2, Field3) VALUES ("Data1", "Data2", "Data3")
```

The field list (Field1, Field2...) contains the names of the fields. The value list ("Data1", etc.) contains the values to be set. These values must be in the same order as the fields. In other words, the field names and values must correspond to each other and be in the same order. If a field is a text or date field, then its corresponding value must be enclosed in quotes. If there are quotes in the actual data being saved, the query will fail (a seemingly foolish situation, but a situation nonetheless).

Next, the query is executed directly via the EXECUTE Method of the database object. The option dbFailOnError creates a trappable error that occurs if the append query fails. If the query was successful, then an HTML confirmation message is sent to the client. This is done with the Send routine, which simply writes the text to the output file. If the query fails, a failure message is returned to the user.

Sending Data to the Client with the Send Command

When sending HTML to the client, the first two lines must consist of a header. In the case of sending HTML, the header should be sent like so:

```
Send "Content-type: text/html"
Send ""
```

The first line defines the content of the transmission as either HTML or straight text or both. The second line is blank, indicating the end of the header. You can also redirect the output to another HTML page by sending the following lines in place of a header and HTML text:

```
Send "URI: <http://your.link.goes.here.html>"
Send ""
```

where the first line is simply "URI: " followed by the HTML address in arrow brackets. Alternatively, you could use the following syntax to redirect output to another HTML file:

```
Send "Location: http://your.link.goes.here.html"
Send ""
```

Either way, this method lets you create "standard" response files, which you can simply tell the HTTP server to display to the client.

If you are sending HTML text, as we are in the Acme example, anything goes after the first two lines. You can send HTML directly, you can mix data from the database with the output text, whatever you want to do. You are the Web Master.

In our example, the confirmation message simply repeats back to the client all the data that was entered by the user:

```
Send "Content-type: text/html"
Send ""
Send "<TITLE>Thank You!</TITLE>"
```

```
Send "<HEAD><CENTER><H1>Thank you for completing our form!</H1></CENTER>"
Send "</HEAD><P><HR SIZE=7><P>"
Send "The following information was saved in our database:"
...
...
```

The Status Code

The status code is a number returned to the HTTP server from the CGI application. If the program runs and exits normally, a status code of 200 is returned. If an error occurs within the CGI mechanism, special status codes are returned. If a runtime error occurs within your CGI application (such as the append query not working) you can specify a status code of 500, which signifies a runtime error. Do this by sending the following line right at the top of the header:

```
Send "Status: 500 Internal Server Error"
```

Optimizing for Speed

It should be obvious that you want your CGI applications to be as fast as possible. With a small to medium-sized web site, you may have 20 to 30 copies of your program running at the same time, all different users. It is therefore imperative that you minimize disk access, minimize code and data in your applications, and write smart code.

When approaching the task of optimizing your Windows CGI application, keep these ideas in mind. First of all, the smaller your application is, the better. Avoid using forms, and write good tight code. I mentioned before that I didn't quite like the way Windows CGI 1.1 reads in all the data as soon as the app is loaded. Remove that code and replace it with only the calls to return the data you are interested in. If you aren't going to use certain pieces of data, why add extra overhead of reading the disk for data you don't need?

One obvious trick is to use a ramdisk for the INI file directory. I didn't find any mention in the WebSite manual of problems that exist when using a ramdisk for this purpose, and I can't personally see any danger in this, except that the size of the ramdisk must be large enough to accommodate all the copies of your CGI application INI files that will be required at any one time. Experimentation and experience are the only things that can determine the magic numbers in this equation. Since I have neither, you will have to experiment yourself.

Other CGI Options

While I have not had a real chance to play with it, WebLink for Visual Basic is a nice alternative to using straight Windows CGI. You can check out the WebLink page at the following URL: http://ciint1.ciinc.com/vbdemo.htm.

The thing that's nice about WebLink is that it works with your Visual Basic program already loaded and running. Your app simply handles requests from the WebLink DLL. With Windows CGI your app must load and run, open any database if necessary, and then handle the request. WebLink makes your site zip along by eliminating the overhead of loading a Visual Basic application, which, as you know, can be quite slow at times.

WebLink works with Windows CGI and also without it. You can use WebLink with any HTTP server, such as WebSite, Purveyor, or MIIS.

Epilogue

WebSite is a fairly decent HTTP server, and the price is right. The manual is well written, and all the sample code is in Visual Basic. HTTPD, the 16-bit version of WebSite, does not have as many features and only works on 16-bit machines, making it unusable for a high-traffic site. However, it works fine for low-traffic servers within an IntraNet if you want to test your pages locally before publishing them on the Net. Both WebSite and HTTPD currently support Windows CGI 1.1, but by the time you read this, updates may be available which use Windows CGI 1.3, the details of which are unkown to me at this time. If you would like more information on WebSite, you can connect to the WebSite Central home page:

```
http://website.ora.com/
```

Windows CGI opens the door to Visual Basic programmers who wish to find a niche in the vastness of the Internet. There are many businesses out there screaming to get on the Net in a big way. You can use these tools to provide data entry forms, search engines, reports, and much more. With just a little extra effort, you can streamline your Windows CGI apps, putting less strain on your HTTP server.

CHAPTER

9

MICROSOFT

INTERNET

INFORMATION SERVER

Although Microsoft has been late in responding to the popularity of the Internet and the World Wide Web, slowly but surely Bill Gates and company have been putting together the pieces of an Internet tools strategy. The two key tools are VB Script, with its capability for coding Internet applications that run inside a web browser, and Microsoft Internet Information Server (MIIS). In this chapter I'll be focusing on the Internet server, with detailed coding examples showing how you can tap its outstanding features to roll your own server with surprisingly little work.

Microsoft's Internet Information Server has many parts. I spent a long weekend exploring a late beta copy of MIIS and found it a bit confusing at first. But once I understood the architecture I was blown away, especially when I grasped the importance of the Internet Database Connector (IDC) and the Internet Server API (ISAPI) technologies that are keys to the power of this package. I had to go sit in a dark room for nearly an hour to let all the incredible possibilities sink in.

In short, IDC bypasses external CGI scripting for data access; and ISAPI (specifically OLEISAPI.DLL) lets users access OLE Automation servers through the web. The power and simplicity of this approach may cause you to rethink your development strategy. A core advantage of this new architecture is less redundancy for us developers, and we all know that redundancy can be really, really, really bad.

Before I go into the technical details, I'll put this new package into perspective. It's easier to access data using the Internet Database Connector than it is using other servers, because the data access is part of the server itself. On the VB side, the Internet Server API does for CGI what IDC does for database access. DLLs written with ISAPI run in the server's address space, requiring less time and resources to be spent processing scripts. Also, OLEISAPI lets you access an OLE Server DLL from the web site.

The first advantage to consider is the Internet Database Connector (IDC). This technology makes it easy to access data from web pages. The simplest way to understand the power of this architecture is by comparison with how VB programmers had to use Common Gateway Interface (CGI) coding not too long ago. If you remember from Chapter 8, a user fills out your HTML form and clicks the Submit button. The server writes the entered data to an INI file and runs your VB application, passing the name of the INI file. The VB app then opens a database, executes a query using the specified data, and returns an HTML result string to the server, which passes it to the user.

However, using MIIS, the server does the work. A user fills out your HTML form and clicks the Submit button. The server reads an IDC script (a small text file) that contains an ODBC data source, username and password, an SQL query, and an .HTX file (Extended HTML). The server then opens the database and executes the query using the specified data. Finally, the server sends back an HTML response that includes the resulting data that is displayed using the HTML Extension file as a template.

Excuse me, but where does Visual Basic fit in? So far, it doesn't. The process never leaves the server! But don't worry, your VB skills aren't becoming obsolete. That's the second half of the story. You can easily integrate VB applications to your server because IDC works smoothly with the ISAPI, as I'll explain later.

Instead of firing up a VB executable to do the database work, the server calls HTTPODBC.DLL, which is already resident in memory, to query the database and return the results. There is no downtime in opening the database because HTTPODBC has its own connection management scheme (Figure 9.1). The power of IDC lies in the use of three types of files:

- *HTM files.* These are standard HTML format files, with no special consideration required except for the fact that they reference an IDC file rather than any other type of CGI script.

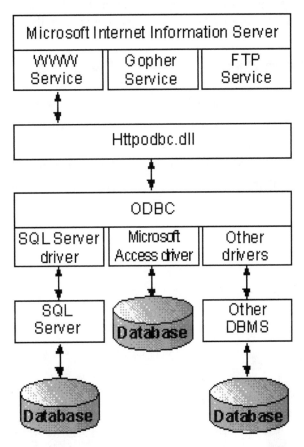

Figure 9.1 Architecturally sound. The Internet Database Connector is tightly integrated into MIIS. Database access occurs from within the server itself using HTTPODBC.DLL to access any ODBC data source.

- *IDC files.* These Internet Database Connector scripts are small text files that contain at minimum: an ODBC data source name, an SQL query, and a reference to an HTX file (see below). By using variables in the query that represent the data passed by the form you can allow users to supply data for the query.

- *HTX files.* At first glance, HTML Extension files look like normal HTML files, but like the IDC file, they contain variables representing data fields. HTML Extension also defines flow control tags so you can return specified results if a certain condition is true, false, or whatever. The HTX file is merely a template—it does not represent the HTML that is sent back to the user. The server uses it to create the final output with the user data.

Understanding File Types

Let me give you an example of each one of these file types, beginning with a simple HTML file that runs an IDC script (see Figure 9.2). I've included a screen capture showing how it looks in the browser (see Figure 9.3). The form for the HTML code in Figure 9.2 consists of one field (Search) and a button that runs TEST.IDC in the \scripts directory off of the web server root. Here are the contents of TEST.IDC:

```
Datasource: Biblio
Template: test.htx
SQLStatement:
+SELECT Name, Address FROM Publishers
+WHERE Name Like "<%Search%>"
```

■■■■■■ **Figure 9.2** This sample HTML form accesses an IDC script.

```
<html>
<body>
<title>Sample IDC Form</title>
<p>
This is a simple example of using the Database Connector
that queries an ODBC data source called Biblio, an Access
database (BIBLIO.MDB).
<p>
```

```
Enter the partial name of a publisher below (ex: "Ran*"
might return "Random House")
<p>
<form action="http:/scripts/test.idc" method="POST">
<input name=Search>
<input type=submit value="Query">
</Form>
<p>
</body>
</html>
```

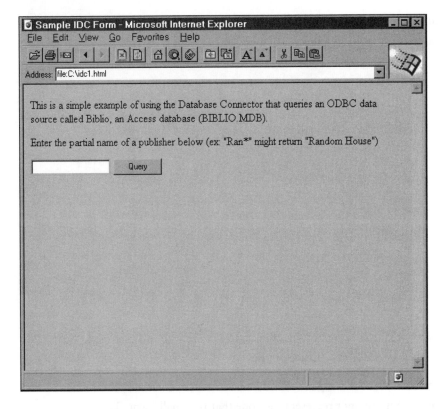

Figure 9.3 A simple HTML form. This simple HTML form calls the IDC
script, TEST.IDC, when the user clicks the Query button.

The Datasource field specifies an ODBC datasource (not the database name), while the Template field specifies an HTML Extension file to be used as the output template, and the SQLStatement field specifies a SQL Query. Although there are a few optional fields, these three fields are required.

You must have a plus sign in front of each line of the query. When the server reads this IDC file, it opens the ODBC data source called "Biblio" and executes the SQL statement:

```
"SELECT Name, Address FROM Publishers
    WHERE Name Like <search term>"
```

The variable <%Search%> is replaced with the contents of the Search field on the form when the query is run. You can reference any of the HTML form's fields within your query in this way.

When the data comes back from HTTPODBC.DLL, it is merged with the TEST.HTX file, which looks like this:

```
<html>
<body>
<title>Query Results</title>
Here are the results of your query:
<p>
<%begindetail%>
<pre>
    Company Name: <%Name%>
        Address: <%Address%>
</pre>
<%enddetail%>
</body>
</html>
```

Figure 9.4 shows what the results of this transaction in the web browser might be if the user had entered "A*" for the search term.

Remember, the HTX file is a template that the server uses to construct the final HTML output, and it does not represent the code that is actually sent. The <%begindetail%> and <%enddetail%> sections delimit where rows returned from

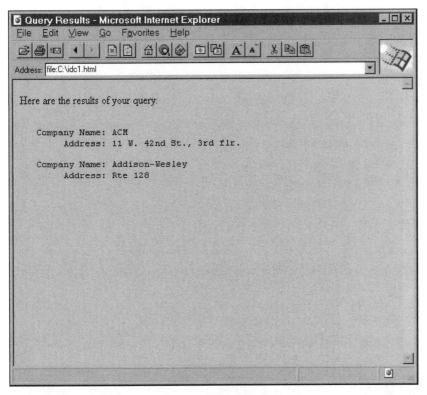

Figure 9.4 Create a standard page. You can automate creation of standard web pages using some code to create a sample form created by an OLE server with a call to the StandardPage string function.

the database will appear in the document. Columns returned from the query are surrounded by <%%>, such as <%Name%> and <%Address%>.

HTML Reserved Words

When writing HTX files you have considerably more control than HTML alone gives you. For example, you can test conditions within the HTX file by using this syntax:

```
<%if condition %>
    HTML text
[<%else%>
```

```
    HTML text]
<%endif%>
```

Where condition is of the form:

```
value1 operator value2
```

and operator can be one of these:

```
EQ          if value1 equals value2
LT          if value1 is less than value2
GT          if value1 greater than value2
CONTAINS    if any part of value1 contains
            the string value2
```

For example, let's say that you want to return a special message if one of the names returned from the query I explained earlier was "Acme":

```
<%begindetail%>
<%If Name EQ "Acme"%>
    <H2>
    Acme is having a sale on all
    size boxes of magnetic
    bird seed!
    </H2><p>
<%EndIf%>
<%enddetail%>
```

The operands value1 and value2 can be column names, one of the built-in variables (CurrentRecord or MaxRecords), an HTTP variable name, or a constant. When used in an <%if%> statement, values are not delimited with <% and %>. The CurrentRecord built-in variable contains the number of times the <%begindetail%> section has been processed. The first time through the <%begindetail%> section, the value is zero. Subsequently, the value of CurrentRecord changes every time another record is fetched from the database. The MaxRecords built-in variable contains the value of the MaxRecords field in the Internet Database Connector file.

You can access parameters from the IDC file in the HTX file by prefixing the name of the parameter with "idc" and a period. For example, if you want to get the actual value the user entered into the Search field on the form, you can do something like this:

```
<%begindetail%>
<pre>
   Company Name: <%Name%>
       Address: <%Address%>
</pre>
<%enddetail%>
<%if CurrentRecord EQ 0 %>
   There are no matches with the term, <%idc.Search%>
<%endif%>
```

Several variables can be used in HTML Extension files that give a lot of information about the environment and the web client connected to the server. There are too many to completely document here in this chapter, but Table 9.1 shows some of the HTTP variables that can be accessed from within an HTML Extension file. MIIS gives you a full CGI header access and more.

████████ **Table 9.1** HTTP Variables Used in an HTML Extension (.HTX) File

CONTENT_TYPE	The content type of the information supplied in the body of a POST request.
HTTP_ACCEPT	Special case HTTP header. Values of the Accept: fields are concatenated, separated by ", "; for example, if the following lines are part of the HTTP header:
	accept: */*; q=0.1 accept: text/html accept: image/jpeg
	then the HTTP_ACCEPT variable will have a value of: */*; q=0.1, text/html, image/jpeg
PATH_INFO	Additional path information, as given by the client. This comprises the trailing part of the URL after the script name but before the query string (if any).
QUERY_STRING	The information which follows the ? in the URL that referenced this script.
REMOTE_ADDR	The IP address of the client.
REMOTE_HOST	The hostname of the client.

REMOTE_USER	This contains the username supplied by the client and authenticated by the server.
REQUEST_METHOD String	The HTTP request method.
SERVER_NAME	The server's hostname (or IP address) as it should appear in self-referencing URLs.

■■■■

Enter VB and ISAPI

Now that you have a sense of how data access works, I'll move on to how you can integrate VB 4.0 applications into your server using the Internet Server Application Programming Interface (ISAPI). It was codeveloped by Microsoft and Process Software Corporation in 1995 to improve the performance of Windows EXE files used as CGI scripts. In short, ISAPI lets Windows programmers write their CGI scripts as in-process DLLs. The DLLs are loaded into the same address space as the server, and the entry points are called by their actual address, not by going through an import library and creating a new process. This method is much faster than loading an EXE file, not only because a DLL stays loaded in memory, but because ISAPI DLLs reside in the same address space as MIIS. Keep in mind that OLE Automation makes ISAPI technology available to any OLE Automation object, which could be created with tools other than VB4 (such as VC++). The key to calling methods in OLE Automation servers as your CGI interface is the OLEISAPI.DLL, written in whole or in part by David Stutz, one of the founding fathers of OLE technology at Microsoft. OLEISAPI.DLL is an ISAPI-based DLL that lets you call OLE methods as CGI programs which execute and return HTML text to the client. OLEISAPI.DLL comes standard with MIIS.

But why use OLE Automation with VB when you can just access data directly using the Internet Database Connector? It's for the same reason there are Access programmers and Visual Basic programmers. With the IDC you can read and write to a database. But tapping VB through OLE Automation gives you much more capability. What if you want a counter on your page? What if you need to access other local or remote objects to get information that's not in your database? What if you want to send email to someone? There are many reasons for using OLEISAPI, and you should evaluate both OLEISAPI and IDC and understand what they can do. This way, you will be prepared to decide what to use when a real-world solution is called for.

Microsoft included a sample program to show how OLEISAPI works, but it wasn't particularly interesting. In lieu of that, I created an OLE server called CFOISAPI—which consists of CFOISAPI.VBP, CFOISAPI.BAS, and CFOISAPI.CLS—that I will show you here for demonstration purposes.

OLEISAPI-callable methods must take two string arguments. The first argument is the request data passed from the server. The second argument is a response string—an HTML reply from your application created by your method. Consider this object definition, which could be called using OLEISAPI.DLL:

```
DLL Name:        OLETEST.DLL
Class Name:      TestClass


Public Sub Method_Get (Request As String, Response As String)
    Response = "Content-Type: text/html" & vbCrLf & vbCrLf & _
        "<html><head><title>" & _
        "<H1>Here is the request " & "string you sent: " & "</H1>" & _
        Request & vbCrlf & "</body></html>"
End Sub
```

Within your HTML form, you might call this method like this:

```
<form
action="oleisapi.dll/OLETEST.TestClass.Method_Get" method="POST">
First Name: <input name="FirstName"><p>
Last Name: <input name="LastName"><p>
<input type="submit" value="Click here">
</form>
```

This is a simple form with a Submit button and two text boxes, one for the first name and one for the last name. When the user clicks the button, the server accesses OLEISAPI.DLL and passes OLETEST.TestClass.Method_Get.

The <form ...> tag defines the action that occurs when you click the Submit button like this:

```
<form action = "[full path to oleisapi.dll]/ [DLL Name].[Class Name].[Method]"
    method = "[Access method: either POST or GET]">
```

The request is passed as a string:

```
[Field1]=[Value1]&[Field2]=[Value2]…
```

Each field/value pair is separated with an ampersand character. Here is an example:

```
FirstName=Joe&LastName=Schmoe
```

Within the fields themselves, spaces are encoded into plus signs. So the string:

```
Joe Schmoe
```

becomes:

```
Joe+Schmoe
```

Clearly then, before you can access this data in your class you need to parse the request string into field/value pairs. I wrote a routine called ParseParameters (included in CFOSAPI.CLS) that does exactly that (see Figure 9.5). ParseParameters requires these declarations in your class:

```
Private Type ParameterType
    Parameter As String
    Data As String
End Type


Dim Pairs()  As ParameterType
Dim NumPairs As Integer
```

■■■■■■ **Figure 9.5** The ParseParameters routine copies all of the field/value pairs specified by the client into a Pairs array, where they can be easily accessed. The szReplaceString function is shown because it is called by ParseParameters.

```
Sub ParseParameters(szRequest As String)


        Dim nPos                As Integer
        Dim szTemp              As String
```

```
Dim szNextParam          As String
'Replace the plusses with spaces
szTemp = szReplaceString(szRequest, "+", " ")
NumPairs = 0
Do
        nPos = InStr(szTemp, "&")
        If nPos Then
                NumPairs = NumPairs + 1
                ReDim Preserve Pairs(1 To NumPairs)
                szNextParam = Left$(szTemp, nPos - 1)
                szTemp = Mid$(szTemp, nPos + 1)
                nPos = InStr(szNextParam, "=")
                If nPos Then
                        Pairs(NumPairs).Parameter = _
                                Left$(szNextParam, nPos - 1)
                        Pairs(NumPairs).Data = _
                                Mid$(szNextParam, nPos + 1)
                Else
                        Exit Do
                End If
        Else
                If Len(szTemp) Then
                        NumPairs = NumPairs + 1
                        ReDim Preserve Pairs(1 To NumPairs)
                        nPos = InStr(szTemp, "=")
                        If nPos Then
                                Pairs(NumPairs).Parameter = _
                                        Left$(szTemp, nPos - 1)
                                Pairs(NumPairs).Data = __
                                        Mid$(szTemp, nPos + 1)
                        End If
                End If
                Exit Do
        End If
```

```
        Loop
End Sub


Function szReplaceString(szOriginal As String, szFind As String, _
szReplace As String)
        Dim szTemp  As String
        Dim nPos        As Integer
        szTemp = szOriginal
        Do
                nPos = InStr(szTemp, szFind)
                If nPos Then
                        szTemp = Left$(szTemp, nPos - 1) & _
                            szReplace & Mid$(szTemp, nPos + Len(szFind))
                Else
                        Exit Do
                End If
        Loop
        szReplaceString = szTemp
End Function
```

Simply call ParseParameters passing the request string and all the Field/Value pairs are copied into the Pairs array. The NumPairs member contains the number of fields.

Consider this practical example. Let's say that you have a form with three text fields on it: Name, EmailAddress, and PhoneNumber. You use ParseParameters to extract these three pieces of data when the Method_Get method is invoked (see Figure 9.6).

Once you have the data from the form, you can run a query against a database and return the results in the Response string. I'll skip over the database part now and show you the next piece of what I consider to be required code for any OLEISAPI-aware object.

■■■■■ **Figure 9.6** Call ParseParameters from within your OLE server. This code retrieves all the parameters sent by the client as discrete strings via the Pairs array.

```
Public Sub Method_Get (Request As String, Response As _          String)
        Dim szName       As String
        Dim szEmail      As String
        Dim szPhone      As String
        Dim szReply      As String
        Dim nIndex       As Integer
        'Copy the returned data into the Pairs array
        ParseParameters Request
        'Set local variables
        For nIndex = 1 to NumPairs
                Select Case UCase$(Pairs(nIndex).Parameter)
                    Case "NAME"
                        szName = Pairs(nIndex).Data
                    Case "EMAILADDRESS"
                        szEmail = Pairs(nIndex).Data
                    Case "PHONENUMBER"
                        szPhone = Pairs(nIndex).Data
                End Select
        Next
        'Create a reply message
        szReply = "Hello, " & szName & "! If we need to " & _
        "contact you we'll either reach you by phone " & _
        "at " & szPhone & " or by email at " & szEmail
        'Send the reply
        Response = "Content-Type: text/html" & _
            vbCrLf & vbCrLf & "<html><head><title>" & _
                szReply & "</body></html>"
End Sub
```

StandardPage is a function that returns a string containing the HTML for a standard document. In other words, you can set up a template for your pages so they all have the same look and feel. Instead of having to custom program the HTML for each and every page, you can just create the critical elements with code, and let the StandardPage routine format it to your standard using this syntax:

```
HTML$ = StandardPage(Title$, TextBody$[, Description$] _
    [, Footer$][, BackgroundImage] [, LogoImage][, LogoURL])
```

The first two arguments (Title$ and TextBody$) are required. All the other arguments are optional. Keep in mind that you can alter StandardPage to suit your needs.

Title$ is the title of the page. This is usually displayed on the TitleBar of the web browser and also at the top of the page. TextBody$ designates the main content of the page—it should be already encoded as HTML text. Description$ is a short description of the contents of the page that will appear at the top under the title. Footer$ is an HTML string that appears at the very bottom of the page (copyright information, text links, things like that). BackgroundImage is the name of an image file that will be used as the background. This should be a small image (maximum of 50 × 50 pixels) because it gets tiled automatically by the web browser. LogoImage is another small bitmap that you can use as a logo. It appears in the upper left-hand corner of the page. If you specify a URL following the LogoImage argument (LogoURL), then clicking on that image will jump to the site at the specified URL. Figure 9.7 shows an HTML page returned by the code in Figure 9.8. The StandardPage function itself is listed in Figure 9.9.

OLEISAPI And Remote Servers

The folks at Microsoft told me that you can't access remote objects with OLEISAPI as of this writing, but this feature may be added in the future. You can, however, create a remote object in your local OLEISAPI object to access the remote object indirectly. For example, consider this object definition:

```
DLL Name:     OLETEST.DLL
Class Name:   TestClass
```

```
Private RemoteObject As New RemoteClass

Public Sub Method_Get (Request As String, Response As String)
   'Access the remote object here and 'return the results
   Response = RemoteObject.GetResults (...)
End Sub
```

Although there is no direct support, you can use your VB class to access the remote object.

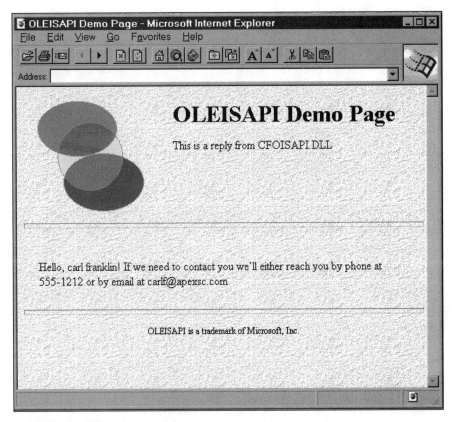

■■■■■ **Figure 9.7** Search results. Results of the sample form shown in Figure 9.8. Here is what the output might look like if the user had entered "A*" for the search term.

■■■■■■■■ **Listing 9.8** The StandardPage function returns the HTML text for a standard web page that contains all the specified elements. The author encourages modification of this function to fit your web page design criteria. This example shows how to call StandardPage.

```
Public Sub Method_Get(Request As String, Response As _ String)
        Dim szName      As String
        Dim szEmail     As String
        Dim szPhone     As String
        Dim szTitle     As String
        Dim szBody      As String
        Dim szDescrip   As String
        Dim szFooter    As String
        Dim nIndex      As Integer
        'Copy the returned data into the Pairs array
        ParseParameters Request
        'Set local variables
        For nIndex = 1 To NumPairs
            Select Case UCase$(Pairs(nIndex).Parameter)
                Case "NAME"
                    szName = Pairs(nIndex).Data
                Case "EMAILADDRESS"
                    szEmail = Pairs(nIndex).Data
                Case "PHONENUMBER"
                    szPhone = Pairs(nIndex).Data
            End Select
        Next
        'Create the title
        szTitle = "OLEISAPI Demo Page"
        'Create a reply message
        szBody = "Hello, " & szName & "! If we need to _
            contact " & "you we'll either reach you by phone_
            at " & szPhone & " or by email at " & szEmail
        'Now the footer.
```

```
        szFooter = "<center><font size=1>OLEISAPI is a " & _
                "trademark of Microsoft, Inc.</font " & _
                    "size=1></center>"
        'Create the description
        szDescrip = "This is a reply from CFOISAPI.DLL"
        'Send the reply
        Response = StandardPage(szTitle, szBody, szDescrip,_
            szFooter, "lyellow.gif", "logo.gif", _
                "http://my.url.com")
End Sub
```

Figure 9.9 The StandardPage function returns the HTML text for a standard web page that contains all the specified elements. You can modify this function to fit your web page design criteria.

```
Function StandardPage( _
        szTitle As String, _
        szBodyText As String, _
        Optional Description As Variant, _
        Optional Footer As Variant, _
        Optional BackgroundImage As Variant, _
        Optional LogoImage As Variant, _
        Optional LogoURL As Variant) As String
            'This is just a work string used internally
            Dim szWorking   As String
            'Flags for the optional arguments
            Dim nBackGroundImage    As Integer
            Dim nLogoImage          As Integer
            Dim nLogoURL            As Integer
            Dim nDescription        As Integer
            'Set the argument flags
```

```
nBackGroundImage = Not IsMissing(BackgroundImage)

nLogoImage = Not IsMissing(LogoImage)

nLogoURL = Not IsMissing(LogoURL)

nDescription = Not IsMissing(Description)

'Start with the HTML header and title

szWorking = "Content-Type: text/html" & vbCrLf & vbCrLf _

        & "<html><head><title>" & szTitle & "</title><body"

'Use background bitmap?

If nBackGroundImage Then

        szWorking = szWorking & " background =" & _

                BackgroundImage & ">"

Else

        szWorking = szWorking & ">"

End If

'Logo image?

If nLogoImage Then

        's there a link in the image?

        If nLogoURL Then

                szWorking = szWorking & "<a href=" & LogoURL & ">"

        End If

        'Here's the image itself

        szWorking = szWorking & "<img src=" & _

                LogoImage & " align=left " & _

                "hspace=20 border=0>"

        'If there's a link then close the anchor.

        If nLogoURL Then

                szWorking = szWorking & "</a>"

        End If

End If

'Display the title

szWorking = szWorking & "<H1>" & szTitle & "</H1>"

'Display the description text

If nDescription Then
```

```
            szWorking = szWorking & Description
        End If
        'Close off the top section
        szWorking = szWorking & "</head><br clear = left><hr size=7>"
        'Display the content and the footer
        szWorking = szWorking & "<DL><DD>" & szBodyText & "</DL><p>" _
            & "<hr size=7><p>" & Footer & "</body>"
        'Return the working copy
        StandardPage = szWorking
End Function
```

Epilogue

In case you couldn't tell, I'm impressed with the technology in MS Internet
Information Server. These tools will make creating a stellar web site a real pleasure.
Performance under a heavy load remains to be seen. I had only seen the second
beta release as of this writing, so I won't comment on the actual performance of
MIIS until I see the release version, as anything else would be unfair.

Add all this up, and your worries about doing powerful CGI scripting should be
long gone. Gary Wisniewski and I are incorporating MIIS into Carl & Gary's Visual
Basic Home Page using these technologies. From what I've seen so far, there is enor-
mous potential for possibilities—some yet to be imagined.

WRITING CUSTOM WINSOCK CLIENT/SERVER APPLICATIONS

Introduction

The code used in this chapter will probably prove to be the most useful to you. It was certainly the most fun for me to write. I got to exploit the features of object-oriented Visual Basic 4.0 to create some code that you can drop into your VB4 applications to write true client/server systems that use the Internet. If you are not familiar with working with objects in Visual Basic 4.0, read Chapter 7 of the *Visual Basic 4.0 Programmer's Guide*, Introduction to Objects.

Note that this chapter does not cover Remote OLE. If you have the Enterprise edition of Visual Basic 4.0 you could use distributed OLE objects to communicate with a server as use the code I am presenting here. The distributed model is more robust than my code, but the enterprise edition currently retails for $999.00, whereas this book cost you less than fifty bucks. Besides, my implementation is simple and straight ahead, and since it is all good code, it is significantly low on resources.

In short, the code presented in this chapter is in two parts. There is a server application that you can use as a starting point for your server application. The second half of the code is an Internet client object. Yes, that's right, an OLE object. It is an OLE automation server that you can use in a Visual Basic, Delphi, Access, or other OLE platform to access and communicate with your server application.

I wrote this chapter because creating remote OLE servers is not as seamless in Visual Basic 4.0 as I think it should be. The premise here is simple. You create an instance of my Winsock OLE class in your VB app. The object connects you to a server application via WinSock (using DSSOCK.OCX). You then send the server commands and data, and the server returns data back to you. Not only that, but the server can send you commands and data without you having to ask for it. Since it is all written in VB 4.0, you can create your own custom OLE objects that accept custom commands (with data) that you specify. On the Internet server side, you can respond to those commands and data, process them, and send back response codes and data to the client.

Now let me illuminate the possibilities here. You have a web site. You're running Microsoft Internet Information Server. You use OLEISAPI to access your custom Winsock object, which then connects to any machine on the Internet which is running your server application. Now you are effectively routing web page requests from your web server to a machine in another location, which has your data on it.

You could also write your own client/server systems using this method. You have at your disposal everything that the web has, such as the ability to send text and graphics through the Internet, and more. The only thing that's missing is a protocol, and that's exactly what this code gives you.

Remember that when you write your own system you control both sides, client and server. What if you could define a set of commands that are sent from the client to the server? The server interprets the commands and sends back data. This is exactly the functionality which this code provides, namely the ability to connect to and communicate using commands that you define at a higher level than the sending and receiving of raw data.

The CFSockClient
OLE Automation DLL

CFSockClient is an OLE DLL written in Visual Basic 4.0. As is, it contains enough properties and methods to get you connecting to an Internet server with security, downloading, and uploading files, as well as receiving unsolicited files (those that you do not ask for).

There are three classes in this DLL: CFSockClient, CFData, and CFEvent. CFData and CFEvent are members of CFSockClient. Figure 10.1 shows the hierarchy.

The CFSockClient class is the interface to your VB4 application. It contains all of the properties and methods for communicating with the server, including binary file transfers.

The CFData class is a wrapper for a two-dimensional string array. An object created from the CFData class can be treated like an array and is thus used to hold data transferred between client and server.

The CFEvent class provides a means for the server to send you unsolicited commands and data. Its Command method is a public sub that is fired whenever your client receives a command from the server. More on this later.

CFData is a public, multiuse class. Its sole purpose is to wrap a two-dimensional string array used as data passed between client and server. The definition of this class is shown in Figure 10.2. It acts just like an array, but has the benefit of being a class. The CFSockClient class contains a CFData class member called Data.

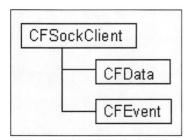

▬▬▬▬ **Figure 10.1** The CFSockClient class hierarchy.

■■■■■■ **Figure 10.2** The CFData class.

Property	Data Type	Description
Cols	Long	Number of Columns
Rows	Long	Number of Rows
DataSet()	String	Two dimensional string property

Method	Description
Resize	Resizes the object given a number of rows and columns

■■■■■■

It is fitting to explain the CFData class first, since CFData is a member of CFSockClient. CFData is easy to understand since it's just a wrapper for a two-dimensional array. You may find it useful for many other applications, not just Internet programming. In the interest of keeping you, the reader, awake through all of this, let's jump right into some sample code. Take a look at the code in Figure 10.3.

In this example, first a new object (MyData) is created. Next, the Resize method allocates two rows and three columns. Inside the CFData class a two-dimensional string array called Data_Set is created. Here is the code for the Resize method in the CFData class:

```
Public Sub Resize(lRows As Long, lCols As Long)

    On Error Resume Next
    ReDim Data_Set(1 To lRows, 1 To lCols) As String

End Sub
```

The statement On Error Resume Next is used to trap an error in case a zero is passed as a row or a column, or a number too large meaning that there isn't enough memory. To determine if an error occurred, check the Rows and Cols properties after invoking the Resize method. The Rows and Cols property handlers use the Ubound function to retrieve the upper boundaries of the array, which will always give you the correct number. Here is the Get code for the Rows property:

```
Public Property Get Rows() As Long


    On Error Resume Next
    Rows = UBound(Data_Set, 1)


End Property
```

Anytime you read the Rows property, this function is called, which gets the upper boundary of the internal Data_Set array's first dimension, or the number of rows.

■■■■ **Figure 10.3** An example use of the CFSockClient class.

```
'-- Create an object from the CFData class
Dim MyData As New CFData


'-- Resize it to 2 rows and 3 columns
MyData.Resize 2, 3


'-- Set row 1, column 1 to "Hello"
MyData.DataSet(1,1) = "Hello"


'-- Set row 2, column 3 to "Good-bye"
MyData.DataSet(2,3) = "Good-bye"


'-- Display the contents of row 1, column 1 in the debug window
Debug.Print MyData.DataSet(1,1)
```

The Rows and Cols property are both read-only, meaning that you cannot set them yourself. The only way to set the number of rows and columns is with the Resize method.

Figure 10.4 shows CFSockClient, the top-level class. An object of this type represents the client half of a client/server application. Essentially, the client application that makes up the OLE server DLL consists of a form with a DSSOCK.OCX control on it, the CFSockClient public class, and the CFData class. Think of CFSockClient like DSSOCK, except that there are higher level commands to communicate real information, not just raw data.

CFSockClient lets you connect with a name and password using the UserName and Password properties. On the server side, you can use the name and password to verify the user against a database, or whatever, simply pass back "OK" to accept the connection and "NO" to not accept it.

Once connected you can send data back and forth using the aforementioned CFData class, essentially a two-dimensional array. You can also send and receive files. The client object and the code on the server side sweat the details of managing connections and getting the data across. All you have to do is respond to the commands.

■■■■■■ **Figure 10.4** The CFSockClient class.

Property	Data Type	Description
SendBlockSize	Integer	Largest possible chunk of transmitted data.
RecvBlockSize	Integer	Largest possible chunk of received data.
CommandTimeout	Integer	Number of seconds before time out when sending commands.
Connected	Integer	True if connected, False if not
Data	CFData (class)	See CFData below
DataSize	Long	Maximum size of data packet

DownloadDir	String	Destination path for downloaded files
ErrorNum	Long	Error number (when an error occurs)
ErrorDesc	String	Description of error, if any
Event	CFEvent (class)	Provides a Command event for server to call.
LocalName	String	Local machine name
LocalDotAddr	String	Local machine IP address
Password	String	Password used to connect to server
ServerName	String	Server machine name
ServerDotAddr	String	Server IP address
ServerPort	Long	Port connected to on server
UserName	String	Username used to connect to server

Method	Description
Connect	Connects you to a server
Disconnect	Disconnects from server
GetFile	Gets a file from the server
RegisterEventObject	Registers a CFEvent object within your local app with CFSockClient
SendCommand	Sends a command to the server
SendFile	Sends a file to the server

Event	Description
Event.Command	Fired when the server sends you an unsolicited command. A couple lines of code is necessary to get this functionality.

You can send files to the server with the SendFile method, download a file with the GetFile method, and handle the receipt of unsolicited files using the Command method. The Command method provides a callback (or an event) for the client object.

But why stop there? The source is included, and I encourage you to expand the code to accommodate your own custom commands. What I consider essential functions are already there: logging on with security, sending and receiving data, and sending and receiving files. Use it as a starting point for your own megadistributed system. Later in this chapter, I will discuss the built-in ODBC code, which lets you access a database at the Internet server from the client machine using CFSockClient.

The CFSockClient Client/Server model

Figure 10.5 shows the client/server model used by CFSockClient. On the client side, your Visual Basic application communicates through the CFSockClient OLE object, which exists outside of your application. The CFSockCLient object contains a DSSOCK OLE control, which communicates via Windows Sockets through the network to the server side.

The server application contains the server (CFServer) code, which consists of a form, a CFData class module, and two code modules. The form contains four DSSOCK OLE controls. You can optionally just use the server code as it is. The project runs by itself; there is no need to modify it as is, unless you want to incorporate it into an existing application. If you are starting from scratch, use the cfserver.VBP project as a starting point and build it up.

You might be wondering why I chose to not use an OLE server for the Internet server side. I considered it, but decided against it because an OLE Server is useful only when more than one application on the local machine is going to use it. Since you would not normally run more than one Internet host application on a single machine, there is really no need for the extra overhead. You want your server to be as fast as possible to be able to handle lots of clients!

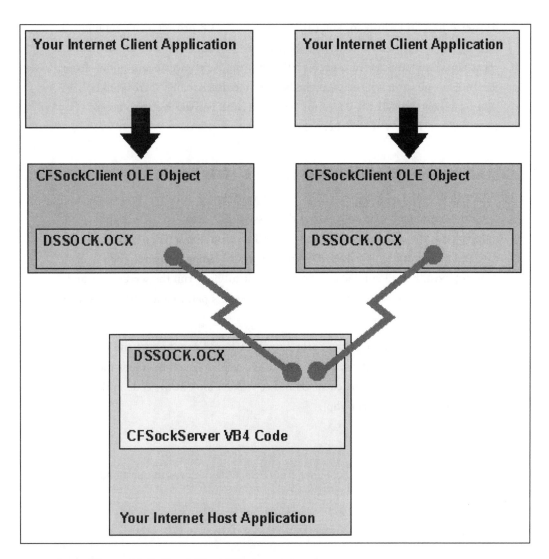

Figure 10.5 The CFSockClient model.

Registering the CFSockClient Object on Your Computer

Before you can use the CFSockClient OLE server, it must be registered. If you are just going to mess around with it and maybe even modify it, you don't have to register it as a DLL. Instead, you can register it as a VB project as it's running. To do this, run a separate instance of VB4 just for CFSockClient. The project name is client.vbp. From another instance of VB, select the References menu option from the Tools menu. You will see near the bottom the description "Carl Franklin's VB Winsock client." Select the checkbox next to it, and you are ready to access CFSockClient from Visual Basic.

Using a CFSockClient Object

Take a look at the code for this hypothetical application. A connection is made using the username "john smith" and the password "password". Once connected, it downloads the daily news file (DailyNews.Txt) from the server's "news" directory and puts it on the Windows Desktop for your reading pleasure. The server does not exist, but all you have to do to bring it to life is run the server code and place the file in a news subdirectory off of the server's path. Figure 10.6 shows an example of this.

You could place this code in the Form_Load of a brand new project and have a complete Internet application. The interface is deceptively simple (that's the idea). The real work is done by the client DLL. Let's take a look at the code in the CFSockClient project (client.vbp).

■■■■■■ **Figure 10.6** Hypothetical usage of CFSockClient class to download daily news.

```
'-- Create a CFSockClient object
Dim MyClient As New CFSockClient


'-- Set the Server's name and the app's port number
MyClient.ServerName = "cf.squiggy.com"
MyClient.ServerPort = 1098
```

```
'-- Specify your username and password
MyClient.UserName = "john smith"
MyClient.Password = "password"


'-- Try to connect by invoking the Connect method.
MyClient.Connect


'-- Could we connect?
If MyClient.ErrorNum Then
    '-- Something went wrong. Display an error.
    MsgBox MyClient.ErrorDesc
Else
    '-- We've connected.
    '-- Download the file "DailyNews.Txt" and
    '   put it on the Windows 95 desktop.
    MyClient.GetFile "\news\DailyNews.Txt", "c:\windows\desktop\DailyNews.Txt"


    '-- Did an error occur?
    If MyClient.ErrorNum Then
        MsgBox MyClient.ErrorDesc, vbExclamation, App.Title
    End If


    '-- Disconnect from the server
    MyClient.Disconnect
End If
```

Inside the CFSockClient OLE Server

The CFSockClient project consists of five files:

cfclient.frm   Form containing a DSSOCK OLE control

cfclient.cls   The CFSockClient class exposed via OLE

cfdata.cls   The data class member of CFSockClient

cfclient.bas   Contains globals and Sub Main for the project

dssock.bas   Contains globals and constants for DSSOCK

The project starts with Sub Main in cfsock.bas. All OLE servers have to start with Sub Main. Our Sub Main simply loads the main form, frmClient (see Figure 10.7). Yes, it's very small and has nothing on it but two DSSOCK controls, but that's okay because you never see it. In fact, the only reason you need a form at all is because Visual Basic does not support controls without forms. You must have a form to use a custom control. You can use OLE automation objects without a form, however. Even if you could use DSSOCK without a form, a window would have to be created somewhere so the control can receive messages and process events. But, be that as it may, there it is. (I've always wanted to say that.)

The first DSSOCK control's name is frmClient.dsSocket1. It uses all of the default DSSOCK property settings except for DataSize, which is upped to 8192 for better throughput. You can adjust this at runtime with the CFSockClient object's RecvBlockSize property, which directly maps to the DSSOCK's DataSize property.

■■■■■ **Figure 10.7** The frmClient form in CFSockClient.

There might be some confusion between the SendBlockSize property and the RecvBlockSize property. The RecvBlockSize property is a direct wrapper for DSSOCK's DataSize property, which controls the maximum number of bytes passed to you via DSSOCK's Receive event. If your app has received 20,000 bytes, and the DataSize is 4,000, then the Receive event could fire as few as five times. If the DataSize is 10,000, then it would be possible for the Receive event to fire only twice. DataSize only represents the maximum size of data. The underlying network really decides how big these chunks of data will be.

The SendBlockSize property is a setting used within the code of the CFSockClient class. When sending data to the server, SendBlockSize is the size of each transmitted chunk of data. If the Data object is populated with 22,000 bytes of data, and SendBlockSize is set to 4,000, then six chunks will be sent. The first five chunks will be 4,000 bytes, and the last chunk will be 2,000 bytes.

Figure 10.8 shows the declarations section of the CFSockData class. The variables that are defined as Public are properties that do not require "Get" and "Let" code. In other words, they are just dynamic values. No action has to be taken when they are set or read. The variables that are created with Dim and the error constants are module-level variables, the same as with a form or a code module.

■■■■■■ **Figure 10.8** CFSockClient declarations section.

```
'-- CFSockClient OLE Class
Option Explicit


#If Win32 Then
    Private Declare Function GetWindowsDirectory Lib "kernel32" Alias _
"GetWindowsDirectoryA" (ByVal lpBuffer As String, ByVal nSize As Long) As Long
#Else
    Private Declare Function GetWindowsDirectory Lib "Kernel" (ByVal _
lpBuffer As String, ByVal nSize As Integer) As Integer
#End If


'-- Windows directory
```

```
Private szWindowsDir    As String


'------------ Public flat Properties and classes -----


'-- This object becomes a means for firing an event at the
'   OLE client application for processing of unsolicited events
'   by the OLE client app.
Public Event As Object


'-- The CFData class wraps a 2-dimensional array for easy
'   data transportation
Public Data As New CFData


'-- Maximum size of outgoing packets. (default = 8K)
Public SendBlockSize As Integer


'-- The Server's Port
Public ServerPort As Long


'-- If RaiseErrors is False (default), then Err is not
'   raised in the client program. If RaiseErrors
'   is True, then Err is raised requiring On Error.
'   Either way, ErrorNum and ErrorDesc will be set.
Public RaiseErrors As Integer


'-- Error Code
Public ErrorNum As Long


'-- Error message
Public ErrorDesc As String


'-- UserName and Password are used to connect to the server app
```

```
'    and are not required to make a socket connection. They are
'    used to identify the client user to the server system. If they
'    are not recognized by the server, the connection will close.
Public UserName As String
Public Password As String


'-- CommandTimeout is the number of seconds to wait after sending
'    a command for a response from the server. The default is 0
'    which means that the client waits forever.
Public CommandTimeout As Long


'------------ Internal Variables -------------------------


'-- Host Name (ex: www.apexsc.com)
Private szHostName As String


'-- Internal Dot Address (ex: 199.257.100.2)
Private szDotAddr As String
```

The statement, Public Data As New CFData, makes the Data object a dependent of the CFSockClient object. Figure 10.9 shows an example of how to access the Data object.

Initialization

When the CFSockClient object is created the Class_Initialize procedure executes. This is where the default values are set. Figure 10.10 shows this code.

The last statement, Set gClientObj = Me, sets a global object variable to the current object, that way the members of the object (namely the Data object) can be accessed from anywhere in the project. Since all the data transfer occurs on the form frmClient, there must be a way for the client form to read and write to the Data object.

Figure 10.9 Accessing the Data object of a CFSockClient class.

```
'-- Create a new CFSockClient object
Dim MyClient As New CFSockClient

'-- Allocate one row and one column in the CFData member
MyClient.Data.Resize 1, 1

'-- Assign a string to this field
MyClient.Data.DataSet(1,1) =  "Hello There"
```

Figure 10.10 CFSockClient initialization code.

```
Private Sub Class_Initialize()

    RecvBlockSize = 8192
    SendBlockSize = 8192

    #If Windows95 Then
        DownloadDir = "C:\WINDOWS\DESKTOP\"
    #End If

    Set gClientObj = Me

End Sub
```

Connecting to the Server

The Connect method connects to the server, the address and port of which must be specified in the ServerName or ServerDotAddr and ServerPort properties. Figure 10.11 shows the code for the Connect method.

■■■■ **Figure 10.11** The Connect method of the CFSockClient class.

```
Public Sub Connect()
    '-- This function connects to a CFServer application

    Dim szAddress    As String

    '-- Initialize the errors
    ErrorNum = 0
    ErrorDesc = ""

    '-- Name specified?
    If Len(szHostName) = 0 Then
        If Len(szDotAddr) = 0 Then
            '-- Neither type of address specified. Error out.
            ErrorNum = vbObjectError + ERR_NOADDRESS
            ErrorDesc = "The server's host name or dot address was " _
                    & "not specified when trying to connect."
            RaiseErr
            Exit Sub
        Else
            szAddress = szDotAddr
        End If
    Else
        szAddress = szHostName
    End If

    '-- Port specified?
    If ServerPort = 0 Then
```

```
    -- No port specified. Error out.
    ErrorNum = vbObjectError + ERR_NOPORT
    ErrorDesc = "The server's port was not specified when trying to connect."
    RaiseErr
    Exit Sub
End If


'-- Attempt to connect.
If SocketConnect(frmClient.dsSocket1, ServerPort, szAddress, (CommandTimeout)) Then
    ErrorNum = vbObjectError + ERR_WINSOCK
    ErrorDesc = "DSSOCK Error" & Str$(Err) & ": " & Error
    RaiseErr
    Exit Sub
End If


'-- Verify the username and password. The server may or may not be
'   using security. If not, then any values are accepted.
Data.Resize 1, 2
Data.DataSet(1, 1) = UserName
Data.DataSet(1, 2) = Password


SendCommand "LOGIN"


If Data.DataSet(1, 1) = "NO" Then
    '-- The user was not allowed access to the system.
    ErrorNum = vbObjectError + ERR_BADUSERPASS
    ErrorDesc = "Your username and password were not accepted " _
        & "by the host. Access denied."
    RaiseErr
End If


End Sub
```

The first two blocks of code (shown separately in Figure 10.12) verify that the port is specified, and that either a remote name or IP address is specified. If one of these conditions are not met, either the NO_ADDRESS or NO_PORT errors are returned.

▬▬▬▬▬ **Figure 10.12** Connect method. The server name and port number are verified.

```
'-- Name specified?
    If Len(szHostName) = 0 Then
        If Len(szDotAddr) = 0 Then
            '-- Neither type of address specified. Error out.
            ErrorNum = vbObjectError + ERR_NOADDRESS
            ErrorDesc = "The server's host name or dot address was " _
                & "not specified when trying to connect."
            RaiseErr
            Exit Sub
        Else
            szAddress = szDotAddr
        End If
    Else
        szAddress = szHostName
    End If


    '-- Port specified?
    If ServerPort = 0 Then
        '-- No port specified. Error out.
        ErrorNum = vbObjectError + ERR_NOPORT
        ErrorDesc = "The server's port was not specified when trying to connect."
        RaiseErr
        Exit Sub
    End If
```

Since this is an OLE server, I figure the best approach for error handling is for the client to poll for errors. By polling, I mean that after you send a command or invoke a method, check the ErrorNum property. If ErrorNum is nonzero then the ErrorDesc will contain a description of the error. Errors in the DSSOCK control are also passed through this way.

Next, an attempt is made to connect to the server by calling SocketConnect. If the connection is not made then CFSockClient raises an error.

The next block of code (shown separately in Figure 10.13) is a good first example of sending a command with data to the server. The LOGIN command, as defined by both client and server, logs the client into the server system. Optionally, the server can verify the client and refuse connection if the UserName and/or password are invalid. The UserName and Password specified here exist only for access to your server. If you wish to grant access to everyone, you do not need to specify them. The LOGIN command accepts one row and two columns of data, namely the UserName, and Password.

To set this data before sending the command, the Resize method is invoked, and the strings are assigned to the DataSet array property. SendCommand is an internal routine that actually sends the command and the data. We'll look at this routine shortly.

■■■■■■ **Figure 10.13** Sending the LOGIN command to the Internet server.

```
'-- Verify the username and password. The server may or may not be
'   using security. If not, then any values are accepted.
Data.Resize 1, 2
Data.DataSet(1, 1) = UserName
Data.DataSet(1, 2) = Password
SendCommand "LOGIN"
```

After the SendCommand routine returns, the Data object will be filled and sized with the data sent back from the server, if any. If the connection is refused by the server, then the server will send back the word "NO", otherwise it will send "OK". Either way, the data is sent in one row and one column. A simple test for the word "NO" determines if we have permission or not. This little piece of code is broken out in Figure 10.14.

Sending Data to the Server

SendCommand is a method of the CFSockClient class. It lets you send a command to the server along with a two-dimensional array of data via the Data object member. This is where the real data transfer protocol is at work. Figure 10.15 shows the SendCommand Method.

The first thing that happens in SendCommand is that the command is identified for documentation purposes. It is first converted to uppercase, and then a Select Case statement is executed. This Select Case really is for documentation, but it's nice to have if you need to do any special processing at the OLE server before a command and data are sent.

The variable gnCommandReturned is set True in the DSSOCK control's Receive event, after a response is received from the server and data has been collected. In this portion of the code, the gnCommandReturned variable is set False.

▬▬▬▬ **Figure 10.14** Testing to see if the server refused your connection.

```
If Data.DataSet(1, 1) = "NO" Then
    '-- The user was not allowed access to the system.
    Me.ErrorNum = vbObjectError + ERR_BADUSERPASS
    ErrorDesc = "Your username and password were not accepted by _
        the host. Access denied."
End If
```

■■■■■■■■ **Figure 10.15** The SendCommand property of the CFSockClient class.

```
Public Sub SendCommand(szCmd As String)
'-- The SendCommand method sends a command string along with the contents
'   of the Data object to the server.

    Dim DoneTime
    Dim szSendMe As String
    Dim lCol As Long
    Dim lRow As Long


    '-- Convert the command to uppercase
    szCmd = UCase$(szCmd)


    '-- What command is being issued? (for documentation only)
    Select Case szCmd
        Case "LOGIN"
            '-- 1,1 = Username
            '   2,1 = Password
        Case "SENDFILE"
            '-- 1,1 = File Name (sans path)
            '   2,1 = File Size (in bytes)
            '   3,1 = File Type
            '           0 = Binary (default)
            '          -1 = Text (one line per row)
            '   4,1 through ?,1 = Data
        Case "GETFILE"
            '-- 1,1 = File Name (full path)
            '   2,1 = File Type
            '           0 = Binary (default)
            '          -1 = Text (one line per row)
    End Select


    '-- Set the internal flag for returned command.
```

```
gnCommandReturned = False


'-- Generate the string(s) to send


'-- The header consists of the command, followed by the number of rows
'   and number of columns in the data set.
szSendMe = Format$(szCmd, "@@@@@@@@@@") _
    & Format$(Trim$(Str$(Data.Rows)), "@@@@@") _
    & Format$(Trim$(Str$(Data.Cols)), "@@@@@")


'-- For each field or cell, send the size of the field (5) followed by
'   the data itself.
For lRow = 1 To Data.Rows
    For lCol = 1 To Data.Cols
        szSendMe = szSendMe _
          & Format$(LTrim$(Str$(Len(Data.DataSet(lRow, lCol)))), "@@@@@") _
          & Data.DataSet(lRow, lCol)
    Next
    '-- If the string is getting too big, send what we've got
    If Len(szSendMe) >= SendBlockSize Then
        If gnDebugMode Then
            Debug.Print "Sending" & Str$(Len(szSendMe)) & " bytes"
        End If
        SendData szSendMe
        DoEvents
        szSendMe = ""
    End If
Next


'-- If there is data to send, send it.
If Len(szSendMe) Then
    If gnDebugMode Then
        Debug.Print "Sending" & Str$(Len(szSendMe)) & " bytes"
```

```
        End If
        SendData szSendMe
        DoEvents
        szSendMe = ""
    End If


    '-- At what time do we timeout?
    If CommandTimeout Then
        DoneTime = DateAdd("s", CommandTimeout, Now)
    End If


    '-- Wait until you get a response or timeout one or the other.
    Do
        DoEvents
        '-- Are we supposed to check for timeout?
        If CommandTimeout Then
            '-- Check for timeout
            If Now >= DoneTime Then
                '-- Time's up. Error out.
                ErrorNum = vbObjectError + ERR_COMMAND_TIMEOUT
                ErrorDesc = "A command was sent to the server, but a
                response was not received in time."
                RaiseErr
                Exit Do
            End If
        End If
    Loop Until gnCommandReturned

End Sub
```

```
'-- Set the internal flag for returned command.
gnCommandReturned = False
```

At this point, the data is prepared to be sent to the server. All the data is copied into a string variable, szSendMe, and sent to the server. The data is sent in chunks, the size of which is determined by the SendBlockSize property. The default size for one block of data sent is 8192 bytes.

Next, a 20-character header is created, formatted as follows:

Command   10 chars

Rows   5 chars

Columns   5 chars

The Rows and Columns values are the number of rows and columns in the Data.DataSet array that will be sent. The variable szSendMe is used to create the string to be sent. First it is initialized as the header as follows:

```
'-- Generate the string(s) to send

'-- The header consists of the command, followed by the number of rows
'   and number of columns in the data set.
szSendMe = Format$(szCmd, "@@@@@@@@@@") _
    & Format$(Trim$(Str$(Data.Rows)), "@@@@@") _
    & Format$(Trim$(Str$(Data.Cols)), "@@@@@")
```

Notice the Format$ function. Format$ is a powerful string function in Visual Basic that performs a variety of string formatting functions. The first argument is the string to format, and the second is a "format string." The at-sign character represents a space. The Format$ statement is essentially padding a string to a number of spaces. The result of the above code might look like this:

```
Data:       LOGIN    4    2
            --------------------
Position:   12345678901234567890
```

The first ten characters are the command, LOGIN. Characters 11 through 15 represent the number of rows being sent. Characters 16 through 20 represent the number of columns. It might seem like I am driving this home, but I want to be clear about how the protocol works.

After the header is created, the data is added to the string. For each field (array element) added, first a five-byte string length is added, then the data. This makes it easy for the server to interpret the incoming data and place it appropriately in its own CFData class object, which you will then access with your server application.

For example, let's say you are sending a command called GETNEWS that gets a specific text file containing news on a particular subject. There are one row and two columns of attached data. The first column is six characters, and describes the type of news (daily or weekly) and the second column is fifteen characters and defines the area of interest (politics or entertainment). Here is a breakdown of the data that will be sent:

```
Description          Length    Data
-----------------------------------
Command              10        GETNEWS
Rows                 5         1
Columns              5         2
Length of (1,1)      5         6
Data in (1,1)        6         DAILY
Length of (1,2)      5         15
Data in (1,2)        15        POLITICS


Total Bytes.......51
```

Since the data is left-padded with spaces, the actual complete 51-byte string sent would look like this:

```
Data:        GETNEWS    1    2    6 DAILY    15         POLITICS
-----------------------------------------------------------
Position:    12345678901234567890123456789012345678901234567890
```

Figure 10.16 shows the code that assembles and sends the data. Note that when the buffer gets too big, as defined by the SendBlockSize property, the data is sent and the buffer cleared.

▬▬▬▬▬ **Figure 10.16** Assembling and sending data (SendCommand).

```
'-- For each field or cell, send the size of the field (5) followed by
'   the data itself.
For lRow = 1 To Data.Rows
    For lCol = 1 To Data.Cols
        szSendMe = szSendMe _
            & Format$(LTrim$(Str$(Len(Data.DataSet(lRow, lCol)))), "@@@@@") _
            & Data.DataSet(lRow, lCol)
    Next
    '-- If the string is getting too big, send what we've got
    If Len(szSendMe) >= SendBlockSize Then
        If gnDebugMode Then
            Debug.Print "Sending" & Str$(Len(szSendMe)) & " bytes"
        End If
        SendData szSendMe
        szSendMe = ""
    End If
Next


'-- If there is data to send, send it.
If Len(szSendMe) Then
    SendData szSendMe
    szSendMe = ""
End If
```

▬▬▬▬

The data is assembled by a loop within a loop. The outside For/Next loop sets lRow from one to the number of rows, and the inside For/Next loop sets lCol from one to the number of columns. Each field is sent prefaced by a five-byte length. In other words: for each field, the first five bytes indicate the number of bytes of data that follow for that field.

The routine that actually sends the data to the server is called SendData. This is a private function of the CFSockClient class. The only reason you need a SendData routine is to catch and resolve the errors that may occur when trying to send data. The only real error (other than losing your connection) to be concerned with is the Winsock 1.1 error 21035, or Operation Would Block. This occurs when the underlying network is busy sending other data, and cannot send your data right away. Blocking, as it is called, is what happens when an application goes into a tight loop waiting for the availability of some other process; in doing so it locks up the system.

Figure 10.17 shows the SendData method, which accepts a string and makes sure it is sent to the server. In this routine, if an Operation Would Block error occurs when trying to send the data (szData), the code goes into a loose loop (for lack of a better

■■■■■■■ **Figure 10.17** The SendData method.

```
Public Sub SendData(szData As String)

    On Error Resume Next
    gnSendReady = False
    frmClient.dsSocket1.Send = szData
    If Err = SOCK_ERR_OPERATIONWOULDBLOCK Then
        Do
            DoEvents
        Loop Until gnSendReady
        frmClient.dsSocket1.Send = szData
    End If

End Sub
```

word), calling DoEvents so the system doesn't lock up. The loop is broken when the gnSendReady global integer variable is set to True, which only occurs when dsSocket's SendReady event is fired after an Operation Would Block error is resolved.

The final portion of the SendCommand routine, shown in Figure 10.18, waits for a response from the server, as signified by the gnCommandReturned variable being set to True.

▬▬▬▬▬▬ **Figure 10.18** Waiting for the server's response (SendCommand).

```
'-- At what time do we timeout?
If CommandTimeout Then
    DoneTime = DateAdd("s", CommandTimeout, Now)
End If


'-- Wait until you get a response or timeout one or the other.
Do
    DoEvents
    '-- Are we supposed to check for timeout?
    If CommandTimeout Then
        '-- Check for timeout
        If Now >= DoneTime Then
            '-- Time's up. Error out.
            ErrorNum = vbObjectError + ERR_COMMAND_TIMEOUT
            ErrorDesc = "A command was sent to the server, but a
            response was not received in time."
            RaiseErr
            Exit Do
        End If
    End If
Loop Until gnCommandReturned
```

Now let's look at what happens elsewhere while we are in this loop after sending the command, waiting for a response.

Receiving Data from the Server

After the client has sent the server a command, the server will send back a response. Even if there is no data required by the server's response, the server sends a header anyway just to notify the client that it received and processed the command.

When either the CFSockClient class or any other OLE client invokes the SendCommand method, the command and data are sent to the server, and then data is passed back to the client from the server. The dsSocket1 OLE control on the frmClient form receives this data. Figure 10.19 shows the Receive event procedure of this control.

Figure 10.19 CFSockClient processes raw data in dsSocket1_Receive.

```
Private Sub dsSocket1_Receive(ReceiveData As String)

    Static lRows As Long
    Static lCols As Long
    Static lCurRow As Long
    Static lCurCol As Long
    Static szLeftOver As String
    Static szCmd As String


    Dim lRow As Long
    Dim lCol As Long
    Dim nLenField As Integer


    '-- Append the leftover data (if any) to the buffer passed in.
    ReceiveData = szLeftOver & ReceiveData


    '-- If this is a response from the server, the first 15
```

```
'    bytes will be "REPLYFROMSERVER", followed by 5 bytes
'    for the number of rows and five bytes for the number
'    of columns, followed by the field data by row, then
'    column. For each field, the length of the field followed
'    by a space and then the data itself is sent.
If Len(szCmd$) = 0 Then
    If Len(ReceiveData) >= 25 Then
        szCmd = Trim$(Left$(ReceiveData, 15))


        '-- szCmd will be "REPLYFROMSERVER" if this is a
        '   response to a client command,
        '   otherwise it is an unsolicited command.


        '-- This is the header. Extract the number of
        '   rows and columns, and redim the Data_Set array.
        lRows = Val(Mid$(ReceiveData, 16, 5))
        lCols = Val(Mid$(ReceiveData, 21, 5))
        lCurRow = 1
        lCurCol = 1
        If lRows Then
            gClientObj.Data.Resize lRows, lCols
        Else
            Set gClientObj.Data = Nothing
        End If
        '-- Trim the header from the received data.
        ReceiveData = Mid$(ReceiveData, 26)
        szLeftOver = ""
    End If
End If


'-- Has the header been received?
If lRows Then
    '-- Have we not processed all the fields?
```

```
If lCurRow <= lRows Then

    '-- Step through the data

    For lRow = lCurRow To lRows

        For lCol = lCurCol To lCols

            '-- Is there enough data to get the next field size?
            If Len(ReceiveData) < 5 Then

                '-- No. Save the remaining data and scoot.
                lCurRow = lRow
                lCurCol = lCol
                szLeftOver = ReceiveData
                Exit Sub

            Else

                '-- Get the length of the next field (5 chars)
                nLenField = Val(Left$(ReceiveData, 5))
                '-- Are we missing any characters?
                If Len(ReceiveData) < 5 + nLenField Then

                    '-- Yep. Save the remaining data and exit.
                    lCurRow = lRow
                    lCurCol = lCol
                    szLeftOver = ReceiveData
                    Exit Sub

                Else

                    '-- Read the data into the Data_Set array
                    gClientObj.Data.DataSet(lRow, lCol) = _
                        Mid$(ReceiveData, 6, nLenField)
                    '-- Is there any more data here?
                    If Len(ReceiveData) > 5 + nLenField Then

                        '-- Is this NOT the last field of the last column?
                        If (lRow < lRows) Or (lCol < lCols) Then

                            '-- Trim this data off the left of ReceiveData
                            ReceiveData = Mid$(ReceiveData, 6 + nLenField)
                            If gnDebugMode Then
```

```
                        Debug.Print "Field Read"
                End If
        Else
                '-- This is the last field, yet there
                '   is more data. This may be indicative
                '   of corrupted string space or a problem
                '   at the data level of the network.
                ReceiveData = ""
                If gnDebugMode Then
                        Debug.Print "Last Field processed"
                End If
        End If
Else
        '-- Is this NOT the last field of the last column?
        If (lRow < lRows) Or (lCol < lCols) Then
                '-- There is no data left in the buffer,
                '   so exit. The Static variables will keep
                '   the position.
                If lRow < lRows Then
                        If lCol < lCols Then
                                lCurCol = lCol + 1
                                lCurRow = lRow
                        Else
                                lCurCol = 1
                                lCurRow = lRow + 1
                        End If
                Else
                        lCurCol = lCol + 1
                        lCurRow = lRow
                End If
                szLeftOver = ""
                If gnDebugMode Then
```

```
                                    Debug.Print "Holding the position _
                                        - saving leftover data"
                                End If
                                Exit Sub
                            End If
                        End If
                    End If
                End If
            Next
        Next


        If lRow = lRows + 1 Then
            '-- Done.
            If szCmd <> "REPLYFROMSERVER" Then
                '-- This is an unsolicited command. Fire the Command method
                '    at the OLE Client application.
                gClientObj.Event.Command szCmd, gClientObj.Data
            End If

            '-- Zero all the static variables.
            lCurRow = 0
            lCurCol = 0
            lRows = 0
            lCols = 0
            szLeftOver = ""
            szCmd = ""
            gnCommandReturned = True
        End If
    End If
Else
    '-- Some unidentified data was received.. print it in
```

```
        '   the debug window if in design mode.
        If gnDebugMode Then
              Debug.Print ReceiveData
        End If
      End If


End Sub
```

This is perhaps the second most complex piece of code in the CFSock library, the
first most complex being the equivalent Receive event on the server side. Let's break
down what is happening here. First of all, this event is called any time the client
receives any type of data from the server. This is the entry point into the client
object for data from the server. The RecvBlockSize property (which is actually
dsSocket1's DataSize property) determines the maximum number of bytes that the
ReceiveData variable can possibly be. The underlying network determines the
actual size for each chunk of data that comes up the stack but RecvBlockSize is the
maximum size.

Since the server's response including data can be larger than the amount of data
able to be passed into the Receive event, multiple Receive events may and often do
occur. The trick is, then, to identify the data as it comes in so it can be processed
properly. The only task in the Receive event is to get the raw data stream into the
Data object, the CFData subordinate class of the CFSockClient class that holds
data.

Even if you are not using the CFSockClient class, and you are writing your own
Internet protocol with DSSOCK or some other communications device, you will
always be faced with the task of interpreting received data. This task is the essence
of communications programming, since no other task is quite as important. Think
about it. If you could rely only on your ears for sensory input, and they were so
damaged that life to you sounded like sideband bleedover on a 40-channel CB
radio or the teacher in Charlie Brown's math class, you would not be able to communicate at all.

The first thing the code does is determine whether this is a new response from the server or data from the current response. When the server sends a response, the first 15 characters are REPLYFROMSERVER. If we receive this, then the first 25 bytes of data will be the header, which is defined as follows:

```
Description      Length    Data
----------------------------------------
Header ID        15        REPLYFROMSERVER
Rows             5         ?
Columns          5         ?
```

If a command (szCmd) has not yet been received, meaning that the client is ready to accept a new command from the server, the first task is to identify the command and break down the header. First, the number of rows and the number of columns are stored in two Static long integer variables, lRows and lCols. When you define a local variable as static its value is retained when the routine is exited, but it only exists within the local procedure. So, once lCols and lRows are set, their values remain until set to zero. Two other static long integer variables, lCurRow and lCurCol hold the next row and column to be read. These are initialized to 1 (the first row and column) when the header is received. Next, the Data object member is resized to the number of rows and columns, and the header is trimmed from the left of the received data string.

I purposely skipped over the top line, which references the szLeftOver variable. I'll discuss that in a moment or two.

The second (bigger) block of code is the meat of the procedure. After determining that the header has been received and there are still fields of data to be read, the remaining fields are extracted and placed into the Data object. This is done in a manner similar to the way the client sends data to the server, by using a loop within a loop.

The variables lRow and lCol (singular) are the current row and column being read, starting from where the reading last left off. Starting with the current row and column, the loops iterate through all rows and columns being received. If at any time there is not enough data left in the ReceiveData string to either determine the length of the next field, or the field itself, the remaining data is saved off in the szLeftOver variable, a static local string variable. The next time the receive event is fired, szLeftOver is tacked onto the beginning of ReceiveData at the top of the procedure.

After all of the data has been received and put in the Data object, the static variables are zeroed, or returned to their default values, and the global flag gnCommandReturned is set to True. If you remember, in the SendCommand method, after the client sends a command to the server, it waits in a loop calling DoEvents waiting for gnCommandReturned to equal True or a timeout to occur, one or the other. This is where the gnCommandReturned flag is set, indicating that the command has been processed by the server and that a response has been received that may or may not include data. You can tell this, of course, by reading the Rows and Columns properties of the client's Data object.

The Debug Flag

You shouldn't need to debug my code, but in case you really want to see what's happening in this code, you can set the global integer variable, gnDebugMode equal to True in the Sub Main. When you run CFSockClient in the Visual Basic environment, debug messages will print in the debug window during operation.

Sending a File to the Server

To send a file to the server, use the SendFile method. SendFile is a wrapper for the SendCommand method in which you specify the local filename and a transfer mode. SendFile places the name of the file into the Data Object and calls the sends the SENDFILE command, which tells the server to prepare for a file transfer. The server sends back a port number for CFSockClient to connect to and send the file data. CFSockClient closes the port after sending the file.

This code shows you how to send a file:

```
'-- Assuming you are connected already!
CFData.SendFile "C:\WINDOWS\WINLOGO.BMP"
```

```
    If CFData.ErrorNum Then
        MsgBox CFData.ErrorDesc, vbExclamation, App.Title
    End If
```

The SendFile method takes one argument, the filename. Figure 10.20 shows the SendFile method code.

■■■■■■■ **Figure 10.20** The SendFile method.

```
Public Sub SendFile(szFileName As String)
'-- Sends a file

    Dim szAddress        As String
    Dim szTemp           As String
    Dim szFileTitle      As String

    Dim nFileNum         As Integer
    Dim nRemainder       As Integer
    Dim nConnectError    As Integer

    Dim lCounter         As Long
    Dim lIndex           As Long
    Dim lNumBlocks       As Long
    Dim lFileSize        As Long
    Dim lPort            As Long


    On Error GoTo SendFileError

    ErrorNum = 0
    ErrorDesc = ""

    '-- Send the SENDFILE Command to tell the server
    '   we want to send a file.
```

```
'    1,1 = File Name (sans path)
'    2,1 = Target Directory (optional)
'    3,1 = File Size
szFileTitle = szJustTheFileName(szFileName)
Data.Resize 3, 1
Data.DataSet(1, 1) = szFileTitle
Data.DataSet(2, 1) = ""
Data.DataSet(3, 1) = Trim$(Str$(FileLen(szFileName)))


SendCommand "SENDFILE"


If Data.Rows Then
    If Data.DataSet(1, 1) <> "OK" Then
        ErrorNum = vbObjectError + ERR_SENDFILE
        ErrorDesc = Data.DataSet(1, 1)
        RaiseErr
        Exit Sub
    End If
End If


'-- Connect to the new port for the data connection
If SocketConnect(frmClient.dsSocket2, Val(Data.DataSet(2, 1)), _
  (frmClient.dsSocket1.RemoteDotAddr), 15) Then
    ErrorNum = vbObjectError + ERR_BADDATACONNECTION
    ErrorDesc = "Could Not Make Data Connection"
    RaiseErr
    Exit Sub
End If


'-- Open the file
nFileNum = FreeFile
```

```
Open szFileName For Binary As nFileNum


'-- Get the size information
lFileSize = LOF(nFileNum)
If lFileSize = 0 Then
    Close nFileNum
    ErrorNum = vbObjectError + ERR_ZEROBYTEFILE
    ErrorDesc = "Zero byte file"
    RaiseErr
    Exit Sub
End If


lNumBlocks = lFileSize \ SendBlockSize
nRemainder = lFileSize Mod SendBlockSize


'-- Send the data
For lIndex = 1 To lNumBlocks
    szTemp = Space$(SendBlockSize)
    Get #nFileNum, , szTemp
    SendData frmClient.dsSocket2, szTemp
Next
If nRemainder Then
    szTemp = Space$(nRemainder)
    Get #nFileNum, , szTemp
    SendData frmClient.dsSocket2, szTemp
End If


'-- Close the file
Close nFileNum


'-- Close the socket
SocketDisconnect frmClient.dsSocket2
```

```
      Exit Sub

SendFileError:

      On Error Resume Next
      '-- Raise the error here
      Close nFileNum
      SocketDisconnect frmClient.dsSocket2
      Exit Sub

End Sub
```

■■■

The first thing that happens is the SENDFILE command is sent to the server with three fields. The first field is the file name with no path information. This will be the name of the file written on the server. The second parameter is an optional path on the server where the file should be stored, and the third parameter is the size of the file in bytes. This is used on the server to display file transfer status information. I will discuss what happens on the server side shortly.

If the server has a problem opening the file for writing on the server, or otherwise any error, it will return a single row with one column containing the error message. If there was no problem, then the first row, column 1 contains OK and the second row, column 1 contains a port number. CFSockClient then connects to the server on the designated port. This is called the data connection. To keep things easy and straightforward, a separate data connection is used for sending and receiving files.

Once the data connection is open, the local file is opened, and the file is sent through the data connection in chunks, the size of which is set with the SendBlockSize property (the default size is 8,192 bytes). The number of chunks is determined by dividing the total size of the file by the block size. Using the Mod operator you can determine the size of the last block, which is always less than the block size (or zero, if the file size is an even multiple of the block size).

Once the file has been completely sent, the local file is closed, the data connection is disconnected, and the routine exits.

Receiving a File from the Server

To receive a file from the server, use the GetFile method. GetFile is a wrapper for the SendCommand property which takes two arguments, the remote filename to send and the local file name to save. Here is a sample use of the GetFile Method:

```
CFData.GetFile "\bin\files\myfile.zip", "c:\windows\desktop\myfile.zip"


If CFData.ErrorNum Then
    MsgBox CFData.ErrorDesc, vbInformation
End IF
```

The remote filename is relative to the server. That is, \bin\files\myfile.zip is a reference to a file on the server, not the client. The second argument specifies a local file name. After the transfer, you can test the ErrorNum property to see if an error occurred, in which case the ErrorDesc property contains a description of the error. Figure 10.21 shows the GetFile method.

After verifying that a local filename was specified CFSockClient prepares to send the GETFILE command to the server application. Internally, the GETFILE command (not the method) accepts only one parameter, the server filename. Just as with the SendFile method, GetFile makes a data connection to the port that is passed back from the server in Data(2,1). However, GetFile interacts with the DSSocket2 control on frmMain, which actually receive the file.

After the data connection is made with frmMain.dsSocket2, the local file is opened, and a carriage return/linefeed is sent on the data connection to tell the server to start sending the file. At that point, the code goes into a loop until gnFileNum (the file number of the received file) is set to zero, which happens either when the data connection is closed or an error occurs. Figure 10.22 shows the dsSocket2_Receive event, which saves the file data to disk.

████████ **Figure 10.21** The GetFile method.

```
Public Sub GetFile(szFileName As String, szSaveFileName As String)


    ErrorNum = 0
    ErrorDesc = ""


    If Len(szSaveFileName) = 0 Then
        ErrorNum = vbObjectError + ERR_GETFILE
        ErrorDesc = "No destination file specified"
        RaiseErr
        Exit Sub
    End If


    '-- Send the GETFILE command.
    '   1,1 = File Name
    gClientObj.Data.Resize 1, 1
    gClientObj.Data.DataSet(1, 1) = szFileName
    SendCommand "GETFILE"
    If Data.Rows >= 2 Then
        If Data.DataSet(1, 1) <> "OK" Then
            ErrorNum = vbObjectError + ERR_GETFILE
            ErrorDesc = Data.DataSet(2, 2)
            RaiseErr
            Exit Sub
        End If
    Else
        ErrorNum = vbObjectError + ERR_GETFILE
        ErrorDesc = "Server did not specify a socket for the data connection"
        RaiseErr
        Exit Sub
    End If
```

```
'-- Open the file
gnGetFileNum = FreeFile
Open szSaveFileName For Binary As gnGetFileNum


'-- Connect to the new port for the data connection
If SocketConnect(frmClient.dsSocket2, Val(Data.DataSet(2, 1)), _
    (frmClient.dsSocket1.RemoteDotAddr), 15) Then
    gnGetFileNum = 0
    Close gnGetFileNum
    ErrorNum = vbObjectError + ERR_BADDATACONNECTION
    ErrorDesc = "Could Not Make Data Connection"
    RaiseErr
    Exit Sub
End If


'-- Send a "Start" byte
SendData frmClient.dsSocket2, vbCrLf


'-- Wait until the file has been received
Do
    DoEvents
Loop Until gnGetFileNum = 0

End Sub
```

■■■■■■

Once the file has been sent, the server closes the data connection. Figure
10.23 shows the dsSocket2_Close event, in which the received file is closed.
The gnGetFileNum variable is set to zero, and the loop at the bottom of the
GetFile method exits.

■■■■■■■ **Figure 10.22** frmMain.dsSocket2 receives file data.

```
Private Sub dsSocket2_Receive(ReceiveData As String)

    If gnGetFileNum Then
        Put #gnGetFileNum, , ReceiveData
    End If

End Sub
```

■■■■■■

■■■■■■■ **Figure 10.23** The received file is written to disk when the data connection closes.

```
Private Sub dsSocket2_Close(ErrorCode As Integer, ErrorDesc As String)

    If gnGetFileNum Then
        Close gnGetFileNum
        gnGetFileNum = 0
    End If

    If ErrorCode Then
        gClientObj.ErrorNum = vbObjectError + ERR_WINSOCK
        gClientObj.ErrorDesc = "DSSOCK Error" & Str$(ErrorCode) & ": " & ErrorDesc
        gClientObj.RaiseErr
    End If

End Sub
```

■■■■■■

The CFServer Application

CFServer, shown in Figure 10.24, is an easily modifiable application that I wrote to compliment the CFSockClient object. There are only two options on the main screen: the port number to listen to and the download directory, where received files are stored. The server service is started by pressing the Start button. Pressing the Pause button causes the server to stop accepting new connections. When the server is paused, the Pause button's Caption says Resume, and pressing it will resume the service. Pressing Stop will close all connections and cause the server to refuse any new connections.

The internal mechanism for communicating with CFSockClient objects is exactly the same as within the CFSockClient class, except that code has been added to handle the requirements of multiple simultaneous connections.

Easy To Modify

When modifying the server, you really only have to be concerned with one internal subroutine, ProcessCommand, which is shown in Figure 10.25.

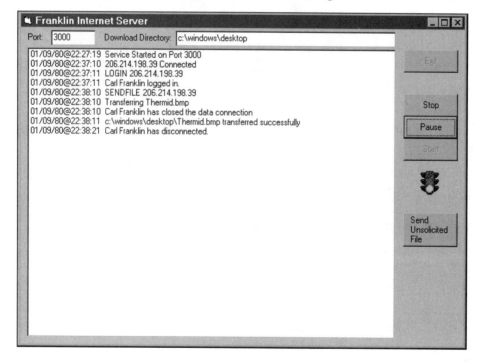

Figure 10.24 The CFServer Application.

▪▪▪▪▪▪▪ **Figure 10.25** CFServer's ProcessCommand routine in the server application.

```
Sub ProcessCommand(Index As Integer, szCmd As String, Data As CFData)
'-- This is where server commands are processed and data
'   is sent back to the server. If no data is to be sent, then
'   one row and one column is sent with the data set to "ACK"


'-- To add a new command to the "repertoire", simply perform a select
'   case on the command string, use the data in the Data object, do your thing,
'   and set the return data in the Data object.
    Dim szUsername  As String
    Dim szPassword  As String
    Dim szDir       As String
    Dim szTargetDir As String


    Dim nCtrlIndex  As Integer
    Dim nThere      As Integer
    Dim nFileNum    As Integer
    Dim lIndex      As Integer
    Dim nIndex      As Integer


    ReDim szSQLData(1 To 1, 1 To 1) As String


    DisplayMessage szCmd & " " & Status(Index).szDotAddress


    Select Case szCmd
        Case "LOGIN"
            '-- Do an optional security check here
            szUsername = Data.DataSet(1, 1)
            szPassword = Data.DataSet(1, 2)


            '-- Do security check against a user database right here ----
```

```
'-- Send back "OK" if logged in, or "NO" if not logged in.
Data.Resize 1, 1
Data.DataSet(1, 1) = "OK"

Status(Index).szUsername = szUsername
Status(Index).szPassword = szPassword

DisplayMessage szUsername & " logged in."

Case "SENDFILE"
    '-- Is the data connection already in use?
    If Status(Index).DataAction Then
        Data.Resize 1, 1
        Data.DataSet(1, 1) = "Data Connection In Use"
        Exit Sub
    End If

    '-- Was a target directory specified?
    szTargetDir = Data.DataSet(2, 1)
    If Len(szTargetDir) Then
        '-- See if the directory exists.
        szDir = Dir$(szTargetDir, vbDirectory)
        If Len(szDir) Then
            Do
                If GetAttr(szDir) And vbDirectory Then
                    If szDir <> "." And szDir <> ".." Then
                        nThere = True
                        Exit Do
                    End If
                Else
                    Exit Do
```

```
                End If
                szDir = Dir$()
        Loop
        If Not nThere Then
            '-- The directory does not exist.
            Data.Resize 1, 1
            Data.DataSet(1, 1) = "Cannot create file on server"
            Exit Sub
        End If
    Else
        '-- The directory does not exist.
        Data.Resize 1, 1
        Data.DataSet(1, 1) = "Cannot create file on server"
        Exit Sub
    End If
End If


On Error Resume Next
'-- Load the data answer and data connection Sockets controls
'   for the file xfer and tell the answer socket to listen
Load frmServer.dssData(Index)
Load frmServer.dssDataAnswer(Index)
Status(Index).DataAction = DATA_ACTION_CLIENT_TO_SERVER
frmServer.dssDataAnswer(Index).Action = SOCK_ACTION_LISTEN


'-- Save the path and filename of the file to be received.
If Len(szTargetDir) = 0 Then
    szTargetDir = frmServer.txtDownloadDir
End If
If Right(szTargetDir, 1) <> "\" Then
    szTargetDir = szTargetDir & "\"
```

```
            End If
            Status(Index).szFileName = szTargetDir & Data.DataSet(1, 1)
            Status(Index).FileSize = Val(Data.DataSet(3, 1))


            '-- Send back the OK, with the port number
            Data.Resize 2, 1
            Data.DataSet(1, 1) = "OK"
            Data.DataSet(2, 1) = Trim$(Str$(frmServer.dssDataAnswer(Index).LocalPort))

        Case "GETFILE"
            '-- Does the file exist?
          If Len(Dir$(Data.DataSet(1, 1))) = 0 Then
                Data.Resize 1, 1
                Data.DataSet(1, 1) = "File Not Found"
                Exit Sub
          End If


          On Error Resume Next
          '-- Load the data answer and data connection Sockets controls
          '   for the file xfer and tell the answer socket to listen
          Load frmServer.dssData(Index)
          Load frmServer.dssDataAnswer(Index)

    On Error GoTo 0


          Status(Index).szFileName = Data.DataSet(1, 1)
          Status(Index).FileSize = FileLen(Data.DataSet(1, 1))
          Status(Index).DataAction = DATA_ACTION_SERVER_TO_CLIENT
          frmServer.dssDataAnswer(Index).Action = SOCK_ACTION_LISTEN


          '-- Send back the OK, with the port number
          Data.Resize 2, 1
```

```
        Data.DataSet(1, 1) = "OK"
        Data.DataSet(2, 1) = Trim$(Str$(frmServer.dssDataAnswer(Index).LocalPort))


    End Select

End Sub
```

The ProcessCommand routine is called after the command and data have been properly received and before the Data object is sent back to the client. In this routine it is
your job to take any action and then set the contents of the Data object to whatever
you want to send back to the client. The process of sending the response is done by
the SendCommandAndData routine in CFSERVER.BAS.

Take a look at the part of ProcessCommand that handles a LOGIN command.
When CFSockClient sends you a LOGIN command, data element (1,1) is the user
name, and element (1,2) is the password. In ProcessCommand you can do a security check with the user name and password. If the user checks out OK, set
Data.DataSet(1,1) to OK, otherwise set it to "NO."

▬▬▬ **TIP**

> You can create your own custom commands in the same way. You don't
> need to modify the CFSockClient object, just the server. Your actual client
> application will send the appropriate commands to the server using
> CFSockClient. Got it?

Receiving Unsolicited Commands from the Server

One of the coolest features of the CFSockClient object is its ability to call back the
client code. Let me explain. One of the main differences between an OCX (OLE

control) and an OLE automation object is that the OCX has events, subroutines that can be called by the OLE object. The programmer can intercept these events and write code handlers accordingly. With an OLE automation object, there are no events.

However, you can easily add this capability to an OLE automation object written in Visual Basic 4.0. Here is how it works. Remember our object model? Take a look at Figure 10.1 again. The CFEvent class is a simple class that has one method, Command. Here is the definition of that method:

```
Public Sub Command(szCommand As String, Data As CFData)
```

The CFSockClient class has a CFEvent class member called Event. Your application can pass a local object reference to CFSockClient via the RegisterEventObject method. Here is the code for that method:

```
Public Sub RegisterEventObject(objAny As Object)


    ErrorNum = 0
    ErrorDesc = ""


    On Error Resume Next
    Set Event = objAny
    If Err Then
        ErrorNum = vbObjectError + ERR_BADOBJECT
        ErrorDesc = Error
        RaiseErr
    End If


End Sub
```

Let's say you create a new project. You are going to use the CFSockClient object to communicate with a server and you want the object to make callbacks to your code. First, you must create the CFSockClient object:

```
Dim CFSock As New CFSockClient
```

Next, load the CFEvent class module into your client application. Create a new object from this class:

```
Dim CFE As New CFEvent
```

Finally, pass the local object to CFSockClient with the RegisterEventObject method:

```
CFSock.RegisterEventObject CFE
```

Now you can respond to commands in the CFE object's Command method, which are called by the server through the CFSock object. Figure 10.26 shows the Command procedure for the CFEvent class. You can, and should, add your own callback commands as needed.

▬▬▬▬▬ **Figure 10.26** The CFEvent.Command method allows the server to "push" commands and data to your application.

```
Public Sub Command(szCommand As String, Data As CFData)
'-------------------------------------------------------------------
'   This is where you process unsolicited commands from the server.
'   The server can send unsolicited commands and data, which you
'   then process here with a Select Case block. The Data object
'   is of the CFData class, and is more or less a wrapper for a
'   two dimensional string array.
'-------------------------------------------------------------------


    Dim szFilePath  As String
    Dim szFileName  As String


    Select Case szCommand


        Case "PUSHFILE" '-- The server is telling you to download a file.


            '-- Obviously, you should change the destination path to
```

```
'    your liking.
#If Windows95 Then
     szFilePath = szWindowsDir & "\desktop\"
#Else
     szFilePath = InputBox("You have received a file. " _
         & "Where do you want it to be saved", App.Title, "\windows\desktop")
     If Right$(szFilePath, 1) <> "\" Then
         szFilePath = szFilePath & "\"
     End If
#End If


'-- Get the file name
szFileName = CFSock.Data.DataSet(1, 1)


'-- Get the file.
CFSock.GetFile szFileName, szFilePath & szJustTheFileName(szFileName)


'-- Display confirmation
If CFSock.ErrorNum = 0 Then
     MsgBox "You have received an unsoclicited file from the server."
End If


     End Select


End Sub
```

This code is set up to act on the PUSHFILE command. When the server wants to send your application a file, it sends the PUSHFILE command to CFSockClient. When CFSockClient receives any command that is not a REPLYFROMSERVER command it fires the Command event in your object, passing the command string and Data object.

In the case of PUSHFILE, the server sends the name of a file on the server. The code simply calls the CFSockClient.GetFile method to retrieve the file.

I wholeheartedly encourage you to take advantage of this technique to write applications in which the server can initiate a conversation just like the client. There are numerous applications for such a system.

You can use the callback to notify email clients when they have mail so that the client doesn't have to poll for this information, polling taking up valuable processor time. You can write a virtual chat program such as Worlds Chat where conversations move from peer to peer through a dedicated server. In general, you can free the client from having to poll for data making your system extremely efficient.

Integration with a WebSite Using Visual Basic Script

Visual Basic Script is not covered in depth in this book simply because of a lack of time. It was just coming out when we were going to print. The next revision of this book, however, will include a chapter on using Visual Basic Script.

In a nutshell, VB Script is a subset of the Visual Basic language that you can use within an HTML document. If the client's web browser supports VB Script (and it should, since MS is giving it away to browser vendors) the VB code executes on the client's machine.

One of the benefits of VB Script is the ability to access OLE Automation servers. I'm going to let you re-read the above paragraphs now so you can make the connection. Go ahead, I'll wait.

Got it? Okay, let me be more specific. Your web page contains a VB Script program that uses either the CFSockClient object or your own OLE DLL (application) that uses CFSockClient to contact your CFServer, which sits right along side your web server. You can use this connection to perform functions that you could not otherwise using VB Script alone.

I promise to go into more detail on this in the next revision of this book.

Remote ODBC

One of the benefits of having this kind of framework in Visual Basic is that you can easily make your ODBC datasources accessible via the Internet. The CFServer application connects to a local ODBC datasource. CFSockClient connects to CFServer (with password protection, of course) and sends a SQL query. The server receives the query and queries the datasource. The resulting data set is then returned to your application through CFSockClient.

Using the callback procedure outlined in the previous section, you can write code on the server to update all clients when the data they are viewing has changed. This is especially important in workgroup applications where the latest data must be accessible at all times.

My remote ODBC code uses the CFSockClient object and an enhanced version of the CFServer application. In that regard, you already know how it works if you read this chapter. The ODBCServ project looks exactly like the Server project, except that it uses a modified version of cfserver.bas, called odbcsrv.bas. This file contains an extended ProcessCommand procedure. The ODBCServ project also includes declares for the ODBC API, which are used to talk to the database. There are a couple of new commands added to ProcessCommand. They are:

1. ODBC_OPEN
2. ODBC_QUERY
3. ODBC_CLOSE

ODBC_OPEN

This command opens a data source on the server. Just as with opening a local database, there are three arguments:

Argument:	Example:
Datasource Name	MyDataSource
User ID	John Smith
Password	higgledy-piggledy

To open a database at the server, use the following syntax:

```
'-- Allocate memory for five arguments
CFSock.Data.Resize 3, 1


'-- These variables are specified by the user
CFSock.Data.DataSet(1, 1) = szDataSource
CFSock.Data.DataSet(2, 1) = szUserID
CFSock.Data.DataSet(3, 1) = szPassword


CFSock.SendCommand "ODBC_OPEN"


If CFSock.Data(1, 1) = "NO" Then
    MsgBox "Could not connect to remote data source", _
      vbInformation
Else
    '-- Success! Save the hdbc (preferably to a global
    '   long integer)
    glhdbc = Val(CFSock.Data.DataSet(1, 1))
End If
```

On the server side, my code uses the ODBC API directly. The routines were originally developed by Andrew J. Brust (70274.1746@compuserve.com) and Michael Love Graves (72240.1123@compuserve.com). You could easily rewrite the code to use any database engine, since the routines for opening, querying, and closing the data source are so clearly defined. At the time of this writing, this direct ODBC method is the fastest way to access an ODBC database, the next fastest method being Remote Data Objects. Figure 10.27 shows the ProcessCommand routine in odbcserv.bas.

■■■■■■■ **Figure 10.27** ODBCServ contains a modified ProcessCommand routine to handle database requests.

```
Sub ProcessCommand(Index As Integer, szCmd As String, Data As CFData)
'-- This is where server commands are processed and data
'   is sent back to the server. If no data is to be sent, then
'   one row and one column is sent with the data set to "ACK"
```

```
'-- To add a new command to the "repertoire", simply perform a select
'   case on the command string, use the data in the Data object, do your
'   thing, and set the return data in the Data object.

    Dim szUsername      As String
    Dim szPassword      As String
    Dim szDir           As String
    Dim szTargetDir     As String

    Dim nCtrlIndex      As Integer
    Dim nThere          As Integer
    Dim nFileNum        As Integer
    Dim lIndex          As Integer
    Dim nIndex          As Integer


    '-- ODBC variables
    Dim szRemotePwd As String
    Dim szDataSource As String
    Dim szUserID As String
    Dim szPwd As String
    Dim nIndex As Integer
    Dim ldbc As Long
    Dim szQuery As String
    Dim szReturn As String
    Dim nRows As Integer
    Dim nColumns As Integer
    Dim nRow As Integer
    Dim nColumn As Integer
    Dim nSentHeader As Integer
    Dim nDummy As Integer

    ReDim szSQLData(1 To 1, 1 To 1) As String
    DisplayMessage szCmd & " " & Status(Index).szDotAddress
```

```
Select Case szCmd
    Case "LOGIN"
        '-- Do an optional security check here
        szUsername = Data.DataSet(1, 1)
        szPassword = Data.DataSet(1, 2)


    '-- Do security check against a user database right here ----

        '-- Send back "OK" if logged in, or "NO" if not logged in.
        Data.Resize 2, 1
        Data.DataSet(1, 1) = "OK"

        Status(Index).szUsername = szUsername
        Status(Index).szPassword = szPassword

        DisplayMessage szUsername & " logged in."

    Case "SENDFILE"
        '-- Is the data connection already in use?
        If Status(Index).DataAction Then
            Data.Resize 1, 1
            Data.DataSet(1, 1) = "Data Connection In Use"
            Exit Sub
        End If

        '-- Was a target directory specified?
        szTargetDir = Data.DataSet(2, 1)
        If Len(szTargetDir) Then
            '-- See if the directory exists.
            szDir = Dir$(szTargetDir, vbDirectory)
            If Len(szDir) Then
```

```
                Do
                    If GetAttr(szDir) And vbDirectory Then
                        If szDir <> "." And szDir <> ".." Then
                            nThere = True
                            Exit Do
                        End If
                    Else
                        Exit Do
                    End If
                    szDir = Dir$()
                Loop
                If Not nThere Then
                    '-- The directory does not exist.
                    Data.Resize 1, 1
                    Data.DataSet(1, 1) = "Cannot create file on server"
                    Exit Sub
                End If
            Else
                '-- The directory does not exist.
                Data.Resize 1, 1
                Data.DataSet(1, 1) = "Cannot create file on server"
                Exit Sub
            End If
        End If
    End If

    On Error Resume Next
    '-- Load the data answer and data connection Sockets controls
    '   for the file xfer and tell the answer socket to listen
    Load frmServer.dssData(Index)
    Load frmServer.dssDataAnswer(Index)
    Status(Index).DataAction = DATA_ACTION_CLIENT_TO_SERVER
    frmServer.dssDataAnswer(Index).Action = SOCK_ACTION_LISTEN
```

```
'-- Save the path and filename of the file to be received.
If Len(szTargetDir) = 0 Then
    szTargetDir = frmServer.txtDownloadDir
End If
If Right(szTargetDir, 1) <> "\" Then
    szTargetDir = szTargetDir & "\"
End If
Status(Index).szFileName = szTargetDir & Data.DataSet(1, 1)
Status(Index).FileSize = Val(Data.DataSet(3, 1))

'-- Send back the OK, with the port number
Data.Resize 2, 1
Data.DataSet(1, 1) = "OK"
Data.DataSet(2, 1) = Trim$(Str$(frmServer.dssDataAnswer(Index).LocalPort))

Case "GETFILE"
    '-- Does the file exist?
    If Len(Dir$(Data.DataSet(1, 1))) = 0 Then
        Data.Resize 1, 1
        Data.DataSet(1, 1) = "File Not Found"
        Exit Sub
    End If


    On Error Resume Next
    '-- Load the data answer and data connection Sockets controls
    '   for the file xfer and tell the answer socket to listen
    Load frmServer.dssData(Index)
    Load frmServer.dssDataAnswer(Index)

    On Error GoTo 0

    Status(Index).szFileName = Data.DataSet(1, 1)
```

```
        Status(Index).FileSize = FileLen(Data.DataSet(1, 1))
        Status(Index).DataAction = DATA_ACTION_SERVER_TO_CLIENT
        frmServer.dssDataAnswer(Index).Action = SOCK_ACTION_LISTEN


        '-- Send back the OK, with the port number
        Data.Resize 2, 1
        Data.DataSet(1, 1) = "OK"
      Data.DataSet(2, 1) = Trim$(Str$(frmServer.dssDataAnswer(Index).LocalPort))

Case "ODBC_OPEN"     '-- Open ODBC Database


        szDataSource = Data.DataSet(1, 1)
        szUserID = Data.DataSet(1, 2)
        szPwd = Data.DataSet(1, 3)


        For nIndex = 1 To nNumDataSources
            If UCase$(typDataSource(nIndex).szDataSource) = UCase$(szDataSource) Then
                '-- The datasource exists!
                Exit For
            End If
        Next


        '-- Prepare to send confirmation
        Data.Resize 1, 1


        If nIndex = nNumDataSources + 1 Then
            '-- No Match Found. Open a new connection.
            If OpenODBCDataBase(szDataSource, szUserID, szPwd) = 0 Then
                '-- Could not open database.. failure
                Data.DataSet(1, 1) = "NO"
            Else
                '-- Successfully opened the database.
                nIndex = nNumDataSources
                '-- Return the hdbc of the open datasource
                Data.DataSet(1, 1) = Str$(typDataSource(nIndex).hdbc)
```

```
                End If
         Else
              '-- Added this Socket connection to the existing database.
              typDataSource(nIndex).nNumConnections = _
                   typDataSource(nIndex).nNumConnections + 1
              '-- Return the hdbc of the open datasource
              Data.DataSet(1, 1) = Str$(typDataSource(nIndex).hdbc)
         End If


    Case "ODBC_QUERY"    '-- Remote Query


         '-- Is this database currently open and available?
         ldbc = Val(Data.DataSet(1, 1))
         For nIndex = 1 To nNumDataSources
              If ldbc = typDataSource(nIndex).hdbc Then
                   Exit For
              End If
         Next
         If nIndex = nNumDataSources + 1 Then
              '-- No it is not. Send back an error
              Data.Resize 1, 1
              Data.DataSet(1, 1) = "NO"
         Else
              '-- Get the query and call it.
              szQuery = Data.DataSet(2, 1)

              If Len(szQuery) Then
                   nRows = LoadArray(szSQLData(), nIndex, szQuery, nColumns)

                   If nRows Then
                        '-- Send back the query results
                        Data.Resize (nRows + 3), (nColumns)
                        Data.DataSet(1, 1) = "OK"
                        Data.DataSet(2, 1) = Val(nRows)
```

```
                        Data.DataSet(3, 1) = Val(nColumns)

                        For nRow = 1 To nRows
                            For nColumn = 1 To nColumns
                                '-- Send each field's size and then the
                                data itself
                                Data.DataSet(nRow + 3, (nColumn)) = _
                                    szSQLData(nColumn, nRow)
                            Next
                        Next
                    Else
                        Data.Resize 1, 1
                        Data.DataSet(1, 1) = "NO"
                    End If
                Else
                    Data.Resize 1, 1
                    Data.DataSet(1, 1) = "NO"
                End If
            End If

    Case "ODBC_CLOSE"      '-- Close Database
        ldbc = Val(Data.DataSet(1, 1))

        For nIndex = 1 To nNumDataSources
            If ldbc = typDataSource(nIndex).hdbc Then
                typDataSource(nIndex).nNumConnections = _
                    typDataSource(nIndex).nNumConnections - 1
                If typDataSource(nIndex).nNumConnections <= 0 Then
                    nDummy = DisconnectFromDataSource(ldbc, _
                        typDataSource(nIndex).hstmt)
                    If nNumDataSources > 1 Then
                        '-- Copy the last entry to this entry, and delete
                        '   the last entry
                        typDataSource(nIndex).hdbc = _
                            typDataSource(nNumDataSources).hdbc
```

```
                                 typDataSource(nIndex).hstmt = _
                                     typDataSource(nNumDataSources).hstmt
                                 typDataSource(nIndex).szDataSource = _
                                     typDataSource(nNumDataSources).szDataSource
                                 typDataSource(nIndex).nNumConnections = _
                                     typDataSource(nNumDataSources).nNumConnections
                                 nNumDataSources = nNumDataSources - 1
                         ReDim typDataSource(1 To nNumDataSources) As DataSourceType
                             Else
                                 Erase typDataSource
                             End If
                         End If
                         Exit For
                     End If
                 Next

         End Select

    End Sub
```

The server has to keep track of connections to the ODBC database. It manages
these connections with an array (typDataSource) of a user-defined type called
DataSourceType. Here is that type:

```
Type DataSourceType
    hdbc                    As Long
    hstmt                   As Long
    szDataSource            As String
    nNumConnections         As Integer
End Type
```

hdbc and hstmt are the database and statement handles returned by ODBC that identify a connection to a datasource. szDataSource is the name of the datasource, and nNumConnections is the number of current WinSock connections to the datasource.

When an ODBC_OPEN command is received by the server, the code first determines whether it needs to open a new connection. First it looks through the Global typDataSource() array to see if the data source is currently open. If it is, it looks at the number of currently connected Winsock clients for that data source. If the datasource is opened or an existing connection is used successfully, the server returns the hdbc of the datasource, a handle that the client must use for all queries and for closing the datasource.

ODBC_QUERY

This command sends a SQL query to the server, which in turn queries the datasource and returns the resultant data set. There are two arguments, the ODBC handle and SQL query:

```
Argument:     Example:
```

hdbc	<long integer returned from ODBC_OPEN>
Query	SELECT * FROM Customer

To send a query to an open database, follow the example in Figure 10.28.

If the query fails on the server, the Data object will have the word "NO" in row 1, column 1, otherwise it contains the resultant data set.

ODBC_CLOSE

ODBC_CLOSE closes a previously opened ODBC connection. In general, you do not need to close a connection. By simply disconnecting, you will close the connection. You should close the connection only if you are done with the database but still wish to remain connected for other reasons.

ODBC_CLOSE takes one argument, the hdbc that was returned from ODBC_OPEN which identifies the datasource connection.

WRITING CUSTOM WINSOCK CLIENT/SERVER APPLICATIONS ■■■■■■

▬▬▬▬▬ **Figure 10.28** Sending a query with ODBC_QUERY.

```
'-- Allocate memory for two arguments
CFSock.Data.Resize 2, 1


'-- The first parameter is the return value of
'    ODBC_OPEN, the hdbc that identifies an open
'    datasource connection.
CFSock.Data.DataSet(1, 1) = Str$(glhdbc)


'-- Create a query and select it into the second row
szQuery = "SELECT * FROM Customer"
CFSock.Data.DataSet(2, 1) = szQuery


'-- Send the query command
CFSock.SendCommand "ODBC_QUERY"


If CFSock.Data(1, 1) = "NO" Then
    MsgBox "Could not query the remote data source", _
        vbInformation
Else
    '-- Success! We have results
    '    Display in the debug window.
    For nRow = 1 to CFSock.Data.Rows
        For nColumn = 1 to CFSock.Data.Cols
            Debug.Print CFSock.Data.DataSet(nRow, nColumn), ", ";
        Next
        '-- Advance the line
        Debug.Print
    Next
End If
```

```
Argument:    Example:
_____

hdbc          <long integer returned from ODBC_OPEN>
```

Here is an example of how to close a data source:

```
'-- Allocate memory for one argument
CFSock.Data.Resize 2, 1


'-- The only parameter is the return value of
'   ODBC_OPEN, the hdbc that identifies an open
'   datasource connection.
CFSock.Data.DataSet(1, 1) = Str$(glhdbc)


'-- Send the close command
CFSock.SendCommand "ODBC_CLOSE"


If CFSock.Data(1, 1) = "NO" Then
    MsgBox "Could not close the remote data source", _
        vbInformation
Else
    '-- Success! The connection is closed.
End If
```

ODBCTest: A Sample ODBC Client Application

ODBCTest, shown in Figure 10.29 is a small program that connects to ODBCServ with CFSockClient. ODBCTest lets the user fill in the datasource name, User ID, and password, and select read-only or exclusive mode. Once connected, ODBCTest lets you submit a query to CFServer. The results are displayed for the user as they come back from the server.

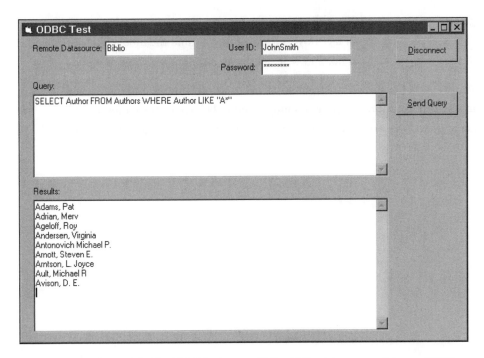

Figure 10.29 ODBCTest uses CFSockClient to connect to an ODBC datasource on the server.

Epilogue

As I sit and write the epilogue to this, the last chapter in my book, my four-month-old daughter is sitting up on the desk looking at my monitor. It blows me away to think of the kind of experiences she will have by the time she's old enough to read this book, if she will be even the least bit interested in what the old man does for a living.

But then it hits me. Her life will always have high technology in it. She may well think of these days like you and I think about the days of Thomas Edison and Henry Ford. Then again, she may decide to move to the moon.

This movement is inescapable, and our lives are changing at a rapid pace because of it. I personally feel lucky to be a part of it, and you should too. You are the "Disney

Imagineers" of tomorrow. Visual Basic and the Internet represent countless possibilities. The real problem we all face now is learning how to find the time in our lives to do all the things we want to do, and write all the applications we want to write.

I hope this book has helped to lift up a few rocks so you can see and understand the murky details of Internet programming. I certainly have learned a lot in the course of its writing. So until the next chapter, do good things and keep in touch.

NNTP

COMMAND LISTING

The following is a listing of both standard and draft NNTP commands. Draft commands are those that do not appear in RFC 977 as of this writing. These commands are indicated with an asterisk. You may find that some servers implement only some of them and not others. This is to be expected.

NNTP Commands (ARTICLE)

Command:	ARTICLE
Description:	Requests the retrieval of a specific article's header and text.
Usage:	ARTICLE [<ArticleNumber	MessageID>] <CRLF>
Parameters:	ArticleNumber is the number of an article in the current newsgroup.
	MessageID is the Message ID of an article in the current newsgroup.

Examples:

```
SendData DSSocket1, "ARTICLE 1123" & vbCrlf
SendData DSSocket1, "ARTICLE <133970@netcom.com>" & vbCrlf
```

Comments: There are three ways to use the ARTICLE Command:

1. ARTICLE

2. ARTICLE <Article Number>

3. ARTICLE <Message-ID>

You can select the current article header and text by not specifying an argument.

You can select a specific article by specifying its article number or message-id as an argument. If either is specified, the current article pointer is updated to the specified article and the header and text are returned.

A blank line (CR/LF) separates the header from the text of the message.

A period on a line by itself indicates the end of the article text.

Return Values (bold indicates success):

- **220 <article #> <msg-ID> Article retrieved—head and body follow**
- **221 <article #> <msg-ID> Article retrieved—head follows**
- **222 <article #> <msg-ID> Article retrieved—body follows**
- **223 <article #> <msg-ID> Article retrieved—request text separately**
- 412 No newsgroup has been selected
- 420 No current article has been selected
- 423 No such article number in this group
- 430 No such article found

NNTP Commands (AUTHINFO *)

Command:	AUTHINFO *
Description:	Used to identify a specific entity to the server using a simple username/password combination.
Usage:	AUTHINFO USER <Username> <CRLF>
	AUTHINFO PASS <Password> <CRLF>
Parameters:	Username and Password are the user's user name and password required for authorization purposes.

Examples:

```
'-- Send your name and password to the server in response to a 480 reply code.
SendData DSSocket1, "AUTHINFO USER JohnSmith" & vbCrlf
SendData DSSocket1, "AUTHINFO PASS MyPassword" & vbCrlf
```

Comments: Sometimes authorization is required to access an NNTP server or a specific command.

When authorization is required, the server will send a 480 response requesting authorization from the client. The client must enter AUTHINFO USER followed by the username. Once sent, the server will cache the username and send a 381 response requesting the password associated with that username. The client must then enter AUTHINFO PASS followed by the password for the username. The server will then check the authentication database to see if the username/password combination is valid.

If the combination is valid, the server will return a 281 response. The client should then retry the original command to which the server responded with the 480 response. The command should then be processed by the server normally. If the combination is not valid, the server will return a 502 response.

Clients must provide authentication when requested by the server. It is possible that some implementations will accept authentication information at the beginning of a session, but this was not the original intent of the specification. If a client attempts to reauthenticate, the server may return 482 response indicating that the new authentication data is rejected by the server.

The 482 code will also be returned when the AUTHINFO commands are not entered in the correct sequence (like two AUTHINFO USERs in a row, or AUTHINFO PASS preceding AUTHINFO USER).

When authentication succeeds, the server will create an email address for the client from the username supplied in the AUTHINFO USER command and the hostname generated by a reverse lookup on the IP address of the client. If the reverse lookup fails, the IP address, represented in dotted-quad format, will be used. Once authenticated, the server will generate a Sender: line using the email address provided by authentication if it does not match the client-supplied From: line. Additionally, the server should log the event, including the email address. This will provide a means by which subsequent statistics generation can associate newsgroup references with unique entities—not necessarily by name.

This is not a standard command as of this writing.

Return Values (bold indicates success):

- **281 Authentication accepted**
- 381 More authentication information required
- 480 Authentication required
- 482 Authentication rejected
- 502 No permission

NNTP Commands (AUTHINFO SIMPLE*)

Command:	AUTHINFO SIMPLE*
Description:	Used to identify a specific entity to the server using a simple username/password combination.
Usage:	AUTHINFO SIMPLE <CRLF>

(Wait for 350 response)

<Username> <Password> <CRLF>

Parameters: Username and Password are the user's username and password required for authorization purposes.

Examples:

```
'-- Send the command in response to a 450 reply code.
SendData DSSocket1, "AUTHINFO SIMPLE" & vbCrlf


'-- Then, after receiving a 350 response.. send the username and password
SendData DSSocket1, "JohnSmith MyPassword" & vbCrlf
```

Comments: AUTHINFO SIMPLE was part of the proposed NNTP V2 specification and is implemented in some servers and clients. It is a refinement of the original AUTHINFO and provides the same basic functionality, but the sequence of commands is much simpler.

When authorization is required, the server sends a 450 response requesting authorization from the client. The client must enter AUTHINFO SIMPLE. If the server will accept this form of authentication, the server responds with a 350 response. The client must then send the username followed by one or more space characters followed by the password. If accepted, the server returns a 250 response and the client should then retry the original command to which the server responded with the 451 response. The command should then be processed by the server normally. If the combination is not valid, the server will return a 452 response.

The response codes used here were part of the NNTP V2 specification and are violations of RFC 977. It is recommended that this command not be implemented, but use either or both of the other forms of AUTHINFO if such functionality is required.

This is not a standard command as of this writing.

Return Values (bold indicates success):

- **250 Authorization accepted**
- 350 Continue with authorization sequence
- 450 Authorization required for this command
- 452 Authorization rejected

NNTP Commands (AUTHINFO GENERIC *)

Command: AUTHINFO GENERIC *

Description: Used to identify a specific entity to the server using a simple username/password combination.

Usage: AUTHINFO GENERIC <Arg1> [<Arg2>...] <CRLF>

Parameters: Username and Password are the user's username and password required for authorization purposes.

Example:

```
'-- Send the command in response to a 380 reply code.
SendData DSSocket1, "AUTHINFO GENERIC" & vbCrlf
```

Comments: AUTHINFO GENERIC is used to identify a specific entity to the server using arbitrary authentication or identification protocols. The desired protocol is indicated by the authenticator parameter, and any number of parameters can be passed to the authenticator.

When authorization is required, the server will send a 380 response requesting authorization from the client. The client should enter AUTHINFO GENERIC followed by the authenticator name, and the arguments if any. The authenticator and arguments must not contain the sequence "..".

The server will attempt to engage the server end authenticator; similarly, the client should engage the client end authenticator. The server end authenticator will then initiate authentication using the NNTP sockets (if appropriate for that authentication protocol), using the protocol specified by the authenticator name. These authentication protocols are not included in this document, but are similar in structure to those referenced in RFC 1731[7] for the IMAP-4 protocol.

If the server returns 501, this means that the authenticator invocation was syntactically incorrect, or that AUTHINFO GENERIC is not supported. The client should retry using the AUTHINFO USER command.

If the requested authenticator capability is not found or there is some other unspecified server program error, the server returns the 503 response code.

The authenticators converse using their protocol until complete.

If the authentication succeeds, the server authenticator will terminate with a 281, and the client can continue by reissuing the command that prompted the 380. If the authentication fails, the server will respond with a 502.

The client must provide authentication when requested by the server. The server may request authentication at any time. Servers may request authentication more than once during a single session.

When the server authenticator completes, it provides to the server (by a mechanism herein undefined) the email address of the user, and potentially what the user is allowed to access. Once authenticated, the server shall generate a Sender: line using the email address provided by the authenticator if it does not match the user-supplied From: line.

Additionally, the server should log the event, including the user's authenticated email address (if available). This will provide a means by which subsequent statistics generation can associate newsgroup references with unique entities—not necessarily by name.

This is not a standard command as of this writing.

Return Values (bold indicates success):

- **281 Authentication succeeded**
- 380 Authentication required
- 501 Command not supported or Command syntax error
- 502 No permission
- 503 Program error, function not performed
- nnn Authenticator-specific protocol

NNTP Commands (DATE *)

Command:	DATE *
Description:	Returns the current date and time from the server's perspective.
Usage:	DATE <CRLF>
Parameters:	<none>
Example:	

```
'-- Send the command in response to a 380 reply code.
SendData DSSocket1, "DATE" & vbCrlf
```

Comments: At the time this command was discussed (1991–1992), the Network Time Protocol (NTP) was not yet in wide use and there was also some concern that small systems might not be able to make effective use of NTP.

This command returns a one-line response code of 111 followed by the GMT (Grenwich Mean Time) date and time on the server in the form YYYYMMDDhhmmss. This is not a standard command as of this writing.

Return Values (bold indicates success):

- **111 YYYYMMDDhhmmss**

NNTP Commands (GROUP)

Command:	GROUP
Description:	Selects a Usenet newsgroup by name.
Usage:	GROUP <Newsgroup> <CRLF>
Parameters:	Newsgroup is the name of a Usenet newsgroup.
Example:	

```
SendData DSSocket1, "Group alt.winsock.programming" & vbCrLF
```

Comments: If the newsgroup exists on the server, the return value indicates the estimated (very important) number of articles available, the first article number, and the last article number in the group. The name of the group is also returned but you don't need this unless you send several GROUP commands at the same time and must identify the newsgroup for each set of statistics.

Return Values (bold indicates success):

- **211 n f l s group selected**

    n = Estimated number of articles in group

    f = First article number in the group

    l = Last article number in the group

    s = Name of the group

- 411 No such newsgroup

NNTP Commands (HELP)

Command:	HELP
Description:	Requests a list of supported NNTP commands.
Usage:	HELP <CRLF>
Parameters:	Newsgroup is the name of a Usenet newsgroup.
Example:	

```
SendData DSSocket1, "HELP" & vbCrLf
```

Comments: If you really want to know if the server supports the commands you intend to send it, you can query the server with the HELP command. The only situation in which I can see this as being useful is for commands that are in the process of being implemented as standards and not supported on all systems. However, it's just as easy to receive an error code and report "function not available" to the user, or some such nonsense.

Return Values (bold indicates success):

- **100 Help text follows**

NNTP Commands (IHAVE)

Command:	IHAVE
Description:	Informs the server that a particular article exists locally. The server reply instructs to either send the article or not send the article.
Usage:	IHAVE <Message-ID> <CRLF>
Parameters:	Message-ID is the message-id of a local Usenet article.

Example:

```
SendData DSSocket1, "IHAVE 192401@domain.com" & vbCrLf
```

Comments: The IHAVE message is for use mainly for server-to-server communication. Its sole purpose is to move existing articles throughout the network. If you are not planning to write an NNTP server, you can ignore this command.

In a perfect world you will receive a 335 reply immediately after sending this command. You should then send the article in the format defined in RFC 850 (at the time of this writing, anyway). You will then either receive a 235 reply indicating success or a 400 series error reply indicating failure. Be aware that just because you receive a 235 reply does not mean the server will post and/or forward the article.

It has become acceptable for NNTP servers to immediately send a 235 reply no matter what, and decide later if the article is appropriate for posting. This behavior will probably change with the next NNTP RFC after 977.

Return Values (bold indicates success):

- **235 Article transferred ok**
- **335 Send article to be transferred. End with <CR-LF>.<CR-LF>**
- 435 Article not wanted—do not send it
- 436 Transfer failed—try again later
- 437 Article rejected—do not try again
- 480 Transfer permission denied

NNTP Commands (LAST)

Command: LAST

Description: Moves the current article pointer to the previous article in the current newsgroup. The previous article is the article previous to the current article.

Usage: LAST <CRLF>

Parameters: <none>

Example:

```
SendData DSSocket1, "LAST" & vbCrLF
```

Comments: If the current article is the first article in the newsgroup an error code is returned and the current article stays selected.

Return Values (bold indicates success):

- **223 <article #> <msg-ID> Article retrieved—request text separately**
- 412 No newsgroup selected

- 420 No current article has been selected
- 422 No previous article in this group

NNTP Commands (LIST)

Command: LIST
Description: Returns a list of valid newsgroups, as well as other associated information.
Usage: LIST <CRLF>
Parameters: <none>
Example:

```
'-- This example does the same as sending just the LIST command.
SendData DSSocket1, "LIST" & vbCrlf
```

Comments: Each newsgroup is sent as a line of text in the following format:

group last first p

<group> is the name of the newsgroup
<last> is the number of the last known article currently in that newsgroup
<first> is the number of the first article currently in the newsgroup
<p> is either 'y' or 'n' indicating whether posting to this newsgroup is allowed

Note that posting may still be prohibited to a client even though the LIST command indicates that posting is permitted to a particular newsgroup. See the POST command for an explanation of client prohibitions. The posting flag exists for each newsgroup because some newsgroups are moderated or are digests, and therefore cannot be posted to; that is, articles posted to them must be mailed to a moderator who will post them for the submitter. This is independent of the posting permission granted to a client by the NNTP server.

Please note that an empty list (i.e., the text body returned by this command consists only of the terminating period) is a possible valid response, and indicates that there are currently no valid newsgroups.

Return Values (bold indicates success):

- **215** List of newsgroups follows

The server sends a period on a line by itself to indicate the end of file.

No error is ever returned. If there are no newsgroups, an empty list will be returned.

NNTP Commands (LIST ACTIVE*)

Command: LIST ACTIVE *

Description: Returns a list of valid newsgroups. If specified, limits the list to a particular pattern of newsgroup.

Usage: LIST ACTIVE [<Wildmat String>] <CRLF>

Parameters: <none>

Examples:

```
'-- This example does the same as sending just the LIST command.
SendData DSSocket1, "LIST ACTIVE" & vbCrlf


'-- This example tells the server to only list those newsgroups that begin
'   with comp.lang.basic
SendData DSSocket1, "LIST ACTIVE comp.lang.basic*" & vbCrlf
```

Comments: LIST ACTIVE does exactly the same thing as the LIST command, except that you can specify a newsgroup pattern. If no pattern is specified the result is the same as if you were to send just a LIST command.

This is not a standard command as of this writing.

Return Values (bold indicates success):

- **215** List of newsgroups follows.

The server sends a period on a line by itself to indicate the end of file.

No error is ever returned. If there are no newsgroups, an empty list will be returned.

NNTP Commands (LIST ACTIVE.TIMES*)

Command: LIST ACTIVE.TIMES *

Description: Returns the contents of the active.times file, which contains information about who created a particular newsgroup and when.

Usage: LIST ACTIVE.TIMES <CRLF>

Parameters: <none>

Example:

```
SendData DSSocket1, "LIST ACTIVE.TIMES" & vbCrlf
```

Comments: The active.times file is only maintained by some news transports systems.

If nothing is matched an empty list is returned, not an error.

This is not a standard command as of this writing.

Return Values (bold indicates success):

- **215 Information follows**

The format of this information generally include three fields. The first field is the name of the newsgroup. The second is the time when this group was created on this newsserver measured in seconds since January 1, 1970. The third is the email address of the entity that created the newsgroup.

The server sends a period on a line by itself to indicate the end of file.

- 503 Data is not available

NNTP Commands (LIST DISTRIBUTIONS*)

Command:	LIST DISTRIBUTIONS *
Description:	Returns the contents of the distributions file, which contains a list of valid values for the Distributions: line in a news article header, and what each value means.
Usage:	LIST DISTRIBUTIONS <CRLF>
Parameters:	<none>

Example:

```
SendData DSSocket1, "LIST DISTRIBUTIONS" & vbCrlf
```

Comments: The distributions file is only maintained by some news transport systems.

If nothing is matched an empty list is returned, not an error.

This is not a standard command as of this writing.

Return Values (bold indicates success):

- **215 Information follows**

  Each line contains two fields, the value and a short explanation on the meaning of the value. The server sends a period on a line by itself to indicate the end of file.

- 503 Data is not available

NNTP Commands (LIST DISTRIB.PATS *)

Command:	LIST DISTRIB.PATS *
Description:	Returns the contents of the distrib.pats file, which contains default values for the Distribution: line in a news article header when posting to particular newsgroups.
Usage:	LIST DISTRIB.PATS <CRLF>
Parameters:	<none>

Example:

```
SendData DSSocket1, "LIST DISTRIB.PATS" & vbCrlf
```

Comments: The distrib.pats file is only maintained by some news transport systems.

This information could be used to provide a default value for the Distribution: line in the header when posting an article.

The information returned involves three fields separated by colons. The first column is a weight. The second is a group name or a pattern that can be used to match a group name in the wildmat format. The third is the value of the Distribution: line that should be used when the group name matches and the weight value is the highest. All this processing is done by the newsposting client and not by the server itself. The server just provides this information to the client for it to use or ignore as it chooses.

If nothing is matched an empty list is returned, not an error.

This is not a standard command as of this writing.

Return Values (bold indicates success):

- **215 Information follows**

The information returned involves three fields separated by colons. The first column is a weight. The second is a group name or a pattern that can be used to match a group name in the wildmat format. The third is the value of the Distribution: line that should be used when the group name matches and the weight value is the highest.

The server sends a period on a line by itself to indicate the end of file.

- 503 Data is not available

NNTP Commands (LIST NEWSGROUPS *)

Command:	LIST NEWSGROUPS *
Description:	Returns the contents of the newsgroups file, which contains the name and a short description of each active newsgroup.
Usage:	LIST NEWSGROUPS [<Wildmat String>] <CRLF>
Parameters:	<none>
Examples:	

```
'-- This example tells the server to display info about all newsgroups
SendData DSSocket1, "LIST NEWSGROUPS" & vbCrlf


'-- This example tells the server to display info about only those newsgroups
'    that begin with "comp.lang"
SendData DSSocket1, "LIST NEWSGROUPS comp.lang*" & vbCrlf
```

Comments: The newsgroups file is only maintained by some news transport systems.

If the optional matching parameter is specified, the list is limited to only the groups that match the pattern (no matching is done on the group descriptions). Specifying a single group is usually very efficient for the server, and multiple groups may be specified by using wildmat patterns (similar to file globbing), not regular expressions.

When the optional parameter is specified, this command is equivalent to the XGTITLE* command, though the response codes are different.

If nothing is matched an empty list is returned, not an error.

This is not a standard command as of this writing.

Return Values (bold indicates success):

- **215 Information follows**

    Each line in the file contains two fields, the newsgroup name and a short explanation of the purpose of the newsgroup.

    The server sends a period on a line by itself to indicate the end of file.

- 503 Data is not available

NNTP Commands (LIST OVERVIEW.FMT *)

Command:	LIST OVERVIEW.FMT *
Description:	Returns the contents of the overview.fmt file, which contains the order in which header information is stored in the overview databases for each newsgroup.
Usage:	LIST OVERVIEW.FMT <CRLF>
Parameters:	<none>
Example:	

```
SendData DSSocket1, "LIST OVERVIEW.FRT" & vbCrlf
```

Comments: The overview.fmt file is only maintained by some news transport systems.

If the header has the word "full" (without quotes) after the colon, the header's name is prepended to its field in the output returned by the server.

If nothing is matched an empty list is returned, not an error.

This is not a standard command as of this writing.

Return Values (bold indicates success):

- **215 Information follows**

    The article header fields are displayed one line at a time in the order in which they are stored in the overview database.

The server sends a period on a line by itself to indicate the end of file.

- 503 Data is not available

NNTP Commands (LIST SUBSCRIPTIONS *)

Command:	LIST SUBSCRIPTIONS *
Description:	Returns a default subscription list for new users of the server.
Usage:	LIST SUBSCRIPTIONS <CRLF>
Parameters:	<none>

Example:

```
SendData DSSocket1, "LIST SUBSCRIPTIONS" & vbCrlf
```

Comments: The order of groups is significant.

This is not a standard command as of this writing.

Return Values (bold indicates success):

- **215 Information follows**

  The server sends a period on a line by itself to indicate the end of transmission.

- 503 Data is not available

NNTP Commands (LISTGROUP *)

Command:	LISTGROUP *
Description:	Returns a listing of all the article numbers in the currently selected newsgroup or a specified newsgroup.
Usage:	LISTGROUP [<Group Name>] <CRLF>
Parameters:	Group Name is an optional parameter. It specifies the name of a newsgroup. If not specified, article numbers for the currently selected newsgroup are returned.

Examples:

```
'-- Asks for a listing of all article numbers in the currently selected group
SendData DSSocket1, "LISTGROUP" & vbCrlf


'-- Asks for a listing of all article numbers in comp.lang.basic.visual
SendData DSSocket1, "LISTGROUP comp.lang.basic.viwual.misc" & vbCrlf
```

Comments: A list of newsgroups may be obtained from the LIST command.

When a valid group is selected by means of this command, the internally maintained "current article pointer" is set to the first article in the group. If an invalid group is specified, the previously selected group and article remain selected. If an empty newsgroup is selected, the "current article pointer" is in an indeterminate state and should not be used.

The name of the newsgroup is case insensitive. It must otherwise match a newsgroup obtained from the LIST command or an error will result.

Return Values (bold indicates success):

- **211 List of article numbers follows**

  The server sends a period on a line by itself to indicate the end of transmission.

- 412 Not currently in newsgroup

- 502 No permission

NNTP Commands (MODE READER *)

Command:	MODE READER *
Description:	Used by the client to indicate to the server that it is a newsreading client.
Usage:	MODE READER <CRLF>
Parameters:	<none>
Example:	

```
SendData DSSocket1, "MODE READER" & vbCrlf
```

Comments: Some implementations make use of this information to reconfigure themselves for better performance in responding to newsreader commands. Some servers require a MODE command before allowing access at all.

The command MODE QUERY is also used sometimes in place of MODE READER. MODE QUERY means exactly the same thing.

Return Values (bold indicates success):

- **200 Hello, you can post**

  Indicates that posting is allowed.

- **201 Hello, you can't post**

  Indicates that posting is not allowed.

NNTP Commands (NEWGROUPS)

Command:	NEWGROUPS
Description:	Retrieves all the newsgroups that were created after a specified point in time.
Usage:	NEWGROUPS <yymmdd> <hhmmss> [GMT] [<distributions>]
Parameters:	The date is specified as six digits in the format YYMMDD, where YY is the last two digits of the year, MM is the two digits of the month (with leading zero, if appropriate), and DD is the day of the month (with leading zero, if appropriate). The closest century is assumed as part of the year (i.e., 86 specifies 1986, 30 specifies 2030, 99 is 1999, 00 is 2000).

The time is specified as six digits HHMMSS with HH being hours on the 24-hour clock, MM minutes 00-59, and SS seconds 00-59. The time is assumed to be in the server's timezone unless the token "GMT" appears, in which case both time and date are evaluated at the 0 meridian. You can use the DATE command to determine the date and time relative to the server.

The optional parameter "distributions" is a list of distribution groups, enclosed in angle brackets. If specified, the distribution portion of a new newsgroup (e.g., 'net' in 'net.wombat') will be examined for a match with the distribution categories listed, and only those new newsgroups that match will be listed. If more than one distribution group is to be listed, they must be separated by commas within the angle brackets.

Example:

```
'-- Returns all newsgroups created since March 1, 1995
'   at exactly 8 PM
SendData DSSocket1, "NEWGROUPS 950301 200000" & vbCrlf
```

Comments: *Note:* an empty list (i.e., the text body returned by this command consists only of the terminating period) is a possible valid response, and indicates that there are currently no new newsgroups.

Return Values (bold indicates success):

- **231** List of new newsgroups follows

  Each line in the file contains two fields, the newsgroup name and a short explanation of the purpose of the newsgroup.

  The server sends a period on a line by itself to indicate the end of file.

NNTP Commands (NEWNEWS)

Command:	NEWNEWS
Description:	Retrieves all articles in a specified newsgroup that were created after a specified point in time.
Usage:	NEWNEWS <newsgroup> <yymmdd> <hhmmss> [GMT] [<distributions>]
Parameters:	The date is specified as six digits in the format YYMMDD, where YY is the last two digits of the year, MM is the two digits of the month (with leading zero, if appropriate), and DD is the day of the month (with leading zero, if appropriate). The closest century is assumed as part of the year (i.e., 86 specifies 1986, 30 specifies 2030, 99 is 1999, 00 is 2000).

The time is specified as six digits HHMMSS with HH being hours on the 24-hour clock, MM minutes 00-59, and SS seconds 00-59. The time is assumed to be in the server's timezone unless the token "GMT" appears, in which case both time and date are evaluated at the 0 meridian. You can use the DATE command to determine the date and time relative to the server.

The optional parameter "distributions" is a list of distribution groups, enclosed in angle brackets. If specified, the distribution portion of a new newsgroup (e.g., 'net' in 'net.wombat') will be examined for a match with the distribution categories listed, and only those new newsgroups that match will be listed. If more than one distribution group is to be listed, they must be separated by commas within the angle brackets.

Example:

```
'-- Returns all new articles in rec.audio.pro since March 1, 1995
'    at exactly 8 PM
SendData DSSocket1, "NEWNEWS rec.audio.pro 950301 200000" & vbCrlf
```

Comments: A newsgroup name containing an asterisk (*) may be specified to broaden the article search to some or all newsgroups. The asterisk will be extended to match any part of a newsgroup name (e.g., net.micro* will match net.micro.wombat, net.micro.apple, etc.). Thus if only an asterisk is given as the newsgroup name, all newsgroups will be searched for new news.

Note: that the asterisk (*) expansion is a general replacement; in particular, the specification of, for example, net.*.unix should be correctly expanded to embrace names such as net.wombat.unix and net.whocares.unix.

Conversely, if no asterisk appears in a given newsgroup name, only the specified newsgroup will be searched for new articles. Newsgroup names must be chosen from those returned in the listing of available groups. Multiple newsgroup names (including an asterisk) may be specified in this command, separated by a comma. No comma shall appear after the last newsgroup in the list. [Implementors are cautioned to keep the 512 character command length limit in mind.]

The exclamation point (!) may be used to negate a match. This can be used to selectively omit certain newsgroups from an otherwise larger list. For example, a news-groups specification of net.*,mod.*,!mod.map.* would specify that all net.<anything> and all mod.<anything> *except* mod.map.<anything> newsgroup names would be matched. If used, the exclamation point must appear as the first character of the given newsgroup name or pattern.

Note: an empty list (i.e., the text body returned by this command consists only of the terminating period) is a possible valid response, and indicates that there are cur-rently no new newsgroups.

Return Values (bold indicates success):

- **230 List of new articles by message-id follows**

  The server sends a list of Message-IDs followed by a period on a line by itself.

NNTP Commands (POST)

Command:	POST
Description:	Requests permission to post a new article.
Usage:	POST <CRLF>
Parameters:	<none>

Examples:

```
'-- Request permission to post an article
SendData DSSocket1, "POST" & vbCrlf


'-- After receiving a 340 reply...
SendData DSSocket1, "From: Carl Franklin <carlf@apexsc.com>"& vbCrlf _
    & "Newsgroup: alt.winsock.programming" & vbCrlf _
    & "Subject: This is a test post" & vbCrlf _
    & vbCrlf _
    & "Hello, this was a posted from a VB program!" & vbCrlf _
    & "." & vbCrlf
```

Comments: After the initial connection to the server is made, the server sends a 200 reply if posting is allowed and 201 reply if not.

After sending the POST command, you will either receive a 340 reply, granting permission to post the article, or a 440 reply denying permission. If you receive a 340 reply then you should immediately send your post.

When posting, there are only three header fields required:

From	Your name and email address
Newsgroup	Newsgroup to post to
Subject	The subject of the article

The subject line is followed by a blank line and that is followed by your article text. End your post with a period on a line by itself.

Return Values (bold indicates success):

- **340 Send your post**
- 440 Do not post

NNTP Commands (XGTITLE *)

Command:	XGTITLE *
Description:	Retrieves newsgroup descriptions for specific newsgroups.
Usage:	XGTITLE [<Wildmat String>] <CRLF>
Parameters:	The optional wildmat string argument specifies a newsgroup pattern such as comp.lang.basic.*, alt.b*, or comp.binaries.s??
	When not specified, data for the currently selected newsgroup is returned.

Examples:

```
'-- Asks for a description of the current newsgroup
SendData DSSocket1, "XGTITLE" & vbCrlf


'-- Asks for a description of all newsgroups that begin with "comp.lang"
SendData DSSocket1, "XGTITLE comp.lang*" & vbCrlf
```

Comments: XGTITLE and LIST NEWSGROUP provide the same functionality, but just return different response codes.

If the optional matching parameter is specified, the list is limited to only the groups that match the pattern (no matching is done on the group descriptions). Specifying a single group is usually very efficient for the server, and multiple groups may be specified by using wildmat patterns (similar to file globbing), not regular expressions.

If nothing is matched an empty list is returned, not an error.

This extension first appeared in ANU-NEWS, an NNTP implementation for DEC's VMS.

This is not a standard command as of this writing.

Return Values (bold indicates success):

- **282 List of groups and descriptions follows**

  Each line in the file contains two fields, the newsgroup name and a short description of the newsgroup.

  The server sends a period on a line by itself to indicate the end of transmission.

- 412 Not currently in newsgroup

- 502 No permission

NNTP Commands (XHDR *)

Command: XHDR *

Description: Retrieves specific header lines from specific articles.

Usage: XHDR <Header> [<Range>|<Message-ID>] <CRLF>

Parameters: Header is the name of a header line (e.g., subject). See RFC 1036 for a list of valid header lines.

The second parameter is optional. This can be either a range of message numbers or a valid Message ID.

The optional range argument may be any of the following:

1. An article number (e.g., 100)

2. An article number followed by a dash to indicate all following (e.g. 100-)

3. An article number followed by a dash and another article number (e.g., 100-105)

If the second parameter is not specified, then information from the current article is displayed.

Examples:

```
'-- Requests the Subject of the current article
SendData DSSocket1, "XHDR subject" & vbCrlf


'-- Requests the email address of article 100's sender
SendData DSSocket1, "XHDR from 100" & vbCrlf


'-- Requests the number of lines in articles from 1 to 100
SendData DSSocket1, "XHDR lines 1-100" & vbCrlf


'-- Requests the date of article with message-id <87623@baz.UUCP>
SendData DSSocket1, "XHDR date <87623@baz.UUCP>" & vbCrlf
```

Comments: The range and message-id arguments are mutually exclusive.

The XHDR command has been available in the UNIX reference implementation from its first release. However, until now, it has only been documented in the source for the server.

This is not a standard command as of this writing.

Return Values (bold indicates success):

- **221 Header follows**

  The server sends a period on a line by itself to indicate the end of transmission.
- 412 No newsgroup current selected
- 420 No current article selected
- 430 No such article exists
- 502 No permission

NNTP Commands (XINDEX *)

Command: XINDEX *
Description: Retrieves an index file in the format of originally created for use by the UNIX TIN newsreader.
Usage: XINDEX <Newsgroup> <CRLF>
Parameters: Newsgroup is the name of a newsgroup. If not specified, then index file for the current newsgroup is returned.

Examples:

```
'-- Requests the index file for the current newsgroup
SendData DSSocket1, "XINDEX" & vbCrlf


'-- Requests the index file for comp.lang.basic.visual.misc
SendData DSSocket1, "XINDEX comp.lang.basic.visual.misc" & vbCrlf
```

Comments: A list of valid newsgroups may be obtained from the LIST command.

When a valid group is selected by means of this command, the internally maintained "current article pointer" is set to the first article in the group. If an invalid group is specified, the previously selected group and article remain selected. If an empty newsgroup is selected, the "current article pointer" is in an indeterminate state and should not be used.

The format of the tin-style index file is discussed in the documentation for the TIN newsreader. Since more recent versions of TIN support the news overview (NOV) format, it is recommended that this extension become historic and no longer be used in current servers or future implementations.

This is not a standard command as of this writing.

Return Values (bold indicates success):

- **218 Tin-style index follows**

  The server sends a period on a line by itself to indicate the end of file.

- 418 No tin-style index is available for this newsgroup

NNTP Commands (XOVER *)

Command:	XOVER *
Description:	Returns reference information about the specified article(s).
Usage:	XOVER <Range> <CRLF>
Parameters:	Range may be any of the following:

1. An article number (e.g., 100)
2. An article number followed by a dash to indicate all following (e.g., 100-)
3. An article number followed by a dash and another article number (e.g., 100-105)

If no argument is specified, the information for the current article is returned.

Examples:

```
'-- Returns information about article #120
SendData DSSocket1, "XOVER 120" & vbCrlf


'-- Returns information about all articles starting from 145
SendData DSSocket1, "XOVER 145-" & vbCrlf


'-- Returns information about articles from 100 to 200
SendData DSSocket1, "XOVER 100-200" & vbCrlf
```

Comments: This is not a standard command as of this writing.

Return Values (bold indicates success):

- **282 XOVER Information follows**

  Each line consists of the article number, followed by reference overview information separated by a tab character. Generally these fields are as follows:

    Message Number

    Subject

    From

Date

Message-ID

Bytes

Lines

The server sends a period on a line by itself to indicate the end of transmission.

- 412 No newsgroup currently selected
- 420 No article(s) selected
- 502 No permission

NNTP Commands (XPAT *)

Command:	XPAT *
Description:	Retrieves specific headers from specific articles in the current newsgroup given one or more search patterns.
Usage:	XPAT <Header> <Range|Message-ID> <Wildmat String> [<Wildmat String>] <CRLF>
Parameters:	Header is the name of a header line (e.g., subject). See RFC 1036 for a list of valid header lines.

The second parameter is either a range of message numbers or a valid Message ID.

Range may be any of the following:

1. An article number (e.g., 100)
2. An article number followed by a dash to indicate all following (e.g., 100–)
3. An article number followed by a dash and another article number (e.g., 100–105)

At least one wildmat string is required. This argument selects a search pattern for the header line being selected. Additional patterns can follow separated by a space.

Examples:

```
'-- Searches all articles starting with 100 and returns all articles
'    where the subject line begins with "RE:"
SendData DSSocket1, "XPAT Subject 100- RE:*" & vbCrlf


'-- Searches all articles from 100 to 200 and returns all articles
'    where the email address contains netcom.com
SendData DSSocket1, "XPAT From 100-200 *netcom.com*" & vbCrlf
```

Comments: The range and message-id arguments are mutually exclusive.

This is not a standard command as of this writing.

Return Values (bold indicates success):

- **221 Header follows**

  Each line consists of the article number, followed by each of the headers in the overview database for that article separated by a tab character.

  The server sends a period on a line by itself to indicate the end of transmission.

- 430 No such article

NNTP Commands (XTHREAD *)

Command:	XTHREAD *
Description:	Retrieves threading information in a format originally created for use by the UNIX TRN newsreader.
Usage:	XTHREAD [DBINIT|THREAD] <CRLF>
Parameters:	The optional parameter is either DBINIT or THREAD.

XTHREAD DBINIT may be issued prior to entering any groups to see if a thread database exists. If it does, the database's byte order and version number are returned as binary data.

If no parameter is given, XTHREAD THREAD is assumed.

Examples:

```
SendData DSSocket1,"XTHREAD" & vbCrlf


SendData DSSocket1, "XTHREAD DBINIT THREAD" & vbCrlf


SendData DSSocket1, "XTHREAD DBINIT" & vbCrlf
```

Comments: This is not a standard command as of this writing.

Return Values (bold indicates success):

- **288 Binary data to follow**

  The format of the trn-style thread format is discussed in the documentation for the TRN newsreader. Since more recent versions of TRN support the news overview (NOV) format, it is recommended that this extension become historic and no longer be used in current servers or future implementations.

- 412 No newsgroup currently selected

- 502 No permission

- 503 Program error, function not performed

SMTP

COMMAND LISTING

The following is a listing of standard Simple Mail Transfer Protocol commands adapted from RFC #821 by Jonathan B. Postel.

SMTP Commands (DATA)

Command: DATA
Description: Requests permission to send message data.
Usage: DATA <CRLF>
Parameters: None
Example:

```
'-- Sends the DATA command
SendSMTPCommand DSSocket1, "DATA"
```

Comments: After sending a DATA command, you will receive a 354 reply from the server which means "Go ahead and send." You then send the message data followed by a period on a line by itself, after which you will receive a 250 reply from the server.
Return Values (bold indicates success):

- **354 Send data**

  Sender sends message data followed by a period on a line by itself, after which the sender receives a 250 reply.

- 421 <domain> Service not available, closing transmission channel
- 451 Requested action aborted: error in processing
- 452 Requested action not taken: insufficient system storage
- 500 Syntax error, command unrecognized
- 501 Syntax error in parameters or arguments
- 503 Bad sequence of commands
- 552 Requested mail action aborted: exceeded storage allocation
- 554 Transaction failed

SMTP Commands (EXPAND)

Command:	EXPN
Description:	Asks the SMTP server to verify a mailing list and returns a membership listing.
Usage:	EXPN <list name> <CRLF>
Parameters:	<list name> is the name of a mailing list.
Example:	

```
'-- Sends the EXPN command
SendSMTPCommand DSSocket1, "EXPN admin"
```

Comments: <list name> is the name of a mailing list. For example, "admin" is generally a mailing list on most networks. Sometimes a mailing list is referred to as an *alias*.
Return Values (bold indicates success):

- **250 OK**

   The server sends a list of members each beginning with a 250 code. There is no period at the end of this list.
- 421 <domain> Service not available, closing transmission channel
- 500 Syntax error, command unrecognized
- 501 Syntax error in parameters or arguments
- 502 Command not implemented
- 504 Command parameter not implemented
- 550 Requested action not taken: mailbox unavailable

SMTP Commands (HELLO)

Command:	HELLO
Description:	Initiates a mail transaction, identifies the sender to the receiver, and tells the server to reset state tables and buffers.

Usage: HELO <sender's domain> <CRLF>

Parameters: The sender's domain is specified as the portion of your email address following the @ sign (e.g., the domain of santa@northpole.com is north-pole.com).

Example:

```
'-- Sends the HELLO command
SendSMTPCommand DSSocket1, "HELO northpole.com"
```

Comments: You should always send the HELO command after receiving the first 220 reply upon connection.

Return Values (bold indicates success):

- **250 OK**
- 421 <domain> Service not available, closing transmission channel
- 500 Syntax error, command unrecognized
- 501 Syntax error in parameters or arguments
- 504 Command parameter not implemented

SMTP Commands (HELP)

Command: HELP

Description: Asks the server for helpful information.

Usage: HELP <CRLF>

Parameters: none

Example:

```
'-- Sends the HELP command
SendSMTPCommand DSSocket1, "HELP"
```

Comments: HELP usually returns a list of supported commands, but there is no standard format for help messages, since they are really meant to be read by a human user. You can usually get an explanation of any supported command by sending HELP followed by the name of the command. Therefore, if you want to determine if a system supports a command, say SOML, you can send "HELP SOML". If you get back a 211 or 214 you know the command is supported. If not, you will get back an error reply.

Return Values (bold indicates success):

- **211 System status, or system help reply**
- **214 Help message**
- 421 <domain> Service not available, closing transmission channel
- 500 Syntax error, command unrecognized

- 501 Syntax error in parameters or arguments
- 502 Command not implemented
- 504 Command parameter not implemented

SMTP Commands (MAIL)

Command:	MAIL
Description:	Initiates a mail transaction and tells the server to reset state tables and buffers.
Usage:	MAIL FROM: <sender's email address> <CRLF>
Parameters:	The sender's email address is specified as a complete email address between a less-than and a greater-than sign (e.g., <santa@northpole.com>).

Example:

```
'-- Sends the MAIL command

SendSMTPCommand DSSocket1, "MAIL FROM: <santa@northpole.com>"
```

Return Values (bold indicates success):

- **250 OK**
- 421 <domain> Service not available, closing transmission channel
- 451 Requested action aborted: error in processing
- 452 Requested action not taken: insufficient system storage
- 500 Syntax error, command unrecognized
- 501 Syntax error in parameters or arguments
- 552 Requested mail action aborted: exceeded storage allocation

SMTP Commands (NOOP)

Command:	NOOP
Description:	Does nothing but request a positive reply from the server.
Usage:	NOOP <CRLF>
Parameters:	none

Example:

```
'-- Sends the NOOP command

SendSMTPCommand DSSocket1, "NOOP"
```

Comments: If you receive back a 250 reply then you have successfully established communication with the server. If nothing comes back then you could be disconnected, or the server could be extremely busy (unlikely).

Using NOOP is a good way to see if you are still talking successfully with the server. If your app has been idle for a while, for example, you may want to establish a clear line of communication before continuing.

Return Values (bold indicates success):

- **250 OK**
- 421 <domain> Service not available, closing transmission channel
- 500 Syntax error, command unrecognized

SMTP Commands (QUIT)

Command:	QUIT
Description:	Tells the receiver of this command to close the connection and terminate the transaction.
Usage:	QUIT <CRLF>
Parameters:	none
Examples:	

```
'-- Sends the QUIT command
SendSMTPCommand DSSocket1, "QUIT"
```

Return Values (bold indicates success):

- **211 System status, or system help reply**

  The server returns a signoff message,
- 500 Syntax error, command unrecognized

SMTP Commands (RECIPIENT)

Command:	RECIPIENT
Description:	Gives a forward-path identifying one recipient. Used in creating a new mail message.
Usage:	RCPT <receiver's email address> <CRLF>
Parameters:	The receiver's email address is specified as a complete email address between a less-than and a greater-than sign (e.g., <santa@northpole.com>).

Examples:

```
'-- Sends the RECIPIENT command
SendSMTPCommand DSSocket1, "RCPT TO: <jaque@southpole.com>"
```

Comments: RCPT

Return Values (bold indicates success):

- **250 OK**
- **251 User not local; will forward to <forward-path>**
- 421 <domain> Service not available, closing transmission channel
- 450 Requested mail action not taken: mailbox unavailable
- 451 Requested action aborted: error in processing
- 452 Requested action not taken: insufficient system storage
- 500 Syntax error, command unrecognized
- 501 Syntax error in parameters or arguments
- 503 Bad sequence of commands
- 550 Requested action not taken: mailbox unavailable
- 551 User not local; please try <forward-path>
- 552 Requested mail action aborted: exceeded storage allocation
- 553 Requested action not taken: mailbox name not allowed

SMTP Commands (RESET)

Command:	RESET
Description:	Resets the server and aborts the current mail transaction.
Usage:	RSET <CRLF>
Parameters:	None

Example:

```
'-- Sends the RESET command
SendSMTPCommand DSSocket1, "RSET"
```

Comments: Any time you encounter an error and wish to abort the current transaction or start over you should first send a RESET command and wait for a 250 reply.

Return Values (bold indicates success):

- **250 OK**
- 421 <domain> Service not available, closing transmission channel
- 500 Syntax error, command unrecognized

- 501 Syntax error in parameters or arguments
- 504 Command parameter not implemented

SMTP Commands (SEND AND MAIL)

Command:	SEND AND MAIL
Description:	Sends a message directly to the recipient and also places the message in the recipient's mailbox.
Usage:	SAML FROM: <sender's email address> <CRLF>
Parameters:	The sender's email address is specified as a complete email address between a less-than and a greater-than sign (e.g., <santa@northpole.com>).

Example:

```
'-- Sends the SEND AND MAIL command
SendSMTPCommand DSSocket1, "SAML FROM: <santa@northpole.com>"
```

Comments: When you SEND (as opposed to MAIL) a message, the message is delivered directly to the user's terminal if the user indeed *has* a terminal and is logged on. SENDing is really only appropriate for terminal-based UNIX shell systems and does not apply throughout the enterprise.

SAML (Send And Mail) performs both a SEND and a MAIL command.

Return Values (bold indicates success):

- **250 OK**
- 421 <domain> Service not available, closing transmission channel
- 451 Requested action aborted: error in processing
- 452 Requested action not taken: insufficient system storage
- 500 Syntax error, command unrecognized
- 501 Syntax error in parameters or arguments
- 502 Command not implemented
- 552 Requested mail action aborted: exceeded storage allocation

SMTP Commands (SEND)

Command:	SEND
Description:	Sends a message directly to the recipient.
Usage:	SEND FROM: <sender's email address> <CRLF>

Parameters: The sender's email address is specified as a complete email address between
               a less-than and a greater-than sign (e.g., <santa@northpole.com>).

Example:

```
'-- Sends the SEND command
SendSMTPCommand DSSocket1, "SEND FROM: <santa@northpole.com>"
```

Comments: When you SEND (as opposed to MAIL) a message, the message is delivered directly to the user's terminal if the user indeed *has* a terminal and is logged on. SENDing is really only appropriate for terminal-based UNIX shell systems and does not apply throughout the enterprise.

Return Values (bold indicates success):

- **250 OK**
- 421 <domain> Service not available, closing transmission channel
- 451 Requested action aborted: error in processing
- 452 Requested action not taken: insufficient system storage
- 500 Syntax error, command unrecognized
- 501 Syntax error in parameters or arguments
- 502 Command not implemented
- 552 Requested mail action aborted: exceeded storage allocation

SMTP Commands (SEND OR MAIL)

Command: SEND OR MAIL
Description: Sends a message directly to the recipient and places the message in the
               recipient's mailbox only if there is a problem sending to the terminal.
Usage: SOML FROM: <sender's email address> <CRLF>
Parameters: The sender's email address is specified as a complete email address between
               a less-than and a greater-than sign (e.g., <santa@northpole.com>).

Example:

```
'-- Sends the SEND OR MAIL command
SendSMTPCommand DSSocket1, "SOML FROM: <santa@northpole.com>"
```

Comments: When you SEND (as opposed to MAIL) a message, the message is delivered directly to the user's terminal if the user indeed *has* a terminal and is logged on. SENDing is really only appropriate for terminal-based UNIX shell systems and does not apply throughout the enterprise.

SOML (Send And Mail) performs a SEND command and performs a MAIL command only if there is a problem with SEND.

Return Values (bold indicates success):

- **250 OK**
- 421 <domain> Service not available, closing transmission channel
- 451 Requested action aborted: error in processing
- 452 Requested action not taken: insufficient system storage
- 500 Syntax error, command unrecognized
- 501 Syntax error in parameters or arguments
- 502 Command not implemented
- 552 Requested mail action aborted: exceeded storage allocation

SMTP Commands (TURN)

Command:	TURN
Description:	Instructs the receiver to switch sender/receiver roles. If a sender receives a TURN command, he or she must become a receiver, and vice versa.
Usage:	TURN <CRLF>
Parameters:	none

Example:

```
'-- Sends the TURN command
SendSMTPCommand DSSocket1, "TURN"
```

Comments: When you connect to an SMTP server and send a TURN command, your process becomes the receiver and the other side becomes the sender of commands. This situation should never present itself when performing the task of sending email. I quote from RFC 821 by Jon Postel:

> Please note that this command is optional. It would not normally be used in situations where the transmission channel is TCP. However, when the cost of establishing the transmission channel is high, this command may be quite useful. For example, this command may be useful in supporting be mail exchange using the public switched telephone system as a transmission channel, especially if some hosts poll other hosts for mail exchanges.

For Windows TCP/IP-based networks, therefore, you shouldn't have to worry about this command at all.

Return Values (bold indicates success):

- **250 OK**
- 500 Syntax error, command unrecognized
- 502 Command not implemented
- 503 Bad sequence of commands

SMTP Commands (VRFY)

Command:	VRFY
Description:	Asks the SMTP server to verify an email address.
Usage:	VRFY carlf <CRLF>
Parameters:	The sender's email address is specified as a complete email address between a less-than and a greater-than sign (e.g., <santa@northpole.com>).

Example:

```
'-- Sends the SEND OR MAIL command
SendSMTPCommand DSSocket1, "SOML FROM: <santa@northpole.com>"
```

Return Values (bold indicates success):

- **250 OK**
- 251 User not local; will forward to <forward-path>
- 421 <domain> Service not available, closing transmission channel
- 500 Syntax error, command unrecognized
- 501 Syntax error in parameters or arguments
- 502 Command not implemented
- 504 Command parameter not implemented
- 550 Requested action not taken; mailbox unavailable
- 551 User not local; please try <forward-path>
- 553 Requested action not taken;mailbox name not allowed

POP3

COMMAND LISTING

The following is a listing of standard Post Office Protocol 3 commands adapted from RFC #1725 by J. Myers.

POP3 Commands (DELE)

Command:	DELE (DELETE)
Description:	Deletes a message from the mailbox.
Usage:	DELE <Message Number> <CRLF>
Parameters:	<Message Number> identifies a message currently in the mailbox.

Example:

```
'-- Sends the DELETE command
SendPOP3Command DSSocket1, "DELE 1"
```

Comments: DELE can be issued only in the TRANSACTION state.

The POP3 server marks the message as deleted. Any future references to the message-number associated with the deleted message in a POP3 command generates an error. The POP3 server does not actually delete the message until the POP3 session enters the UPDATE state.

Return Values (bold indicates success):

- **+OK Message deleted**
- -ERR No such message

POP3 Commands (LIST)

Command:	LIST
Description:	Returns the header of a specified message (or all messages).
Usage:	LIST [<Message Number>] <CRLF>
Parameters:	<Message Number> is an optional argument that identifies a message currently in the mailbox. If not given then the server returns header lines for all available messages.

Example:

```
'-- Sends the LIST command
SendPOP3Command DSSocket1, "LIST 1"
```

Comments: LIST may be given only in the TRANSACTION state.

After the initial +OK, for each message in the maildrop, the POP3 server responds with a line containing information for that message. This line is also called a "scan listing" for that message.

A scan listing consists of the message-number of the message, followed by a single space and the exact size of the message in bytes.

Messages marked as deleted are not listed.

Return Values (bold indicates success):

- **+OK Scan listing follows**

  <Message Number> <space> <message size (bytes)>

- −ERR No such message

POP3 Commands (NOOP)

Command:	NOOP
Description:	This command does nothing but invoke an +OK response from the server.
Usage:	NOOP <CRLF>
Parameters:	None

Example:

```
'-- Sends the NOOP command
SendPOP3Command DSSocket1, "NOOP"
```

Return Values (bold indicates success):

- **+OK**

POP3 Commands (PASS)

Command:	PASS
Description:	Specifies a password for access to the POP3 server.
Usage:	PASS <password> <CRLF>

Parameters: <password> is the user's password.

The username is specified with the USER command, which is issued prior to the PASS command.

Example:

```
'-- Specify the USER name
SendPOPCommand DSSocket1, "USER jsmith"
'-- Wait for an +OK response here.
'-- Specify the PASS name
SendPOPCommand DSSocket1, "PASS MyPassword"
```

Comments: PASS may be given only in the AUTHORIZATION state after a successful USER command.

Since the PASS command has exactly one argument, a POP3 server may treat spaces in the argument as part of the password, instead of as argument separators.

Return Values (bold indicates success):

- **+OK Maildrop locked and ready**
- -ERR Invalid password
- -ERR Unable to lock maildrop

POP3 Commands (QUIT)

Command: QUIT
Description: Logs off of the POP3 server.
Usage: QUIT <CRLF>
Parameters: None

Example:

```
'-- Sends the QUIT command
SendPOP3Command DSSocket1, "QUIT"
```

Comments: You should send the QUIT command prior to logging off. One advantage to sending a QUIT command as opposed to simply closing the socket is that the POP3 server closes the connection, which results in a Close event (when using DSSOCK). You can simply put your exit code in the Close event.

Return Values (bold indicates success):

- **+OK**

POP3 Commands (RETR)

Command: RETR (RETRIEVE)
Description: Retrieves a message from the mailbox.

Usage: RETR <Message Number> <CRLF>

Parameters: <Message Number> identifies a message currently in the mailbox.

Example:

```
'—Retrieve the first message in the mailbox
SendPOP3Command DSSocket1, "RETR 1"
```

Comments: RETR may be given only in the TRANSACTION state.

   If you get an +OK back from the server, the server will send the message one line at a time ending with a period on a line by itself.

Return Values (bold indicates success):

- **+OK Message follows**
- -ERR No such message

POP3 Commands (RSET)

Command: RSET

Description: Resets the mailbox to its state prior to your connection.

Usage: RSET <CRLF>

Parameters: None

Example:

```
'-- Resets the mailbox
SendPOP3Command DSSocket1, "RSET"
```

Comments: RSET may be given only in the TRANSACTION state.

   If any messages have been marked as deleted by the POP3 server, they are unmarked.

Return Values (bold indicates success):

- OK

POP3 Commands (STAT)

Command: STAT

Description: Returns a single line, called a "drop listing," from the server containing information for the maildrop.

Usage: STAT <CRLF>

Parameters: None

Example:

```
'-- Sends the STAT command
SendPOP3Command DSSocket1, "STAT"
```

Comments: STAT may be given only in the TRANSACTION state.

   The positive response consists of "+OK" followed by a single space, the number of messages in the maildrop, a single space, and the size of the maildrop in bytes.

Messages marked as deleted are not counted in either total.

Return Values (bold indicates success):

- **OK <space> <message count> <space> <total bytes>**

  <message count> is the number of messages available.

  <total bytes> is the total size of all messages combined in bytes.

POP3 Commands (TOP *)

Command:	TOP
Description:	Returns the header lines and a given number of lines of the message body for a given message.
Usage:	TOP <Message Number> <Number Of Lines> <CRLF>
Parameters:	

1. <Message Number> identifies a message currently in the mailbox.
2. <Number Of Lines> is the (maximum) number of lines to return from the top of the message.

Example:

```
'-- Retrieve the header and top 10 lines of message 1
SendPOP3Command DSSocket1, "TOP 1 10"

'-- The POP3 server sends the headers of the message, a blank line,
'-- and the first 10 lines of the body of the message>
```

Comments: TOP may be given only in the TRANSACTION state.

TOP is not implemented in all POP3 implementations.

If the POP3 server issues a positive response, then the response given is multiline.

After the initial +OK, the POP3 server sends the headers of the message, the blank line separating the headers from the body, and then the number of lines indicated message's body.

If the number of lines requested by the POP3 client is greater than the number of lines in the body, then the POP3 server sends the entire message.

Return Values (bold indicates success):

- **+OK Top of message follows**

  The server sends the header lines followed by a blank line followed by the top x number of lines of the message body all ending with a period on a line by itself.

- -ERR No such message

POP3 Commands (UIDL *)

Command:	UIDL (Unique ID Listing)
Description:	Returns a "unique ID listing" for a given message (or all messages).

Usage: UIDL [<Message Number>] <CRLF>

Parameters: <Message Number> is an optional argument that identifies a message
               currently in the mailbox. If not given then the server returns header
               lines for all available messages.

Example:

```
'-- Get a Unique ID Listing for all messages
SendPOP3Command DSSocket1, "UIDL"
```

Comments: UIDL may be given only in the TRANSACTION state.

A unique-id listing consists of the message-number of the message followed by a single space and the unique-id of the message.

The unique-id of a message is an arbitrary server-determined string, consisting of characters in the range 0×21 to $0 \times 7E$, which uniquely identifies a message within a maildrop and which persists across sessions. The server never reuses a unique-id in a given maildrop for as long as the entity using the unique-id exists.

If no argument is given the server returns an -OK reply followed by a list of unique-ids for (one for each current message) all ending with a period on a line by itself.

Return Values (bold indicates success):

- **+OK Unique-id listing follows**

  <message number> <space> <unique-id>

- -ERR No such message

POP3 Commands (USER)

Command: USER

Description: Specifies the username required to log onto the POP3 server.

Usage: USER <username> <CRLF>

Parameters: <username> is the name of the user logging on.

Example:

```
'-- Specify the USER name
SendPOPCommand DSSocket1, "USER jsmith"

'-- Wait for an +OK response here.

'-- Specify the PASS name
SendPOPCommand DSSocket1, "PASS MyPassword"
```

Comments: The USER command is immediately followed by the PASS command.

Return Values (bold indicates success):

- **+OK Name is a valid mailbox**

- -ERR Never heard of mailbox name

FTP COMMAND

LISTING

The following is a listing of standard File Transfer Protocol commands adapted from RFC #929 by Postel and Reynolds.

FTP Commands (ABOR)

Command: ABOR (Abort)

Description: Tells the server to abort the previous FTP service command and any associated transfer of data.

Usage: ABOR <CRLF>

Parameters: None

Example:
```
SendData DSSocket1, "ABOR" & vbCrlf
```

Comments: The abort command may require "special action" to force recognition by the server (See RFC 959 for details). No action is to be taken if the previous command has been completed (including data transfer). The control connection is not to be closed by the server, but the data connection must be closed.

There are two cases for the server upon receipt of this command: (1) the FTP service command was already completed, or (2) the FTP service command is still in progress.

In the first case, the server closes the data connection (if it is open) and responds with a 226 reply, indicating that the abort command was successfully processed.

In the second case, the server aborts the FTP service in progress and closes the data connection, returning a 426 reply to indicate that the service request terminated abnormally. The server then sends a 226 reply, indicating that the abort command was successfully processed.

Return Values (bold indicates success):

- **225** Data connection open; no transfer in progress
- **226** Closing data connection; Requested file action successful
- 421 Service not available, closing control connection

  This may be a reply to any command if the service knows it must shut down.

- 426 Connection closed; transfer aborted
- 500 Syntax error, command unrecognized

  This may include errors such as command line too long

- 501 Syntax error in parameters or arguments
- 502 Command not implemented.

FTP Commands (ACCT)

Command:	ACCT (Account)
Description:	Specifies the user's account information. This command should be sent only after receiving a 332 code after sending a PASS command.
Usage:	ACCT <Account > <CRLF>
Parameters:	Account is the user's account, which may be additionally required to access certain services.

Example:

```
SendData DSSocket1, "ACCT N322s" & vbCrlf
```

Comments: When account information is required for login, the response to a successful PASS command is reply code 332. On the other hand, if account information is *not* required for login, the reply to a successful PASS command is 230; and if the account information is needed for a command issued later in the dialogue, the server returns a 332 or 532 reply depending on whether it stores (pending receipt of the ACCT command) or discards the command, respectively.

Return Values (bold indicates success):

- 202 Command not implemented, superfluous at this site
- **230 User logged in, proceed**
- 421 Service not available, closing control connection

  This may be a reply to any command if the service knows it must shut down.
- 500 Syntax error, command unrecognized

  This may include errors such as command line too long.
- 501 Syntax error in parameters or arguments
- 502 Command not implemented
- 503 Bad sequence of commands
- 530 Not logged in

FTP Commands (ALLO)

Command:	ALLO (Allocate)
Description:	Allocates x number of bytes on the server before a file is sent.
Usage:	ALLO <NumBytes> [<MaxSize>] <CRLF>
Parameters:	NumBytes is an integer representing the number of bytes (using the logical byte size) of storage to be reserved for the file.
	MaxSize is an optional maximum record or page size when using record or page data structures.

Example:

```
SendData DSSocket1, "ALLO 3000 128" & vbCrlf
```

Comments: This command may be required by some servers to reserve sufficient storage to accommodate the new file to be transferred. For files sent with record or page structure a maximum record or page size (in logical bytes) might also be necessary; this is indicated by a decimal integer in a second argument field of the command. This second argument is optional, but when present should be separated from the first by the three ASCII characters <SP> R <SP>. This command is followed by a STORe or APPEnd command. The ALLO command should be treated as a NOOP (no operation) by those servers that do not require that the maximum size of the file be declared beforehand, and those servers interested in only the maximum record or page size should accept a dummy value in the first argument and ignore it.

Return Values (bold indicates success):

- **200 Command okay**
- 202 Command not implemented, superfluous at this site

- 421 Service not available, closing control connection

  This may be a reply to any command if the service knows it must shut down.

- 500 Syntax error, command unrecognized

  This may include errors such as command line too long.

- 501 Syntax error in parameters or arguments

- 504 Command not implemented for that parameter

- 530 Not logged in

FTP Commands (APPE)

Command:	APPE (Append with create)
Description:	Prepares the server to receive a file and instructs it to append the data to the specified filename, or create the specified file if it does not already exist.
Usage:	APPE <FileName> <CRLF>
Parameters:	FileName is a fully qualified path and filename at the server site.
Example:	

```
SendData DSSocket1, "APPE " & szFileName & vbCrlf
```

Return Values (bold indicates success):

- 110 Restart marker reply

  In this case, the text is exact and not left to the particular implementation; it must read:

  MARK yyyy = mmmm

  where yyyy is User-process data stream marker, and mmmm server's equivalent marker (note the spaces between markers and "=").

- **125 Data connection already open; transfer starting**

- **150 File status okay; about to open data connection**

- **226 Closing data connection; The requested file action was successful**

- **250 Requested file action okay, completed**

- 421 Service not available, closing control connection

  This may be a reply to any command if the service knows it must shut down.

- 425 Can't open data connection

- 426 Connection closed; transfer aborted

- 450 Requested file action not taken; file unavailable (e.g., file busy)
- 451 Requested action aborted: local error in processing
- 452 Requested action not taken; insufficient storage space in system
- 500 Syntax error, command unrecognized

  This may include errors such as command line too long.

- 501 Syntax error in parameters or arguments
- 502 Command not implemented
- 530 Not logged in
- 532 Need account for storing files
- 550 Requested action not taken; file unavailable (e.g., file not found, no access)
- 551 Requested action aborted: page type unknown
- 552 Requested file action aborted; exceeded storage allocation (for current directory or dataset)
- 553 Requested action not taken; filename not allowed

FTP Commands (CDUP)

Command: CDUP (Change to Parent Directory)

Description: Changes the current directory to the root of the remote file system without altering login, accounting information, or transfer parameters.

Usage: CDUP <CRLF>

Example:

```
SendData DSSocket1, "CDUP" & vbCrlf
```

Comments: The CDUP command changes to the parent directory. The MS-DOS equivalent of the command is *cd *. This command was created to accommodate the different operating systems that incorporate FTP.

Return Values (bold indicates success):

- **250 Requested file action okay, completed**
- 421 Service not available, closing control connection

  This may be a reply to any command if the service knows it must shut down.

- 500 Syntax error, command unrecognized

  This may include errors such as command line too long

- 501 Syntax error in parameters or arguments

- 502 Command not implemented
- 530 Not logged in
- 550 Requested action not taken; file unavailable (e.g., file not found, no access)

FTP Commands (CWD)

Command: CWD (Change Working Directory)
Description: Changes the current directory to the specified path of the remote file system without altering login, accounting information, or transfer parameters.
Usage: CWD <Path> <CRLF>
Parameters: Path is a working directory on the remote system.
Example:

```
SendData DSSocket1, "CWD /pub/cgvb/uploads" & vbCrlf
```

Return Values (bold indicates success):

- **250 Requested file action okay, completed**
- 421 Service not available, closing control connection

  This may be a reply to any command if the service knows it must shut down.
- 500 Syntax error, command unrecognized

  This may include errors such as command line too long.
- 501 Syntax error in parameters or arguments
- 502 Command not implemented
- 530 Not logged in
- 550 Requested action not taken; file unavailable (e.g., file not found, no access)

FTP Commands (DELE)

Command: DELE (Delete)
Description: Causes the file specified in the pathname to be deleted at the server site.
Usage: DELE <FileName> <CRLF>
Parameters: FileName is a fully qualified path and filename on the server side.
Example:

```
SendData DSSocket1, "DELE temp.fil" & vbCrlf
```

Comments: If an extra level of protection is desired (such as a "Do you really wish to delete this file?" option), it should be provided by the client software.

Return Values (bold indicates success):

- **250 Requested file action okay, completed**
- 421 Service not available, closing control connection

  This may be a reply to any command if the service knows it must shut down.

- 450 Requested file action not taken; file unavailable (e.g., file busy)
- 500 Syntax error, command unrecognized

  This may include errors such as command line too long.

- 501 Syntax error in parameters or arguments
- 502 Command not implemented
- 530 Not logged in
- 550 Requested action not taken; file unavailable (e.g., file not found, no access)

FTP Commands (HELP)

Command:	HELP (Help)
Description:	Causes the server to send helpful information regarding its implementation status over the control connection to the client.
Usage:	HELP [<Topic>] <CRLF>
Parameters:	Topic is an optional command or other argument concerning which help text is requested.

Example:

```
SendData DSSocket1, "HELP" & vbCrlf
```

Comments: HELP may take an argument (e.g., any command name) and return more specific information as a response. The reply is type 211 or 214. It is suggested that HELP be allowed before entering a USER command. The server may use this reply to specify site-dependent parameters, e.g., in response to HELP SITE.

Return Values (bold indicates success):

- **211 System status, or system help reply**
- **214 Help message**

  Describes how to use the server or the meaning of a particular nonstandard command. This reply is useful only to the user as there is no standard format for help messages.

- 421 Service not available, closing control connection

  This may be a reply to any command if the service knows it must shut down.

- 500 Syntax error, command unrecognized

  This may include errors such as command line too long.

- 501 Syntax error in parameters or arguments

- 502 Command not implemented

FTP Commands (LIST)

Command:	LIST (List)
Description:	Causes a list to be sent from the server to the client.
Usage:	LIST [<PathName>] <CRLF>
Parameters:	PathName is a valid path and filespec on the server system.
Example:	

```
SendData DSSocket1, "LIST /pub/*.*" & vbCrlf
```

Comments: If the pathname specifies a directory or other group of files, the server should transfer a list of files in the specified directory. If the pathname specifies a file then the server should send current information on the file. A null argument implies the user's current working or default directory. The data transfer is over the data connection in type ASCII or type EBCDIC (the user must ensure that the *type* is appropriately ASCII or EBCDIC).

Since the information on a file may vary widely from system to system, this information may be hard to use automatically in a program, but may be quite useful to a human user.

Return Values (bold indicates success):

- **125 Data connection already open; transfer starting**

- **150 File status okay; about to open data connection**

- **226 Closing data connection;** requested file action successful (for example, file transfer or file abort)

- **250 Requested file action okay, completed**

- 421 Service not available, closing control connection

  This may be a reply to any command if the service knows it must shut down.

- 425 Can't open data connection

- 426 Connection closed; transfer aborted

- 450 Requested file action not taken; file unavailable (e.g., file busy)

- 451 Requested action aborted: local error in processing

- 500 Syntax error, command unrecognized

  This may include errors such as command line too long.

- 501 Syntax error in parameters or arguments

- 502 Command not implemented

- 530 Not logged in

FTP Commands (MKD)

Command:	MKD (Make Directory)
Description:	Causes the directory specified in the pathname to be created as a directory (if the pathname is absolute) or as a subdirectory of the current working directory (if the pathname is relative).
Usage:	MKD <Path> <CRLF>
Parameters:	Path is a valid path on the server side.

Example:

```
SendData DSSocket1, "MKD /users/johnsmith" & vbCrlf
```

Return Values (bold indicates success):

- **257 "PATHNAME" created**

- 421 Service not available, closing control connection

  This may be a reply to any command if the service knows it must shut down.

- 500 Syntax error, command unrecognized

  This may include errors such as command line too long.

- 501 Syntax error in parameters or arguments

- 502 Command not implemented

- 530 Not logged in

- 550 Requested action not taken; file unavailable (e.g., file not found, no access)

FTP Commands (MODE)

Command:	MODE (Transfer Mode)
Description:	Specifies the transfer mode.
Usage:	STRU <Mode> <CRLF>
Parameters:	Mode is one of the following ASCII values:
	S - Stream (Default)
	B - Block
	C - Compressed

Example:
```
SendData DSSocket1, "STRU B" & vbCrlf
```

Return Values (bold indicates success):

- **200 Command okay**
- 421 Service not available, closing control connection

  This may be a reply to any command if the service knows it must shut down.

- 500 Syntax error, command unrecognized

  This may include errors such as command line too long.

- 501 Syntax error in parameters or arguments
- 504 Command not implemented for that parameter
- 530 Not logged in

FTP Commands (NLST)

Command:	NLST (Name List)
Description:	Causes a directory listing to be sent from server to client.
Usage:	NLST [<PathName>] <CRLF>
Parameters:	PathName is a valid path and filespec on the server system.

Example:
```
SendData DSSocket1, "NLST /pub/cgvb" & vbCrlf
```

Comments: The pathname should specify a directory or other system-specific file group descriptor; a null argument implies the current directory. The server will return a stream of names of files and no other information. The data will be transferred in ASCII or EBCDIC type over the data connection as valid pathname strings separated by <CRLF> or <NL> (again the user must ensure that the *type* is correct.)

NLST is intended to return information that can be used by a program to further process the files automatically; for example, in the implementation of a "multiple get" function.

Return Values (bold indicates success):

- **125 Data connection already open; transfer starting**
- **150 File status okay; about to open data connection**
- **226 Closing data connection; requested file action successful (for example, file transfer or file abort)**
- **250 Requested file action okay, completed**

- 421 Service not available, closing control connection

  This may be a reply to any command if the service knows it must shut down.

- 425 Can't open data connection

- 426 Connection closed; transfer aborted

- 450 Requested file action not taken; file unavailable (e.g., file busy)

- 451 Requested action aborted: local error in processing

- 500 Syntax error, command unrecognized

  This may include errors such as command line too long.

- 501 Syntax error in parameters or arguments

- 502 Command not implemented

- 530 Not logged in

FTP Commands (NOOP)

Command:	NOOP (NOOP)
Description:	This is a nonaction command. It does nothing.
Usage:	NOOP <CRLF>
Parameters:	None

Example:

```
SendData DSSocket1, "NOOP" & vbCrlf
```

Comments: NOOP does not affect any parameters or previously entered commands. It specifies no action other than that the server send an OK reply.

Return Values (bold indicates success):

- **200 Command okay**

- 421 Service not available, closing control connection

  This may be a reply to any command if the service knows it must shut down.

- 500 Syntax error, command unrecognized

FTP Commands (PASS)

Command:	PASS (Password)
Usage:	PASS <Password> <CRLF>
Description:	Sends the user's password to the remote system. Use after a USER command.

Parameters: Password is the password of the registered user as specified by the
                USER command.

Example:

```
SendData DSSocket1, "PASS mypassword" & vbCrlf
```

Comments: The USER command is sent immediately after connecting to an FTP server
on port 21 after receiving a line that starts with the code 220, indicating that the server
is ready for you to send it USER and PASS commands to log into the FTP server.

The PASS command should immediately follow the USER command.

If you have an account on the FTP server, you can specify your username and password. If you would like to log in anonymously, specify "anonymous" for the username
and your email address for the password.

Return Values (bold indicates success):

- 202 Command not implemented, superfluous at this site
- **230 User logged in**
- **332 Need account for login** (see ACCT command)
- 421 Service not available, closing control connection

    This may be a reply to any command if the service knows it must shut down.

- 500 Syntax error, command unrecognized

    This may include errors such as command line too long.

- 501 Syntax error in parameters or arguments
- 530 Not logged in

FTP Commands (PASV)

Command: PASV (Passive)
Description: Tells the server to listen for a data connection on a nonstandard port.
Usage: PASV <CRLF>
Parameters: This command requests the server-DTP to "listen" on a data port (which
               is not its default data port) and to wait for a connection rather than ini-
               tiate one upon receipt of a transfer command. The response to this com-
               mand includes the host and port address this server is listening on.

Example:

```
SendData DSSocket1, "PASV" & vbCrlf
```

Return Values (bold indicates success):

- **227 Entering Passive Mode (h1,h2,h3,h4,p1,p2)**

The return value includes a HOST-PORT specification for the data port to be used in data connection. The argument is the concatenation of a 32-bit Internet host address and a 16-bit TCP port address. This address information is broken into 8-bit fields and the value of each field is transmitted as a decimal number (in character string representation). h1 is the high-order byte of the Internet host address and p1 is the high-order byte of the port.

- 421 Service not available, closing control connection

  This may be a reply to any command if the service knows it must shut down.

- 500 Syntax error, command unrecognized

  This may include errors such as command line too long.

- 501 Syntax error in parameters or arguments

- 502 Command not implemented

- 530 Not logged in

FTP Commands (PORT)

Command:	PORT (Data Port)
Description:	Specifies an IP address and local port for a data connection.
Usage:	PORT \<Socket> \<CRLF>
Parameters:	Socket is a HOST-PORT specification for the data port to be used in data connection. There are defaults for both the user and server data ports, and under normal circumstances this command and its reply are not needed. If this command is used, the argument is the concatenation of a 32-bit Internet host address and a 16-bit TCP port address. This address information is broken into 8-bit fields and the value of each field is transmitted as a decimal number (in character string representation). The fields are separated by commas. A port command would be:

> PORT h1,h2,h3,h4,p1,p2

where h1 is the high-order byte of the Internet host address and p1 is the high-order byte of the local port.

Example:

```
SendData DSSocket1, "199,199,199,0,33,1" & vbCrlf
```

Return Values (bold indicates success):

- **200 Command OK**

- 421 Service not available, closing control connection

  This may be a reply to any command if the service knows it must shut down.

- 500 Syntax error, command unrecognized

  This may include errors such as command line too long.

- 501 Syntax error in parameters or arguments

- 530 Not logged in

FTP Commands (PWD)

Command:	PWD (Print Working Directory)
Description:	Causes the name of the current working directory to be returned in the reply.
Usage:	PWD <CRLF>
Parameters:	None

Example:
```
SendData DSSocket1, "PWD" & vbCrlf
```

Return Values (bold indicates success):

- **257 "PATHNAME" returned**

- 421 Service not available, closing control connection

  This may be a reply to any command if the service knows it must shut down.

- 500 Syntax error, command unrecognized

  This may include errors such as command line too long.

- 501 Syntax error in parameters or arguments

- 502 Command not implemented

- 550 Requested action not taken; file unavailable (e.g., file not found, no access)

FTP Commands (QUIT)

Command:	QUIT (Logout)
Description:	Terminates the connection.
Usage:	QUIT <CRLF>

Example:
```
SendData DSSocket1, "QUIT" & vbCrlf
```

Comments: QUIT terminates the USER and if file transfer is not in progress, the server closes the control connection. If file transfer is in progress, the connection will remain open for result response and the server will then close it. If the user-process is transferring files for several USERs but does not wish to close and then reopen connections for each, then the REIN command should be used instead of QUIT.

An unexpected close on the control connection will cause the server to take the effective action of an abort (ABOR) and a logout (QUIT).

Return Values (bold indicates success):

- **221 Service closing control connection**
- 500 Syntax error, command unrecognized

FTP Commands (REIN)

Command:	REIN (Reinitialize)
Description:	Terminates a user.
Usage:	REIN <CRLF>
Example:	

```
SendData DSSocket1, "REIN" & vbCrlf
```

Comments: REIN flushes all I/O and account information, except to allow any transfer in progress to be completed. All parameters are reset to the default settings and the control connection is left open. This is identical to the state in which a user finds himself immediately after the control connection is opened. If you are going to log in afterwards, send a REIN command before sending a USER command.

Return Values (bold indicates success):

- 120 Service ready in nnn minutes
- **220 Service ready for new user**
- 421 Service not available, closing control connection

  This may be a reply to any command if the service knows it must shut down.

- 500 Syntax error, command unrecognized

  This may include errors such as command line too long.

- 502 Command not implemented

FTP Commands (REST)

Command:	REST (Restart)
Description:	Identifies the data point within the file from which the file transfer will resume.
Usage:	REST <Marker> <CRLF>

Parameters: Marker represents the server marker at which file transfer is to be restarted.

Example:

```
SendData DSSocket1, "REST 244" & vbCrlf
```

Comments: REST does not cause the file transfer but skips over the file to the specified data checkpoint. REST is immediately followed by the appropriate FTP service command, which causes the file transfer to resume.

Return Values (bold indicates success):

- **No response indicates success**
- 350 Requested file action pending further information
- 421 Service not available, closing control connection

  This may be a reply to any command if the service knows it must shut down.

- 500 Syntax error, command unrecognized

  This may include errors such as command line too long.

- 501 Syntax error in parameters or arguments
- 502 Command not implemented
- 530 Not logged in

FTP Commands (RETR)

Command: RETR (Retrieve)

Description: This command causes the server to transfer a copy of the file, specified in the pathname, to the client. The status and contents of the file at the server site are unaffected.

Usage: RETR <FileName> <CRLF>

Parameters: FileName is a fully qualified path and filename at the server site.

Example:

```
SendData DSSocket1, "RETR /pub/cgvb/misc/somefile.zip" & vbCrlf
```

Return Values (bold indicates success):

- 110 Restart marker reply

  In this case, the text is exact and not left to the particular implementation; it must read:

  MARK yyyy = mmmm

  where yyyy is User-process data stream marker, and mmmm server's equivalent marker (note the spaces between markers and "=").

- 125 Data connection already open; transfer starting
- 150 File status okay; about to open data connection
- 226 Closing data connection; the requested file action was successful
- 250 Requested file action okay, completed
- 421 Service not available, closing control connection

  This may be a reply to any command if the service knows it must shut down.

- 425 Can't open data connection
- 426 Connection closed; transfer aborted
- 450 Requested file action not taken; file unavailable (e.g., file busy)
- 451 Requested action aborted: local error in processing
- 500 Syntax error, command unrecognized

  This may include errors such as command line too long.

- 501 Syntax error in parameters or arguments
- 504 Command not implemented for that parameter
- 530 Not logged in
- 550 Requested action not taken; file unavailable (e.g., file not found, no access)

FTP Commands (RMD)

Command:	RMD (Remove Directory)
Description:	Causes the directory specified in the pathname to be removed as a directory (if the pathname is absolute) or as a subdirectory of the current working directory (if the pathname is relative).
Usage:	RMD <Path> <CRLF>
Parameters:	Path is a fully qualified path on the server side.
Example:	

```
SendData DSSocket1, "RETR /users/johnsmith" & vbCrlf
```

Return Values (bold indicates success):

- **250 Requested file action okay, completed**
- 421 Service not available, closing control connection

  This may be a reply to any command if the service knows it must shut down.

- 500 Syntax error, command unrecognized

  This may include errors such as command line too long.

- 501 Syntax error in parameters or arguments

- 502 Command not implemented
- 530 Not logged in
- 550 Requested action not taken; file unavailable (e.g., file not found, no access)

FTP Commands (RNFR)

Command:	RNFR (Rename From)
Description:	The first half of the file renaming process. Specifies the old path and filename name of the file being renamed.
Usage:	RNFR <FileName> <CRLF>
Parameters:	FileName is a fully qualified path and filename at the server site.
Example:	

```
SendData DSSocket1, "RNFR source.zip" & vbCrlf
```

RNFR must be immediately followed by a "rename to" command (RNTO) specifying the new path and filename.

Return Values (bold indicates success):

- **No response indicates success**
- 350 Requested file action pending further information
- 421 Service not available, closing control connection

   This may be a reply to any command if the service knows it must shut down.

- 450 Requested file action not taken; file unavailable (e.g., file busy)
- 500 Syntax error, command unrecognized

   This may include errors such as command line too long.

- 501 Syntax error in parameters or arguments
- 502 Command not implemented
- 530 Not logged in
- 550 Requested action not taken. File unavailable (e.g., file not found, no access)

FTP Commands (RNTO)

Command:	RNTO (Rename To)
Description:	The second half of the file renaming process. Specifies the new path and filename of the file being renamed.
Usage:	RNTO <FileName> <CRLF>
Parameters:	FileName is a valid filename at the server site.

Example:

```
SendData DSSocket1, "RNTO destination.zip" & vbCrlf
```

Comments: RNTO must be preceded by a "rename from" command (RNFR). Together RNFR and RTNO rename a file on the server.

Return Values (bold indicates success):

- **250 Requested file action okay, completed**
- 421 Service not available, closing control connection

  This may be a reply to any command if the service knows it must shut down.

- 500 Syntax error, command unrecognized

  This may include errors such as command line too long.

- 501 Syntax error in parameters or arguments
- 502 Command not implemented
- 503 Bad sequence of commands
- 530 Not logged in
- 532 Need account for storing files
- 553 Requested action not taken; file name not allowed

FTP Commands (SITE)

Command:	SITE (Site parameters)
Description:	SITE is used by the server to provide services specific to the system that are essential to file transfer but not sufficiently universal to be included as commands in the protocol. The nature of these services and the specification of their syntax can be stated in a reply to the HELP SITE command.
Usage:	SITE <String> <CRLF>
Parameters:	String is any string argument.

Example:

```
SendData DSSocket1, "SITE chmod 646 myfile.zip" & vbCrlf
```

Comments: You could use SITE, for example, to change permission attributes of a file using the following syntax:

```
SITE CHMOD<Attribute><Filename>
```

Return Values (bold indicates success):

- **200 Command okay**
- 202 Command not implemented, superfluous at this site

- 500 Syntax error, command unrecognized

  This may include errors such as command line too long.

- 501 Syntax error in parameters or arguments

- 530 Not logged in

FTP Commands (SMNT)

Command:	SMNT (Structure Mount)
Description:	Allows the user to mount another file system data structure without altering login, accounting information, or transfer parameters.
Usage:	SMNT <Path> <CRLF>
Parameters:	Path is the path of another file data system.
Example:	

```
SendData DSSocket1, "SMNT /users/johnsmith" & vbCrlf
```

Return Values (bold indicates success):

- 202 Command not implemented, superfluous at this site

- **250 Requested file action okay, completed**

- 421 Service not available, closing control connection

  This may be a reply to any command if the service knows it must shut down.

- 500 Syntax error, command unrecognized

  This may include errors such as command line too long.

- 501 Syntax error in parameters or arguments

- 502 Command not implemented

- 530 Not logged in

- 550 Requested action not taken; file unavailable (e.g., file not found, no access)

FTP Commands (STAT)

Command:	STAT (Status)
Description:	Causes a status response to be sent over the control connection in the form of a reply.
Usage:	STAT [<PathName>] <CRLF>
Parameters:	PathName is a valid path on the server.
Example:	

```
SendData DSSocket1, "STAT /users/johnsmith/myfile" & vbCrlf
```

Comments: STAT may be sent during a file transfer (along with the Telnet IP and Synch signals—see the RFC 959 Section on FTP Commands) in which case the server will respond with the status of the operation in progress, or it may be sent between file transfers. In the latter case, the command may have an argument field. If a full pathname is specified, STAT is analogous to the LIST command except that data shall be transferred over the control connection. If a partial pathname is given, the server may respond with a list of file names or attributes associated with that specification. If no argument is given, the server should return general status information about the server FTP process. This should include current values of all transfer parameters and the status of connections.

Return Values (bold indicates success):

- **211 System status, or system help reply**
- **212 Directory status**
- **213 File status**
- 421 Service not available, closing control connection

  This may be a reply to any command if the service knows it must shut down.
- 450 Requested file action not taken; file unavailable (e.g., file busy)
- 500 Syntax error, command unrecognized

  This may include errors such as command line too long.
- 501 Syntax error in parameters or arguments
- 502 Command not implemented
- 530 Not Logged In

FTP Commands (STOR)

Command:	STOR (Store)
Description:	Prepares the server to receive a file via the data connection.
Usage:	STOR <FileName> <CRLF>
Parameters:	FileName is a fully qualified path and filename at the server site.

Example:
```
SendData DSSocket1, "STOR newfile.zip" & vbCrlf
```

Comments: The Store command causes the server to accept the data transferred via the data connection and to store the data as a file at the server site. If the file specified in the pathname exists at the server site, then its contents shall be replaced by the data being transferred. A new file is created at the server site if the file specified in the path-name does not already exist.

Return Values (bold indicates success):

- 110 Restart marker reply

   In this case, the text is exact and not left to the particular implementation; it must read:

   MARK yyyy = mmmm

   where yyyy is User-process data stream marker, and mmmm server's equivalent marker (note the spaces between markers and "=").

- **125 Data connection already open; transfer starting**

- **150 File status okay; about to open data connection**

- **226 Closing data connection; the requested file action was successful**

- **250 Requested file action okay, completed**

- 421 Service not available, closing control connection

   This may be a reply to any command if the service knows it must shut down.

- 425 Can't open data connection

- 426 Connection closed; transfer aborted

- 450 Requested file action not taken; file unavailable (e.g., file busy)

- 451 Requested action aborted; local error in processing

- 452 Requested action not taken; insufficient storage space in system

- 500 Syntax error, command unrecognized

   This may include errors such as command line too long.

- 501 Syntax error in parameters or arguments

- 504 Command not implemented for that parameter

- 530 Not logged in

- 532 Need account for storing files

- 550 Requested action not taken; file unavailable (e.g., file not found, no access)

- 551 Requested action aborted: page type unknown

- 552 Requested file action aborted

   Exceeded storage allocation (for current directory or dataset).

- 553 Requested action not taken; file name not allowed

FTP Commands (STOU)

Command:	STOU (Store Unique)
Description:	Prepares the server to receive a file and instructs the server to save the file with a unique name in the target directory.
Usage:	STOU <CRLF>
Parameters:	None

Example:

```
SendData DSSocket1, "STOU " & vbCrlf
```

Comments: The Store Unique command works exactly like STOR except that the resultant file is to be created in the current directory under a name unique to that directory. The 250 Transfer Started response must include the name generated.

Return Values (bold indicates success):

- **110 Restart marker reply**

  In this case, the text is exact and not left to the particular implementation; it must read:

  MARK yyyy = mmmm

  where yyyy is User-process data stream marker, and mmmm server's equivalent marker (note the spaces between markers and "=").

- **125 Data connection already open; transfer starting**

- **150 File status okay; about to open data connection**

- **226 Closing data connection; the requested file action was successful**

- **250 Requested file action okay, completed** (unique filename included on this line)

- 421 Service not available, closing control connection

  This may be a reply to any command if the service knows it must shut down.

- 425 Can't open data connection

- 426 Connection closed; transfer aborted

- 450 Requested file action not taken; file unavailable (e.g., file busy)

- 451 Requested action aborted; local error in processing

- 452 Requested action not taken; insufficient storage space in system

- 500 Syntax error, command unrecognized

  This may include errors such as command line too long.

- 501 Syntax error in parameters or arguments
- 504 Command not implemented for that parameter
- 530 Not logged in
- 532 Need account for storing files
- 550 Requested action not taken; file unavailable (e.g., file not found, no access)
- 551 Requested action aborted; page type unknown
- 552 Requested file action aborted; exceeded storage allocation (for current directory or dataset)
- 553 Requested action not taken. File name not allowed

FTP Commands (STRU)

Command:	STRU (File Structure)
Description:	Specifies the structure type of transmitted data.
Usage:	STRU <StructureType> <CRLF>
Parameters:	StructureType is one of the following ASCII characters:
	F - File structure (default)
	R - Record structure
	P - Page structure
	See RFC 959 for information on using nonfile structures

Example:

```
SendData DSSocket1, "STRU R" & vbCrlf
```

Return Values (bold indicates success):

- **200 Command okay**
- 421 Service not available, closing control connection

  This may be a reply to any command if the service knows it must shut down.

- 500 Syntax error, command unrecognized

  This may include errors such as command line too long.

- 501 Syntax error in parameters or arguments
- 504 Command not implemented for that parameter
- 530 Not logged in

FTP Commands (SYST)

Command:	SYST (System)
Description:	SYST is used to find out the type of operating system at the server.
Usage:	SYST <CRLF>
Parameters:	None

Example:

```
SendData DSSocket1, "SYST" & vbCrlf
```

Comments: Supposedly, the reply has as its first word one of the system names listed in the current version of the Assigned Numbers document [4]. However, I don't see this as being something you can count on. New systems are popping up all the time. The public documentation may or may not keep up with it.

Return Values (bold indicates success):

- **215 NAME system type**

  NAME is an official system name from the list in the Assigned

  Numbers document.

- 421 Service not available, closing control connection

  This may be a reply to any command if the service knows it must shut down.

- 500 Syntax error, command unrecognized

  This may include errors such as command line too long.

- 501 Syntax error in parameters or arguments

- 502 Command not implemented

FTP Commands (TYPE)

Command:	TYPE (Representation Type)
Description:	Determines how data will be transmitted.
Usage:	TYPE <DataType Code> <CRLF>
Parameters:	DataType Code is an ASCII character (or characters) that identifies a data representation type.

Example:

```
' -- Set binary mode
SendData DSSocket1, "TYPE I" & vbCrlf
```

Comments: Typically you will use the TYPE type command to toggle ASCII or binary mode (Image). Use the image type when sending and receiving files of any kind. Use the ASCII type only when transmitting text.

Several types take a second parameter. The first parameter is enoted by a single ASCII character, as is the second Format parameter for ASCII and EBCDIC; the second parameter for local byte is a decimal integer to indicate Bytesize. The parameters are separated by a <SP> (Space, ASCII code 32).

The following codes are assigned for type:

A - ASCII *

E - EBCDIC *

I - Image (use this for binary file transfers)

L <byte size> - Local byte Byte size

---

* A and E types take any one of these three second **Parameters:**

N - Non-print

T - Telnet format effectors

C - Carriage Control (ASA)

The default representation type is ASCII Non-print. If the Format parameter is changed, and later just the first argument is changed, Format then returns to the Non-print default.

Return Values (bold indicates success):

- **200 Command okay**

- 421 Service not available, closing control connection

  This may be a reply to any command if the service knows it must shut down.

- 500 Syntax error, command unrecognized

  This may include errors such as command line too long.

- 501 Syntax error in parameters or arguments

- 504 Command not implemented for that parameter

- 530 Not logged in

FTP Commands (USER)

Command:	USER (User Name)
Description:	Specifies the user's name on the remote system. Use with the PASS command to log in.
Usage:	USER <UserName> <CRLF>

Parameters: UserName is the name of the registered user on the FTP system.

Example:

```
SendData DSSocket1, "USER johns" & vbCrlf
```

Comments: The USER command is sent immediately after connecting to an FTP server on port 21 after receiving a line that starts with the code 220, indicating that the server is ready for you to send it USER and PASS commands to log into the FTP server.

The PASS command should immediately follow the USER command.

If you have an account on the FTP server, you can specify your username and password. If you would like to log in anonymously, specify "anonymous" for the username and your email address for the password.

You can send the USER and PASS commands at any time during the session to change control to a new user.

Return Values (bold indicates success):

- **230 User logged in**
- **331 User name okay, need password**
- 332 Need account for login
- 421 Service not available, closing control connection

  This may be a reply to any command if the service knows it must shut down.

- 500 Syntax error, command unrecognized

  This may include errors such as command line too long.

- 501 Syntax error in parameters or arguments
- 530 Not logged in

CARL & GARY'S

VISUAL BASIC

HOME PAGE

Carl & Gary's Visual Basic Home Page (http://www.apexsc.com/vb) is a public system on the World Wide Web that exists for the purpose of providing Visual Basic programmers with timely information and files related to Visual Basic Programming. Most of all, Carl & Gary's is a place where members of the Visual Basic community can share information with each other. We will publish anything related to Visual Basic as long as it is done in good taste. The site exists for you, and we encourage you to send us material for publishing. At the time of this writing, Carl & Gary's is considered to be the most comprehensive site for Visual Basic programmers, if not the busiest. We currently get around 40,000 hits a day. It's not surprising, though, since we were the first VB page on the Internet, and we've had a lot of time to grow and refine. As of this writing we have over 100 links just to other Visual Basic–related sites on the Internet, and that doesn't include the other 110 or so pages full of links.

Figure E.1 shows Carl & Gary's main screen (http://www.apexsc.com/vb). This is the first page you see when you connect. Figure E.2 shows the same screen but scrolled down a bit, so you can see some of the sections of the page that are listed here. We update the page usually around the first of the month unless we are both too busy (hey, it's a volunteer effort). We have a mailing list to which we send a "what's new this month" notice every time we update the page. Also, there is a *What's New* page shown in Figure E.3 (http://www.apexsc.com/vb/whatsnew.html) where you can see what we've recently

Figure E.1 Main screen.

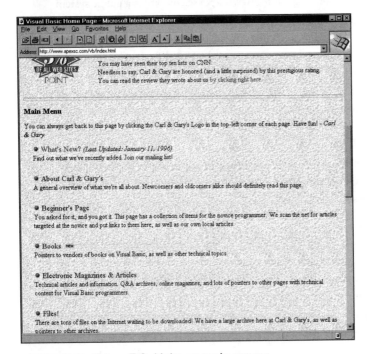

Figure E.2 Links on main screen.

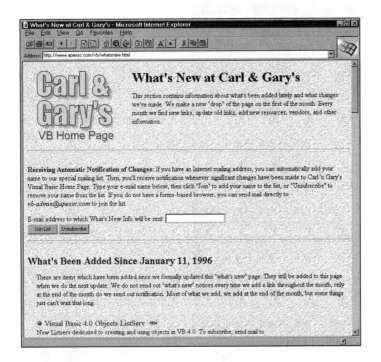

Figure E.3 *What's New* page.

added, and add your name to our mailing list. Figure E.4 shows some of the links that appeared on the *What's New* page for January 1995. I think the most links we've ever added in one month was around 40.

Our Internet Development page, shown in Figure E.5 (http://www.apexsc.com/vb/internet.html), has links to sites that deal with Internet development issues (not just in Visual Basic). This page points to a ton of information on topics like Java, VB Script, VRML, Netscape, WinSock, and Microsoft's Internet Information Server (MIIS).

Carl & Gary's also has an extensive collection of shareware and freeware files, some of which are Visual Basic related. Figure E.6 shows a few of the files on the local Visual Basic File Archive page (http://www.apexsc.com/vb/ftp1.html). In addition to these, we have lots of pointers to other archives throughout the Internet.

One of the most popular pages is the Usenet Newsgroup Archives page (http://www.apexsc.com/vb/vb-bin/ngsearch), shown in Figure E.7. We have been archiving Usenet news since January 7, 1995. You can search in the Visual Basic and related Usenet newsgroups for articles that relate to your particular interest. For example, if you are having a problem with the MCI control you can search for "MCI," and you will be presented with a list of all messages where the word MCI appears in the subject line.

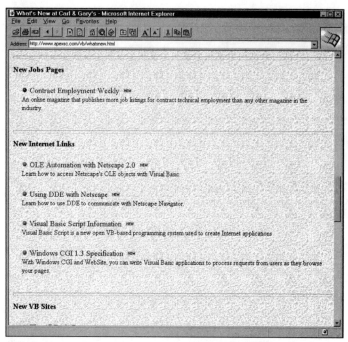

Figure E.4 Links on *What's New* page.

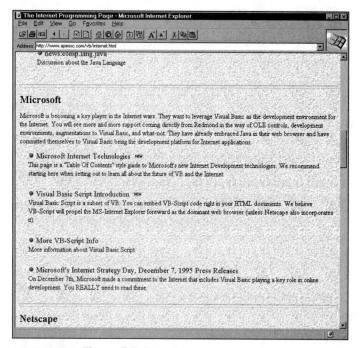

Figure E.5 Internet page.

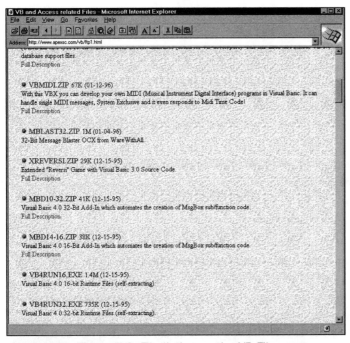

Figure E.6 File listing on the VB Files page.

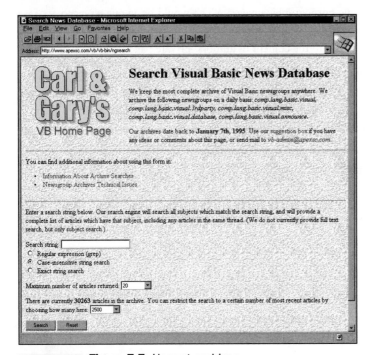

Figure E.7 Usenet archives.

A new page in 1996 is the Jobs page (http://www.apexsc.com/vb/jobs.html), shown in Figure E.8. This page has lots of links to online job search agencies, job listings, contract brokers, and the like. However, in order to make our list they have to list openings for VB developers. Also, if you are looking for a programmer, the Jobs page has links to consulting agencies and private contractors, as well as a link to Carl & Gary's very own Consultant's Corner (http://www.apexsc.com/vb/consult.html), which lists hundreds of developers, their specialties, and contact information (free of charge). If you are a developer looking for work, you can add yourself to the list.

On the subject of the job market, we also have a Training page, shown in Figure E.9, with links to training companies (http://www.apexsc.com/vb/training.html). There are lots of companies that offer live, video, or even CD–ROM based training for Visual Basic and other programs. We list them here.

Figure E.10 shows *The Library* (http://www.apexsc.com/vb/library.html), an online magazine at Carl & Gary's where you can read technical articles written by today's hippest gurus, including Gary and myself, of course. Anyone can write an article for *The Library*, as long as you can write (don't laugh) and have something of relative importance to say to the VB community. In exchange for an article, we give authors their own private area with 5 MB of disk space for whatever HTML pages they would like to set up. Of course, there are some reasonable limitations to the content of these pages. (For example, we don't want someone publishing pornographic images, which would bring our server to a grinding halt, not to mention making us look unprofessional.) In general, as long as it's in good taste, we have no objections to the content of authors' private pages.

Finally, Carl & Gary's offers the tool vendor industry free listings of their web sites and email addresses on our Market Place page (http://www.apexsc.com/vb/market.html), shown in Figure E.11. Any vendor can just send their web site address and a short description to us at vb-admin@apexsc.com, and we will add it to the page.

There's always something cooking at Carl & Gary's. Plenty of reading material, great files, great pointers, and lots of current information. Stop by anytime and pay us a visit.

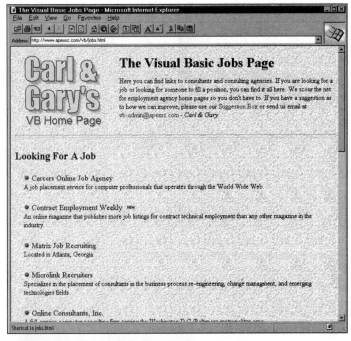

■■■■ **Figure E.8** Jobs page.

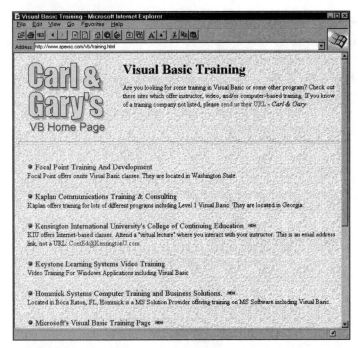

■■■■ **Figure E.9** Training page.

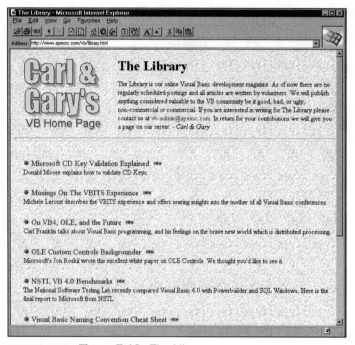

■■■■■■■ **Figure E.10** *The Library.*

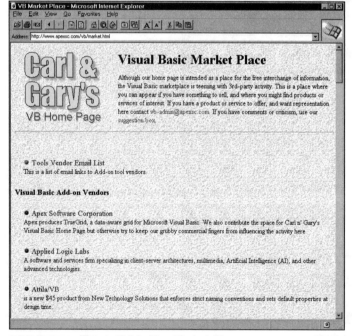

■■■■■■■ **Figure E.11** The Market Place.

ABOUT THE

SOFTWARE

What's on the Companion CD-ROM?

The companion CD-ROM contains sample code, Internet client applications, Internet Server applications, the entire Request For Comments library, and three songs recorded by the author. You can listen to the music with any standard CD player.

What Is Freeware/Shareware?

Freeware is software that is distributed by disk, through BBS systems, and the Internet free. There is no charge for using it, and can be distributed freely as long as the use it is put to follows the license agreement included with it.

Shareware (also known as user-supported software) is a revolutionary means of distributing software created by individuals or companies too small to make inroads into the more conventional retail distribution networks. The authors of Shareware retain all rights to the software under the copyright laws while still allowing free distribution. This gives the user the chance to freely obtain and try out software to see if it fits his or her needs. Shareware should not be confused with Public Domain software even though they are often obtained from the same sources.

If you continue to use Shareware after trying it out, you are expected to register your use with the author and pay a registration fee. What you get in return depends on the author, but may include a printed manual, free updates, telephone support, and so on.

Another common type of software distribution is Evaluation. The rules vary from title to title, but the basic idea is that the software is complete in features, but has a limited life span. In other words, the user may be prevented from use after a certain number of days.

Hardware Requirements

Hardware requirements for the included shareware and freeware are unique to each program. Consult the on-line documentation or the software vendor for exact requirements.

The sample code requires a connection to the Internet. The connection can be via modem, ISDN, direct connection, or any other valid means of connectivity. As well, TCP/IP is required in order for the DSSOCK custom control to function. Windows 95 (Plus Pack) and Windows NT both ship with TCP/IP drivers. Contact Microsoft for options.

A CD-ROM drive is required to access the code. You can access the music on the CD with any standard audio CD player.

Sample Code

The Sample Code is located in the \Code directory. Each project is designed for Visual Basic 4.0 32-bit, but has a 16-bit sub-directory that contains the same project for VB4 16-bit. The only difference is that the 32-bit versions use DSSOCK32.OCX and the 16-bit versions use DSSOCK.VBX. The two controls are compatible.

If you experience problems with or have questions about the sample code, please do not send email before you check out this book's web site: (http://www.apexsc.com/vb/vbip). The site has any and all updates to the code, as well as answers to questions you might have about it. As well, an up-to-date README is available on-line. If you can't resolve your problem/question via the web site, you can send me email at carlf@apexsc.com.

Here is a list of all the projects by chapter, their locations on the CD-ROM, and a brief description.

Chapter 2

Project: TERMINAL
Description: Sample Winsock Terminal application
Location: \Code\Terminal

Project:	WINSOCK
Description:	Starter Project for any Winsock application
Location:	\Code\Winsock

Chapter 3

Project:	GETFILE
Description:	Simple application to retrieve a file from a gopher server
Location:	\Code\Gopher\GetFile

Project:	GOPHCLNT
Description:	Sample Gopher Client application
Location:	\Code\Gopher\Gopherclnt

Chapter 4

Project:	NNTP
Description:	Sample Usenet News client application
Location:	\Code\Usenet

Chapter 5

Project:	BRAINDED
Description:	Sample application that sends an email message with no error checking
Location:	\Code\Smtp

Project:	POP3
Description:	Sample application that retrieves email from a mail server
Location:	\Code\Pop3

Project:	SMTP
Description:	Sample application that sends an email message with full SMTP support
Location:	\Code\Smtp

Project:	UUCODE
Description:	Sample application to encode and decode binary files using UU encoding and decoding
Location:	\Code\UUCoding

Chapter 6

Project:	FTPDEMO
Description:	Sample FTP client program
Location:	\Code\Ftp

Chapter 7

Project: MAP
Description: Sample application that returns a custom map from the Tiger Mapping
                Service
Location: \Code\Map

Project: NETPAPER
Description: Sample application that retrieves BMP and GIF files from gopher and
                web sites and displays them as the Windows desktop wallpaper image
Location: \Code\NetPaper

Project: WEBDEMO
Description: Sample application that retrieves a text file from Carl & Gary's Visual
                Basic Home Page
Location: \Code\WebDemo

Chapter 8

Project: ACME
Description: Sample CGI application that uses Windows CGI to communicate with
                WebSite or HTTPD web servers
Location: \Code\WinCGI

Chapter 9

Project: OLEISAPI
Description: Sample OLE Object callable via OLEISAPI with Microsoft Internet
                Information Server
Location: \Code\CFOIsapi

Chapter 10

Project: CFSDEMO
Description: Sample application that uses CFSockClient to communicate with
                CFSERVER
Location: \Code\CFSocket

Project: CFSERVER
Description: Server application to compliment the CFSockClient Object
Location: \Code\CFSocket

Project: CLIENT
Description: CFSockClient OLE Object
Location: \Code\CFSocket

Project: ODBCSERV
Description: Enhanced version of CFSERVER that allows for remote ODBC access
Location: \Code\CFSocket

Project: ODBCTEST
Description: Sample application that uses CFSockClient to communicate with
                \Code\CFSocket
Location: ODBCServ

Miscellaneous

Project: FINGER
Description: Simple Finger and WhoIs program
Location: \Code\Finger

Internet Client Applications

Several shareware client applications are included on the CD-ROM. These can be found under the \Clients subdirectory. Every one of these tools could have been written using the code in this book.

Name: HGOPHER
Description: Winsock Gopher Client application
Location: \Clients\Gopher\HGopher
Provider: Martyn Hampson
Email: m.hampson@ic.ac.uk
Installation: Copy all files to an empty directory on your hard drive

Internet Server Applications

These servers are all available publicly on the Internet. Since they are pretty large in size, though, I thought it would be nice to include them on the CD-ROM.

Name: EMWAC Internet Mail Server
Description: SMTP/POP3 Server for Windows NT
Location: \Servers\Email\Emwac
Provider: European Microsoft Windows NT Academic Centre
Email: <none>
Installation: Copy all files to an empty directory on your hard drive

Name:	EMWAC Gopher Server
Description:	Gopher Server for Windows NT
Location:	\Servers\Gopher\Emwac
Provider:	European Microsoft Windows NT Academic Centre
Email:	<none>
Installation:	Copy all files to an empty directory on your hard drive

Name:	EMWAC HTTP Server
Description:	HTTP Server for Windows NT
Location:	\Servers\Web\Wmwac
Provider:	European Microsoft Windows NT Academic Centre
Email:	<none>
Installation:	Copy all files to an empty directory on your hard drive

Name:	HTTPD
Description:	HTTP Server for 16-Bit Windows
Location:	\Servers\Web\Httpd
Provider:	Robert Denny
Email:	<none>
Installation:	Copy all files to an empty directory on your hard drive

Internet Development Tools

This collection of publicly available Internet development tools represents the state of the art in Internet tools as of this writing. Please contact the vendors of these tools for more information regarding these and other products.

Product:	PowerTCP-32 Standard OLE Toolkit
Description:	32-Bit TCP/IP, Telnet, FTP, SMTP, POP3 and VT220 Tools
Location:	\DevTools\Dart
Vendor:	Dart Communications
Email:	info@dart.com
Installation:	\DevTools\Dart\PT32-109.EXE

Product:	PowerTCP-32 Specialty OLE Toolkit
Description:	32-Bit SNMP, TFTP and UDP Tools
Location:	\DevTools\Dart
Vendor:	Dart Communications
Email:	info@dart.com
Installation:	\DevTools\Dart\PT32-110.EXE

Product:	PowerTCP-16 Standard OLE Toolkit
Description:	16-Bit 32-Bit TCP/IP, Telnet, FTP, SMTP, POP3 and VT220 Tools
Location:	\DevTools\Dart
Vendor:	Dart Communications
Email:	info@dart.com
Installation:	\DevTools\Dart\PT16-109.EXE

Product:	PowerTCP-16 Specialty OLE Toolkit
Description:	16-Bit SNMP, TFTP and UDP Tools
Location:	\DevTools\Dart
Vendor:	Dart Communications
Email:	info@dart.com
Installation:	\DevTools\Dart\PT16-110.EXE

Product:	IP*Works
Description:	A large collection of TCP/IP development tools.
Location:	\DevTools\devSoft
Vendor:	devSoft
Email:	devsoft_sales@devlink.com
Installation:	\DevTools\devSoft\Setup.EXE

Product:	DSSocket (OCX)
Description:	Winsock client/server/UDP control
Location:	\DevTools\Dolphin\DSSocket\Ocx
Vendor:	Dolphin Systems
Email:	stephenc@idirect.com
Installation:	Copy OCX file to \Windows\System

Product:	DSSocket (VBX)
Description:	Winsock client/server/UDP control
Location:	\DevTools\Dolphin\DSSocket\Vbx
Vendor:	Dolphin Systems
Email:	stephenc@idirect.com
Installation:	Copy VBX file to \Windows\System

Product:	GIF2BMP
Description:	DLL that converts a GIF file to a BMP file
Location:	\DevTools\Dolphin\Gif2Bmp

Vendor:	Dolphin Systems
Email:	stephenc@idirect.com
Installation:	Copy DLL files to \Windows\System

Product:	Finger Control
Description:	Custom control for the Finger protocol
Location:	\DevTools\Mabry
Vendor:	Mabry Software
Email:	mabry@halcyon.com
Installation:	\DevTools\Mabry\Finger.EXE

Product:	GetHost Control
Description:	Custom control for name resolution
Location:	\DevTools\Mabry
Vendor:	Mabry Software
Email:	mabry@halcyon.com
Installation:	\DevTools\Mabry\Gethst.EXE

Product:	Time Control
Description:	Custom control for the returning accurate GMT
Location:	\DevTools\Mabry
Vendor:	Mabry Software
Email:	mabry@halcyon.com
Installation:	\DevTools\Mabry\Time.exe

Product:	Whois Control
Description:	Custom control for the Whois protocol
Location:	\DevTools\Mabry
Vendor:	Mabry Software
Email:	mabry@halcyon.com
Installation:	\DevTools\Mabry\Whois.EXE

Product:	Socket Control
Description:	Winsock Control
Location:	\DevTools\Mabry
Vendor:	Mabry Software
Email:	mabry@halcyon.com

Installation: \DevTools\Mabry\Socket.Exe

Product: Mail Control
Description: Custom control for SMTP and POP3 protocols
Location: \DevTools\Mabry
Vendor: Mabry Software
Email: mabry@halcyon.com
Installation: \DevTools\Mabry\Mail.Exe

Product: FTP Control
Description: Custom control for the File Transfer Protocol
Location: \DevTools\Mabry
Vendor: Mabry Software
Email: mabry@halcyon.com
Installation: \DevTools\Mabry\Ftp.EXE

Request For Comments (RFC) Files

Included with the CD-ROM is an Access database containing all of the RFC documents available on or before March 15, 1996. A search program is included (with full source code, of course) that lets you search for and read these files.

Database Specifics

Filename: \RFCs\RFCS.MDB
Tables: Documents
Fields:

Field Name	Data Type	Description
RFCNumber	Long	The RFC document number
FileName	Text (50)	The RFC filename
Title	Memo	Title of the document
Text	Memo	Text of the document

Search Program: \RFCs\RFCFind.EXE

Music

I couldn't resist this. I have been playing in bars with my older brother since we were 15 and 16 years old. I've been writing songs since before I can remember, and probably have over 100 pieces of original music in my collection. My instruments are voice, guitar (acoustic and electric), bass, keys, drums, baritone horn, and trumpet (in order of proficiency). In the early 1990s I developed good delta blues finger style skill, and have released a few collections on tape to family and friends.

One of those tracks, The Last Steam Engine Train, is a favorite of mine. It's the third of the three tracks on the disc. The recording is a little harsh and hissy because it was recorded in a basement, but it's a pretty good performance. The first song (St. James Infirmary) was recorded AAD, with the electric guitar being added later on ADAT. St. James Infirmary is known to be the oldest blues song, although such a claim is impossible to prove. It's one of my all-time favorite songs. The second song, Bear, is an original. It was recorded in New York on a Sansui 6-track cassette multi-track deck and mixer. It took a lot of tweaking to get it that quiet. I used an SM-58 as a vocal mic because we didn't have anything else at the time.

You can play the CD with any standard audio CD player, but make sure you start at track two because the first track is software.

User Assistance and Information

The software accompanying this book is being provided as is without warranty or support of any kind. Should you require basic installation assistance, or if your media is defective, please call our product support number at (212) 850-6194 weekdays between 9 am and 4 P.M. Eastern Standard Time. Or, we can be reached via e-mail at: wprtusw@jwiley.com.

To place additional orders or to request information about other Wiley products, please call (800) 879-4539.

INDEX

CUSTOMER NOTE: